Other great books from Veloce –

Essential Buyer's Guide Series
Porsche 928 (Hemmings)

General
Porsche 356 (2nd Edition) (Long)
Porsche 908 (Födisch, Neßhöver, Roßbach, Schwarz & Roßbach)
Porsche 911 Carrera – The Last of the Evolution (Corlett)
Porsche 911R, RS & RSR, 4th Edition (Starkey)
Porsche 911, The Book of the (Long)
Porsche 911 – The Definitive History 1963-1971 (Long)
Porsche 911 – The Definitive History 1971-1977 (Long)
Porsche 911 – The Definitive History 1977-1987 (Long)
Porsche 911 – The Definitive History 1987-1997 (Long)
Porsche 911 – The Definitive History 1997-2004 (Long)
Porsche 911SC 'Super Carrera' – The Essential Companion (Streather)
Porsche 914 & 914-6: The Definitive History of the Road & Competition Cars (Long)
Porsche 924 (Long)
Porsche 928 (Long)
Porsche 944 (Long)
Porsche 964, 993 & 996 Data Plate Code Breaker (Streather)
Porsche 993 'King Of Porsche' – The Essential Companion (Streather)
Porsche 996 'Supreme Porsche' – The Essential Companion (Streather)
Porsche Racing Cars – 1953 to 1975 (Long)
Porsche Racing Cars – 1976 to 2005 (Long)
Porsche – The Rally Story (Meredith)
Porsche: Three Generations of Genius (Meredith)

From Veloce Publishing's new imprints:

BATTLE CRY!

Battle Cry!
Soviet General & field rank officer uniforms: 1955 to 1991 (Streather)
Soviet military and paramilitary services: female uniforms 1941-1991 (Streather)

Hubble & Hattie

Hubble & Hattie
Know Your Dog – The guide to a beautiful relationship (Birmelin)
My dog is blind – but lives life to the full! (Horsky)
Smellorama – nose games for your dog (Theby)
Waggy Tails & Wheelchairs (Epp)
Winston ... the dog who changed my life (Klute)

www.veloce.co.uk

First published in 2005, reprinted in 2007 and January 2010 by Veloce Publishing Limited, Veloce House, Parkway Farm Business Park, Poundbury, Dorchester, Dorset, DT1 3AR, England. Fax 01305 268864/e-mail info@veloce.co.uk/web www.veloce.co.uk or www.velocebooks.com.
ISBN: 978-1-904788-65-2 UPC: 6-36847-00365-4

Readers with ideas for automotive books, or books on other transport or related hobby subjects, are invited to write to the editorial director of Veloce Publishing at the above address.
British Library Cataloguing in Publication Data – A catalogue record for this book is available from the British Library. Typesetting, design and page make-up all by Veloce Publishing Ltd on Apple Mac. Printed in India by Imprint Digital.

Porsche 911 3.2 Carrera

The last of the evolution

Tony Corlett

VELOCE PUBLISHING
THE PUBLISHER OF FINE AUTOMOTIVE BOOKS

Porsche 911 3.2 Carrera
The last of the evolution
Tony Corlett
Foreword by Peter W. Schutz

Contents

About the author

Although I've been involved with sports cars for many years (including Ferraris, Alfa Romeos, Lotus, McLarens and Porsches), as time's gone by I've found myself becoming increasingly interested in the cars produced in the nineteen-eighties (the last of what I regard as the 'true grit' sports machines). Chief among these is the Porsche 911, and, in particular, the last of the 911 evolution, the 3.2 Carrera.

In the early 'eighties I was employed as a time keeper by Scuderia Ferrari, working alongside such greats as Gilles Villeneuve, Didier Pironi, Patrick Tambay and Rene Arnoux, as well as Mauro Forgheiri, the then Ferrari team boss. I returned to Ferrari as a project manager in the late eighties, and I headed the development of Ferrari's United Kingdom Formula One design facility, working directly as a consultant to John Barnard and Peter Reinhart.

After this period with Ferrari, I went to work for McLaren Cars as a consultant overseeing the development of the McLaren F1 road car production factory (reporting directly to Jeff Hazell, ex-team manager from Williams Grand Prix Engineering).

I've contributed articles and photographs for various publications, journals and books during the eighties and, in 1983, while performing a stint with Charles Ivey and the Group B Porsche 930 Turbo, I appeared in the video *In Car 962* with Derek Bell.

I've been the Register Secretary of the Porsche Club Great Britain, 911 3.2 Carrera, for four years now, and have amassed a great deal of information on, and photographs of, these great cars. This book, then, which is based on that experience, is a nostalgic wander back through the nineteen-eighties with one of the greatest cars ever built. I hope you enjoy reading it as much as I have enjoyed writing it.

Tony Corlett with his 1984 Carrera.

Foreword by Peter W Schutz (CEO Porsche AG 1981-1987)

The Porsche 924, 944 and 928, the vehicles intended to replace the unorthodox 911, were like figure skaters with their arms extended for slow spins. The engine in the front and transmission in the rear were designed to optimise stability instead of manoeuvrability. This resulted in stable touring cars that were outstanding technical achievements, but not real Porsches in the eyes of the Porsche faithful.

None of these new vehicles was able to replace the about-to-be-discontinued Porsche 911 in the hearts of customers and dealers. It was essential for us to recognize what our faithful customers were looking for, and to make sure we gave it to them.

A deep sense of loss, a grieving that was almost heartbreaking, was gathering like a storm. The new Porsche offerings could not replace the revered 911. To me, a newcomer, the feeling of impending catastrophe was overpowering.

The decision to keep the 911 in the product line occurred one afternoon in the office of Dr Helmuth Bott, the Porsche operating board member responsible for all engineering and development. I noticed a chart on the wall of Professor Bott's office. It depicted the ongoing development schedules for the three primary Porsche product lines: 944, 928 and 911. Two of them stretched far into the future, but the 911 program stopped at the end of 1981. I remember rising from my chair, walking over to the chart, taking a black marker pen, and extending the 911 program bar clean off the end of the chart. I am sure I heard a silent cheer from Professor Bott, and I knew I had done the right thing. The Porsche 911, the company icon, had been saved, and I believe the company was saved with it.

Peter W Schutz, CEO of Porsche AG, 1981 to 1987, with a 911 Carrera.

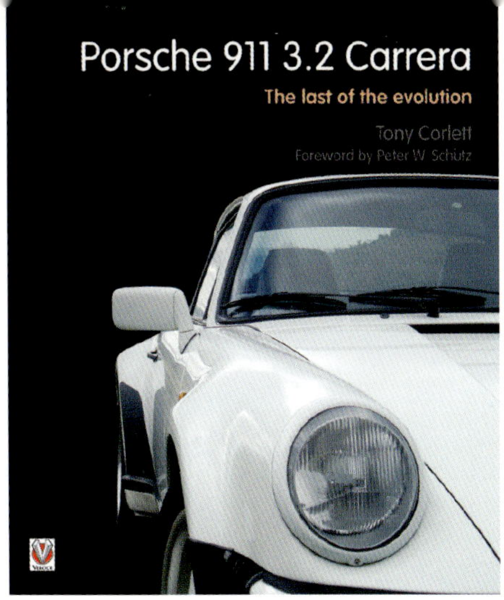

Introduction

"Driving in its purest form," is how the sales brochure describes the 3.2 Carrera. With regard to the engine performance, it goes on to say, "The advanced specification has resulted in the 3.2 litre engine of the 911 Carrera model developing 231bhp (DIN) at 5900rpm with a 10.3:1 compression ratio. The 3164cc engine's maximum torque of 284Nm at 4800rpm indicates its excellent flexibility, enabling 0-62.5mph acceleration in 6.1 seconds and a maximum speed of 152mph, regardless of body style".

When considering that the 3.2 Carrera has none of the later electronic aids, nor any special safety features like ABS or power steering, perhaps the sales brochure is right, and it is indeed driving in its purest form.

The confidence you feel in a well set up Carrera is something quite special. While there is a tendency towards mild understeer in harder cornering situations, generally the car feels as if it's on rails. It turns in with sharp precision and, once through the apex of the curve, the power can be applied quite harshly.

Savour the sound of the (glorious) flat six engine and watch the needle, in the massive centrally-mounted rev counter, climb round into the red. Power delivery is smooth, and then at a little over 4000rpm the engine note changes and it digs a little deeper right up to the red line. Speeds in excess of 120mph can be achieved without really trying. Road conditions and safety considerations allowing, you'll feel at one with the progressive power and the overall tautness of the chassis. Once you've taken a 911 Carrera to the limit, you'll want to turn around and do it all again.

Although the steering is heavy, the chassis hard, and the gear change demanding, driving a 911 is a memorable experience - the feeling of man and machine in complete harmony.

Model versions

• Carrera: Standard Body with Teledial cast alloy wheels.
Sport Equipment (SE)
•'Carrera Sport: Package' As standard but with front and rear aerodynamic spoilers, sport shock absorbers and wider road wheels (lightweight cast or forged) with low profile tyres.
• Turbo-Look (TL) or Supersport Equipment (SSE): As standard, but with the wider Turbo body, front and rear aerodynamic spoilers as fitted to the Turbo, an ultra-high performance braking system, uprated suspension and shock absorbers, wider lightweight forged road wheels with ultra-low profile tyres.
• Club Sport (CS): A lighter and simplified variant of the Sport-equipped Coupé.
• Speedster: A lowered variant of the Cabriolet with Turbo-Look optional body.
• Silver Anniversary and Celebration models celebrating 25 years of the 911 and the 250,000th 911.

Body types

Coupé: All steel roof incorporating a sun-roof as an option.
Targa: Removable full-width roof panel and wraparound rear screen.

Factory photograph of the 911 Carrera Coupé.

Cabriolet: Electrically operated folding Mohair soft-top roof.

Production years

1984 - E Program
1985 - F Program
1986 - G Program
1987 - H Program
1988 - J Program
1989 - K Program

Upgrades

1987 (H Program) replaced Porsche 915 gearbox with Getrag G50, the latter having a shorter shift and hydraulic clutch operation.

Options

Many options were offered, varying from car to car. Option codes for each chassis number are listed in the car's original handbook and on a sticker under the bonnet lid. The option codes are also available from Porsche (as related to specific chassis numbers).

Acknowledgements

This book was written with the assistance and support of Dr Ing hc F Porsche (Porsche AG) in Stuttgart, for which I am extremely grateful. I am particularly indebted to Klaus Parr (Archive), Tilman Brodbeck (Excellence), Annemarie Reinhardt (Legal).

Special thanks goes to Peter W Schutz, ex-Porsche AG Chairman/CEO, who not only wrote the foreword for this book, but also offered me inside knowledge into the exact moment the 911 was saved from discontinuation. After six World Sports Car Championships, three Formula One World Championships, and seven profitable years, Peter retired from Porsche at the end of 1987.

Thanks to Otto Fuchs KG, Bosch, Getrag, RUF, and the Porsche Club Great Britain.

Amongst the many individual enthusiasts who contributed to this book, my sincere thanks goes to:

Paul Dangerfield: Technical and background assistance, technical checking.
Paul Cadrobbi: USA Turbo-Look assistance.
Michael Chadwick: Club Sport assistance.
Steve Darnell: Club Sport assistance.
Chris Davenport: Speedster assistance.
Richard Bernau: Upgrade assistance.
Jorg Ludwig: Fuchs assistance.
Alois Ruf and Marc Bonger: RUF assistance.

I am very grateful to the many owners and photographers whose cars

Factory photograph of the 911 Carrera Coupé with 'Turbo-Look' option.

and photographs appear in the book: Jamie Brundell, Mike Chadwick, Mark Clair, Alan Cordery, (Tony Corlett), Steve Darnell, Chris Davenport, Darren Fink, John Gaisford, Island Photographics, Brice Kadel, Masaru Kagami, Lloyd Langley, Jonathan Madden, Bernie Magee, Gordon McKay, Steve Miller, Paul Narcisse Jr, Kevin Post, Peter Robain, Dale Smith, Andy Tims, Tom Trudell, Steve Upsdell, Salvador Valiente, William Vogl and Bill Waite.

Cover shot: Bernie Magee's Grand Prix White Supersport - photographer: Tony Corlett.

For general assistance: Geoff Ives, Bernie Magee, Mario Lusardi, Gordon McKay, Julian Trinder and Steve Upsdell.

I am indebted to all the other Carrera owners around the world with whom I have communicated over the years, all of whom share the same passion.

The 'Carrera' script, reproduction of the driver's handbook, official Carrera promotional photographs, 1964 911 promotional photograph, and 1984 Paris to Dakar poster are all (officially) used with the kind permission of Porsche AG The 1984 Paris to Dakar screen captures were reproduced by and used with kind permission from Duke International Limited.

Tony Corlett, Isle of Man

Handbook cover.

911 Carrera

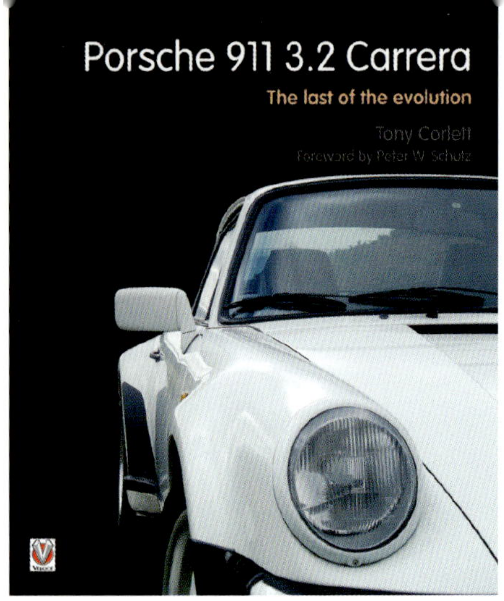

Chapter 1

911 The complete evolution

1963
Model 901 launched on 12th September 1963 at the Frankfurt Show.

1964
'O' Series
Model 911 goes into production - type number changed from 901 to 911.
911 2.0: 130bhp
Engine capacity is 1991cc
Price DM 21,900

1965
911 2.0: 130bhp
Targa model introduced

1966
911 2.0: 130bhp
100,000th 911 rolls off the production line

1967
911 2.0: 130bhp
911S: 160bhp
Forged alloy wheel rims (Fuchs) introduced

1968
'A' Series
911 T: 110bhp - replaced 912
911 L: 130bhp
911 S: 160bhp
Sportomatic gearbox introduced

1969
'B' Series
911 T: 110bhp
911 E: 130bhp
911 S: 160bhp
Wheelbase increased on all 911 models from 2211mm to 2268mm

1970
'C' Series
Engine capacity increases to 2195cc

1971
'D' Series
911 T: 125bhp
911 E: 155bhp
911 S: 180bhp

1972
'E' Series
Engine capacity (Capacity) increases to 2341cc
911 T: 130bhp
911 E: 165bhp
911 S: 190bhp
915 4-speed gearbox introduced

1973
'F' Series
911 T: 130bhp
911 E: 165bhp
911 S: 190bhp
911 RS Carrera 2.7: 210bhp
Wheelbase increased on all 911 models from 2268mm to 2272mm
Carrera name used for the first time
Rear 'ducktail' spoiler introduced

1974
'G' Series
Engine capacity increases to 2687cc
911 2.7: 150bhp
911 2.7 S: 175bhp
Impact bumpers introduced

1975
'H' Series
911 2.7: 150bhp
911 2.7 S: 175bhp
911 Turbo 3.0: 260bhp

911 Carrera

The first production sports car to have an exhaust-driven turbocharger
Long-term corrosion protection introduces galvanised zinc coating

1976
'I' Series
Engine capacity increased to 2994cc
911 2.7: 150bhp
911 2.7 S: 175bhp
911 Carrera 3.0: 200bhp
911 Turbo 3.0: 260bhp

1977
'K' Series
911 2.7: 150bhp
911 2.7 S: 175bhp
911 Carrera 3.0: 200bhp
911 Turbo 3.0: 260bhp
250,000th Porsche rolls off the production line - 911 2.7

1978
'L' Series
911 SC: 180bhp
911 Turbo 3.3: 300bhp
Bosch 'K' Jetronic Injection
11 blade fan
Cast alloy wheels optional

1979
911 SC: 180bhp
911 Turbo 3.3: 300bhp
Catalytic converter introduced to 911 range

1980
'A' Programme
911 SC: 180bhp
911 Turbo 3.3: 300bhp
915 5-speed gearbox introduced

1981
'B' Programme
911 SC: 204bhp
911 Turbo 3.3: 300bhp

1982
'C' Programme
911 SC: 204bhp
911 Turbo 3.3: 300bhp
911 SC Cabriolet
The first 911 Cabriolet

1983
'D' Programme
911 SC: 204bhp
911 Turbo 3.3: 300bhp

1984
'E' Programme
Engine capacity increases to 3164cc
911 3.2 Carrera: 231bhp
911 Turbo 3.3: 300bhp
911 4x4 wins the Paris to Dakar rally
Turbo or wide body option included - known as Turbo-Look (TL) and Supersport Equipment (SSE)

1985
'F' Programme
911 3.2 Carrera: 231bhp
911 Turbo 3.3: 300bhp

1986
'G' Programme
911 3.2 Carrera: 231bhp
911 Turbo 3.3: 300bhp

1987
'H' Programme
911 3.2 Carrera: 231bhp
911 Carrera Club Sport: 231bhp
911 Turbo 3.3: 300bhp
G50 gearbox introduced

1988
'J' Programme
911 3.2 Carrera: 231bhp
911 Carrera Club Sport: 231bhp
911 Turbo 3.3: 300bhp

1989
'K' Programme
911 3.2 Carrera: 231bhp
911 Carrera Club Sport: 231bhp
911 3.2 Speedster: 231bhp
911 Turbo 3.3: 300bhp

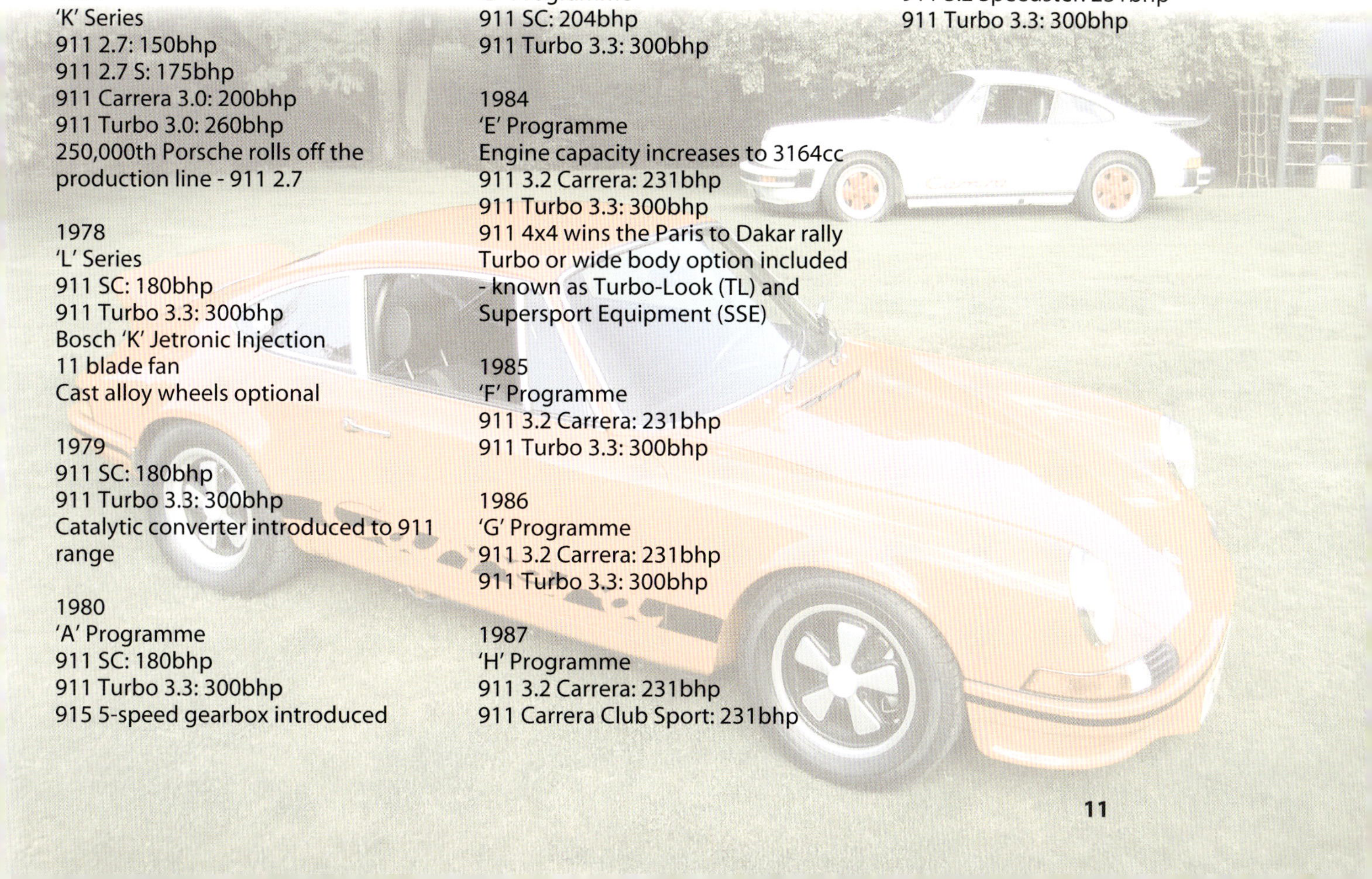

CHAPTER 2

HISTORY

From its inception in 1963, the Porsche 911, which went from strength to strength under the control of Fritz Bezner and Bernd Kahnau, was the subject of one of the longest periods of continuous development of any car. However, although there were development drawings and specifications, no-one really ever 'designed' a new 911, which is why the basic concept remained throughout its evolution. Each evolution really only meant a bigger engine and more power. Handling, comfort and accessories were improved, but the established formula remained (indeed, the body design was considered to be beyond improvement, only requiring cosmetic changes to keep it up to date).

By 1984, though, when the 911 was 21, the design was regarded as being rather dated and old fashioned, and the intention was for it to be discontinued. It was pure chance that secured the continuation of the 911 and thus the creation of the 3.2 Carrera.

The distinctive rear aerodynamic spoiler was fitted to the Sport equipped Carrera. Reshaped for the Carrera in 1984, this gave the then new 911 a fresh visual identity compared to its predecessor the 911 SC. This rear tail was designed to be aerodynamically smoother and less of a dirt trap.

1984 Carrera Coupé with Sport Equipment.

Claimed to be substantially new, the 3.2 litre Carrera was hailed as an altogether improved car over its predecessor, the 3 litre SC. The biggest change was the engine, 80 per cent of which Porsche claimed was new. Still using the 95mm bore of the SC, it now incorporated the stroke of the 930 Turbo, increasing the capacity to 3164cc and lifting the power to 231bhp. Marrying this engine to the Bosch Motronic DME (Digital Motor Electronics) controlled fuel injection system allowed the compression ratio to be raised from 9.8:1 to 10.3:1. It also created a very fuel-efficient unit, improving power output, torque, pollution levels, and cold start operation. To eliminate the ongoing problem with the 911 engine chain tensioners, the Carrera chain tensioners became hydraulically-operated. The cylinder designed to keep the chain under tension was now fed directly by an engine oil pressure circuit.

The braking system was also improved. The front and rear discs were increased by 4mm to 24mm thick, and the rear calliper pistons were increased to 42mm diameter. A pressure regulator was included in the rear brake circuit.

The basic bodywork, suspension configuration, and most of the interior were copied from the SC, but the Carrera was more luxurious. Other differences included a rear engine lid 'Carrera' logo, integrated front fog lights, a more streamlined rear wing, a new ventilation system, new seats, and various interior modifications.

During its six years of production, the biggest improvement came in 1987 with the introduction of the newly-designed type G50 gearbox, manufactured by Getrag. This replaced the old and generally more bulky Porsche-built type 915 gearbox. The new G50 used Borg-Warner synchronisers and provided an improved gear change and shortened shift distance. At the same time, an hydraulically-operated clutch was introduced to replace the original cable-operated system. The diameter of the clutch was increased from 225mm

Carrera Club Sport.

Carrera Cabriolet 1984 to 1989.

Carrera Speedster 1989.

Carrera Turbo-Look 1984 to 1989.

1984 to 1986 rear light cluster with under-bumper fog lights for European cars and full width Porsche script logo.

India Red Carrera Coupé: Sport Equipment, with front and rear aerodynamic spoilers and Fuchs alloy wheels. The car is fitted with 16in diameter wheels finished in standard black paint.

The Carrera Cabriolet was the brainchild of the then new Porsche chairman Peter W Schutz.

to 240mm. The incorporation of this new gearbox also brought about rear floorpan and torsion bar modifications.

The Carrera was also available with the Turbo-Look option, which used the standard Carrera power plant and drivetrain, but featured larger brake callipers and turbo-style rear trailing arms.

For 1987 and 1988, and in limited numbers for 1989, the Carrera Club Sport was introduced. This was a limited production run, lightweight option, weighing 50kg less than the standard sport-equipped Coupé. Ready for racing, the Club Sport was stripped of fog lights, air-conditioning, power seats, rear seats, undercoating and sound deadening, but included stiffer Bilstein Special dampers, sports seats, hollow stem valves, and a re-programmed ECU chip.

In 1988 and 1989, to celebrate both the 25th year since the original 901 presentation and the production of the 250,000th 911, Porsche produced special edition models know as 'Silver Anniversary' and 'Celebration' models. The latter Celebration model for 1988 was not too different from the standard Sport-equipped Coupé, this Carrera came in (special) Diamond Blue Metallic paint, colour-coded wheels, and a Silver Blue leather interior. It also had an imprint of Ferry Porsche's signature on the headrests, in recognition of his ongoing involvement with the 911.

In 1989, the Carrera Speedster was introduced. This design succeeded in capturing the character of previous and historic Porsche Speedsters. With an even lower windscreen, 'speedster humps' and soft top roof, it was a combination of Club Sport and Cabriolet. Unlike the Club Sport, however, the Speedster also came with a popular wide body option.

In 1989 the 3.2 Carrera was discontinued and the evolution based on the original 911 ended with it. It made way for the newer technology and aerodynamic sophistication of the new 964 (designated 911 for marketing purposes only, which means that the 3.2 Carrera was the last Porsche to carry the 911 brand as a factory designated production number).

CHAPTER 3

MODEL SPECIFICATIONS

COUPÉ

Chassis code 10 or 12. The Coupé was, of course, the original 901 design from the pen of Alexander 'Butzi' Porsche. Apart from some minor changes, the shape of the Coupé remained the same from its inception in 1963 to the last of the 3.2 Carreras in 1989.

The term coupé describes a two-door car with a sweeping rear screen. The 'C' posts usually incorporate a set of rear seats and a luggage compartment. Porsche chose to use the luggage compartment to house the engine, but the basic sloping design was maintained. Unbelievably, no other motor manufacturer has successfully copied the 911 Coupé shape, which leaves this masterpiece with a monopoly in an otherwise copy-cat world. Very much drawn from the original Volkswagen Beetle and the later Porsche 356 shapes, the 911 Coupé shape is iconic and unmistakable.

USA specification Coupé, Targa and Cabriolet.

Factory promotional photograph of a 1987 Sport equipped Coupé.

Targa

Chassis code 14 or 16. Introduced in 1965, the Targa was Porsche's response to the demand for open-top motoring from customers who favoured the 356 cabriolets. Faced with two major problems (the cost of tooling up for a new car, and a lack of body rigidity once the roof was removed from the Coupé) Porsche retained as many of the Coupé body panels as possible, and incorporated a stainless steel roll-over bar. All the panels below the waist line remained the same, thus saving tooling costs, although the incorporation of the roll-over bar required some minor reinforcements in the floorpan. This produced an acceptably rigid open-top car without a major weight gain.

The Targa, with its removable lateral panel between the top of the windscreen and the 'B' post roll-over bar (or, as it's more commonly known, the 'Targa Bar') was a popular Carrera option. In order to incorporate the Targa Bar into the Coupé shape, Porsche chose to increase the size of the rear screen. Originally a zip out plastic screen, this was later changed to glass and wrapped around to the 'B' posts, thereby eliminating the 'C' post altogether. This gave a more airy feel to the cabin and, once the Targa roof was removed, an almost total cabriolet feel could be achieved.

Factory promotional photograph of a 1984 Targa.

Factory promotional photograph of a 1984 Cabriolet.

Cabriolet

Chassis code 15 or 17. The brainchild of Peter Schutz and engineered by an original 356 Cabriolet engineer, Herr Bauer, the 911 Cabriolet was born from the carcass of a 911 Targa. First shown in 1981 at Frankfurt, interestingly as a four-wheel drive Turbo, the Cabriolet entered production in 1982.

Bauer almost achieved perfection with soft-top design in the 911 Cabriolet. This was a 911 with a soft-top that maintained a lot of the classic Coupé lines. Leaving the Coupé windscreen and 'A' posts in place, the Carrera Cabriolet looked as good with the roof up as it did with it folded down. In order to maintain the stiffness of the chassis, Porsche incorporated reinforcements within the lower chassis sills, thus eliminating much of the chassis twist associated with roof removal. Scuttle-shake and chassis-sag were thus avoided, and the doors on the Cabriolet operated as perfectly as they did on the Coupé.

In 1985, Porsche showed a Turbo-Look Cabriolet with an aluminium detachable hardtop at the Swedish Motor Show. The style of this was such that, at a glance, it could easily be mistaken for a Coupé. Referred to in the Porsche literature from 1986, a galvanised steel hardtop was made available.

One further addition made to the Cabriolet was an engine vibration damper. This was a strut that sat to the rear left of the engine and was designed to eliminate engine vibration through the chassis.

Since Targa and Cabriolet production was carried out in conjunction with the Coupé, Porsche was able to maximise its manufacturing process in one sequence.

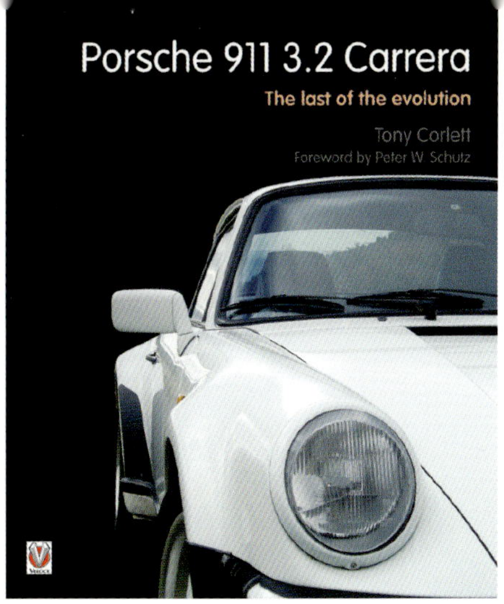

CHAPTER 4

THE CARRERA - DESIGNED TO DRIVE

Because the basic 911 shape remained much the same from 1963 through to 1989, it is understandable that Porsche chose to keep the 911 factory designation during this period. The rear engine configuration was not new in 1963, of course, as both Porsche and Volkswagen used the Ferdinand Porsche layout to great effect in the Porsche 356 and VW Beetle. The 911, however, or 901 as it was originally named, was an attempt to achieve the optimum form in a configuration no other manufacturer was even contemplating. The 356, albeit a great little car, was never going to be a supercar, but with the 911, Porsche has never really looked back.

Following on from the 911 SC, the 3.2 Carrera brought even better performance and roadholding to the 911 evolution, whilst maintaining the essence of a practical 2+2 sports car. The heart of the new 911 was a 3.2 litre, flat-six air-cooled engine which remained faithful to the original engine concept. With consistent development, the engine was one of the most efficient, economical, and environmentally acceptable performance engines available. Capable of stunning performance, this engine also returned fuel economy never before seen in a performance car. The flat-six configuration was always exceptionally smooth, and the 3.2 litre version was no exception.

The 911 rear wheelarches are legendary, blending with the wings and flanks in perfect harmony.

Unconventional, perhaps, but respected, definitely. The 3.2 flat-six was compact and relatively light, due to the lightweight silicon aluminium alloy engine block and light alloy cylinders and cylinder heads. With superbly balanced crankshaft (forged steel) and connecting rods, achieved using twelve counterweights with eight main bearings, the 3164cc (cubic centimetre) engine was exceptionally smooth. With two valves per cylinder in a 'V' configuration, the intake and exhaust valves were positioned perfectly to ensure maximum flow of inlet and exhaust gases. The double overhead camshafts, oil scavenger and pressure pumps were chain driven. The chain was kept at the correct tension by way of force-feed lubrication and self-adjusting, maintenance free chain tensioners (a vast improvement over earlier 911 engines).

The 3.2 Carrera had a 42 per cent to 58 per cent weight distribution, front to rear, the 911 Turbo narrowly beating it at 38 per cent to 62 per cent. With nearly 60 per cent loading over the rear driving wheels, due mainly to the rear-mounted engine, the Carrera had almost unequalled power transfer to the road. It delivered power without any appreciable loss of grip, ensuring good overall traction on all road surfaces.

The engine was cooled by a distinctive, centrally-mounted, direct-

The standard Carrera Coupé came without the aerodynamic front and rear spoilers. The rear engine cover incorporated a slatted grille where the spoiler would be fitted. The fan sucks the air through this grille and onto the engine.

drive axial flow fan which produced a massive 1500 litres of air per second at 6000rpm across the entire engine surface. Air was sucked in through the grill in the top of the engine cover by the fan located behind the engine. In front of the fan was a shroud that directed the air over the crankcase and cylinder barrels. Deflector panels were fitted around each barrel to ensure even cooling. These deflectors directed the air downwards and across the exhaust to aid exhaust cooling. The air was then deflected downwards and away from the engine towards the road surface.

The air cooling was complemented by a dry-sump oil lubrication system. The mass of the engine oil was stored in a remote oil reservoir, a design feature taken directly from motor racing success, which ensured a continuous oil supply even under severe lateral cornering. The oil was cooled twice, once through a crankcase-mounted oil cooler located within the 'fan' air-flow, and secondly, via a front-mounted oil cooler located under the right front wing. The oil circulated from the engine via the oil cooler radiators and was delivered back to the reservoir. In all 911 engines, the oil assisted in maintaining engine temperature, and it was essential that the oil was of a sufficiently high quality.

The gearbox was mounted directly to the front of the engine. Power was delivered through the flywheel and single dry-plate clutch combination, and transmitted to the drive wheels via articulated halfshafts.

Fully independent, the Carrera suspension remained faithful to the original 901 design, offering precise handling and comfort in unison with the power output. From the start, bushing was kept to an absolute minimum. A very rigid body and chassis monocoque design, married to an uncompromising suspension layout, ensured that body roll was kept to a minimum during cornering. This ensured that the tyres had maximum adhesion under adverse lateral conditions.

Porsche expected that, in most cases, a normal 911 driver would only utilise about 40 to 50 per cent of the Carrera's cornering abilities. On a 190 meter radius track, the 3.2 Carrera achieved 85 per cent gravitational acceleration, in other words 0.85g, meaning that the Carrera would reach its cornering limits very late. The average limit for other competitive marques was stated as 0.76g, indicating that the Carrera outperformed most of its rivals.

Precise and responsive steering was achieved using a traditional rack and pinion system. The steering rack formed part of the track-rod and was self correcting, with no play whatsoever from lock to lock. Driver contact with the front wheels and the road was perfect, with every movement transferred directly through the steering wheel. This gave the driver a complete 'feel' for the car's road behaviour.

Stopping power was provided by a race-proven, servo-assisted, hydraulic dual circuit braking system with ventilated discs all round. The standard Carrera had cast-iron, two-piston brake callipers, while the Supersport version had aluminium four-piston brake callipers, all located so as to get maximum air-flow for cooling. The callipers were also positioned on the hub to minimise rotation forces from the wheels. The servo-assistance ensured maximum braking performance from minimal brake pedal pressure. The handbrake operated on the rear wheels only, via a

The duck tail was first introduced on the 911 2.7 RS in 1973, increased in size with the introduction of the Turbo in 1975, further increased in size to cope with the Turbo intercooler in 1978, and streamlined for the Carrera in 1984.

The 911 impact bumpers first made an appearance in 1974, and were carried through to the end of Carrera production in 1989. The front and rear aerodynamic spoilers greatly reduce lift, and provide much improved straight line stability. The aerodynamic effect was such that the chin spoiler was not fitted to Carreras without the rear spoiler, and vice versa.

separate drum inside the disc housing. This ensured that any excessive heat built up in the discs could still dissipate when the handbrake was applied, thus avoiding problems of disk warping.

As for aerodynamics, Porsche claimed a drag coefficient of Cd 0.39 and a frontal area, for the standard car, of 1.77 square meters.

The body and overall appearance of the 911 Carrera was something to behold. Unsurpassed finish quality and fitment ensured the 911 experience began long before its performance was appreciated. A single piece monocoque shell, incorporating the body, floor pan and chassis components, was completely hot-dip galvanized (a quenching process which applied a rust-inhibiting zinc coating to the steel). The front wings, doors, boot lid and engine cover, also hot-dip galvanised, completed the full body. The main flanks, rear wings and roof formed part of the single piece body shell.

To front and rear were wraparound aluminium bumpers, painted to match the body colour. They were made from 5-6 millimetre thick aluminium sheet and were mounted remotely to the main body. This provided a slip-plane in which they were able to move laterally to the body in case of crash impact. These 'impact-bumpers', first introduced to the 911 in 1974 to suit American safety legislation, were mounted on shock-absorbing dampers and designed to operate when bumped at low speed. Following stringent testing under both low and high speed conditions, the results showed that at low speed, no damage at all was done to the body, while at high speed, damage was kept to a minimum.

The most important aspect of this safety technology was the front crumple zone, which absorbed energy in the case of a frontal crash. The bonnet was designed to deform in a predetermined way, and the firm hinge mountings prevented the bonnet intruding into the passenger cabin. Because the impact resistant fuel cell was mounted at the front, it incorporated a closed evaporation system and protected pipes to prevent fuel escaping in roll-over crashes. Attention was also paid to the layout of the front radius arms, or lower wishbones, which provided protection to the cell.

The safety cell of the Carrera was extremely strong, and would withstand impact from front or side. The side doors were fitted with 'safety-locks', designed to keep them closed and in position during impact. In a 30mph frontal impact, the safety cell performed well enough to ensure that the doors could be opened after the incident and that the seat belt fixing points did not fail.

The integral roof and strong side pillars provided exceptional roll-over protection. In crash test simulations, the Carrera was catapulted sideways at 30mph and repeatedly rolled over, simulating a critical crash condition. The results showed that the entire safety cell performed admirably. Both doors remained firmly shut, ensuring integrity of the safety cell, and opened freely afterwards.

The interior of the Carrera was just as safe, with energy absorbing material incorporated at all critical points. All the instrument panel switches and the glove compartment lock, for example, were made from deformable materials. The rear view mirror was mounted on a deformable stalk, and all materials used were flame retardant. Inertia reel seat belts and safety glass all round completed the internal safety features. Outside the car, foldable rubber-edged mirrors and rubber body extremities ensured pedestrian injury was kept to a minimum.

At the front, external lighting was by way of large, H4 halogen headlamps, two valance-mounted driving lamps and two bumper-mounted indicators. The rear had a lateral lighting cluster incorporating brake lights, indicators

Exacting body panel fit.

and reversing lamps. On the early Carreras, a high density rear fog lamp was positioned under the rear bumper, whereas on the later Carreras two fog lamps were incorporated into the lighting and reflector cluster. The Porsche script logo across the rear of the lighting cluster was also reduced in width on later cars to allow the fog lamps to be fitted.

The Carrera body shape was classic 911, the pure lines of which were only interrupted three times during its history. The first time was in 1973 with the addition of the rear 'duck-tail'; the second time was when the bumpers were changed in 1974; and the third time was when the body was widened for the turbo in 1975. Although the aerodynamic additions of rear wing and chin spoilers developed through various stages of design and development, the overall shape remained the same.

Amongst the many options, the Carrera was available with the more modern rear wing and chin spoiler for the Sport Equipment cars. The rear wing was redesigned to be more streamlined than that of the Turbo or SC. Shaped for smoother air-flow and to prevent the build up of dirt, this resulted in sleeker and lower side up-stands. This feature set the Carrera apart from the SC at a glance, the latter sporting the full turbo wing. However, the Carrera Supersport, bred from its turbo sister, did carry the full turbo rear wing.

Wind tunnel testing showed that the Carrera's chin spoiler and rear wing greatly reduced lift at high speeds. Porsche claimed that the front chin spoiler reduced underbody turbulence and that the large rear spoiler enhanced the Carrera's straight-line running performance in reducing wind resistance, increasing stability, and reducing lift at high speed. These wind tunnel-developed aerodynamic aids, when fitted to the Carrera, reduced overall drag by 2 per cent, and reduced

The pure lines of the 911 remained largely unchanged from its introduction in 1963. Only three major changes were made throughout its life: the rear ducktail in 1973; the impact bumpers in 1974; and the wide body of the Turbo in 1975.

lift from 180kg at 150mph to just 17kg. Extensive wind tunnel testing also improved engine cooling and the position of passenger compartment ventilation inlets, as well as optimising noise reduction for the rubber door and window seals, mirrors and windscreen wipers.

The front and rear aerodynamic aids were designed to work together. Where the Carrera was marketed without the rear wing, Porsche found that the chin spoiler had to be removed because the pitching moment at high speeds would have upset the balance, causing serious oversteer. Also, it's worth noting that a Carrera could not be ordered without a chin spoiler if the rear wing was fitted, because the understeer would have been too great.

The 911 3.2 Carrera was marketed throughout the world in different formats and with a variety of options. In its basic form, the standard Carrera - or 'non-sport' as it became affectionately known - was a 'pure' 911 shape without the additional aerodynamic features of the Sport Equipment cars. The Sport Equipment option included the chin and rear spoilers, sport shock absorbers, and wider road wheels with low profile tyres. The Supersport Equipment option included extended or wide wheelarches front and rear, with front and rear aerodynamic spoilers as fitted to the Turbo. Also included was an ultra-high performance braking system, uprated suspension and shock absorbers, wider road wheels and low profile tyres.

In identifying the Carrera, Porsche chose to be discrete. The standard Porsche Stuttgart Shield took pride of place on the very front of the bonnet, as is the case with all 911 Porsches, and there was a 'Porsche' script logo across the rear light cluster and a delicate 'Carrera' script logo on the rear engine cover. Although bearing the name 'Carrera', chosen after racing successes in the Mexican 'La Carrera Panamericana' road race, only the Club Sport model carried the 'Carrera' script on the lower flanks and doors.

Although Porsche offered many optional extras, none of these detracted from the beauty of the Carrera - rather, in many ways, they served to enhance the already evolved car. Whether it was a limited slip differential or cruise control, leather trim or air conditioning, the Carrera could be made into an executive express with all the trappings of luxury, sophistication and comfort.

Traditionally entirely hand-built, the 3.2 Carrera also benefited from a largely hand-assembled engine. The end result was a car of such quality that Porsche was able to offer extensive mechanical and body warranties (a ten year anti-corrosion body warranty, and a two year or twelve thousand mile mechanical warranty).

The Carrera specification catered for all tastes. The purists could opt for the standard model, whereas the more sport inclined could opt for the Sport Equipment or Supersport Equipment. Regardless of which you chose, the basic 911 shape was recognisable and brought with it a sense of defying the establishment.

United Kingdom C16 specification India Red Sport equipped Coupé. India Red was only used from 1984 to 1986 (changed to Indian Red from 1987). Although many believe otherwise, Porsche never produced the Carrera in Guards Red.

Polite Notice
Please do not dispose of litter in this area as it presents a danger to aircraft

CHAPTER 5

M491 TURBO-LOOK/ SUPERSPORT EQUIPMENT: WIDE BODY

Although the Turbo-Look was born from the Carrera in 1984, investigation into early Turbo-Look documentation shows that some of the early cars didn't actually carry the 491 option code at all. This is a bit of a mystery, as the 1984 Carrera price reports: "*Turbo-Look (Karosserie, Fahrwerk, Bremsanlage wie 911 Turbo)*", and the 1984 Carrera handbook states: "*Fur den 911 Carrera mit Turbo-Look gelten, wenn nicht gesondert aufgefuhrt, die Angaben des 911 Carrera*". In other words, the Turbo-Look was definitely a recognized option from that date as a factory produced wide body. Exactly why option 491 was not previously stated still remains unclear. For this reason, the birth of the Turbo-Look, later known as 'Supersport Equipment' in Europe, is somewhat open to speculation.

While it's possible to determine the overall Carrera production numbers from official computer records at Porsche AG, including body types and international variants, the Turbo-Look was never specifically listed in Porsche production figures. Because of the apparent ambiguity surrounding the early European factory M491 Carreras, not even the option code listings can be relied upon. Since the chassis numbers for all Carreras do not differentiate options, the earlier Turbo-Look is not specifically denoted or easily spotted on paper. This problem is almost non-existent in America, however, as Porsche Cars North America did make a sustained effort to keep relatively accurate records of imports.

Unlike the Club Sport and Speedster, the latter also having the M491 option, the Turbo-Look or European Supersport did not get an official chassis recognition. This now legendary production code was not

Both pages: The Carrera Turbo-Look option was introduced by Porsche in 1984 to combat unofficial wide body copies built by independent coachbuilders. The M491 option code was used to denote the Turbo-Look. This is a later UK specification Supersport Coupé with the G50 gearbox.

This 1984 Turbo-Look in Platinum is thought to be the first imported into the USA. The American Turbo-Look came without the Carrera script on the engine cover. Only 421 Turbo-Look Coupés were imported into America in 1984.

The Turbo-Look or Supersport Equipment option for the Carrera used the wide body, suspension, wheels and brakes from the Turbo 911.

just a simple option number, unlike most of the other option codes that often represented only a single factor or accessory. Option M491 covered quite a bit more. Put simply, this was not just a wide body placed on a standard car.

As well as the rear suspension modifications and the wide front and rear wheelarches, the Turbo-Look also incorporated a Turbo rear spoiler, a wraparound Turbo chin spoiler, and Turbo wheels. Brake technology, derived from the 917 racing program, featured 285mm diameter cross-drilled discs to the front, and 290mm diameter cross-drilled discs to the rear, both with four-piston aluminium callipers. 1984 and 1985 Turbo-Look Carreras had 7x16 rims at the front and 8x16 rims at the rear, with the rears upsized to 9x16 from 1986 onwards, as was the case with the 911 Turbo.

The M491 option code was first used in the fabrication of the legendary 1973 RSR 2.8. Ingenious relocation of suspension pick-up points and modified trailing arms and wheel bearings allowed the cars to accommodate much wider wheels and tyres, keeping them firmly planted on the road. This option, created by Porsche engineers, was used on various wide-body competition 911s which remained at the cutting edge of international motorsport for a decade. Most notable were the 2.8 RSR and RS 3.0. Interestingly, from their inception in 1974, the iconic 911 Turbo Carreras were produced by installing a turbo engine and a stronger 4-speed gearbox into M491 optioned Carreras.

As the early 1975 911 Turbo Carrera quickly became an international sensation, many private coachbuilders recognized a niche market for transforming standard-bodied 911s into wide-bodied, Turbo-Looking cars. Porsche, not wanting to lose out, responded by returning to the pre-turbo production M491 optioned Carrera, and officially introducing it to the product range in 1984. Porsche's timing was in direct response to losing revenue due to independent tuners cashing in on Turbo Look 'knock-offs'. This was also Porsche's answer to a temporary withdrawal of the 911 Turbo from its largest market, North America. From 1980 onwards, more restrictive emissions controls in America saw the end of the 911 Turbo until 1986. Porsche had a growing void to fill. Many customers were left desperately wanting what they couldn't have, a fact which is backed-up by the American Turbo-Look sales figures for 1984 and 1985 of 423 and 391 respectively. When the 911 Turbo was reintroduced in 1986, Turbo-Look sales dropped to

1986 Supersport in Grand Prix White with colour-coded Fuchs alloy wheels.

just 15 in 1986, 30 in 1987, 155 in 1988, and 66 in 1989.

Although the 911 Turbo stayed in production for the European and the RoW markets until 1989, a growing number of discerning European customers, who liked the Turbo for its looks, preferred the more drivable and flexible Carrera engine. This may have been a key factor for Porsche's official recognition of the Turbo-Look as more than just a factory option or marketing tool for America. Hence the official European 'Supersport' designation from 1987 onwards.

Although an ideal option for those who like the look of the 911 Turbo, the Turbo-body Carrera was quite expensive. It cost some DM26,000 more in Germany and $10,000 more in America than the standard Carrera in 1984, rising to DM30,000 and $14,000 more in 1989. When officially named the Supersport in 1987, it was £10,000 more expensive than a Sport Equipment car in the United Kingdom. These prices were, however, considerably less than those of the private coachbuilders attempting to match factory quality, some of whom charged as much as $35,000 for a complete conversion, including the necessary suspension modifications, 917 brakes, callipers, wheels, body and paintwork. Hence, Porsche effectively stole the market back.

The Turbo-Look cars had an additional option to delete the standard aerodynamic front and rear spoilers. These cars were known as 'without spoilers' or 'spoiler delete' under separate option code M470 for 1984, changing to P59 for 1985 to 1987, and P22 for 1988 and 1989. As with the Speedster, revised front quarter panels were incorporated replacing the wraparound chin spoiler. American Turbo-Look Carreras came without the rear engine lid 'Carrera' script logo as standard, whereas the RoW had it fitted as standard, though cars could be ordered without the script as option M498.

The 911 Carrera Supersport was not an independent model, but later Porsche literature has the SSE variant listed under Optional Equipment and says: "For drivers with even more sporting aspirations ..." Being approximately 70kg heavier than the standard Carrera due to wider wheels, tyres and wheelarches, the Turbo-Look aerodynamic drag was also increased due to the larger overall body area. The SSE acceleration figures were slightly lower than a standard Carrera. Test results showed them to be over a second slower to 100mph.

The interior was identical to the standard Carrera, as were key dimensions like wheelbase, length and height. When ordered, the car

American Turbo-Look Carrera with option code M470 – 'without spoilers/spoilers delete'.

The full 911 Turbo aerodynamic front and rear spoilers were fitted to the Turbo-Look and Supersport Carreras.

Left: Two American spec Turbo-Look Coupés. 421MADE is a fitting registration plate as it represents the number of Turbo-Look Coupés imported into the United States during 1984.

had all the standard options available, including the 491 code, and these were listed in the handbook, in the front boot compartment, and, for American cars only, on a window sticker (which also referred to '930 performance body/chassis'). The body, which was 123 millimetres wider than standard, incorporated standard doors, boot lid and bonnet lid, as well as the wider front and rear wings, wider 'shaped' bumpers, a fully wraparound front chin spoiler and the Turbo rear wing.

Technically, the engine (types 930/20, 930/21, 930/25 and 930/26) and transmission (type 915) were the same as the standard Carrera. From 1987 onwards, the Turbo-Look also benefited from the much improved G50 gearbox and hydraulic clutch mechanism.

The suspension design and fitments were uprated to match the 911 Turbo. 18.8mm torsion bars and a 22mm anti-roll bar were fitted at the front, and 26mm torsion bars and a 20mm anti-roll bar were fitted at the rear, although larger 27 millimetre rear torsion bars were introduced with the G50 cars. It also had larger semi-trailing arms at the rear; some 50mm wider than standard.

16 inch Fuchs alloy wheels were standard for the Turbo-Look. The front and rear rim widths being 7, 8 and 9 inches wide respectively. There were no 'Turbo-Look' identifying body markings used other than the standard 'Carrera' or 'Porsche' badges on the nose, rear light cluster and engine cover.

As an option to the standard Carrera, the 491 code was probably the most comprehensive and certainly the most expensive. Porsche was keen to offer the more discerning driver the latest styling, wider and arguably more aggressive looking Turbo aesthetics. Although straight line performance was slightly slower, the brakes were considerably better than those on the standard Carrera.

The Carrera Turbo-Look (option M491) replaced the 911 Turbo from 1984 to 1986 in America. This was due to restrictive emission control laws dating from 1980.

421 MADE

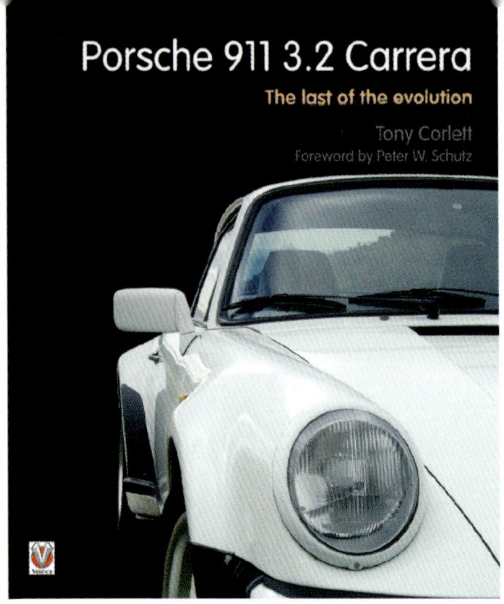

Chapter 6

M637 Club Sport: blueprinted

India Red Fuchs wheels as standard on a United Kingdom specification Club Sports.

The Club Sport (CS) was a lightened and simplified variant of the 3.2 Carrera Coupé. Porsche took an already established and well engineered package and, in the face of some criticism that the 911s were 'too padded', produced a lighter and more sporting car to suit its more competitive customers. Two areas of the standard Carrera Coupé were targeted in order to create a car that was special enough to have it's own name; weight reduction and engine balance, the latter resulting in a 'blueprinted' version of the standard 3.2 Carrera engine, specially designated with 'SP' on the crankcase. The Club Sport was introduced in 1987 to provide a more sporting road car suitable for regular track use or, with further modifications, to form the basis of a club racer.

The Club Sport was a reminder that the 911 was still a raw sports car that could be used and enjoyed on the road during the week, yet could be raced on a track in club events at the weekend. Whilst the 959 demonstrated Porsche's advanced technical prowess with sophisticated new systems that would be incorporated into the forthcoming new generation cars, the Club Sport, in contrast, was the essence of a purely functional sports Coupé, in keeping with the spirit of the revered 1973 Carrera 2.7RS.

Based on the 1987 Coupé which was already fitted with the improved G50 gearbox and hydraulic clutch, the Club Sport came with none of the luxury items associated with the standard Coupé. The specification put the emphasis on the critical areas of weight reduction and optimising the performance and handling characteristics. It carried the lightened chassis specification 'M637', and the chassis numbers started at 105000 for years 1987 (H) and 1988 (J). However, the 1989 (K) cars were only available by special order, and the chassis numbers ran in sequence with the standard Carrera Coupé.

The exact specification varied slightly for different markets, but the principal modifications to the standard Carrera Coupé included:

M637 chassis specification

- Deletion of electric sunroof
- Deletion of Carrera logo on engine lid
- Deletion of rear and sidewall trim panels
- Deletion of central locking
- Deletion of rear wiper
- Deletion of front fog lights
- Deletion of headlamp washers
- Deletion of PVC underseal
- Deletion of heavy duty sound insulation (except for engine and roof lining)
- Deletion of passenger sun visor
- Deletion of boot/engine courtesy lights
- Deletion of glove box lock (some markets only)
- Deletion of coat hooks
- Deletion of rear speakers
- Deletion of lids for door storage compartments
- Replacement of electric window lifts with mechanical winders
- Replacement of electric front seats with manually adjusted sports seats

Official factory promotional photograph of the 1987 Club Sport.

A typical UK specification Carrera Club Sport in Grand Prix White with India Red trim.

The Carrera Club Sport was almost identical to the standard Sport-equipped Coupé. Visual differences include the lack of front fog lamps and the inclusion of flank or front wing decals.

- Replacement of rear seats and belts with carpeted rear shelf
- Simplified manual heating system
- Simplified radio system
- Simplified, lightweight wiring harness
- Lightened, non-recoil bumper mountings
- Lightened space-saver spare wheel
- Fuel tank without PVC coating
- Modified, sculpted front bumper to admit more air to oil cooler

Engine
- Manufactured to 'blueprint' specification
- Lightened, hollow intake valve stems
- Modified Bosch DME, extending peak revs from 6520rpm to 6840rpm
- Modified engine/gearbox mounts
- Modified air cleaner with carbon canister plug
- Crankcase and cylinder head stamped 'SP' to differentiate the Club Sport engine from the standard Carrera unit

Transmission
- Limited slip differential
- Short throw gear lever
- Revised 4th and 5th gear ratios

Suspension, wheels, tyres
- Bilstein sports dampers
- 6Jx16 front and 7Jx16 rear Fuchs forged alloy wheels
- 205/55 VR front and 225/50 VR rear tyres

Aerodynamics
- Front and rear Sport Equipment spoilers

Although there was no special racing technology used, the engine components were carefully selected and matched from the standard parts so as to provide uniform output and reliability. This, together with the other subtle engine modifications and the lighter chassis, provided a power to weight ratio of over 200bhp/tonne.

Although the standard Sport Equipment Coupé performance figures were officially quoted for the Club Sport, it is widely accepted that these cars, in European specification, produced over 240bhp. A revised version of the standard Bosch Motronic injection and engine management system was used which raised the peak revs from 6520rpm to 6840rpm. It came with a short-shift gear linkage and a limited slip differential as standard. Apart from a slightly modified air intake, Porsche chose not to revise the standard throttle bodies and exhaust system.

The brakes and suspension were identical to the Sport Equipment but the Club Sport ran Bilstein Sport dampers as standard.

Opposite: The Club Sport had a limited production run from 1987 to 1989 of just 340 cars in total. Although Porsche officially produced the Club Sport in 1989, they were not specifically noted, unlike the 1987 and 1988 cars which had chassis numbers starting at 5000. The +5000 designation was reserved for the Speedster in 1989, so the Club Sport was produced within the usual Coupé chassis numbers.

Carrera
91 WON

91 WON
Carrera

Great White meets great white.

Performance figures for the Club Sport were as follows:

0 - 30mph	2.0 seconds
0 - 50mph	4.0 seconds
0 - 60mph	5.1 seconds
0 - 100mph	13.1 seconds
0 - 120mph	19.6 seconds
50 - 70 (5th gear)	7.4 seconds
50 - 70 (4th gear)	5.6 seconds
Maximum speed	152.1mph

The Club Sport's straight line performance was slightly better than the standard Carrera's, and it was quicker than the 2.7RS and the, then new and very quick, 250bhp 944 Turbo SE. In addition, the reduced weight and better chassis specification provided much sharper dynamics, enabling the Club Sport to handle with greater agility. The Club Sport also benefited from improved braking and lower fuel consumption.

The kerb weight of the Club Sport was quoted at 1160kg, a claimed saving of 50kg over a standard Carrera Coupé. However, it is likely that most European Club Sports weighed closer to 1135kg, and were, in fact, around 75kg lighter than a typically-specified Carrera Coupé with Sports Equipment.

The precise specification of the production Club Sports varied slightly for different markets. In the majority of cases, they were offered in a choice of colours, mostly non-metallic, with discreet CS Club Sport graphics on the left-hand front wing. However, all but one of the UK Club Sports were finished in distinctive Grand Prix White, with Indian Red wheel centres and prominent red Carrera CS script along the lower flanks of each door, mimicking the Carrera 2.7RS from 1973. The exception was exactly the opposite, finished in Indian Red with Grand Prix White detailing.

There was a choice of interior trim colours, although most cars had black leatherette with pinstripe cloth front seats.

Despite the sporting designation, it was possible to specify additional equipment from the options list. Most cars remained standard, though, as a higher specification would have contradicted the basic, sporting nature of the car.

A total of only 340 Club Sports were built by the factory, 81 in 1987, 169 in 1988 and 90 in 1989. Just 53 right-hand drive examples were imported into the United Kingdom and only 28 'federalised' examples were imported into America during 1988 and 1989. It is thought that all 81 cars from 1987 remained in Germany.

The Club Sport was a noisier, less comfortable car, with little really to distinguish it from the normal roadgoing, sport-equipped Carrera. Side by side, the Club Sport and the Coupé with Sports Equipment were identical, apart from the additional 'CS' decals and the absence of front fog lights on the former.

When the Club Sport was launched it received mixed reaction. The 1980s had seen a new generation of Porsche customer, with new wealth emerging from a booming economy. Many of these customers wanted to be part of the 911's sporting heritage, but couldn't live without the creature comforts of air-conditioning, electric windows, sunroof, central locking, etc. Purists were disappointed that the Club Sport hadn't gone further, with lightened panels and glass, and an even more basic specification in keeping with the original Carrera 2.7RS 'lightweight'. But this was late in the Carrera 3.2's life cycle, and an 'RS' variant couldn't be justified. Instead, the Club Sport bridged the gap.

A most desirable 911 variant, the Club Sport offered arguably the best marriage of 911 road car to 911 race car, and with it came all the flavour of a raw 911 with just a hint of sophistication. It's a shame that the 911 3.2 Carrera never made it to RS status, but the Club Sport filled the gap admirably and was, perhaps, in many ways, more appropriate for the time.

The Carrera Club Sport was a lightweight version of a Sport-equipped Coupé. Some 50kg lighter, the Club Sport was designed to offer occasional club racing. This is a typical United Kingdom specification RHD car in Grand Prix White with red 'Carrera CS' decals. There are thought to have been only 53 right-hand drive Club Sports imported into the United Kingdom.

Distinctive Club Sport graphic on the front left fender of American Club Sports.

This is an American specification LHD Club Sport in black: it's thought to be one of only three.

Thought to be the only Diamond Blue Club Sport in the world, this is a 1989 American specification Carrera with the later type 930/26 low compression 217bhp engine. There are thought to have been only 28 'federalised' Club Sports imported into America.

A row of American specification Club Sports. Whilst all but one of the United Kingdom specification Club Sports were Grand Prix White with red trim, American specification cars came in a variety of colours. They also did not carry the flank script, but did have a distinctive Club Sport logo on the front left fender.

An American Club Sport in Silver with black headlamp surrounds. Note the side reflectors within the front bumper forming an extension to the indicator lens for US specification Carreras.

CHAPTER 7

M503 911 SPEEDSTER: BOTT'S CREATION

The 911 Speedster was introduced in 1989 as a radically different Carrera, aimed at capturing the spirit of the historic 356 Speedsters. Drawn from the traditional Porsche 'Speedster' design, it came with a lowered windscreen and cabriolet roof. It was also available in both wide body and narrow body versions, the most popular being the wide body or Turbo-Look M491 option.

Soon after the launch of the Cabriolet in 1981, Porsche recognised the (largely American) requirement

Official 1989 Porsche promotional photograph showing a Speedster with a standard body.

Official 1989 Porsche promotional photograph showing the Speedster with a Turbo-Look body.

for a simple, light, and fine weather-use 911. Originally based on an SC chassis, the 911 Speedster made its way into production in 1983 under the direction of Prof. Helmuth Bott. Bott developed the prototype 911 Speedster in a little under six weeks, but it was subsequently shelved and locked away. This car became known as 'Bott's Speedster'.

Officially launched at the 1987 Frankfurt Motor Show, it wasn't until 1989 that Bott's creation was allowed to venture forward. By that stage it was considered unsuitable for production without some modifications, which included a taller windscreen capable of having a windscreen wiper fitted. The 911 Speedster finally went into production in 1988 as a 1989 'K' programme car, within the body of the 3.2 Carrera but without the aerodynamic front and rear spoilers.

Knowing by then that the 911 Carrera production run was due to end in 1989, Porsche still chose to introduce the Speedster as a 3.2 Carrera. Perhaps this was a pre-launch special for the eventual 964 chassis or, more likely, an easier adaptation of Bott's SC based car. Either way, only 2104 3.2 based Speedsters were produced in 1989, of which only 161 were narrow bodied and only 139 were right-hand drive.

The wide body Speedster was effectively a Supersport in non-sport guise. Without an aerodynamic front chin spoiler, two outer valance quarter panels were fitted to the Speedster in order to make up the width in the wider front wings and wheelarches. These quarter panels also incorporated the standard recessed fog lights.

Strictly a two-seater, the Speedster was a great combination of the Club Sport and the Cabriolet. As with the original 356 Speedsters, this 911 aimed to capture the essence of open top

The Speedster was a lowered variant of the Carrera Cabriolet. The brainchild of Helmuth Bott, the Speedster was developed and shelved in 1983, but was later shown at the 1987 Frankfurt Motor Show and went into production in 1989 as a limited run. The Carrera Speedster was the only 911 Speedster made, following in the spirit of the original 356 Speedsters.

The Speedster 'humps'.

motoring and, to some extent, was never designed to have the soft top raised. The Speedster looked best with the roof down, keeping the low windscreen and the 'speedster' humps prominent.

The Speedster was the Club Sport alternative for the Cabriolet lover and, with that, came a spirit of the traditional open top roadster. The windscreen was designed to be unscrewed and replaced by a small aero-screen in front of the driver for track events. However, even though the windscreen could be removed, Porsche never produced the aero-screen. The seats were lowered to offer better headroom with the lowered roof line and, as with the Club Sport, a lot of the unnecessary weighty items were removed.

Porsche designed a radically lower windscreen, and raked it some 5 degrees flatter than the standard screen, which was fitted within a slimline aluminium structure. The quarter-lights were also removed from the standard Cabriolet doors. To capture the original 'Speedster' image, two humps were placed directly behind the front seats, over the area where the rear seats would ordinarily have been, and across the cabriolet roof aperture at the rear of the car. This created a very low sweeping effect. The Speedster

Next two pages: The Speedster was designed for the sunshine. An emergency folding roof was provided, but came with a disclaimer from Porsche that the roof was not entirely weatherproof. The roof was stowed under the 'humps' and was raised manually.

'humps' were moulded in polyurethane and colour matched to the body.

In reality, the Speedster was a lowered Cabriolet, albeit that the unpretentious soft-roof was neither lined nor electrically operated. The Speedster was designed for sunny climates and, although it did have

Speedster

The Speedster cockpit had lowered windscreen and no side quarter-lights.

a roof, this was neither effective in keeping weather out, nor easy to raise and collapse. The roof nestled below the Speedster humps when stowed. In raising the roof, the hump panel hinged backward and the roof then hinged forward, from where the bottom of the 'B' post would normally be located, allowing the hump panel to be lowered again. The roof was then pulled backward over the hump panel and forward to the top of the windscreen and clipped into place, forming a taut cover. Although the Speedster looked tidy with its roof up, the roof wasn't completely weatherproof, nor did very little in reducing wind noise and, with very low sides, it obstructed the driver's lateral vision. It's clear that this car was never intended to be used with its roof up. In fact, Porsche made prospective owners sign a weather damage waiver prior to purchase.

This 911 variant was never designed to be practical, nor to sell in its thousands. Instead, it represented a pure fashion statement that only Porsche could capture. It was a great example of eccentric motoring for those who wanted to stand out in a crowd, and captured the essence of the much loved 356 predecessors.

The Speedster was probably *the* jewel in the Carrera crown and fitting that it should see out the final days of the last factory-designated 911. It was a wonderful variant and we should be very thankful that it was manufactured at all, let alone as part of the 3.2 Carrera production run.

The Speedster was available with a standard or Turbo-Look body and without the aerodynamic front and rear spoilers. The Turbo-Look option incorporated an infill lower front quarter panel up to the front wheelarches.

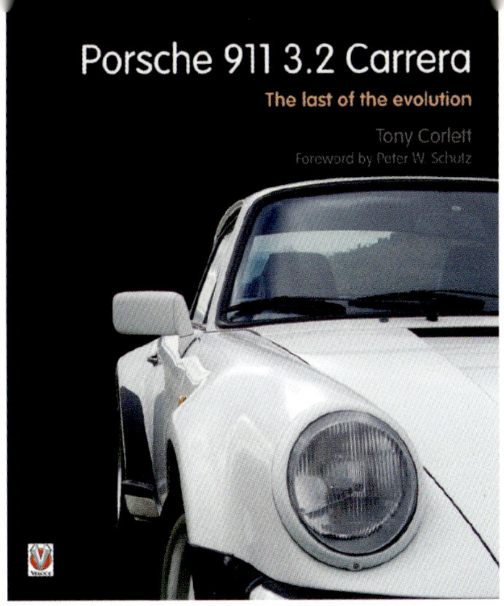

Chapter 8

The engine - type 930

The Carrera engine was available in two basic guises, the type 930/20 and 930/26 with a compression ratio of 10.3:1, and type 930/21 and 930/25, with a compression ratio of 9.5:1.

Derived from the RS 3.0, the 930 had a die-cast aluminium crankcase, 95mm diameter Nikasil cylinders, an aluminium camshaft box (the camshafts running on four bearings), forged pistons cooled directly by oil squirted from crankcase jets, forged connecting rods, and a forged steel crankshaft. The crankshaft ran on eight main bearings, increased from seven with the revised 3.3 litre Turbo type 930/60.

The improved type 930/60 3.3 litre Turbo engine (type 930/66 from 1983) formed the basis of the SC type 930/03 and, subsequently, the 3.2 type 930/20.

The use of Nikasil is an important factor in the Carrera engine as it provided a substantial level of protection to the cylinder bores. Nikasil is an exceptionally hard surface nickel and silicone carbide coating, normally less than 0.1 millimetre thick, which is applied directly to the aluminium bore. Within the nickel coating are particles of silicon carbide, less than 4 microns in size, making up something like 4 per cent of the Nikasil coating and forming adhesion points for oil collection. An extremely tough surface with low friction was achieved, ensuring excellent cylinder lubrication and longevity.

Developed in the early nineteen-eighties, the original 3164cc flat-six engines were twin turbo-charged, developing some 700bhp, and were used in limited numbers in race cars only. These original development engines used the crankshaft from the 930 Turbo and the cylinder bores of the SC, offering a 74.4mm stroke and a 95mm bore. Porsche actually went even further, using 100mm bores with a capacity of 3.5 litres and, although tried and tested, these never made it into production.

The 3.2 litre naturally-aspirated Carrera engine was, therefore, a natural development of the 911 power plant. However, without the advanced development of the Bosch Motronic engine management system, it may have been compromised in terms of the power boost falling foul of increased fuel consumption. The two main elements worked well together and Porsche engineers produced a mighty package with little or no compromise.

Together with the capacity increase over the predecessor's 3.0 litre engine, the 3.2 engine had one other major improvement. The timing chain tensioner cylinders were permanently fed with oil from the engine, thus preventing failure (a regular and expensive problem with earlier 911 engines). This was seen as a major step forward and, in many ways, made the 3.2 Carrera engine almost totally reliable. Another major change was the size increase for the inlet and exhaust ports, although the same size valves were used. That increase, together with the use of a larger diameter exhaust system, meant that the engine breathed more efficiently, producing 73bhp per litre, compared to the 68bhp per litre of the earlier 3.0 litre engine.

The Carrera was produced with four different 930 flat-six air-cooled engine units. With a capacity of 3164cc, the power output was a strong 231bhp, reduced to 207 or 217 for the American market in lower compression format. This is a Porsche 1986 promotional photograph of a type 930/20 with optional air-conditioner pump.

The modifications over the 3.0 litre engine brought the 3.2 dry engine weight up to 219kg, compared to the 190kg of the 3.0 litre. Although the 3.2 engine weighed over 35kg heavier than the original 901 engine, it could still be housed in an original 901 engine bay without modification to either.

With its new engine and revised ratios in the 915 gearbox, the 1984 930/20 European Carrera hit the road running. Porsche claimed a top speed of 152mph and a staggering fuel consumption figure of 41.6mpg at a steady 55mph. At a steady 75mph, the Carrera's efficiency really showed, with Porsche claiming 31.4mpg, a truly remarkable return for a car with such performance reserves.

For the American, Canadian and Japanese markets, all running on lead-free fuel, the 930/20 engine was fitted with flatter pistons and re-named 930/21. It had a lower compression ratio (9.5:1) and was tuned to run on 91 octane fuel. This engine, which had a three-way catalytic converter and lambda sensor but maintained the same type of engine management system and valve timing, produced only 207bhp at 5900rpm. The type 930/21 was replaced by the type 930/25 in 1987, to coincide with the new G50 gearbox. The new type 930/25 used a different Motronic engine management system and ran on 95 octane fuel, and power output increased to 217bhp.

Engine type 930/26 was specifically introduced in 1985 for the Swiss market only. Although exactly the same as the 930/20 except for the inclusion of an air pump blowing into the exhaust ports, the power and torque were identical to that of the 930/20.

The type 930/20 engine ran for the entire life of the Carrera and was sold throughout the world except for America, Canada, Japan and Switzerland. Type 930/26 ran from 1985 to 1989 for the Swiss market only. The low compression type 930/21 ran from 1984 to 1986, and the type 930/25 ran from 1987 to 1989 for America, Canada and Japan. Later 930/20 engines were also fitted with three-way catalytic converters and Lambda sensors, for markets such as Germany, where government tax incentives were offered for cleaner emissions.

Apart from the inclusion of chrome-plated valve stems (from 1986) and the Club Sport 'blueprinted' engine specification, the type 930/20 engine didn't change.

Chapter 9

Ignition and fuel injection

Bosch Motronic ML 3.1

Porsche maximised the performance of the Carrera engine by way of an effective ignition system, providing smooth delivery of power, optimum fuel efficiency, and minimum exhaust emissions. Very much a complete solution, the fuel injection and flat-six engine worked in total harmony, having undergone exhaustive testing with the aim of achieving a power plant of almost perfect proportions.

Porsche retained the tried and tested Bosch petrol injection system, but upgraded to the Motronic system (Bosch L-Jetronic with Digital Motor Electronics - DME) on the Carrera, a type of fuel injection commonly referred to as a pulsed injection system.

This fuel injection system sprayed fuel into the intake manifold when required in the combustion cycle. This way, the fuel delivery was accurately controlled to achieve the most efficient stoichiometric air/fuel ratio of 14/7 (mass of air/mass of fuel). The stoichiometric or 'theoretical combustion' is the ideal combustion process during which the fuel is burned completely. A complete combustion is a process which burns all the carbon (C) to (CO_2), all hydrogen (H) to (H_2O), and all sulphur (S) to (SO_2). If there are any unburned components in the exhaust gas the combustion process is incomplete.

The Motronic setup incorporated an engine management system that controlled the ignition and fuel injection, enabling the Carrera engine to function at its optimum level. The Motronic system timed and metered the fuel and dictated when to fire the spark to create combustion at exactly the correct time. The DME computed input from various sensors in the engine (engine speed was measured from the rpm sensor, the amount of air being induced into the engine was measured from the airflow sensor, the exhaust gasses were measured by an oxygen sensor and additional information was gained from the timing and cylinder head sensors). The DME then calculated the optimum ignition timing and fuel delivery to produce the most horsepower with the least amount of emissions.

Constant monitoring and instantaneous adjustment to the fuel/air mixture and ignition timing to over four thousand possible combinations produced durability, reliability and performance without compromise. The DME computer's chip contained a data map based upon dynometer and emissions tests carried out by Porsche. At any split second, the DME could read all of the data input from the engine sensors, compare it to the original data map, and dictate how much fuel to deliver and when to fire the ignition.

The Motronic system also controlled the maximum engine revolutions, cutting off the fuel supply at 6520rpm, and an idling speed stabilization function ensured an even-running engine.

CHAPTER 10

TRANSMISSION - 915 TO G50

Derived from the Porsche type 916 racing gearbox, the type 915 unit was first introduced in 1971 as a four-speed unit, before being uprated to a five-speed. Originally cast in magnesium alloy for a lighter casing, from 1978 onwards the type 915 was cast in aluminium for greater strength. This laid a good foundation for the powerful 3.2 output in 1984, though the type 915 was stretched to its limits.

For the 3.2 engine, the type 915 gearbox was fitted with an oil cooler, and the fourth and fifth gear pinions were modified. This was to keep the gearbox oil cooler under the higher power and torque load of the type 930/20 engine. The oil cooler was mounted on the left side of the gearbox housing just ahead of the driveshafts.

Ironically, the problems associated with cooling the oil in the type 915 gearbox effectively caused its demise in 1986. As well as being an expensive solution, Porsche realized that its own synchronizers, durable and reliable as they were, were not going to cope with the increasing gear shifting forces, so it chose the tried and tested 924/944 Audi-based Borg-Warner synchronisers for an all new gearbox for 1987.

The new G50 gearbox, with the Borg-Warner synchronisers and without the need for an oil cooler, was produced by Getrag, an independent manufacturer, in 1987. The new gearbox was a completely new design and had great potential in terms of torque loading, so much so, in fact, that Porsche used the new G50 gearbox in its 911 Turbo in 1989, the very first five-speed gearbox to be used in a 911 Turbo. A further development ensured that, if required, Porsche could save weight with the G50 by going back to a magnesium housing, though an aluminium housing went into production.

The switch from type 915 to type G50 was an important step, and one which carried with it a whole new approach to gear change. The G50 unit was a far more efficiently-designed unit, and substantially improved ease of operation and gear shift throw.

Several gearbox combinations were offered throughout the life of the Carrera. From 1984 to 1986, types 915-67, 915-68, 915-69, 915-70, 915-72 and 915-73 were used and, from 1987 to 1989 with the G50 gearbox, types G50-00, G50-01 and G50-02 were used.

From 1984 to 1986 with the type 915 gearbox, Porsche used a cable-operated clutch and plate diameter of 225mm. For the type G50 gearbox from 1987 to 1989, the clutch was uprated to hydraulic operation and the plate diameter was increased to 240mm, the same size as that used in the 911 Turbo.

Gearbox type: 915-72/915-67/915-69		
Final drive	8:31	3.875:1
1st gear	11:35	3.182:1
2nd gear	18:33	1.833:1
3rd gear	23:29	1.261:1
4th gear	29:28	0.966:1
5th gear	38:29	0.763:1
Maximum rpm in 5th gear	6520	

Gearbox type: 915-73/915-68/915-70		
Final drive	8:31	3.875:1
1st gear	11:35	3.182:1
2nd gear	18:32	1.778:1
3rd gear	23:29	1.261:1
4th gear	26:26	1.000:1
5th gear	38:30	0.789:1
Maximum rpm in 5th gear	6520	

Gearbox type: G50-00: Europe and rest of world (inc. Club Sport)		
Final drive	9:31	3.444:1
1st gear	12:42	3.500:1
2nd gear	17:35	2.059:1
3rd gear	22:31	1.409:1
4th gear	27:29	1.074:1
5th gear	36:31	0.861:1
Maximum rpm in 5th gear	6520	

Gearbox type: G50-01: USA, Canada and Japan (inc. Club Sport)		
Final drive	9:31	3.444:1
1st gear	12:42	3.500:1
2nd gear	17:35	2.059:1
3rd gear	22:31	1.409:1
4th gear (Lower)	32:36	1.125:1
5th gear (Lower)	36:32	0.889:1
Maximum rpm in 5th gear	6520	

Gearbox type: G50-02: Switzerland		
Final drive	9:31	3.444:1
1st gear (Higher)	13:41	3.154:1
2nd gear (Higher)	19:36	1.895:1
3rd gear (Higher)	24:32	1.333:1
4th gear (Higher)	28:29	1.036:1
5th gear	36:31	0.861:1
Maximum rpm in 5th gear	6520	

Chapter 11

Suspension

Fully independent to all corners, the 911 Carrera was weighted on torsion bars all round, positioned longitudinally at the front and laterally at the rear. This basic torsion bar design remained unchanged from 1963 to 1989.

The 911 torsion bars were engineered to operate with resistance to a turning moment. That turning moment was applied to the torsion bars via leverage from lower wishbones at the front, and the trailing or radius arms at the rear. Whereas the front wishbones operated sideways, the rear trailing arms operated backwards. An axle control arm was fitted at the rear which picked up the trailing arm and lower damper mounting and ran back towards the middle of the car, pivoting off the floorpan. For 1984 and 1985, the factory standard torsion bar diameter at the front was 18.8mm and the rear was 24mm. From 1986 to 1989, the factory standard torsion bar diameter at the front was 18.8mm and the rear was 25mm.

The entire weight of the car was taken through the turning moment on the torsion bars, and the ride heights were dependent upon the splines within the rigid housings of the torsion bar. Secondary to the torsion bars and wishbones/trailing arms were the dampers, otherwise described as self-levelling, hydro-pneumatic suspension struts. These provided the damped stiffness between the lower mounting point of the control arm at the rear, or wishbones at the front, and the rigid top fixing point of the body. The damper or strut provided the level of stiffness required for varying types of driving styles or comfort. Between the torsion bars and the dampers, the 911 Carrera suspension set up was quite simple. From 1984 to 1989, the factory standard damper was either Boge for the comfort setting or Bilstein for the sport setting.

At the front of the car, the torsion bars were housed within the wishbone or transverse control arm, fixed at the very front to a light alloy crossmember which tied both left and right wishbones together. At the rear of the car, the torsion bars were housed within the floorpan, and ran out towards the side of the car where they connected to the trailing arm. A distinctive body feature of the 911 was the two circular rear torsion bar removal plugs which were positioned in the lower skirt line in front of the rear wheelarches. Removing these allowed access for removal and replacement of the rear torsion bars.

There were only eight main suspension bushes in the entire suspension. Two on each corner, one at either end of the wishbones at the front, and two at the pivot point of the control arms to the floorpan at the rear.

Anti-roll bars were fitted to the front and the rear of the car. These were each fixed through four rubber bushes which were the only ancillary suspension bushes on the car. For 1984 and 1985, the factory standard anti-roll bar diameter was 20mm at the front and 18mm at the rear. From 1986 to 1989, the factory standard anti-roll bar diameter was 22mm at the front and 21mm at the rear.

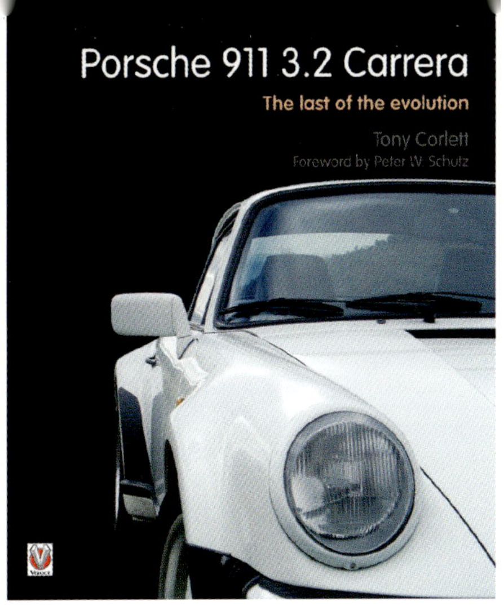

CHAPTER 12

FUCHS FELGE

In the nineteen-sixties, German industrialist Otto Fuchs produced the earliest forged aluminium wheels. These, officially known as '*Fuchs Felge*' in German and 'Fuchs Alloy' in English, went on to become one of the distinctive 'trademarks' of the 911. More recently referred to as the '*Flügel-Rad*' or 'Vane-Type', the word 'Fuchs' is used to describe the wheel synonymous with Porsche 911s. Otto Fuchs KG went on to produce forged wheels for many other manufacturers, but the name 'Fuchs' remains as sole description for the most famous and distinctive Porsche wheel of all.

The forging process is basically a method of shaping heated metal by compression. The Fuchs process for the 911 *Fuchs Felge* starts with a single aluminium alloy billet (aluminium, silicon, magnesium and manganese) before being pressured into the wheel shape with a massive press. This single-billet-forged process provided a very strong wheel which performed with little or no distortion about the hub.

The Fuchs alloy was phased out at the end of Carrera production in 1989, never again to be used by Porsche. It was replaced by the light alloy pressure cast Design 90 and Cup alternatives on the 964. There were good engineering reasons why Porsche dropped the people's favourite wheel, and in some ways the more modern approach to alloys suited the new era of 964 design.

FUCHS OFFSETS:

6J x 15 H2 36.0mm
7J x 15 H2 23.3mm
8J x 15 H2 10.6mm
9J x 15 H2 3mm

6J x 16 H2 36.0mm
7J x 16 H2 23.3mm
8J x 16 H2 10.6mm
9J x 16 H2 15mm

The Fuchs forging process shaped the wheel from one single aluminium alloy billet, to the final shape, under compression. This official Fuchs image shows five random stages during compression from the billet on the left to the final wheel on the right.

A typical forged Fuchs alloy wheel. The name Fuchs has become synonymous with the Porsche 911.

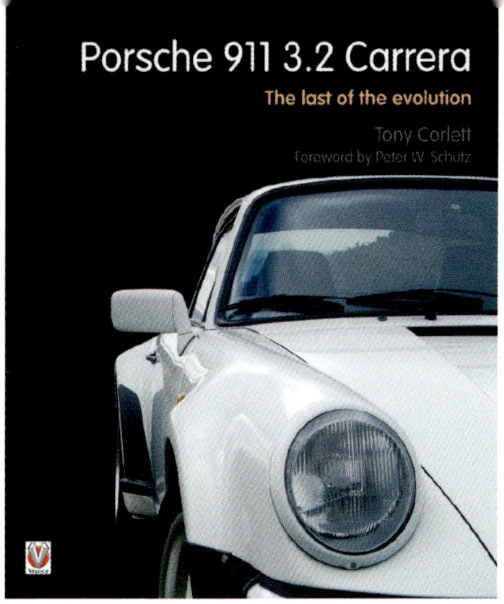

Chapter 13

Chassis numbers

WPO ZZZ 91 Z X S 1 Y NNNN

WPO	World manufacturer's code: 'Porsche'	
ZZZ	Replaced with ABO or EBO codes for USA models only, body, engine and restraints as follows:	
ABO	A:	Body code USA/CDN: Carrera Coupé
EBO	E:	Body code USA/CDN: Carrera Targa and Cabriolet
	B:	Code for USA engine variants
	O:	Restraint system: O: Belts
91	First two digits of vehicle type (i.e. 91 for all 911s)	
Z	Check character	
X	Model year:	
	E:	1984
	F:	1985
	G:	1986
	H:	1987
	J:	1988
	K:	1989
S	Plant of origin (S = Stuttgart for all 911s)	
1	Last digit of vehicle type (i.e. 1 for all 911 models)	
Y	Code for body:	
	0:	911 Coupé
	2:	911 Coupé USA and Canada
	4:	911 Targa
	5:	911 Cabriolet and Speedster
	6:	911 Targa USA and Canada
	7:	911 Cabriolet and Speedster USA and Canada
NNNN	Sequential chassis number	

Official 1984 Porsche promotional photograph showing from left to right, Targa, Coupé and Cabriolet for the American market.

911 Carrera

CHAPTER 14

FACTORY PRICES

Prices as quoted from official Porsche price lists (all prices in *deutschmarks*)					
	Coupé*	Targa*	Cabriolet*	Club Sport	Speedster**
1984	68,560	71,660	75,980		
1985	72,000	76,000	82,000		
1986	72,250	79,250	85,250		
1987	80,500	84,600	90,800	80,500	
Cat	82,075	86,175	92,375	82,075	
1988	83,700	88,000	94,200	83,700	110,000
Cat	85,275	89,575	95,775	85,275	111,575
1989	86,000	90,500	96,800		110,000
Cat	87,575	92,075	98,375		111,575

* Standard body without spoilers
* Teledial wheels up to 1988
** Turbo-Look

Sport Equipment options (in *deutschmarks*)				
	F/R Aero Spoilers M473	6x16/7x16 Fuchs M395	7x15/8x15 Fuchs M401	Turbo-Look M491
1984	+2730	+3085	+1850	+25,950
1985	+2850	+3195	+1915	+27,950
1986	+2990	+3355	+2100	+29,350
1987	+2995	+1370	N/A	+29,350
1988	+2995	standard	N/A	+29,750
1989	+2995	standard	N/A	+29,790

Interior equipment options				
	Leather seats M562	Full leather	Customer leather	Air conditioning M559
1984	+1850	+3950	+4350	+3290
1985	+1990	+4090	+5070	+3450
1986	+2130	+4380	+6950	+3620
1987	+2205	+4535	+6990	+3750
1988	+2300	+4715	+7250	+3900
1989	+2300	+4715	+7250	+3900

Exterior paint options		
	Metallic paint	Customer paint
1984	+1380	+2510
1985	+1380	+2650
1986	+1435	+2760
1987	+1485	+2855
1988	+1545	+2965
1989	+1545	+2965

By comparison, in 1984 a Turbo-Look Carrera Coupé would have cost DM94,510 compared to a 911 Turbo Coupé at DM114,000, correspondingly rising to DM115,790 compared to DM138,800 for similar cars in 1989.

Late in 1988, the newly introduced 964 Carrera 4 Coupé could be ordered. It was priced at DM114,500 for availability later in 1989.

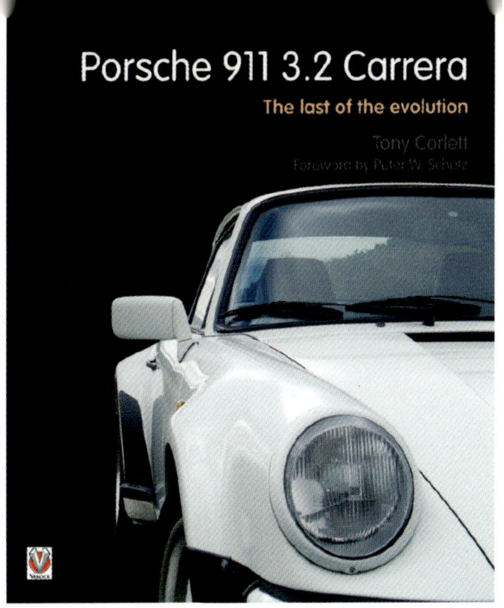

Chapter 15

Manufacture codes

The first code on the identification label is a 'C' code which identifies the market for which the car was produced. This appears not always to have been used on the earlier European cars.

International 'C' codes	
C00	Germany
C02	Equipped with catalytic converter
C03	California type car
C05	France
C07	Italy
C09	Sweden
C10	Swiss version - post 1986 with cat
C11	Austria
C15	Hong Kong
C16	United Kingdom
C20	Holland
C22	Belgium
C23	Australia
C24	Greece
C26	Singapore/South Africa
C32	Saudi Arabia
C36	Canada

Below are examples of standard equipment for UK and USA markets in 1987:

Standard UK Specification for 1987 (C16)*
5-speed manual transmission
Forged alloy road wheels, black with anti-theft device
Sport shock absorbers
Front and rear anti-roll bars
Front and rear aerodynamic spoilers
Integral front and high intensity rear fog lamps
Brake pad wear indicator
2-stage heated rear window (Coupé and Targa only)
3-speed windscreen wipers, variable intermittent wipe settings with heated,

electrically operated windscreen washers and additional heavy duty windscreen wash system
Internally adjustable headlamps
Headlamp washers
Rear window wiper (Coupé and Targa only)
Impact absorbing bumpers
Electrically operated windows
Central door locking
Tinted, heat insulating glass
Electrically operated sunroof (Coupé only)
Electrically operated roof (Cabriolet only)
Heated, electrically adjustable mirrors for driver and passenger doors
Thermostatic heating control
Electrically adjustable front seats (partial leather)
Leather covered steering wheel (380mm diameter)
Blaupunkt Toronto digital self-seek stereo radio with combined auto-reverse cassette player with Dolby and metal tape facilities, cassette programme search, anti-theft code protection, 4x20 watt output. 8 speaker system (6 on Cabriolet) and integral windscreen aerial

Standard USA Specification for 1987*

Oil cooler, front
Four-wheel independent torsion bar suspension with stabilizer bars, front and rear
Welded, unitary construction; double sided zinc-galvanised body
Dual circuit four-wheel vented disc brakes, power assisted
Forged alloy wheels
Aluminium spare tire rim with space saving tire
Electrically adjustable and heated outside rear-view mirrors
Brake pad wear indicator light
Upshift indicator light
Integrated fog lights
Anti-theft device on wheels
Windshield with graduated tint
Halogen headlights
Heatable windshield washer nozzles
Steel belted radials
Rack and pinion steering
Inertia reel 3-point seat belts, front and lap belts, rear
Driver seat with electric height and backrest adjustment
Reclining bucket seats
Choice of partial leather seats

Leather covered steering wheel
Transistorized tachometer
Trip odometer
Sun visors with covered vanity mirrors
Quartz analog clock
Electric rear window defroster, two stage (Coupé and Targa)
Power windows
Tinted glass all round
Deep cut carpeting
Carpeted luggage compartment
Electric windshield wiper with intermittent wiper cycle
Air conditioning
Blaupunkt Portland digital FM/AM cassette radio
Windshield antenna, 4 loudspeakers, suppression kit

* As listed in official Porsche literature for UK and USA - 1987

It is not unusual on the earlier cars to find only the 'C' code listed in the handbook.
Later cars also had further 'M' Option Codes listed as well as the 'C' code.

Option 'M' Codes (Mehrausstattungs Nummer)

Official Porsche 911 Carrera Option List : 1984 to 1989		
M Code	Description	Associated M Code
018	Sport steering wheel with elevated hub	
058	Bumpers with impact absorbers	
070	Tonneau cover - Cabriolet	
139	Seat heating - left	
197	88Ah battery	
220	Locking differential (40%)	
243	Shorter gear shift lever	
261	Passenger side mirror electric plain	528
286	High intensity windscreen washer	
288	Headlight washer	
298	Prepared for unleaded fuel, manual transmission	
326	Radio Blaupunkt Berlin IQR 86/IQR 88	328, 330, 686, 688, 494, 690

Official Porsche 911 Carrera Option List : 1984 to 1989		
M Code	Description	Associated M Code
327	Radio Blaupunkt Köln SQR 23	330, 686, 688
328	Radio Blaupunkt Bremen SQR 45/SQR 46	330, 686, 688, 326, 690
330	Radio Blaupunkt Atlanta SQR 23/Toronto SQR 24/SQR 46	327, 686, 688, 328, 326, 690
340	Seat heating - right	
341	Central locking system	
348	Forged wheels in Grand Prix White	485
379	Series seat, left electrical vertical adjustment	383, 437, 586
380	Series seat, right electrical vertical adjustment	387, 438, 513
383	Sport seat - left	437, 586, 980, 379
387	Sport seat - right	438, 513, 980, 380
395	Light metal wheels forged	401, 455, 491, P59
401	Light metal wheels	395, 455, 491, P59
419	Rear luggage compartment instead of rear seats	
425	Rear wiper	559
430	Rectangular fog light yellow lens	
437	Full power seat - left	383, 379
438	Comfort seat - right	387, 380
439	Electric Cabriolet roof	
451	2 speakers on back shelf	
454	Cruise control	
455	Wheel locks	395, 401, 491
462	Sekuriflex windshield	
463	Clear windshield	567
470	Without spoilers, in conjunction with Turbo-Look	
473	With spoilers	491, P59, P22
474	Sport shock absorbers - Bilstein	491, P59, P22
485	Forged wheels in gold metallic	348
490	Hi-Fi sound system	
491	Turbo-Look	P59, 395, 401, 455, 473, 474, 49
494	Amplifier system	326, 686
496	Prepared for cellular telephone	
498	Without rear model designation	491, P59
513	Lumbar support - right seat	387, 380
526	Cloth door panels	980
528	Passenger side mirror convex	261
533	Alarm system	

Official Porsche 911 Carrera Option List : 1984 to 1989		
M Code	Description	Associated M Code
559	Air conditioner	425
567	Windshield green graduated tint	463
586	Lumbar support - left seat	383, 379
605	Vertical headlight adjustment	
650	Sunroof	
686	Radio Blaupunkt Hamburg SQM 24/ Ludwigsburg SQM 26	327, 330, 688, 328, 326, 494, 690
688	Radio Blaupunkt Boston SQM 23	327, 330, 686, 328, 326, 494
690	Porsche CD-10 with radio	326, 328, 330, 686
975	Velour carpet in luggage compartment	
980	Seat cover ruffled leather	383, 387
P22	Turbo-Look without spoilers	473, 474
P40	Forged wheels	
P59	Without spoilers	491, 395, 401, 473, 474, 498
There were many more Porsche 'M' option codes available but not officially denoted within Porsche literature, option lists and price lists for 1984 to 1989.		

Official 1985 Porsche promotional photograph showing a Turbo-Look Cabriolet without front and rear aerodynamic spoilers. Note how the modified front lower quarter panels differ from production models.

Please note that colour reproduction may not be completely accurate.

Chapter 16

Colours

1983/1984				
Colour	Metallic	Codes		
Grand Prix White		908		P5
India Red		027	L M3A	G8
Black		700	L 041	A1
Alpine White			L 90E	
Pasadena Yellow			L Y1L	
Glacier Blue		32Z		K4
Chiffon White		182		
Pewter	Metallic	956		U3
Platinum	Metallic	655	L M8U	U1
Moss Green	Metallic	20C		Y8
Slate Blue	Metallic	661		X6
Quartz Grey	Metallic	662		X5
Kiln Red	Metallic	811		X3
Ruby Red	Metallic	810	L M3V	X7
Light Bronze	Metallic	966	L M1V	R6
Sapphire	Metallic		L Y5V	
Montego Black	Metallic		L Y9V	
Gemini Grey	Metallic		L Z7Z	
Zermatt Silver	Metallic		L Y7Y	

1985/1986				
Colour	Metallic	Codes		
Grand Prix White		908		P5
India Red		027	L M3A	G1
Black		700	L 041	A1
Alpine White			L 90E	
Marble Grey		673		A8
Pastel Beige		536	LM1N	D4

1985/1986				
Colour	Metallic	Codes		
Dark Blue		347		K5
Nutmeg Brown	Metallic	492		S1
Garnet Red	Metallic	822	L M3Y	S2
Iris Blue	Metallic	33P		S3
Prussian Blue	Metallic	33X		S4
Crystal Green	Metallic	33N	L M6Y	S5
White Gold	Metallic	539		S6
Silver	Metallic	936		S7
Moss Green	Metallic	20C		Y8
Meteor Grey	Metallic	961		Y5
Sapphire	Metallic		L Y5V	
Zermatt Silver	Metallic		L Y7Y	
Mahogany Brown	Metallic		L B8Z	
Kalahari Beige	Metallic		L A1Y	
Slate Grey	Metallic		L Y7U	
Pearl White	Metallic		L OA9	

1987/1988				
Colour	Metallic	Codes		
Grand Prix White		908		P5
Black		700	L 041	A1
Dark Blue		347		K5
Cherry/Carmine Red		80F		
Citrus Yellow		10W		
Ceramic/Caramel Beige		499		
Turquoise		21M		M7
Indian Red		80K	LM3A	G1
Alpine White			L 90E	
Summer Yellow			LM1A	B1
Silver	Metallic	980		S7
Laguna Green	Metallic	35Y		F2
Granite Green	Metallic	699		F3
Nougat Brown	Metallic	40B	L M8V	F4
Diamond Blue	Metallic	697	LM5U	F6
Espresso Brown	Metallic	40D		F5
Navy Blue	Metallic	35V		
Venetian Blue	Metallic	35U		F8
Cassis Red	Metallic	80D		F9
Zermatt Silver	Metallic		L Y7Y	
Slate Grey	Metallic		L Y7U	

1987/1988				
Colour	Metallic	Codes		
Nautit/Ocean Blue	Metallic		L Y5Z	
Flamingo	Metallic		L Y4Z	
Maraschino Red	Metallic		L Y3V	
Almond Beige	Metallic		L Y1Y	

1989				
Colour	Metallic	Codes		
Grand Prix White		908		P5
Black		700	L 041	A1
Dark Blue		347		K5
Indian Red		80K		G1
Linen		60M	L MIU	E2
Apricot Beige		548		E4
Murano Green		22C		N6
Alpine White			L 90E	
Silver	Metallic	980		S7
Diamond Blue	Metallic	697		F5
Dove Blue	Metallic	37B	C7	
Stone Grey	Metallic	693		U8
Slate	Metallic	22D		
Velvet Red	Metallic	81L		U6
Linen Grey	Metallic	550		W5
Pine Green	Metallic	22E		W7
Cognac Brown	Metallic	40L		Z7
Salmon/Coral	Metallic	81K		Z9
Zermatt Silver	Metallic		L Y7Y	
Slate Grey	Metallic		L Y7U	
Glacier Blue	Metallic		L Y5U	
Bamboo	Metallic		L Y1Z	
Baltic Blue	Metallic	37B		C7
Forest Green	Metallic	22E		W7

Targa Roof and Cabriolet Hood Colour Codes		
Colour	Code	Model
Dark Brown	V4	Cabriolet
Burgundy	V5	Cabriolet
Mahogony	V6	Cabriolet
Grey Green	V7	Cabriolet
Dark Blue	V8	Cabriolet
Black	V9	Targa & Cabriolet

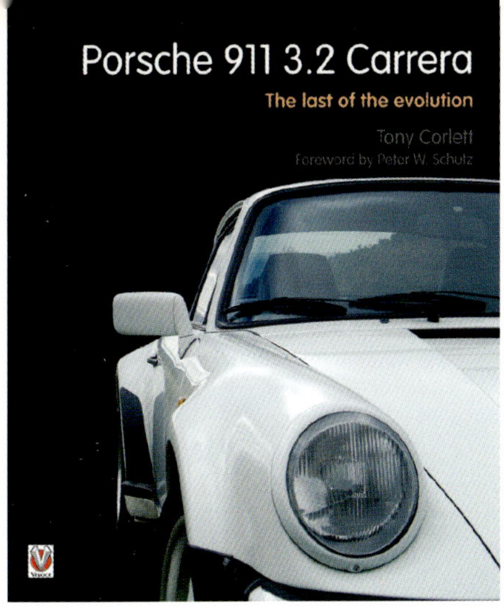

Chapter 17

Official factory production numbers

Model year 1984 (E-Program)		
911 Model	**Chassis number range**	**Production**
Carrera Coupé	91 ES 10 0001 - 91 ES 10 4033	3973
Carrera Coupé Japan	91 ES 10 9501 - 91 ES 10 9717	157
Carrera Coupé US and CDN	91 ES 12 0001 - 91 ES 12 2282	2222
Carrera Targa	91 ES 14 0001 - 91 ES 14 1469	1409
Carrera Targa Japan	91 ES 14 9501 - 91 ES 14 9564	4
Carrera Cabriolet	91 ES 15 0001 - 91 ES 15 1835	1775
Carrera Cabriolet Japan	91 ES 15 9501 - 91 ES 15 9577	17
Carrera Targa US and CDN	91 ES 16 0001 - 91 ES 16 2260	2200
Carrera Cabriolet US and CDN	91 ES 17 0001 - 91 ES 17 1191	1131
Total for 1984		12888

Model year 1985 (F-Program)		
911 Model	**Chassis number range**	**Production**
Carrera Coupé	91 FS 10 0001 - 91 FS 10 3529	3469
Carrera Coupé Japan	91 FS 10 9501 - 91 FS 10 9722	162
Carrera Coupé US and CDN	91 FS 12 0001 - 91 FS 12 1959	1899
Carrera Targa	91 FS 14 0001 - 91 FS 14 1435	1375
Carrera Targa Japan	91 FS 14 9501 - 91 FS 14 9564	4
Carrera Cabriolet	91 FS 15 0001 - 91 FS 15 1583	1524
Carrera Cabriolet Japan	91 FS 15 9501 - 91 FS 15 9575	15
Carrera Targa US and CDN	91 FS 16 0001 - 91 FS 16 1942	1882
Carrera Cabriolet US and CDN	91 FS 17 0001 - 91 FS 17 1050	990
Total for 1985		11320

Model year 1986 (G-Program)		
911 Model	**Chassis number range**	**Production**
Carrera Coupé	91 GS 10 0001 - 91 GS 10 4031	3984
Carrera Coupé Japan	91 GS 10 9501 - 91 GS 10 9733	173
Carrera Coupé US and CDN	91 GS 12 0001 - 91 GS 12 2619	2559
Carrera Targa	91 GS 14 0001 - 91 GS 14 1758	1698
Carrera Targa Japan	91 GS 14 9501 - 91 GS 14 9579	8
Carrera Cabriolet	91 GS 15 0001 - 91 GS 15 2358	2300
Carrera Cabriolet Japan	91 GS 15 9501 - 91 GS 15 9580	20
Carrera Targa US and CDN	91 GS 16 0001 - 91 GS 16 1976	1916
Carrera Cabriolet US and CDN	91 GS 17 0001 - 91 GS 17 1986	1926
Total for 1986		14584

Model year 1987 (H-Program)		
911 Model	Chassis number range	Production
Carrera Coupé	91 HS 10 0001 - 91 HS 10 3381	3341
Carrera Coupé Japan	91 HS 10 9501 - 91 HS 10 9808	248
Carrera Coupé US and CDN	91 HS 12 0001 - 91 HS 12 2916	2856
Carrera Targa	91 HS 14 0001 - 91 HS 14 1354	1295
Carrera Targa Japan	91 HS 14 9501 - 91 HS 14 9579	19
Carrera Cabriolet	91 HS 15 0001 - 91 HS 15 1464	1407
Carrera Cabriolet Japan	91 HS 15 9501 - 91 HS 15 9585	25
Carrera Targa US and CDN	91 HS 16 0001 - 91 HS 16 2232	2172
Carrera Cabriolet US and CDN	91 HS 17 0001 - 91 HS 17 2653	2593
Total for 1987		13956

Model year 1988 (J-Program)		
911 Model	Chassis number range	Production
Carrera Coupé	91 JS 10 0001 - 91 JS 10 3580	3524
Carrera Coupé Japan	91 JS 10 9501 - 91 JS 10 9930	370
Carrera Coupé US and CDN	91 JS 12 0001 - 91 JS 12 2066	2066
Carrera Targa	91 JS 14 0001 - 91 JS 14 1281	1223
Carrera Targa Japan	91 JS 14 9501 - 91 JS 14 9580	20
Carrera Cabriolet	91 JS 15 0001 - 91 JS 15 1501	1444
Carrera Cabriolet Japan	91 JS 15 9501 - 91 JS 15 9581	21
Carrera Targa US and CDN	91 JS 16 0001 - 91 JS 16 1500	1440
Carrera Cabriolet US and CDN	91 JS 17 0001 - 91 JS 17 2116	2056
Total for 1988		12164

Model year 1989 (K-Program)		
911 Model	Chassis number range	Production
Carrera Coupé	91 KS 10 0001 - 91 KS 10 3532	3472
Carrera Coupé US and CDN	91 KS 12 0001 - 91 KS 12 1156	1096
Carrera Targa	91 KS 14 0001 - 91 KS 14 1063	1003
Carrera Cabriolet	91 KS 15 0001 - 91 KS 15 2787	1442
Carrera Targa US and CDN	91 KS 16 0001 - 91 KS 16 0860	800
Carrera Cabriolet US and CDN	91 KS 17 0001 - 91 KS 17 1361	1301
Total for 1989		9114

'Special' Production (1984 to 1989)			
911 Model	year	Description	Production
953 4x4	1984	91 ES 10 0020 - 91 ES 10 0022	3
Club Sport	1987	Row	81
	1988	Row	148
		USA	21
	1989	Row	83
		USA	7
Speedster	1989	Row: Turbo-Look	1124
		Row: Narrow Body	161
		USA & CDN: Turbo-Look	819
Total			2447

Total production number: 76473

No specific production figures are available for M491 Turbo-Look/ Supersport.

Production numbers as supplied by Porsche AG.

CHAPTER 18

ZUFFENHAUSEN - 1984 TO 1989

In 1984, coinciding with the introduction of the new 911 Carrera, Porsche, despite being a family-owned company, offered non-voting preference shares on the stock exchange for the first time, and thus became Porsche Aktiengesellschaft (AG).

Dr Ing hc Ferry Porsche, son of the company's founder Dr Ing Ferdinand Porsche, had headed the company until 1972. Since then, a series of chairmen took over the reins, notably Professor Ernst Fuhrmann, who took over from Ferry Porsche and stayed until 1980. It was under his leadership that the 924, 944 and 928 cars were developed which, had he stayed in charge, would have seen the death of the 911 after the SC production run. After apparent disagreements with Ferry Porsche regarding the longevity of the 911, Fuhrmann resigned to make way for Peter W Schutz.

Very early in his leadership, Schutz met with Dr Helmuth Bott, the board member responsible for research and development, and, with a single stroke of his marker pen on Bott's production chart, Schutz indicated that 911 production would continue, much to the joy of Bott and his team at Porsche.

The 911 was resurrected, and the 3.2 Carrera was sanctioned to go ahead. This car had very nearly never made it to life, but for the intervention of Ferry Porsche and the then new Chairman Schutz. Schutz later said: "The Porsche 911, the company icon, had been saved, and I believe the company was saved with it".

By the mid-eighties, the number of Porsche employees had multiplied from a little over 1500 in 1965 to a little over 8000 in 1986. Correspondingly, the number of cars produced per year had increased from a little over 10,000 cars in 1965, to a little over of 50,000 cars in 1986. Porsche had undoubtedly come a long way in just twenty-one years, and this was largely due to the success of the 911.

The boardroom at Zuffenhausen in 1986 was filled by six men: Peter Schutz; his deputy, Heinz Branitzki, who subsequently took over as Chairman when Schutz retired in 1987; Professor Helmutt Bott was head of research and development; Kurt Femppel was head of personnel; Professor Rudi Noppen was head of production quality control; and Hans Halback was head of marketing.

Although Ferry Porsche had been, somewhat suprisingly, moved from the main factory by Schutz's predecessor Fuhrmann, Schutz chose to bring him back to the main headquarters, and kept him and the Porsche family close at hand in the business.

During the mid-eighties the Porsche company produced nine models: 924S, 944, 944S, 944 Turbo, 911 Carrera Coupé, 911 Targa, 911 Cabriolet, 911 Turbo and 928S4. The 911 and 928 ranges were built entirely at the Porsche factory at Zuffenhausen, while the 924 and 944 ranges were built in Neckarsulm.

For the 1985/86 financial year, the American market took the lion's share of Porsche cars. American exports claimed a huge 53.9 per cent of

An official 1986 Porsche photograph of an American specification Carrera Coupé with Sport Equipment. A 911 Carrera has over 6000 spot welds and more than 10 meters of seam welding.

production, ahead of Germany at 21.1 per cent, Great Britain at 7.2 per cent, France at 3.1 per cent, Switzerland at 2.9 per cent, Canada at 2.3 per cent. All other countries were at 9.5 per cent.

For the same period, the 944 range accounted for 48 per cent of total cars made, ahead of the 911 at 31.7 per cent, the 924 at 11.5 per cent, and the 928 at 8.8 per cent.

Research and development

Research and development played a big part in the success of Porsche cars. The Carrera was developed, as with all Porsche models, at Porsche's Weissach technical factory, where every element of a new or development model was researched, designed and developed into a production part. With facilities capable of producing full-size clay models, Weissach covered an extensive area of almost 50 hectares, which included 10 kilometres of road testing facilities. Weissach boasted 2200 employees, representing 30 per cent of the total Porsche staff, of which 1000 were engineers and 800 were specialists in prototype construction. A team of 45 filled the styling department and, with a full-size wind tunnel facility, Weissach represented a great base from which to launch the new 911 3.2 Carrera.

The Weissach R&D facility was started in the early nineteen-sixties and, by 1974, Porsche had moved all research and development there from Zuffenhausen. Weissach continued to expand through the nineteen-seventies and early nineteen-eighties to provide a state-of-the-art facility, not only for Porsche in the pursuit of 'Driving in its Purest Form', but also for outside contracts. Porsche claimed that something over 10 per cent of its annual costs was spent on research and development. During the nineteen-eighties, Weissach had seen investment of over DM1100 million, which included a full-scale wind tunnel, environmental test centre, a crash-test facility, and race-car test centre.

Crash testing was an important feature as Porsche developed the Carrera. Although earlier 911s still passed the then current legal crash-test requirements, the new facility introduced exacting records. Photographic records, taken at 1000 frames per second, allowed Porsche to individually monitor the level of adverse disturbance in a crash situation. Up to ten cameras would record the exact time of impact at 110 kilometres per hour, lasting no longer than one tenth of a second. The 911 Carrera was extremely rigid, and crash-test simulation only served to improve the already excellent design. Extra stiffening was introduced to the roof and door design to improve safety in side impact collisions.

To meet the tough American emissions controls, the Carrera was subjected to exhaustive testing in the new environmental test facility. Over two hundred technicians and engineers were available in this facility for continual testing and recording. These people were responsible for the development of Porsche's three-way catalytic exhaust system, fitted as standard to all US specification Carreras. Engine management was also under the control of the environmental facility where, with the aid of Bosch's Motronic injection system and Porsche's own data-fed

A Porsche promotional photograph of a 1989 Carrera Cabriolet.

E-Prom (Erasable Programmable Read Only Memory) microchip, the Carrera showed improved power with no increase of fuel consumption or emissions. The Carrera could be tested under simulated conditions of climate, altitude, and humidity, to satisfy emissions criteria for any given geographical location.

The introduction of the galvanised body in 1975 saw Porsche's Weissach facility all but combat rust in steel-bodied cars. In 1973, as part of Porsche's development programme, the engineers at Weissach hot-dip galvanised a 911, which they then left un-painted and exposed outside the factory in all weathers. This 911 was still in place during the nineteen-eighties without any degradation. With the introduction of new materials, Porsche suggested at the time that the expected lifespan of its cars was a minimum of twenty years, and one hundred and eighty thousand miles.

Prior to Weissach's new wind tunnel facility in 1986, all Porsche aerodynamic testing and development was undertaken at Stuttgart University. The Carrera's aerodynamic styling,

A Porsche promotional photograph of a 1984 Carrera Targa.

A Porsche promotional photograph of a 1988 Carrera Targa.

The Carrera Targa was a strong seller for Porsche throughout the world, offering the best of both the Coupé and Cabriolet.

The Targa, developed in 1965, retained as many of the Coupé production panels as possible to reduce tooling costs.

A Porsche promotional photograph of a 1988 Carrera Cabriolet.

including the development of the Sport Equipment front and rear spoilers, was carried out there. The Carrera, when tested in the Stuttgart University wind tunnel, was given a Cd value of 0.385.

Amongst the many diverse and interesting development programmes, Weissach developed a 3.2 flat-six based aircraft engine, the PFM 3200, which was due for production in 1987 but never made it.

In 1986, Porsche was building on average 30 911s per day, for which were between 70 and 100 customer options were available from the Porsche options list. Although Porsche offered 13 basic colour shades for the 911 Carrera, approximately every twentieth 911 was painted in a specific colour requested by the customer.

Approximately 500 sheet metal parts made up a 911 Carrera, all of either galvanised steel or aluminium. The build process of a 911 Carrera had approximately 6000 spot welds and approximately 10 meters of seam welding in each car which, together, made up 35 hours of production time.

The Carrera was manufactured almost entirely by hand; the newly installed robots were only used to feed and empty the machines for crankcase machining. Every spot weld, each stitch, and every drop of paint was carried out and/or applied by hand, by a technical workforce of the highest capability. This, in Porsche's opinion, was the vital feature of production. Porsche claimed that, along with quality, it was flexibility in the production process which hand work ensured. At the time, no technology matched the flexibility of a well-motivated Porsche production team.

Statistics at the time indicated that it was extremely rare to have two 911 Carreras built identically in any given month, such was the extent of the Porsche options and colour choices.

As part of the overall Porsche quality control, a computerised parts acceptance system was in place. This checked each and every part before it was made available to the production line. Massive importance was placed on quality by Porsche and, as a result, the 3.2 Carrera was produced during a time when 'hand-made' was at its optimum. Parts were made to exacting standards and before the advent of robotised assembly; this car really was put together by engineers.

Mechanical components of the flat-six engine were machined by up to 200 specialist machine technicians. Machining was vital, and accounted for 15 per cent of the cost of the entire engine. The machined parts would then be taken to the engine department for final assembly. Although every engine technician was capable of building an entire engine on his own, in order to ensure continuity with all the engine ranges, each would work at 3 to 4 of the total 20 stations, switching between them every four weeks. This gave Porsche a great deal of versatility in its engine production which, at the time, was made up of 50 variations across the range.

As for the interior trim, each Carrera was individually produced using the best leather (or simulated leather and cloth), cut and stitched by hand. Banks

A Porsche promotional photograph of the 1987 Frankfurt Show Speedster.

of (mainly) women, all wearing a blue short-sleeved jacket type overalls with the distinctive Porsche logo on the pocket, fed thousands of yards of material through small industrial tabletop sewing machines. The body and engine production departments were staffed almost entirely by men, wearing green or grey dungarees with the Porsche logo across the front. Hard hats were worn during final assembly of body, engine and running gear.

Each Carrera was mounted on special cradle frames and painted as a whole car. The main body, front valance and bumper, boot lid, doors, engine cover, rear bumper, and skirts, were all located in the cradle for spraying together. The ancillary parts were positioned slightly away from the main body in order to allow paint to flow into concealed areas. After final quality checks and finishing, all edges were bound with protective tape and sent into the assembly area for trimming.

Final assembly of a Carrera required several thousand separate operations before every finished car was sent out for a 30 kilometre road test. Without exception, each Carrera was carefully tested by 40 experienced engineer drivers who checked the cars in the city, country and motorways, covering more than 40 control points. These engineer drivers were responsible for driving every Carrera manufactured with the aim of judging the behaviour of the car. Their feedback was critical in ensuring that the 911 Carrera was as driveable on the road as the technical statistics implied.

The finished Carreras were then sent to dispatch, for shipping to their ultimate destinations.

Randomly selected Carreras were also chosen from the production run for further testing on the test tracks and skid pans at Weissach. Handling tests were carried out on 40, 60 and 190 metre diameter skid pan circles. Each test was carefully monitored and recorded to test lateral 'g' force acceleration, braking 'g' forces, roll angles and steering forces.

On the 'paved and mountain track' at Weissach, the Carreras were tested for production faults relating to performance, acceleration, braking, handbrake operation, and fuel consumption. On the test track, the Carreras were checked for percentage speedometer and rev counter errors.

Long range testing of the Carrera included 16,000 kilometres at Weissach, incorporating the above, plus a further 80,000 kilometres, including 12,000 kilometres of town driving, 20,000 kilometres of country driving, 24,000 kilometres of *autobahn* driving, 6000 kilometres at the long Nürburgring track, and 18,000 kilometres at the Nardo track in Italy. Every element was carefully recorded and measured and compared to the predetermined 'expected' data.

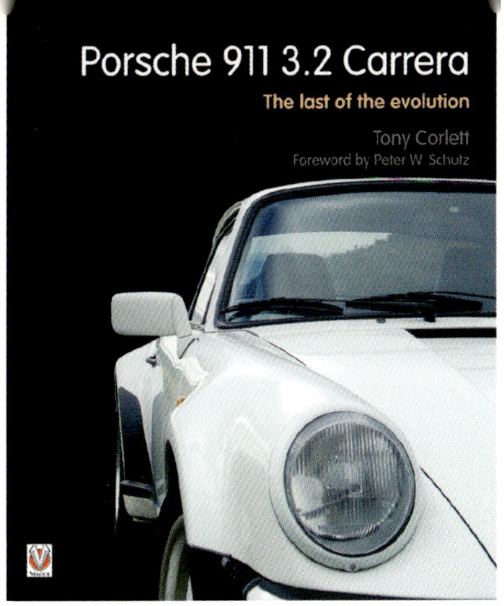

Chapter 19

Exterior aesthetics

The exterior of the Carrera was all about aesthetics. The shape, the stance, the luxurious paintwork, the panel fit; everything about the Porsche Carrera was sheer perfection.

There is no doubt that Porsche paintwork is amongst the best automotive finishes in the world, and the finish on the Carrera was no exception. The deep lustre of the paint finish showed off the sweeping lines of the 911 in the best possible way, and the first encounter with a Carrera left one with an extraordinary desire to experience more.

In design terms, the 911 shape could almost be described as two different cars moulded together. Although the front is rather upright and stern, and the rear sweeping and relaxed, the two married together in a way that conveyed purpose and resolve.

As an overall package, the 911 Carrera was more practical than most sports cars. The very fact that it had a decent-sized boot, could seat two large adults and two children with relative comfort, and still notch up 150mph in a straight line really does speak volumes. Although relatively small in stature, the layout of the car provided the utmost use of space in a very matter-of-fact way.

Introduced to provide impact absorption for American legislation, the wraparound impact-bumper design was a strong feature of the 911 from 1974, the Carrera looking particularly imposing with them. Using rubber collapsible 'bellows', these impact-bumpers allowed the large cross-body member to move freely in the event of an accident.

Although Porsche provided 'federalised' engines to suit the American market, standing side by side, the bodies of European and American Carreras were virtually indistinguishable. The only identifying features of the American cars was the rear bumper, which was fitted with very much larger over-riders, the front indicator lenses, which incorporated a reflector and wrapped around to the bellows, and the red rear indicator lenses.

Blending the rather smoother body lines with the somewhat sturdier bumpers was carried out with great

The exterior quality of the Carrera was exacting in every respect. All body panels fitted with exceptional accuracy, and all opening panels functioned with perfect engineering precision.

Pages 82-84: Exterior detailing was carried out to perfection.

skill. Meeting the legal requirement to satisfy Porsche's largest single market, the integral and aesthetically-pleasing 'impact-bumper' solution was adopted on all Carreras. These colour-coded sectional bumpers comprised a large cross-body aluminium member, lower quarter panels, front and rear valance, a wraparound rubber bump-strip, side 'bellows', rubber over-riders to the rear bumper only, and a rubber connecting strip or 'smile' to the front. At the rear, the vertical lights and central reflector cross panel cluster sat snugly above the bumper, with wraparound indicator lenses meeting at the 'bellows' line. A single, large diameter exhaust pipe protruded from a cutout between the lower left quarter panel and the rear lower valance, and was angled for exit. At the front, indicator lenses were incorporated into the rubber bump-strip line, fog-light clusters were moulded into the lower valance, and a flat rubber strip, also affectionately known as the 'smile', was used to mask the gap between the cross-body bumper member and the leading edge of the bonnet.

Flowing up from the flat top surface of the front bumper and 'smile', the bonnet swept evenly up and widened out to the scuttle panel and lower windscreen. Two folds in the bonnet directed fresh air into the cabin air-intake grill. The intake grill was positioned directly below and centrally about the windscreen wiper pivots, and slightly inside the two windscreen washer jets. Everything was symmetrical and, apart from the windscreen wipers which rested towards the driver's side, for both left- and right-hand drive cars, the overall design was in complete balance.

The one piece front wings protruded forward and above the bonnet line, taking in the widening bonnet, front wheelarches and doors. On the left-hand wing, and set flush into the body line, was the fuel filler flap. This blended perfectly into the car's smooth lines, and was remotely operated, hinging forward to reveal

Impact bumpers move freely laterally without damage to the bodywork under light crash impact. The 'bellows' are designed to collapse and spring back to shape.

Later 1987 to 1989 Carreras incorporated the rear fog lamps into the reflector panel above the bumper. Carrera front light clusters were continued without change from the 911 SC, but incorporated two lower front driving lamps in the valance.

the fuel filler throat. The headlights sat upright, laying back only slightly.

The windscreen, too, was in perfect harmony with the rest of the front.

From the top edge of the rather stubby upright windscreen, a transformation occurred. The roof line swept over to the top of the very large and shallow-raked rear screen, then passed over the engine cowling to the top edge of the vertical light and cross panel cluster at the rear.

In profile, the Carrera's upper waist line ran almost horizontally, and added presence to the front end. This line ran along the top of the wing, below the side glass area, under the 'A' post, narrow 'B' post and sweeping 'C' post, with a definite downward sweep to the very corner of the rear light cluster. The 'C' posts flowed seamlessly into the rear wings, which in turn incorporated the flared rear wheelarches and flanks, stretching forward to the rear edge of the doors.

The shape of the doors echoed the design change from front to rear. The leading edge was vertical, whilst

A discreet 'Carrera' script logo was fitted on the engine cover. Cars were supplied without the logo under option M498 which was standard for the American market.

1984 to 1986 Porsche script rear reflector panel.

the rear edge was almost at a tangent to the sweeping roof line. The doors made up most of the car's flanks, and incorporated delicate sidescreen window frames with fixed quarter-lights. The mirrors were large and oblong, as opposed to sporting and rounded, yet somehow suited the overall bullish look of the Carrera.

The rear wheelarches were flared all round, whereas the front wheelarches had a smaller eyebrow design.

Most Sports Equipment cars, and all of the Supersport Equipment cars, were fitted with the robust Fuchs alloy wheels. Generally speaking, however, the standard cars had the more elegant Teledial alloys. The Carrera adopted a very purposeful stance on either design.

The finishing touches to the body were limited to practical accessories rather than flamboyant features. The door handles, side repeater indicators and screen wipers, front and rear, were

Quality did not stop at external looks.

all discreet and not overpowering. A black sill-line rubber stretched between the wheelarches and separated the lower flanks from the lower side-skirts. These lower skirts housed the manual jacking point which was also the balancing point or centre of gravity along the length of the car.

The door operation is like no other car; the distinctive and solid 'clunk' sound of a 911 door closing is instantly recognisable. The door handles were appropriate for such a gutsy car, and the squeeze lever handle operated with great precision, springing the door open cleanly and smoothly. The hinges, latches and strike plates worked together beautifully, and really made the first venture into 911 territory a pleasure. Shutting the doors required more than just a gentle nudge, more like a solid push actually, but once closed they fitted perfectly. The same was true of all the movable panels, which operated with precision and had perfect fit.

The engine cover and the bonnet lid were released via remote handles: a lockable pull release under the dashboard for the bonnet, and a simple lever within the left-hand door jamb for the engine cover.

In 1987, when the Carrera was updated, the external aesthetics remained largely unchanged (the windscreen washer jets were modified, and the rear light cluster was redesigned to incorporate fog lights). There was no longer any need for the lower rear fog lamp attachment, and the size of the Porsche logo script across the rear of the car was reduced.

A 16 inch diameter Fuchs alloy rear wheel as fitted to Sport equipped and Turbo-Look cars.

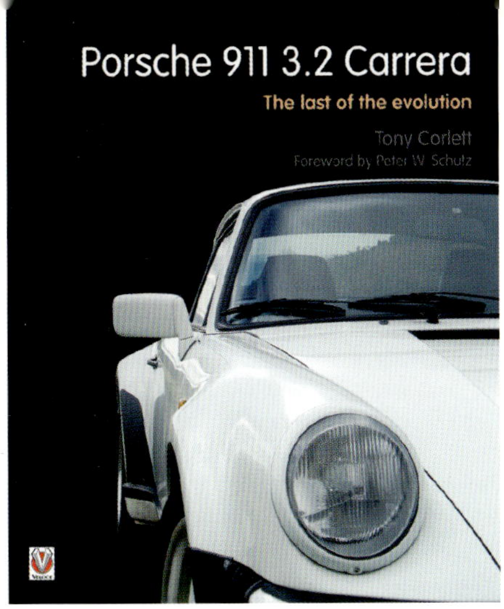

Chapter 20

Interior

The interior of the Carrera was, as you might expect of a German sports car, very functional, of high quality, and very well trimmed. Although entering a Carrera was easier than most low-slung sports cars, it still took a bit of practice, as getting your leading leg under the steering wheel was difficult and uncomfortable. A typical entry procedure would be as follows: lead leg in, bottom down, lead leg under the steering wheel, and then the other leg in.

Once in, the Recaro design sports seats did a great job of hugging the occupants. The front seats could slide backward and forward quite a long way, and could quite easily accommodate occupants of varying heights. Headroom was also very good. The same, however, could not be said of the rear seats, which comprised a small squab and back rest. Despite having more space than most sports cars, the rear seats were only adequate for small adults or children, and for shorter trips.

The rear seat rests could be hinged forward and laid flat, forming a luggage shelf (once again, showing that practicality was an important consideration for the designers). The earlier cars had a leather strap and popper to hold the seat-back in the upright position, clipping to the rear parcel shelf, whereas later cars had a mechanical pin at the hinge point which did the same job.

An interesting link between Porsche and Recaro is worthy of note. In 1963, Reutter Carzozzerie Coachbuilders sold its body company to Porsche K.G. so that, in 1964, the bodies would be built by Karmann and Porsche. The Reutter family continued to build the seats, under the company name 'Recaro', which was a combination of 'Reutter' and 'Carzozzerie'.

The trim was of exceptional quality and finish. Basically two upholstery specifications were offered with the Carrera: standard cloth, or full leather. The standard finish had soft cloth pinstripe design inserts in the centre of the front seats, the door panels and the rear seats. As fitted as standard to the 911 Turbo, or as an option on the Carrera, the full leather finish included the front seats and door panels, with matching leather or leatherette for the rear seats. With both trims, the rear parcel shelf, dashboard, fascia and door tops were finished in a matching leatherette. A great many trim variations were offered on the Carrera, including full leather for some or all of the above, and colour contrasting 'piping' to the front seats.

Expertly manufactured, the luxurious thick woollen pile carpets were generally loose fitting, with all exposed edges trimmed with leatherette to match the colour of the carpet or optional seat 'piping'. The backs of the fold-down rear seats were also trimmed with carpet, which meant that the parcel shelf was in keeping with the finish when folded flat.

The cabin headlining was leatherette, as were the two sun visor covers, each fitted with a vanity mirror.

The dashboard and fascia were neat and functional. A soft, leatherette or optional leather, roll-top dashboard cushion extended across the top of the

Although the basic 911 interior format was adopted for the 1984 Carrera, a number of modifications and luxury additions were made to later cars.

A 1984 Coupé with half-leather seats and pinstripe cloth inserts. There were smaller fresh air vents on earlier Carreras.

Rear seats had a seat base and independent seat-back which hinged forward to provide a flat luggage area.

fascia, around the top of the instrument binnacle, and rolled over to meet the simple black fascia. Immediately in front of the driver was the instrument binnacle, housing five instrument gauges. In the centre of the dashboard, within the roll-top cushion, were the fresh air vents, below which were a group of three switches and three warning lights. Below these was the radio/tape audio equipment. The glove box was on one side of the radio, and the ventilation controls were on the other. There were fresh air ventilation outlets at eacch end of the black fascia, and along the lower edge of the black fascia was a leatherette or optional leather trimmed bump-strip, with a centrally-positioned ashtray.

The dashboard and fascia layout on right-hand drive cars was essentially a mirror image of that on left-hand cars, with the exception of the instrument binnacle, glove box lid, and the petrol flap pull release.

There were some subtle changes to the dashboard and fascia of later 1987 to 1989 Carreras. These included substantially larger ventilation outlets, and a relocated internal temperature thermostat.

A variety of controls and switches were located on the fascia panel and in and around the instrument binnacle. On the fascia were the ignition switch, headlight switch, hazard light switch, ventilation controls, radio/tape player, rear window demister switch, fog light switch, cigarette lighter, glove box, and warning lights for seatbelts, handbrake and brake pad wear. Located within and under the instrument binnacle fascia were the rear screen wiper switch (when fitted), the headlight washer switch, the intermittent flick wipe rheostat switch, the sunroof switch (when fitted), and the left/right door mirror switch (when fitted).

The ventilation sliders operated dampers behind the dashboard, directing hot or cold air to various outlets for driver comfort and window demisting.

In front of the gear lever, on the floor in the centre of the car, was a small utility/console unit which provided space for audio cassettes

A 1986 Cabriolet with roof folded.

A 1988 Coupé with full leather interior, larger air vents and a leather gear stick surround.

1984 Coupé with full leather interior.

Rear seat-backs fixed in upright position. Early Carreras had a leather tag and popper-clip to hold them back against the rear shelf.

Rear seat-backs laid down to form a luggage shelf. Later Carreras had a mechanical fixing at the pivot.

Door lock thumb-turn in leather door trim.

and switches for audio speaker control and air-conditioning (when fitted). The gear lever itself was quite basic; a tall slender tube bent over slightly at the top, with a neat bulb handgrip, running down into a small rubber boot at the bottom. Later cars had a leatherette, or optional leather wrap. Behind the gear lever, between the seats, was the handbrake lever.

The main hot air control switch was positioned between the seats, behind the handbrake lever. A circular switch, with ten individual cold to hot settings, controlled the hot air coming into the cabin from the heat exchangers on the underside of the engine. The older, SC dual levers were used for the lighter Club Sport and Speedster, one each for the driver and passenger.

An option on the Carrera (standard on the 911 Turbo) the fully-automatic air-conditioning system offered combined heating, ventilation and cooling, maintaining a pre-selected temperature.

The dashboard binnacle carried a five-dial display. In the centre, and directly in front of the driver, was the large, and somewhat legendary, circular 911 tachometer. To either side of the tachometer was the speedometer and the oil-pressure/temperature gauges. To either side of these were the clock and the fuel/temperature dials.

The steering wheel came in two designs: the earlier, three-spoke design had the Stuttgart crest motif in the centre, whereas the later four-spoke 'sport' design featured the Porsche script logo. There were two levers mounted on the steering column, one to either side. The left-hand lever controlled the indicators and headlight dip and main beam,

In celebration of the 25th year of the 911 and the 250,000th 911 to roll of the production line, the 1988 Carrera was available with special 'Celebration' livery, including Diamond Blue metallic paintwork and matching interior leather. An image of Ferry Porsche's signature was incorporated into the front seats.

As part of the weight saving package, the Club Sport did not have the rear seats fitted, nor the rear side trim panels and rear parcel shelf.

the right-hand lever controlled the windscreen wiper functions and the windscreen washers.

The sunroof (when fitted), the door mirrors, the front windows and, in most later cars, the front seats, were all electrically-operated. A Blaupunkt radio/tape player was fitted as standard, and output was through four audio speakers, two on the back shelf and one in each door. The front seatbelts were inertia-reel items, whereas the rear were lap belts.

The way the doors operated demonstrated the overall high quality of the 911 Carrera. The vertical locking button, which closed flush and couldn't be lifted, was fitted on top of the door, immediately behind the quarter-light. Directly below the button was a recessed knurled wheel that, when turned, forced the button back up, thus unlocking the door. The door release handle was incorporated within an armrest/door pull handle, which also contained a flip-top storage bin.

The windows were electrically-powered, except on the Club Sport and Speedster which had manual window winders. The electric window winder switches were mounted on the doors, the driver's door carrying switches for both windows.

Internal storage was by way of the lockable glove locker, and 'bins' on each door. The Speedster also had two lockable compartments below the rear shelf.

Everything operated in a very positive and reassuring manner. The interior of the Carrera was as well engineered as the rest of the car, and using the controls was a delight. Comfort was good, visibility was good, and the driving position was good.

The Carrera's luggage compartment was located between the front wings, above the fuel tank and spare wheel well. It was fully carpeted and remarkably large, and got progressively wider towards the windscreen. Luggage needed to be carefully chosen, however, but the space was not as restrictive as it might seem at first. The carpet for the boot lining comprised four basic mats, all moulded to fit around the floor, two wings and rear scuttle cover. An option of upgrading the carpet from the standard tight weave, to the luxurious wool as used within the passenger cabin, was offered.

Chapter 21

Attention to detail

The overall quality of the Carrera was evident in the detailing. The best engineers in the world designed and built this car, and every aspect was carefully engineered and designed to give maximum operational capability, longevity and aesthetics. From the operation of the control switches, to the neatness of the moulded fuel cell, nothing about the Carrera was left to chance.

To underline Porsche's dedication to quality, Prof Dr ing Rudi Noppen, the then board member responsible for Production, Quality Control and Supply Economics, said: "A high quality level is the primary goal in the actual production process. When business is good, manufacturers are easily tempted to raise production numbers at the expense of quality. This is not our way - quality quite obviously takes priority".

Technically, every Porsche benefited from the team of development engineers at Weissach. With regard to Weissach, Prof. Helmuth Bott, the then board member responsible for Research and Development said: "Our main task is to develop new products for our own company and to maintain our production cars at a high technical level".

A staunch dedication to achieving perfection drove both the development and production lines, which worked hand in hand to achieve an exceptional standard of quality for every car produced. Customers came to expect this level of quality, and Porsche excelled in meeting its customers' expectations.

The then Chairman Peter W Schutz said: "The synthesis of common taste with individual demands is the basis for close ties between all Porsche drivers". And he was right. It's not just for the elite few, but rather a quality that permeates through each and every Porsche ever made. And it all boils down to one simple phenomenon - attention to detail. Once this is understood and entrenched, anything is possible. Porsche cars are proof of that.

Porsche's attention to detail was second to none.

An engineering and production quality driven policy ensured that every Carrera manufactured was of the highest possible standard in every respect.

Official Porsche cut-away drawing shows both earlier 915 (left) and later G50 (above) gearbox-equipped cars. Differences include wheels, gearbox and side impact protection bars. Note the chassis changes behind the rear seat for the different gearboxes.

Chapter 22

At the controls

The 911 Carrera is a very comfortable car. The driver's seat, the steering wheel, the gear lever, and the pedal positions are extremely well situated, and inspire the sort of confidence that comes from being properly in command of the controls.

As with the windscreen, the steering wheel is quite steeply raked. This reinforces the sense of sitting up, as opposed to laying back, and improves visibility to the four corners of the car. Gear changes are comfortable, as is the steering, though this can be heavy when the wide Sport Equipment tyres are fitted.

The classic 911 dashboard layout is very evident in the Carrera. The large diameter, centrally-mounted tachometer, and the four flanking dials, give the impression that this is a place to conduct the business of driving fast. The tachometer, which dominates the driver's view of the information array, was drawn straight from the world of racing.

There are two steering column-mounted levers. The indicators and the headlight dip and main beam lever is on the left, the windscreen wiper and windscreen washer lever is on the right. Both are at finger length, are very comfortable to use, and operate very firmly and precisely.

The accelerator, brake and clutch pedals are floor-mounted and can take a bit of getting used to. The operation is, however, very positive, and the clutch is not heavy. The position of the brake in relation to the accelerator does not easily allow for heel and toe down shifts, which is a shame. The gear lever is functional and stands high from a low centre console, and the handbrake lever rests between the seats and is easily operated.

Right-hand drive Carreras have a pedal-box offset. The pedals are closer to the centre of the car than of those on the left-hand drive cars. This can take a little time to get used to, with the brake pedal being where the clutch pedal would ordinarily be.

Glass area is relatively large, visibility is good, and there are no major blind spots. It has to be said that the 911 Carrera is exceptionally relaxing as sports cars go, and really does inspire confidence in the driver. The view behind is also good, both door mirrors and the rear view mirror offering good visibility for rear view observation and reversing.

The typical 911 dashboard layout was carried forward for use in the Carrera. The display is dominated by the large centrally-mounted rev counter. This is a 1984 Coupé with a three-spoke steering wheel.

1988 Coupé with four-spoke steering wheel.

1989 Club Sport with four-spoke steering wheel fitted as standard.

Official factory photograph of a 1984 dashboard with four-spoke leather steering wheel.

Right-hand drive Speedster dashboard showing the typical layout of later Carreras. Note the manual door window winder as fitted to the Speedster and Club Sport.

Carrera

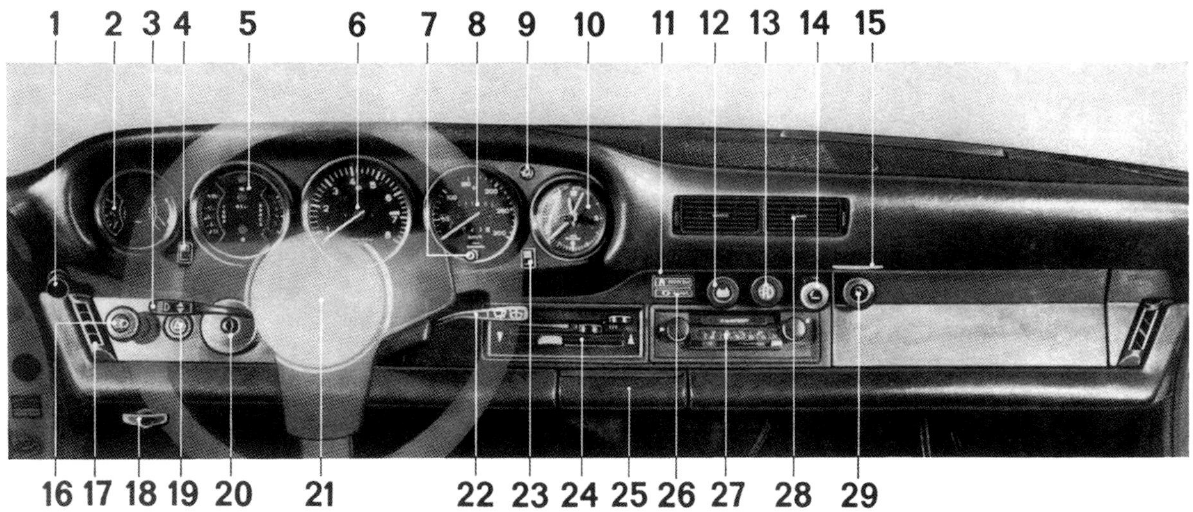

THE STANDARD LAYOUT OF A 1984 DASHBOARD AND CONTROLS AS SHOWN IN THE PORSCHE HANDBOOK:

1. Fuel flap release pull.
2. Small combination instrument dial.
3. Indicator stalk.
4. Rear screen wiper switch.
5. Large combination instrument dial.
6. Tachometer.
7. Odometer trip button.
8. Speedometer.
9. Intermittent windscreen wiper timer switch.
10. Clock.
11. Seatbelt indicator light.
12. Heated rear window switch.
13. Front and rear fog lamp switch.
14. Cigarette lighter.
15. Map light.
16. Light switch.
17. Fresh air intake vent.
18. Luggage compartment release knob.
19. Hazard lights button.
20. Ignition switch.
21. Steering wheel.
22. Windscreen wiper stalk.
23. Headlamp washer switch.
24. Heater and ventilation slide controls.
25. Ashtray.
26. Brake warning lights.
27. Audio player.
28. Fresh air inlet vents.
29. Glove locker.

Chapter 23

Driving impressions

For a good driver, a well set up 911 Carrera is a joy to drive. A poor driver, on the other hand, may never get near the car's limits (which is probably just as well) but will certainly have a lot of fun. I believe that the 911's reputation for being 'tail-happy' has a lot to do with the poor quality of the drivers who 'think' they can drive fast, and inevitably end up in trouble.

For everyday use, and compared to other, more brutish sports cars, the 911 Carrera is actually quite easy to drive. For most drivers, the 911 Carrera will go where it is pointed (up to a point) and accelerate more than adequately. However, things get a little more complicated when driving a 911 quickly turns into driving it fast. That's when all the car's adverse idiosyncrasies start to manifest themselves.

The key to driving a 911 Carrera fast (and safely) is knowing about and understanding the car's characteristics. For example, the two basic 'rules' for driving a 911 are: never lift off the

Official 1987 Porsche photograph of a Club Sport undergoing road tests.

On the road, the Carrera is a very confidence building sports car to drive fast. Handling is precise and power delivery is strong all the way to the red line.

throttle in a corner, and; don't turn-in under braking. It's a learned 911 driver who gets away with breaking either of these rules.

The engine is the heaviest object in any car, and it's usually mounted within or over the axle lines. For the 911 Carrera, however, the engine was mounted in an 'outboard' position, behind the rear axle line. This is fine in normal circumstances but, when cornering, gravitational forces can cause a pendulum effect and spin the car. The 911 will actually spin about its front wheels, which would effectively be the fulcrum point of the pendulum.

As the 911 was developed to deliver more power, the suspension, roadholding and handling were also improved. The earlier, 'loose' handling car gradually evolved into something that stuck like glue until the moment it reached maximum gravitational pull (whereupon it would let go in one giant swing, rather than a gentle and controllable slide). Because the maximum gravitational pull point is extremely high, 0.85g, once reached, there is very little that can be done to prevent the car from letting go.

Driving a Carrera on the limit really does require total commitment. It takes a thorough understanding of how a 911 behaves to really appreciate how it handles. The feeling of holding a Carrera under control as the rear end lightens up under hard braking is fabulous.

Under normal driving conditions, understeer - where the front end washes away during cornering, and is rectified only by controlled power-off

- is the Carrera's worst characteristic. Understeer is, however, built into the handling of the Carrera, and is there to provide a safety margin for the average driver. With understeer built in, and under normal road use, the heavy tail would first have to overcome the front of the car before spinning around. For example, if you arrive at a corner too quickly, turning-in will result in understeer, and most drivers would lift off the throttle (normally a mistake). However, provided the car is still under control, lift-off oversteer will counteract the understeer. Without the built in understeer, the tail would come round under exactly the same cornering situation.

Although a skilled driver may be able to trail the brake pedal when cornering, and even brake quite hard into corners, it's generally best to brake in a straight line to prevent the tail coming round. Although the understeer will provide some degree of safety against unavoidable late braking, if you get it all wrong, the Carrera will oversteer and spin, and there's very little you can do about it. Don't let that put you off, though; the Carrera's limits are a long way off and, provided you keep things tidy, you'll not run into trouble.

With the exception of the most severe oversteer conditions, you should never attempt to correct oversteer

With a 40/60 front to rear weight distribution, the Carrera has excellent traction under acceleration.

using the steering wheel. Instead, stay on the throttle, and ride it out, letting the natural understeer do its job. The feeling of controlling a rampant Carrera is second to none. When you reach this stage of total commitment, you'll experience the real beauty of a 911 chassis and walk away with a grin.

The Carrera brake and accelerator pedals are not positioned for heel and toe driving as the the brake pedal is much higher. This was either an oversight on the part of the Porsche engineers or, more likely, a way of preventing both pedals being depressed at the same time.

The gear changes on the earlier type 915 gearboxes, as fitted during 1984, 1985 and 1986, are rather long, and can be a little cumbersome. However, the later type G50 gearbox, as fitted during 1987, 1988 and 1989, has a shorter throw and better selection which make gear changes a little more comfortable. The purists will argue that the Porsche type 915 gearbox is more true to the 911 package, and, therefore, should be more rugged and tough in keeping with the rest of the car. Although I have a lot of sympathy with that, the Getrag type G50 is slick and does select a lot more positively, making the later G50 cars a little easier on the driver.

For normal day to day driving, the 911 Carrera is one of the easiest sports cars to drive. You can see most of the front end, it provides good all round visibility, and the driving position is such that you sit up, as opposed to slumping down. The steering wheel is very vertical, and reach is not compromised by the pedal positions. The 911 Carrera is an all-round comfortable car, which makes it all the better for confident driving.

The Carrera is subject to traditional rules for driving a 911. Under normal road driving conditions, brake in a straight line and don't lift off the throttle in a bend.

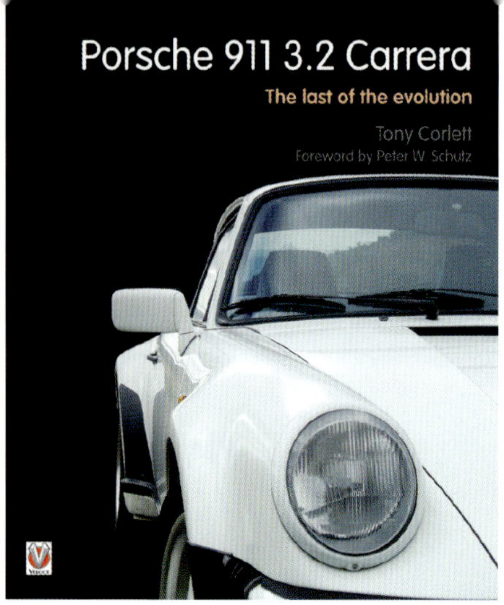

CHAPTER 24

ON THE TRACK

Driving a Carrera on a race track is probably the best driving experience you'll ever have behind the wheel of a 911.

IN THE DRY

The first thing you'll notice, which is far more pronounced on a circuit than on a road, is the understeer. This is most evident on fast sweeping corners. Lifting-off the throttle is required to induce oversteer to tame the lateral pull, but this will compromise your lap time, of course. You can modify the suspension settings and stiffness to overcome cornering understeer, but I'm primarily discussing standard Carrera specifications here.

It can be quite hard work keeping a rampant 911 Carrera on the limit. The lightening up of the tail, it has to be said, is a major feature of the overall experience and can be a little tricky under braking, particularly if you like to trail the brake pedal or simply brake under turn-in.

Understeer is the Carrera's biggest handling trait, and no more so than on the circuit where long fast curves will require lift-off oversteer.

Club Sports are used regularly on circuits around the world. Here is a typical example at Leguna Seca in America.

In the hands of the experienced, wet track driving can produce some of the Carrera's finest moments.

Club Sports compete all over the world. This is a UK specification Carrera in Australia.

That's what it's all about, however, the feeling of taking the car to the limit, but remaining squarely in control. You'll know when you get there, as you will be hard on the brake, turning the car in and balancing the tail on the steering, probably locking up the inside front, the rear just begging to lead the way.

A Carrera will only take so much sideways motion before it goes completely, however, and when that happens, it happens fast, usually allowing no time to gather it all up. But then that's what you're on the circuit for, to find the cars limits and to enjoy this wonderful chassis and power balance.

A Carrera will deliver its power right up to the red line. The trick is to change up just before the inbuilt Bosch rev limiter spoils the fun. Typical track gears would be third, fourth and fifth (depending upon the length of the straight) which will provide good acceleration. Keeping the tachometer needle above 4000rpm is the objective here, but the torque range is so good in this car that it will catapult forward from just about any rev.

The track braking capacity of a standard Carrera is good. Compared to more modern cars, however, particularly with larger callipers, it's quite a task to get the braking points right. Obviously, as you learn, you can brake later and later into a corner, trailing the pedal with turn-in, but you'll reach the limit sooner or later.

At something like 125mph in fourth gear, a braking distance of at least 100 meters would be required for a fast third gear bend. Compare this with a lighter, more nimble race or track car and you'll find the Carrera needs twice as much for braking.

The pedal will remain quite firm, but brake fade will start to creep in as the standard, original equipment discs and pads start to glaze and the brake fluid gets hotter. Eventually, you'll run out of good pressure after several laps at hard speeds, but, generally, the pedal will stay quite confident if you ease back for a lap or two and let things cool down.

The steering is very responsive and provides a very good feel to the front of the car. Initial turn-in is strong and can lead to a false sense of security later in a longer sweeping bend as the understeer takes over.

Body roll is actually quite extensive on a Carrera and it can drag the car off line if you get a little over-enthusiastic. With uprated torsion bars and harder dampers it is possible to reduce this, but the overall sharpness of turn-in is inherent within the chassis.

The rear outside tyre, as you might expect, takes most of the load on 911 circuit driving. It is important to keep an eye on the temperatures of the rear tyres, especially on normal roadgoing tyres, and to ensure they are not wearing too harshly.

Generally speaking, the 911 Carrera is an easy car to drive quickly on a circuit, although it does get harder the more you push it. I guess that's the same with any track car, the Carrera is just that little more anarchic. There is no substitute for track driving and track experience. Anyone who really wants to experience a 911 would be well advised to take it to a track and play. You'll be amazed at just how fast a Carrera can be around a circuit, and, where it loses out over lighter cars, on overall cornering speed, braking, grip and acceleration, the straight line grunt will make up for it.

Kinks and chicanes probably offer the most exhilarating part of track driving a Carrera; the ability to brake right into the turn, turning-in towards the first apex, then using the car's pendulum effect to set it up for the next apex, in effect, catching a 911 out at its own game. The switch in direction can really be sharp, allowing full power through and out of the second apex. For a chicane, it's just a matter of doing this twice, dumping the car into the third apex quite harshly, again using the pendulum pull to great effect. Manhandle the car and it seems to know who's boss under these conditions and simply hangs on, despite all the feelings to the contrary. You're dumping all the weight to the

The best way to experience a Carrera is on the track.

Part of the joy of experiencing a 911 Carrera on the circuit is to firstly understand how it reacts under pressure.

outside wheels and turning into the slide, but that's exactly where you want to go. You've caught it out again.

Things are relatively predictable in the dry, of course, but add a slip-plane and a measure of adverse weather, and things get much more complicated.

In the wet

I've always been a lover of wet driving; in fact, the wetter the better. It's the only way to really challenge the limits of car and driver. Different lines, sometimes odd braking and turn-in points, and cautious throttling and braking make wet track driving quite exhilarating.

Braking and acceleration have to be carefully balanced with steering control. You're on the limit when you find the right balance, and finding the Carrera's 'sweet-spot' in the wet is sometimes better than dry and sticky racing.

Some people shy away from driving a 911 in the wet, which is definitely a shame (some of my finest moments have been in the wet, and as for the spray off the rear wing, well that's just fantastic).

On a wet track, all your actions, both in the cockpit and on the track surface, must be gentle. If you can avoid harsh and sharp movements you'll be fine. A light shower after a warm period will make the circuit very slippery and sometimes impossible to read. Get a good downpour, however, and the grip comes back, that's if you know where to find it and how to handle it.

Take a few laps to understand the track surface. The first few laps will feel greasy and generally unpleasant, but as you begin to find grip and feel the car's attitude, you'll get quicker.

I particularly remember one wet track day, where, after some heavy rain, some grip had returned. Through standing water, continual rain and spray, I was spinning the rear wheels on the straight in fourth, my focus firmly fixed on the two red spots visible through the spray in front. It was fellow Carrera owner Mike Chadwick, this time

Body roll in a standard Carrera is quite severe under hard cornering. Some detailed modifications to the suspension set up will reduce this for regular circuit use.

out in his Caterham Road Sport. Usually a good few seconds quicker than me in the dry, here I was slowly reeling him in. I had found the sweet-spot, was braking early, running wide looking for grip, and powering on without upsetting the rear end; my Carrera was buzzing. My Dunlop Sport tyres, with very scrubbed (just how I like them for dry sessions) were far from ideal for shifting the water, but never once compromised the enjoyment.

After several fast and demanding laps, and with the Caterham almost within my grasp, I missed my early brake point into the sharp right-hander at the end of the main straight. I ran into the standing water too fast, locked up, missed the apex, ran way too wide, just missed a few cones, and those red lights were a distant blur again. I pitted a few laps later, sweat pouring from me such was my concentration. Such experiences really bring the joys of a 911 Carrera to the fore, and the memories never fade.

If you do a lot of track drives, a number of simple modifications will make a difference. One is to have a strut brace fitted to the tops of the front turrets, and another is to replace the standard Porsche brake pads with a set that will handle and disperse the heat more efficiently. Other good ideas include using a brake fluid with better viscosity at high temperatures, and fitting tyres with a compound that works better at hotter temperatures, perhaps even go for a semi-slick road tyre. Naturally, the stiffer the suspension the better, but that involves major work and might not necessarily suit your road driving conditions.

Whatever you do in a Carrera, the car needs to be set up correctly in the first place. Spend time on that and you'll never look back: you're never going to find buckets more power, the standard engine is good to start with, so enjoy what the Porsche engineers spent a lot of time and effort perfecting.

A change of torsion bars, anti-roll bars, and dampers can eliminate body roll.

A well set up Carrera will be a thrill to drive in the wet.

911 Carrera

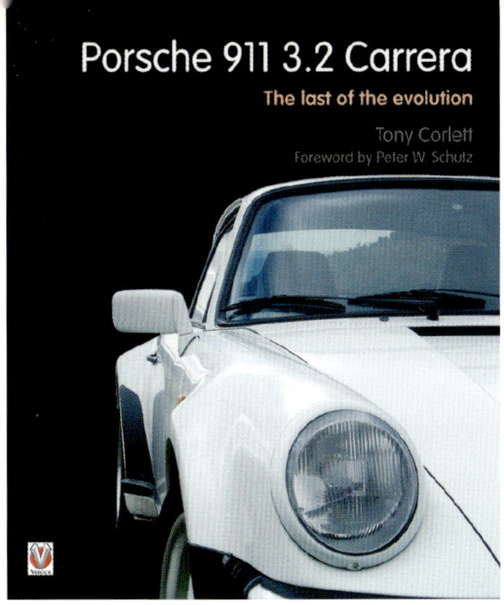

CHAPTER 25

953 4X4 PARIS TO DAKAR

The toughest race of them all ... survival of the fittest, not necessarily the fastest, but the Paris to Dakar Rally is a tough nut to crack. Jacky Ickx was determined to match his 1983 rally victory, this time with his own development programme Porsche 911 Carrera.

In 1983, Ickx and a Porsche development crew spent two months in Algiers trying and testing the new and radical Porsche four-wheel-drive system in the desert. It was an ambitious project and Ickx was confident that the 3.2 litre four-wheel-drive 911 would conquer the tough conditions of Africa.

Under the leadership of Porsche works driver Jacky Ickx, Porsche engineered three four-wheel-drive 911 Carreras to successfully tackle the 1984 Paris to Dakar Rally.

Linked with Rothmans tobacco sponsorship from the Porsche track endurance cars, and under the team management of Porsche's head of race sport development, Peter Falk, Porsche officially entered three identical 911 Carreras, code named 953, in the 1984 Paris - Dakar Rally, with backup coming in the form of an entire racing crew with large service vehicles.

In Paris, Jacky Ickx said " ... it's an off-road rally; most of the tracks we are using are used sometimes only two or three times a year, so there are really no roads. You have to be so careful and you have to be so aware of the problems of the road itself, so the tension during the rally is very high. As you know, we have to race between six and nine hours a day, on off-road racing, with a four-wheel-drive car ..."

And about the car he said " ... it is a Porsche 911, it looks like a Porsche but it has four-wheel-drive and it's prepared for the desert and off-road racing, so it means the ground clearance is very high, it's nearly thirty centimetres. It has a 3.2 litre engine, and it has 330bhp ..."

The three 911 Carreras, built using 1984 'E' program 911 chassis, were WPOZZZ91ZES100020 (car 175), WPOZZZ91ZES100021 (car 176) and WPOZZZ91ZES100022 (car 177). Car 175 was driven by world endurance champion and ex-formula one driver Jacky Ickx, partnered by French film star Claude Brasseur. Car 176 was driven by 1981 rally winner and French saloon car champion Rene Metge, partnered by Dominique Lemoyne. Car 177, the team chase-car car, was driven by Porsche factory engineers Roland

Ickx at speed in the desert.

Service area.

Kussmaul at speed in the desert.

Rally winner Rene Metge in car number 176.

Kussmaul tackling a river crossing.

The winning car at rest on the beach at Dakar.

Kussmaul and Erich Lerner.

The 953 variant, derived from the SC RS (954), used a stock, flat-six 3.2 Carrera engine producing over 300bhp. This car was effectively an all-wheel-drive version of the 911 SC RS, which later provided the platform for the 959 four-wheel-drive system. The 953 used a manually-operated four-wheel-drive system, the driver being able to operate the drive wheels using a series of levers. This was superseded in the 959 with a variable torque split function.

The race was dominated by the Porsches, with a clear victory for Metge in car number 176, Ickx bringing his 911 home in sixth place, having had by far the majority of the failures and bad luck of the three. The chase-car of Roland Kussmaul came home in 26th place, having suffered two rolls and a few lengthy time delays in performing his team duties of helping the two other 911s.

The 953 Carrera 4x4 has, to some extent, missed out on Porsche racing history (the 1984 Paris to Dakar Rally being its only competition). It may be the case that it was only ever regarded as a development tool for the 959.

911 Carrera

Official Porsche publicity poster following the 1984 Paris to Dakar win. "Rally Paris-Dakar '84: A victory for Porsche technology and reliability".

Chapter 26

CTR Yellow Bird

Group C Turbo Ruf (CTR)

It was extremely unlikely that Porsche could ever have built this 911, because it went against the company's mission statement of providing "prudent and refined" sports cars. It could be argued that Porsche *should* have built this car, but it chose to develop the 959, with its all-wheel-drive system and somewhat 'comprehensive' specification, instead.

For a small private engineering concern which could throw caution to the wind and ignore the rulebook, however, taking a 911 to the absolute limits of everything known to man at the time was an indulgence just waiting to happen.

The technically advanced 450bhp 959 Group B-based 911, developed under the control of Helmuth Bott, was first shown by Porsche in 1983, and went into limited production in 1987. In the same year, Ruf introduced the 469bhp CTR based on a standard Carrera chassis and body (though that's where the similarity ends). Whereas Porsche used a mallet to accurately crack the nut, Ruf used a sledgehammer.

CTR Yellow Bird: on its way into the record books at Nürburgring in 1987.

The story of Ruf Automobile GmbH begins in 1939, when founder Alois Ruf Senior started Auto Ruf. Over the following years he built up a relationship with Volkswagen and offered its VW customers attention to detail. In 1955, Ruf developed a full-sized passenger bus, and then went on to build up a bus manufacturing company. In 1958, Ruf diversified into Fiats and, in 1963, he added BMW to his list of specialist cars. With his son taking a keen interest, it was inevitable that when, in 1974, Ruf Senior died, Alois Ruf Junior would take over the company, concentrating on the Porsche brand with which Auto Ruf had been involved since 1963.

The first Ruf-enhanced Porsche was introduced in 1977. The car featured a 3.3 litre turbo-charged engine which offered vastly improved performance over Porsche's current 3.0 litre Turbo. This was followed in 1978 by a 217bhp, 3.2 litre, normally-aspirated 911 engine, based on Porsche's standard 3.0 litre unit. In 1981, in response to customer requests, Ruf introduced a five-speed gearbox to replace Porsche's own four-speed gearbox. In 1983, Ruf produced what it called its first "work of art", the Ruf BTR (Group B Turbo Ruf), a 3.4 litre, 374bhp, turbo-charged 911. This

Group C Turbo Ruf (CTR) Yellow Bird.

911 was a bare chassis construction, and represented a complete package of engine, transmission, chassis, and brakes.

In 1985, Ruf developed a 17 inch wheel fitted with Dunlop's newly-developed Denloc System tyres (a high-performance safety tyre originally intended for use on Porsche's 200mph 959). The Denloc system prevented the tyre from leaving the rim when deflated, and also allowed the car to be driven on the flat tyre. Ironically, Porsche did not use the Dunlop tyre, but chose instead to use the Bridgestone RE71 as original equipment. Ruf, however, used the Dunlop Denloc Sport D40 to great effect on its 200mph plus CTR.

In 1987 Alois Ruf Junior brought out the next generation of Ruf-enhanced 911s. Here was a 911 that benefited from every minute development detail and was not compromised by conservative thinking.

Ruf named this the CTR, Group C Turbo Ruf, paying tribute to the Porsche 956 and 962 Group C sports prototype race cars of the eighties. 'Yellow Bird' was a nickname given to the car in recognition of its colour.

Following on from the BTR, the CTR was also a bare chassis build. Although Ruf used its own chassis numbers, the original CTR (registration no. MN P 911) was taken from an 'H' programme Porsche chassis, Ruf choosing to opt for the narrow-bodied Carrera as opposed to the wide-bodied Turbo.

A lightweight 911 coupé with a high-technology, twin-turbo engine, it produced 496bhp and recorded a top speed of an incredible 342km (214mph) on the Nardo Racetrack in Italy. Engine capacity was increased from 3164cc to 3367cc by retaining the 74.4mm Carrera stroke, but the bore was increased from 95mm to 98mm. Adding twin KKK (Kühnle, Kopp & Kausch) turbocharger units boosted the power to 496bhp at 5950rpm. This gave an output of 139.3bhp/litre compared to the standard Carrera's output of 73bhp/litre.

Porsche actually managed to get almost 20bhp more per litre from its 959 930 Turbo-based engine than Ruf did with its CTR, but the latter was lighter and less comfortable. Using lightweight materials, such as aluminium, for the doors and bonnet, the body alone weighed 200kg less than the standard Carrera body. Weighing in at 1150kg (2535lb) the power to weight ratio was 407.8bhp/ton. The 959S, the lightweight version, weighed in at 1566kg (3452lb) and had a substantially lower power to weight ratio of 287.3bhp/ton.

Maintaining the 40/60 front to rear weight distribution, the CTR had excellent traction and power delivery to the rear drive wheels. The 17 inch wheels allowed massive 330mm diameter Brembo cross-drilled brake discs to be used. Compared to the 959, the CTR brake disc diameter was considerably larger.

Substantially stripped of all its extra weight, the original CTR was very basic in its final form. Standard Carrera body, fibreglass bumpers, 6-point roll cage, Carrera/Ruf twin-turbo engine, twin intercoolers, uprated Bosch Motronic electronic fuel injection

The sum of the Yellow Bird's parts make up something rather more than just a fast Porsche 911.

Brembo cross-drilled discs and Dunlop Denlok tyres.

In the right hands, power slide oversteer is made to look easy in the Yellow Bird.

MN P911 at Nürburgring.

CTR's 3.4 litre, twin-turbo, flat-six Carrera-derived engine pumps out a staggering 496bhp.

Even under extreme cornering, body roll on the CTR is minimal.

The CTR Yellow Bird in good company - easily capable of out-gunning Ferrari's Testarossa, Lamborghini's Countach and Porsche's 959.

and ignition system, Ruf-developed 5-speed gearbox, uprated suspension, Bilstein dampers, Ruf lightweight alloy wheels (front 8x17 DL with 215/45 VR 17 tyres, rear 10x17 DL with 255/40 VR 17 tyres), driver's seat, full harness seat belts, and not a lot else. The fuel capacity was increased from 85 to 105 litres, adding 72kg to the weight of the car when full.

The body shape of the Carrera was maintained, including the original rear aerodynamic spoiler. Lightweight bumpers replaced the original impact bumpers, the door mirror was integral to the quarter-light and above each rear wheel, set in the flared arches, were two air-intake ducts with direct air feed to the throttle bodies (on top of the engine) and twin turbo intercoolers (each side of the engine). The Fuchs alloys were also replaced with Ruf, five-spoke design, 17 inch wheels, and twin exhaust pipes made up the rear of the otherwise standard Carrera look.

Ruf data states, 0 to 60mph in 4.1 seconds, 0 to 125mph in 11.4 seconds, and a top speed of 339kph (214mph). Here was a car that in its day, quite easily out-performed a Ferrari F40, and showed the world what a Porsche 911 could really do if pushed. Ruf decided to use the standard Carrera body instead of the more flamboyant Turbo body because of weight considerations, despite the direct head-to-head with Porsche's own 930 Turbo.

Officially, Ruf built 29 CTRs using original factory-supplied Carrera chassis. It also converted a number of existing customer Carreras to CTR specification. These modified cars, unlike the original 29, still have the official Porsche chassis numbers.

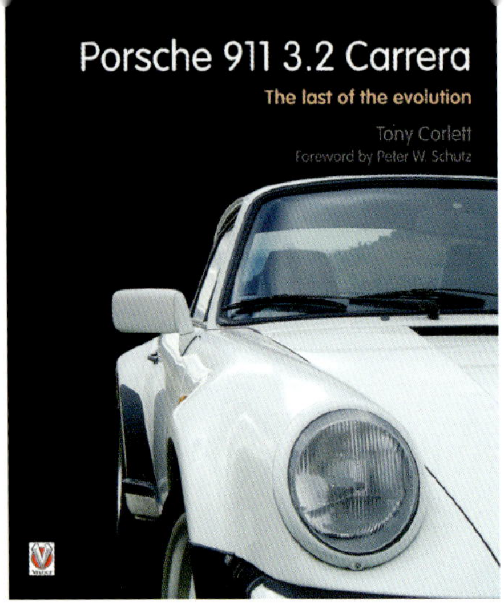

CHAPTER 27

PORSCHE VS FERRARI

CARRERA VS 328

Both cars come from an era when traditional design features mattered. One comes with passion, however, the other with brute force; one was born from the heart, the other was born from the head. Porsche showed the way in the great 'mid-range' battle by introducing a 3.2 litre engine first, but Ferrari, not to be out-gunned in the 'affordable' supercar market, soon uprated its 3.0 litre car to 3.2 litres.

Whereas the Ferrari is low, traditionally swept and sleek, the Porsche is more upright and bullish. The Ferrari sweeps by, barely disturbing the surrounding air as it goes; the Porsche takes a more aggressive approach, confronting the air and forcing it apart with a mighty lunge. Where the Ferrari slaps you; the Porsche punches you.

So how do these two great cars stack up against one another? Both come with 3.2 litre power plants and both have fuel injection. Both cars carry the name of the company founder, Ferdinand Porsche and Enzo Ferrari, who approved production of these cars whilst still overseeing their respective factories. That's where the similarities end, though, as the cars are so distinctly different that it's hard to go from one to the other without taking stock.

The layout of the two cars is radically different: one is a mid-engined, strictly two-seater arrow; the other a rear-engined, 2+2 seater cannonball. However, as an art critic might compare the brush strokes of Picasso with those of Dali, so we can compare the automotive differences in such a way as to show that these two cars are exceptional in their own right.

One key detail separates the two, however, a small badge of distinction which places the 328 in the realms of 'designer' package. The Ferrari was born from the Pininfarina pen, whereas the Carrera evolved from the original Ferdinand Alexander 'Butzi' Porsche 901 design. This is significant if you are to assess the design qualities of both cars.

Interestingly, both were followed by arguably lesser cars, not in respect of their qualities, but rather in design evolutions. The Carrera was followed by the rather 'stocky' 964, an altogether different 911, and the 328 by the rather 'hostile' 348, also an altogether different car.

Before we consider the heart of each car, we can tell a lot about the engineers who designed them just by opening or closing the doors. The Ferrari immediately gives the impression of having to take care when opening the door, such is the daintiness of the handle, whereas closing the Porsche doors requires some effort. Then there's the sound of the doors, the instantly recognisable, deep-throat clunk of the Porsche door which releases as if ready for military duty, and the lazy, almost limp action of the Ferrari door which shows little inclination of opening, let alone allowing you to get in. The Porsche wants you to grab it firmly and deal with it, the Ferrari seems more languid. It's all about design versus practicality, with Porsche opting for the latter, of course, though with such high engineering quality, you can't fail to be

It's been argued that Ferrari launched its 3.2 litre engined 328 as a direct response to Porsche's 3.2 Carrera.

impressed. The Ferrari's designer door handles are soon forgotten, whereas operation of the Porsche door brings a smile every time.

The steeply-raked windscreen and steering wheel on the Carrera, together with the hugging leather seats promote a feeling of total confidence in the car. The long and sloping screen on the 328, on the other hand, complements the oppositely-raked steering wheel to great effect, providing a greatly lower roof-line and far sleeker lines from nose to tail. However, the Ferrari is not immediately comfortable, and does not promote the same level of confidence as the 911. It could be said that Ferrari designed its cars and then, almost as an afterthought, thought about where the driver would sit. How true that seems when considering the driving position of the 328. The Carrera pitches you upright, and lets you see far more of the overall car. The 328 lays you back and leaves you with very little idea of where the corners of the car are. The Carrera's steering wheel is right where it should be, ergonomically, and the layout will suit most drivers. The Ferrari's steering wheel stretches away from the driver, and the driving position is much less comfortable.

The interiors of both cars are impeccable. The Carrera came with the option of leather or part-leather, the 328 only came in leather but, compared to the Carrera, there is a suppleness not present in the German car. Once again, there is a design versus practicality debate, with the robust 911 winning hands down. The Ferrari seems much more delicate, to the extent that a stray fingernail might scratch or a sturdy shoe may cause irreparable damage to the tender finish.

The 328 has a cluster of instruments in a binnacle that sits high above the almost flat dashboard. The Carrera, on the other hand, has a wide instrument cluster, dominated by the tachometer, incorporated within the fascia.

There is one item that sets the Ferrari way out ahead, and that is the standard fitment steering wheel. I say standard fitment because Porsche offered two alternatives, both large diameter. The typical brushed aluminium triple-spoke, leather-rimmed steering wheel fitted to the 328 is sheer poetry in motion and lovely to use.

The Carrera is slightly longer, considerably higher, but lighter than the 328.

Frontal styling is also very different.

The smooth lines of the 328 vs the bullish stance of the Carrera.

The seats in both cars are very good and offer great support. The Carrera has the ability to comfortably seat taller drivers, and the seats can recline fully. The 328 is strictly a two-seater cockpit, whereas the Carrera can arguably be called a four-seater, the rear seats offering space for children or small adults. When not used as seats, the rears fold flat to provide a very useful luggage shelf. From a cockpit practicality point of view, the Carrera is way ahead in the battle, but this is to be expected given that the Ferrari engineers put the engine where the rear seats would normally be; the Porsche engine hangs out the back, allowing for considerably more cockpit space. The Ferrari is a mid-engine layout, born from the 206 Dino in the nineteen-sixties, and the Porsche is a rear-engine layout, born from the 356 in the nineteen-fifties. Both manufacturers were pioneers in mid- and rear-engine design, respectively, and both have a thoroughbred background.

Lifting the engine covers on both cars reveals ... well ... not a lot really, as the engines are largely concealed on both cars. The Carrera engine is dominated by the cooling fan, and the 328 by the injection box. The large engine cover on the 328 also spans a reasonable boot space, behind the engine. At the front of both cars is what might be referred to as a boot, housing the spare wheel, the 328 holding a good deal less than the Carrera in bulk. To be fair, the Carrera boot is not a bad size and will hold a remarkable amount of luggage.

Technically, both 3.2 litre units produce solid power, the water-cooled 'V' (33° 30') configuration, eight-cylinder 328 producing some 50bhp more than the air-cooled 'Boxer' or 'Flat' (180°) six-cylinder Carrera. Official factory figures show the 328 producing 270bhp at 7700rpm, whereas the Carrera produces 231bhp at 5900rpm, the Ferrari engine able to rev considerably higher. The Carrera also lags behind on torque, at 284Nm at 4800rpm compared to the 328 at 304Nm at 5500rpm. The bore and stroke of the 328 is 83mm x 73.6mm, and the Carrera is 95mm x 74.4mm, cylinder displacement being 3185 cm^3 for the 328 and 3164 cm^3 for the Carrera.

The 328 GTS Variant (1272kg), is heavier than the Carrera (1210kg), a difference of 62kg, effectively the extra weight of a passenger. This shows

Comparing the Carrera's 231bhp flat six with the 328's 270bhp V8 will not tell the whole story.

up in the standing 0 to 60mph times, the Carrera being quicker at just 6.1 seconds whereas the 328 records 6.4 seconds. Top speeds are quoted as 163.4mph for the 328 and 152mph for the Carrera.

Both cars are driven via the rear wheels, the 328 from a transversely-mounted engine, its gearbox below and behind the engine, whereas the Carrera is driven from a longitudinally-mounted engine, its gearbox ahead and in-line with the engine. Both have five forward gears plus reverse, driven through single plate dry clutches.

The Carrera is slightly longer than the Ferrari (4291mm compared to 4255mm) but the 328 is considerably lower (1128mm compared to the Carrera at 1320mm). The 328 also has a longer wheelbase (2350mm compared to the Carrera at 2272mm) though the Porsche has a smaller turning circle (10.95m compared to 12m).

At 1730mm, the 328 is wider than the standard-bodied Carrera, but narrower than the Supersport or Turbo-bodied versions. Ferrari never offered a 'sport' option for the 328.

In conclusion, both cars have their own unique qualities, and benefit from design and engineering supremacy to suit their own needs. They are exceptional cars, and very capable of producing stunning performance. Does it matter that the Carrera has more room in the cockpit, or that the 328 has a tenderly-crafted soft leather finish? Well, yes actually, these are important to the overall feel of the cars, and preclude us from ever trying to say that one is better than the other.

Porsche sold over seventy-five thousand Carreras, whereas Ferrari sold almost two thousand 328s, and in a way this is the only real comparison that can be made. The Carrera was virtually a mass-produced supercar, whereas those elite 328 owners could rightly claim exclusivity.

These days, you're far more likely to find high mileage Carreras than you are 328s. In fact, the galvanised Carrera is of such sturdy construction that it would well outlast the 328 in a straight head-to-head longevity battle. However, run both down the High Street and see which one turns heads. The Carrera is a head-banger and announces its presence with some force; the 328, on the other hand, seems to generate a different, more considerate reaction.

The Carrera wasn't designed, it evolved, the 328 was designed by the world's greatest car stylist ... but remember, beauty is only skin deep.

The radically different design philosophies of Pininfarina and 'Butzi' Porsche.

The Carrera's rear engine layout and the 328's mid-engine layout can both claim a long ancestry.

Porsche produced over seventy-five thousand Carreras, whereas Ferrari produced under two thousand 328s.

CHAPTER 28

IMPROVING EXCELLENCE: UPGRADING

There is a very strong argument which suggests that the Porsche engineers did their job so well that trying to improve upon their know-how and experience is going to be difficult. It must not be forgotten that Porsche builds reliability, longevity and economy into the overall package, so modifications to any factory settings will have a detrimental affect on one or more of these.

The Carrera was primarily designed for road use and, as such, has in-built limitations intended to create the perfect balance for day-to-day use. It was not developed as a race car and, although Porsche went some way toward this in producing an occasional track-day car in the Club Sport, the overall Carrera package is one of roadgoing excellence with little compromise.

The 3.2 litre engine is already near its expansion limits, so there's really nothing to be added here, except to say that simply upgrading one or two elements is not going to achieve much in terms of power, speed or handling. In fact, most upgrades will reduce the in-built Porsche excellence for sporting road use.

You should note that engine output needs to be as close to the 231bhp optimum as possible. Trying to overcome a lower power output with enhancements is never going to work.

ENGINE

Air filter - Fitting a cone filter or drilling holes in the airbox will only cause an increase in noise levels. The restriction in the standard intake is not the filter.

Exhaust - The standard exhaust works very well on a 3.2 Carrera engine. This engine likes back pressure, and changing to a sports back box, or even the early style or SSI type system, will not produce more horsepower without a complementary chip change. Cars with an SSI exhaust, sports 2-in 2-out muffler, and custom chip have been known to produce as much as 255hp at the flywheel. If you don't change the chip as well, you're likely to lose mid-range torque when changing to a sports exhaust. If you have a catalytic converter fitted, then changing to a pre-muffler will produce a little more hp than the catalytic converter alone. A complementary chip is required to realise maximum gains of 10-15hp.

Porsche Cup replica wheels are available with the Carrera offsets.

Split Rim BBS style wheels can be customised with Carrera offsets.

DME computer chip - You can upgrade the DME chip using a custom chip mapped on a dynometer. It would be difficult to gauge the effect of just changing a chip, though, as an extra 10hp in a 231hp car is less than most people would notice.

Engine management - A Motec system will control fuel and ignition requirements more precisely than a Motronic system, and can produce 260bhp to 270bhp if used with an SSI type exhaust and larger fuel injectors on a healthy engine.

Camshafts - There's not too much scope for performance camshafts in a 3.2 engine. Because of the shape of the pistons, there is limited valve to piston clearance. This means you cannot run something like an 'S' cam profile from the 2.4S or 2.7RS engines unless you invest in new pistons. A 3.2 engine with high compression race pistons and 'S' cams would be lovely. The 3.2 engine has enough displacement to avoid being peaky like the 2.4S, but an 'S' cam would give it a lovely 5000rpm kick. To get the maximum benefit you would then need to think about stronger rod bolts and racing valve springs with titanium retainers in order to run a little more rpm (perhaps a 7200rpm red line). In a standard 3.2 Carrera without piston modifications, the best camshafts seem to be the 964 M64 3.6 litre camshaft profile or equivalent. These will fatten the torque curve in the mid-range and allow the engine to rev a little more freely above 5000rpm.

Throttle bodies - This is the ultimate way to enhance the intake of the 3.2 engine. Six independent throttle bodies (ITBs) with six throttle butterflies allow a virtually unrestricted path to the inlet valves. They also sound wonderful. In the nineteen-seventies, the way to get maximum horsepower was via high butterfly slide valve MFI. These are great on a racing engine (like the 1974 RSR) but aren't practical for lower revs and road use. Independent throttle bodies together with a Motec, or similar, EMS control, is the most effective way to get 100bhp per litre without drawbacks.

A Carrera with independent throttle bodies, a Motec EMS, 964 camshafts and an SSI exhaust should make close to 280hp. Add in 'S' camshafts and racing pistons and the Carrera 3.2 engine is good for 300-320hp!

Engine capacity - It's possible to increase the capacity to 3.4 or 3.5 litres (with piston and crankshaft upgrades, using either 98mm or 100mm pistons). Going to 3.5 litres involves some crankcase machine work, so it is more difficult. The horsepower increase is basically proportional to the displacement increase. So 3.4 litres is probably only a 6-7 per cent increase. It's been shown, however, that lightweight racing pistons will produce a little more horsepower than the displacement increase alone would suggest. Combined with a camshaft change and SSI exhaust, the gains seem to be exponential. Porsche Special Works offered these conversions, so they're quite reliable. Helmuth Bott, for instance, drove a 3.5 litre 911 SC as his personal car.

Transmission - Type 915 vs Getrag G50. The G50 weighs about 40lb more than the 915, but has a more accurate shift. A good 915 may be nearly as good - in fact many Porsche fans prefer it - but there's always a little more risk of a missed gear change. There are 'short-shift' kits that create a more strongly sprung and 'gated' feel for the 915. There is also a completely gated shift to create a G50 feel.

Limited slip differential - Nice if you have one, but not worth the money if you don't. The reason is that the weight distribution of the 911 (60 per cent to the rear) means that, under power the rear squats very evenly coming out of corners, and there is very little chance of spinning the inside wheel. The only time you get inside wheel spin is in steeply off-camber corners, more so in the wet. If you have massive horsepower increases, then a plate-type or torque sensing LSD makes sense. 500bhp Turbos, for example, need such a differential.

Gearing - With a close ratio gear set installed, it will feel like you've added

30+bhp. An 'active' gear set will have a tall first gear, that is, one you actually use on the race track for slow corners rather than just for starting, and then closely stacked ratios thereafter (maybe not so practical for street use). Alternatively, you can lower the top gears, and have shorter 3rd, 4th and 5th gears. This will sacrifice some top speed, maybe only 10mph, but give a closely stacked 2nd, 3rd, 4th and 5th. Running a chip with the Club Sport rev limit of 6850rpm will go some way towards eliminating the pick-up in the gear spacing.

Clutch - The standard clutch works well unless you like drag racing starts. A racing clutch with a lightweight pressure plate and flywheel is a bit like an on/off switch, and makes street driving harder. Unless you need to replace the clutch, it should not be high on the list of priorities.

Handling

Alignment - Alignment settings involve a trade-off between corner grip and wear. Modern radial race tyres like a lot of camber - some as much as 5 degrees of negative camber. Porsche designed the Carrera to have some built-in understeer for safety, and the standard alignment settings are very conservative. They are fine for road use, but if you're performance-minded you'll want a little more negative camber. The more negative camber, however, the more the inside of your tyres will wear.

With a low ride height, you can almost get 2 degrees of negative camber in the front. The rear has more adjustment, achieving 3.5 degrees easily. More is not necessarily better, though, and most experts advise that you set the front camber first, and then set the rear at 0.5-1.0 degree more negative camber. A fast road setting, for example, would be 0.75 degrees negative at the front, and 1.25 degrees negative at the rear. This is about the most you will get at the front at standard ride heights.

To get more negative camber, you could fit adjustable camber plate top mounts to the front struts, lower the ride height, and use an adjustable strut brace to pull the shock towers together a little. Rear wheel toe-in should always be left at factory settings (likewise at the front, unless you want a very 'pointy' front end that responds very quickly to turn-in, in which case you can run zero toe at the front). Castor should be set to the maximum possible since more castor gives more negative camber as the wheels are turned.

Ride height - This depends on your preference for aesthetics and road clearance. Very low will adversely affect the front and rear geometry and, in particular, increase bump steer, requiring steering rack spacers. The tie-rods should be basically horizontal when the car is at rest. A lower height will lower the roll centres, which has a cornering benefit. Too low will mean the suspension operates outside its optimal arc of travel, though, and there will be adverse camber changes and the possibility of the dampers running out of travel. Adjustments are easily made on the front using the ride height adjustment screws, while small adjustments on the rear can be achieved using the eccentric bolts on the spring-plate. Bigger adjustments on the rear require re-indexing and removal of the rear torsion bars. Whenever ride height is changed, you'll need to re-align the car, as ride height affects the geometry.

Dampers - Your choice of damper will always involve a compromise between comfort and stiffness, in relation to road conditions. Most Carreras had Boge gas dampers fitted as standard. Porsche deemed them good enough and, provided they are in good working order, they work very well. For road use, these dampers provide a nice ride/handling balance. A stiffer damper would provide better body control and less weight transfer. The sportier dampers supplied by Bilstein for the Carrera come in two alternatives: Heavy Duty and Sport. Heavy Duty is slightly too hard when used with standard torsion bars, but worthwhile for track use. Sport is less hard, but provides a very stiff setting for everyday road use on standard torsion bars. If used in conjunction with larger diameter torsion bars, the Sport dampers are very good. A combination of Hard and Sport (front and rear, respectively) when upgrading to large diameter torsion bars is not uncommon in America. Bilstein also makes inserts to fit the Boge strut.

Torsion bars - These are effectively the springs on the 3.2 Carrera. Increasing the diameter of the torsion bar increases the spring rate. A traditionally-recommended fast road set up would be to install 26mm 911 Turbo torsion bars on the rear and leave the front as standard. This will help counter the understeer, but will have little effect on ride. To virtually eliminate body roll will require the use of larger diameter torsion bars (though some front/rear combinations can make the car too firm for road use). A good compromise would be a 22/29 front to rear setup. While this won't result in a move towards oversteer, it will have a noticeable understeer balance much like the factory car, it will mean very little weight transfer due to the roll stiffness. A 22/29 torsion bar platform is certainly a much stiffer setup than standard, but the ride remains quite tolerable for road use if the damping is unchanged.

Anti-roll bars - Changing these is a relatively inexpensive way of making your car corner with less roll. An adjustable bar offers the ability to increase or decrease roll stiffness by changing the leverage on the bar itself. Bigger is not necessarily better, however, as anti-roll bars have a detrimental affect on ride. A nice upgrade would be to add an adjustable rear anti-roll bar, of a slightly bigger diameter than stock - say a 22mm diameter. This small increase in rear roll stiffness goes some way towards dialling out the inherent understeer and, together with new shocks and a fast road alignment, might be a good starting point if you want to compete in more than just the occasional track day.

Steering arms - The upgrade to Turbo tie-rods is popular. The theory is that by using a tie-rod with monoball type joints and no rubber, you get more precise execution of your steering inputs. If, for example, you needed to replace your steering rack, then it might be a good time to do the tie-rods as well.

Strut brace - Under certain stresses the front strut towers may spread apart or compress together. Hard cornering, for example, has been shown to spread the towers apart. It is this spreading that the strut brace is designed to correct, as even a very small movement may translate into a relatively large camber change. Targas and Cabriolets seem to benefit more from a brace than Coupés, but the difference my be so marginal as to be difficult to detect.

Suspension bushes - Worn bushes allow excess and uncontrolled movement. Whenever analysing suspension changes, you must remember that the goal is to minimise geometry change so that the contact patch of the tyre is maximised.

Using new rubber bushes will provide good compliance and isolation from noise. For the ultimate precision, however, a monoball upgrade provides free movement but zero compliance and noise isolation, though these are more suited to race cars where they can be regularly inspected for wear. In everyday road use, dirt, road grime and grit can cause failures.

A further option is plastic or Teflon impregnated plastic. These have to be fitted very carefully, and regularly lubricated to avoid friction and squeaking. A more costly option is polybronze bushings. These have zero friction, are easy to fit and to lubricate without removal, and they provide precise location.

The key bushing in the 911 suspension system is the rear spring-plate. These are large donut-shaped bushings, vulcanised to the spring-plate, and can deform over time with the constant load they experience. They are key because the toe and camber for the rear wheels are set from the eccentric bolts in the spring-plate. Sloppy bushings here result in sloppy rear wheel control, and adverse toe changes, in particular, result in oversteer. The cheapest and most popular change here is to use a harder rubber bushing.

Brakes

Although the standard brakes on a Carrera are really very good, one limitation is that they are designed to fit within 15-inch wheels. As a result, are very similar to the brakes fitted to the original 911, which had roughly half the horsepower of the Carrera, and weighed a lot less.

Fluid - To avoid brake fade, use fresh brake fluid (preferably with a high boiling point). While the Carrera brakes are very good for road use, on a track day they will experience much greater demands than on the road, and will, therefore, generate a lot more heat. Using a race-type fluid is a good first step towards preventing brake fade.

Cooling - Better cooling will help to prevent brake fade and will also help to prolong the lifespan of brake pads, callipers, seals, etc. The first step is to remove the dust shields from the back of the disc. The next step is to duct some air to the brakes. Fitting a kit with scoops that collect air from the

Later 'modern' wheels can also be fitted to Carreras.

air stream below the A-arm and duct it to the centre of the disc is a good start, and although they don't collect a huge amount of air, they will probably collect enough.

Hoses - A popular upgrade is to change the OE rubber hoses for braided stainless hoses as these don't expand under pressure.

Pads - A pad upgrade involves fitting pads that operate at a higher temperature. It is a compromise again, however, as high temperature pads will not work as well when cold, their coefficient of friction is lower when cold. They may have little bite when cold, may create lots of dust, may squeal, and may even accelerate disc wear. They will, however, work at temperatures as high as 700-800 Fahrenheit. The cold performance of a race pad is never quite as bad a some people will have you believe, and will be tolerable on the street if you are careful, aware of the limitations, and drive accordingly. Porsche used Pagid pads in all its factory race cars, and these are very highly regarded. The 'Blue' compound is acceptable for street and track, and the 'Orange' and 'Black' compounds are more race oriented.

Discs - There are two ways of improving the brake discs. The first is to use the 911 Turbo brakes (which are very good, and their origins go back to the 917), but these are expensive, and the callipers are difficult to come by. The Turbo discs are 32mm thick (front) and 28mm thick (rear), and offer a much greater heat sink capacity. Another option is to use the brakes from an early 944 Turbo or 964. The 28mm thick 944 Turbo front discs and the 4-piston callipers from either the 944 Turbo or the 964 can be adapted to fit on the front, provided the standard Carrera proportioning valve is removed. This will result in an acceptable bias when used with the standard rear brakes. You need to run a 16x7 front wheel with this set-up, as the diameter of the disc and thickness of the calliper will not fit within a 16x6 or a 15-inch wheel.

Master cylinders - In general terms, the standard 3.2 master cylinder is fine for upgrades up to and including the 944 Turbo brakes. However, once you go to 911 Turbo brakes then you need the bigger, 930 master cylinder to push enough fluid around.

Wheels and tyres

Although the Fuchs wheel is very strong and lightweight, the design is quite poor for brake cooling. Using 50 profile tyres on the 7 or 8x15 inch wheels gives a nice gearing reduction for better acceleration, but the 205/50x15 front tyre, is quite small for the Carrera.

For the 16 inch wheels, you have a couple of options. The first would be to stick with the standard wheel and tyre sizes, 205/55x16 at the front and 225/50x16 at the rear, and add 20mm spacers front and rear to fill out the wheelarches and provide a slightly wider track. The second would be to fit some 8x16 or 9x16 wheels to the rear, and move the 7x16 wheels to the front. You can run the standard tyre sizes on these rims, which will give you a nice increase in track, but this will also stretch out the tyres so they perform closer to their optimum.

You also have the option to go 'plus 1' on 16-inch rims by running 245/45x16 at the rear and 225/50x16 at the front. Clearance at the rear is no problem, but you have to be careful at the front. Even a 205/55 on a 7x16 can foul the wheelarch at the front, and a 225/50 will be even tighter. You may need to roll the lip of the fender and run some negative camber to avoid fouling. A strut brace is useful for pulling in a little more negative camber, and using a 225/45x16 on the front also helps as it's not such a tall tyre.

If you use a 9x16 rear wheel, it's better to run the plus 1 size tyre (245/45x16) as this rim is a little too wide for a 225 section tyre. Most of the extra offset is on the inside of the 9x16 wheel, so clearance is not a problem, though you should check that there's no rubbing on the oil lines, spring-plate bolts, and on the wheelarches. If you're inclined to play around with wheels and tyres, it's very useful to fit longer wheels studs with steel wheel nuts, and have a few 7mm spacers available. This way you can make adjustments until you find the right setting.

The easiest wheel upgrades involve fitting the Cup replicas, in Cup 1, 2 or 3 styles. These are made specifically for pre-964 911s with the correct offsets. The later cars, 964s and 993s, have a different offset. The wheels fitted to those later cars need very big spacers in order to work on a 911 Carrera. The replica wheels have two disadvantages, however, in that they're very heavy, and they're not very strong.

Other options that work are the three-piece, split-rim style. Because these can be built from different rim sections, the offsets can be customised. Another possibility is the one-piece, 17-inch wheels from Ruf.

Tyres - The biggest decision, in terms of the compromise involved, is whether to go for R-compound, often referred to as track day tyres, or with normal road tyres. R-compound tyres will be very lightly treaded, and will have a very soft compound and stiff sidewalls. They can wear out in as little as 2000-5000 miles of road driving, but may last longer than road tyres for pure track miles as they are not so prone to overheating. In damp conditions, sticky R-compound tyres will have more grip than road tyres, but in the wet they are prone to aquaplaning due to minimum tread and shallow tread depth.

Tyre pressure - Porsche recommends very high rear tyre pressures, which presumably are well suited to sustained high speed running on the autobahns. Most people recommend that rear pressures should be around 2-4psi higher than front pressures, with front pressures somewhere around the 29-31psi mark. There is no absolute right answer though.

You need to regularly check pressures and wear across the tyre. Alignment settings, particularly camber, will change wear patterns. You will tend to wear the insides of the tyres more quickly with lots of negative camber, for example. Track days will put much higher demands on your tyres. With higher speeds, heavy braking and acceleration, higher g-loads and more friction, the tyres generate lots of heat and, accordingly, pressures rise. You need to monitor this temperature-related pressure increase when at a track day. This will be around 6-10psi above cold pressures. The optimum hot pressure will vary from tyre to tyre but, for most road tyres, the ideal is around 36psi, and around 32psi for R-compounds.

Once you find the optimum pressures, you can start to measure inside, outside and centre temperatures with a pyrometer, as a more accurate way to fine tune pressures and camber settings, but there is neither time nor space to cover that here.

Interior

There are usually two main goals when upgrading the interior: reducing weight and improving safety.

Seats - Changing to shell-type race seats with sliders to allow simple forward and aft adjustment will net a weight saving of around 40kg. Shell-type race seats may not work so well with standard seat belts, and they make entry and exit from the car more difficult, but they do help to locate you securely in the seat so you don't have to grip the steering wheel so hard to stop sliding around.

If you add proper harnesses, it's a good idea to add a roll bar or cage, as you can be more vulnerable in a roll-over situation with harnesses and a shell-type seat. The thing to keep in mind is that your safety depends on many aspects of the car's design and set-up. Once you start changing one area, you need to consider its effect on other areas.

Seat belts - Although 4, 5 or 6 point harnesses hold you in place in your seat better than normal seat belts, particularly when used with a race seat, there are safety concerns surrounding their use. Harnesses have to be properly and securely mounted, either from a proper roll bar or from the existing factory seat belt mounts using a harness guide bar to control the angles. This is an area where professional advice will have a large impact on your safety.

Steering wheel - Many people change the standard wheel for something a little smaller, usually a 350mm wheel. This obscures the speedometer a little, but the feel of a slightly smaller wheel with a large leather rim is very nice.

Weight reduction - You could, of course, remove everything in the interior, other than the seat and steering wheel, in an effort to reduce weight. The Club Sport, for example, has had many of the interior luxuries removed, but you can go further. Comfort levels inevitably dictate to what extent you are going to save weight; that and the increase in noise levels which will result by removing all the sound deadening and absorbing materials, such as the carpets. Door panels can be replaced with aluminium skins, and the side and rear glass can be replaced with Perspex. The rather heavy impact-bumpers can either have their impact absorbers removed, or entirely replaced with lighter fibreglass alternatives. The same can be said for the front wings, doors, engine cover and hood/boot lid.

Chapter 29

Over the mountain

The Carrera has impeccable manners on fast twisty roads, and can be driven with confidence.

Set in the middle of the Irish Sea there is an oblong piece of land steeped in motorsport history: so much so that, today, it is known as the road racing capital of the world. Long since the dust of the very first motor race to be held in Great Britain has drifted into the annals of history, the sound of racing machines resonates around a circuit that has become a true legend in every sense of the word.

Still using some of the original 1905 motor racing circuit, the track has become a remarkable landmark that openly slaps the face of the conformist world in which we live. It stands out as a radical 'bad-boy' in an otherwise politically correct world and, in many ways, goes hand in hand with Porsche's 911. The TT course wraps speed with adversity, rolled into one dynamic package in which we can indulge. Is this the best Carrera road in the world ...?

The climax of this circuit is known as the 'mountain course' which winds itself up into a finale second to none. A finishing touch that leaves only the brave and the daring with a feeling of complete domination over one of the trickiest pieces of road in the world.

Mix the unorthodox with the unconventional and you get an explosive cocktail of adversity - step up the Porsche 911 Carrera and bring on a lap of the TT Course - welcome to chisel vs stone ... welcome to the Isle of Man ...

Twice a year, the entire TT Course is closed off for two of the world's greatest motorcycle road races, the Manx TT and the Manx Grand Prix. At all other times, the TT Course is a normal

911 Carrera

road with normal traffic and normal drivers. It is one of the main arteries of the island and provides circulation routes for everyday life. But beneath that lies the real animal, brought to life by those who know how, brought to life by those who can.

I want to take you over the mountain in a 911 Carrera.

Thrown in at the deep end really, the Ramsey Hairpin signals your first real dose of the Mountain Course. Just after the 24th Mile Marker, attack it hard, brake hard, too fast and you'll dig the nose in on the apex and get the tail out; too slow and it leaves you wanting. It turns sharp left, back on itself and climbs steeply through the apex. A stiffly set up Carrera will lift the inside wheel and traction is lost. Brake hard and square on the central white line, find second gear in good time, and turn the car in sharply, almost brutally: you need both hands here. Lay down the power carefully, too much and you'll swap ends, hit the throttle hard when the car is almost straight, the adverse camber will keep you pointing ahead and the climb up the hill will tame the horses.

It's gloomy at the hairpin, you're shrouded in trees and the side of a mountain stares darkly from beneath the shadows. Even in the warm sunshine, the hairpin can be damp and ready to catch out and punish the uninitiated. Punch a hole through the gloom, flat in second, up to the rev limiter and shove it well into third. Ignore the right sweep, keep it flat, it straightens slightly into another right, you might snatch fourth if you are cruising, brake hard and let the car run into the first of two right-hand turns, holding the throttle for the second tight right, stay in third, but watch the understeer on the way out.

You're travelling quickly now, climbing gently, lay the power on fully as you head out onto a short straight into a blind right, left sweep, nail the throttle in as it opens out up the hill past the waterworks. Fast in third through the left, right, left sweeps, lifting only to control the nose, and into the braking zone for the Gooseneck at the 25th Mile Marker.

The Gooseneck is tight and needs a big slow for careful negotiation. It's on a steep incline on a very tight right-hand bend which can be tempting to take too fast. Don't. Find second before you turn in, you will need both hands again here as you muscle the car in, taking care not to lose either end in the process. Too late on the brakes and you'll understeer wide into an awaiting bank, too early on the power and you'll spin.

You can plant the throttle almost immediately on the apex and sit and wait as the power comes back, gravity is tugging you back, all 60 per cent weight is squatting over the back wheels, and the 911 is shaking its head, surging forward onto the open sweeping sections of the Mountain Course.

Driving the Mountain Course fast is very much a matter of understanding the road and carrying the speed through bends. Keep it tidy, the smoother the better, don't cut the blind corners and on many occasions let adverse gravity, on the uphill sections, do the slowing down for you. You can save your brakes on the way up that way, you'll need them on the way down. A fast driver is not necessarily the guy who needs to brake everywhere, rather pace the car, roll off the throttle early.

The secret to acceleration in a 911 Carrera is to change up just before the rev limiter spoils the fun, and that's exactly how you snatch third, at around 6000rpm, out of the gooseneck as you head quickly into a blind crest left sweep. Hold it in third as the road keeps on sweeping left, into a short straight, left sweep, short straight. Stay in third for a tight right and hit the throttle hard for a long uphill run, sweep to the right, into a short straight, into fourth, over a blind crest and brake, back to third, for a tight left/right 's' curve at Guthrie's Memorial, the 26th Mile Marker.

Open out into a short uphill straight, blind left, short straight, flat in third through tricky right, into a left sweep, through a left bend onto the famous Mountain Mile, between the 27th and 28th Mile Markers, a long straight section in fourth and fifth. This is where the speed really begins to build up. It's all or nothing now, the Mountain Course is there for the taking, and where you were cautious with speed in the lower gears to begin with, you will stay on it now, catching fifth only for comfort and safety.

Into fourth through a long right-hand sweep, flat through a left sweep, the road keeps sweeping to the right as you climb up past the 28th Mile Marker. Stay flat up to the braking zone for a blind tight left curve at Mountain

On track or road, the secret to acceleration in a Carrera is to change up just before the rev limiter spoils the fun.

Hut, straight line the right kink and aim for the hut and brake hard. Accelerate through a second left sweep onto a long right/left/right combination, past the 29th Mile Marker. Stay on it in fourth, sweeping right into a short straight. The road flattens out a bit here as you head towards the summit of the mountain through a series of fast sweeps. You can stay in fourth here or choose fifth for comfort.

From here, there is a great view across the valley to the right, looking out for oncoming traffic to the Black Hut. This is important at this point, because of a very tricky right-hand turn, which can be taken fast in fourth using the whole road, otherwise it's brake time, and keeping the car on the left of the road is tricky on the adverse camber which has a tendency to pull you wide.

Assuming a clear road, you can accelerate down a short straight to the Black Hut very quickly indeed, flat in fourth, before easing the car out to the extreme right of the road and feathering off. No need to brake, Black Hut is a fast left-hand bend with good grip and visibility. Roll the car off the right kerb, brush the apex, flatten the throttle and let it run wide across the road to the right, before bringing it back to the left to set up for the first right-hand sweep into the Veranda, past the 30th Mile Marker.

Stay in fourth, ease off the throttle for a long sweeping blind right with four effective apexes and onto the fast Veranda straight in fourth. A long fast straight with a blind right sweep into a short straight. As you straighten out, the whole road comes into view and you can see across to the left through the next combination of bends. Once again, if there is no traffic, bring the car out smoothly as far as you can to the right turn, run the car to the apex and flatten the throttle for a short straight, let the nose drift out to the right, but no more than the middle of the road, you need to bring it back to the left smartly for a blind long right into the Bungalow. A very short straight into the Bungalow, used mostly for braking and finding third. The Bungalow is a deceptively slow corner.

Look across the series of Bungalow turns and up Hailwood Rise to Brandywell. Loads of braking on the right of the road, wash off more speed than you think, the Bungalow tightens back on itself and will catch you out if you're not careful. Stay in third, wait for the right moment, it is a long apex, before squeezing the throttle and letting the car have its head.

Suddenly you seem to have acres of road to play with, and you pay the price for the slow Bungalow. Onto Hailwood rise is a tricky off-camber right sweep which can only be taken flat on the wrong side of the road, but the car will still understeer, seemingly wanting to bury you into the banking on the left, but stay with it, feather off understeer for the timid, but you can plant the throttle as you head up the fast Hailwood Rise, past the 31st Mile Marker, flat into fourth and roll into fifth. Sweep right and feather off for the fast right into the tight left at Brandywell, brake hard, back to third, and keep the car tight.

Sweep left again and through a fast right, brake, stay in third for a combination of two left turns, at the 32nd Mile Marker, feather the power between the two and wait for the fast straight down to Windy Corner.

Look out across the valley and watch for traffic. At this point you can see for at least two miles and can assess the road ahead. This is important, it is here that you plan your approach to Windy Corner, another deceptively slow corner. The name of the corner gives you a clue, and yes, it can blow you all over the place up here.

Flat in third, and well into fourth before standing on the brakes, there is a slight hump and left sweep into the braking zone for Windy, but a great overtaking point under braking as you slip up the inside of the bend, the grip under braking is fantastic. Take as much of the left of the road as you can, bring it back into third and turn-in sharply, get the nose tucked in, the understeer will again drag you out. Stay off the power, it feels like an eternity, but eventually you will have the understeer under control and you can plant the power again for a long flat straight into fourth, flat left sweep and right sweep, brake for a long blind left, double apex, holding the car on the throttle between the two.

A short straight and fast right sweep, through the 33rd Mile Marker, tightening into a tricky braking zone for the tight left-hand curve at Kepel Gate. You will need to brake while turning in, it's quite easy to throw it all away here. Care is needed and some speed has to be forfeited in fourth through the right sweep. Stand on the brakes, select third, you can trail the brakes into Kepel but be careful, on a hot day the grip is not there and the car will slide around. Stay in third and hold it on the throttle along the short straight to Kate's Cottage. Keep it tidy in third through Kate's before hitting the throttle for the long fast downhill run to the Creg ny Baa.

Off the straight from Kate's and you can give it everything, shove the revs to the gunnels, you can hit the rev limiter very easily here, gravity is tugging you forward and your own blood pressure is rising. Then, sooner than perhaps you might like, stand on everything you have to slow down, you'll need it to get around the blind and very tight right-hand Creg ny Baa. Third is best here, albeit slow. It is at this turn that the brakes have to be in top condition, if you're inexperienced with the mountain and you've hammered them too hard on your way over, some fade might be apparent; be careful, you may like to dab the brakes with your left foot on the way down the hill.

Too brave and too late on the brakes and you'll go straight through the front doors of the Creg ny Baa hotel, too fast on turn-in and you'll go backwards through the establishment's car park. This is one of the slowest points on the course and, ironically, comes off one of the faster straights. It demands respect. Accelerate too quickly off the apex and you will understeer into the wall on the way out.

The final downhill run from the Creg ny Baa to Hillberry is very fast, narrow, downhill. A long straight, a blind right sweep, a short straight before hard braking for Brandish.

Nasty would be the best description of Brandish. Brake hard, bring it back into third, and don't underestimate the tightness, it's blind, but you can feather in the power on the apex before flattening the throttle for the last straight, a long run into the restricted areas. You can gun it all the way and let the speed wash off on the slight uphill run out of Hillberry and past the 36th Mile Marker.

You've come off the mountain. Just under twelve miles and it all happened in less than ten minutes. If you've driven it fast, your mouth will be dry and the adrenaline pumping - there really is nothing quite like a spirited trip over the mountain in a 911.

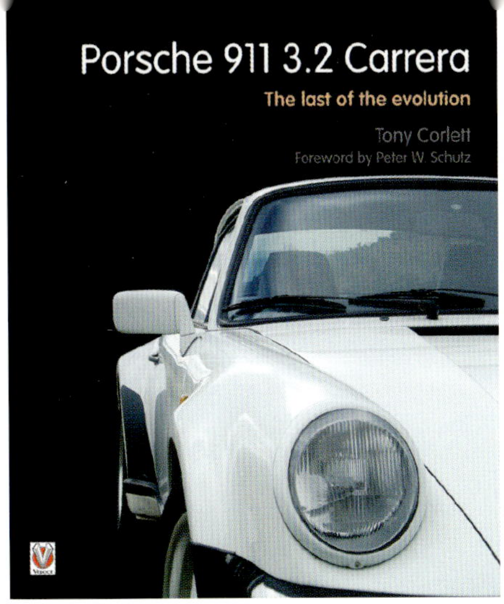

CHAPTER 30

SPIRIT OF CARRERA

So why is it that these cars exude such spirit? Perhaps it's the engineering quality, or perhaps it's the fact that no matter what, they give an immense sense of pleasure. Whether standing still or moving, the Carrera spirit never lifts, it's always there to grab you by the scruff of the neck and make you feel like something really special is going on.

It's generally known that the name Carrera was adopted by Porsche from the 'La Carrera Panamericana' road race that took place in Mexico between 1950 and 1954. Porsche won the 1953 event with a 550 Spyder, and it seems that, as a result, it took up the name and started using it on the competition-based cars, with road car derivatives carrying the Carrera name as a mark of sporting tradition. It is fitting, therefore, that Porsche chose to name the new 1984 911 a Carrera.

A spirit of competition is there, bred so deeply into the car that it's impossible not to feel the emotion that Porsche drew on in evolving its icon 911 into one of the greatest race-based road cars.

It is that same spirit which provokes the driver into challenging the very car that is seemingly infallible, by stepping over the thin line of 911 adversity. Pressed hard, the Carrera just keeps giving more and more until you instinctively know that you have wrung it by the neck and beaten it at its own game.

Like man and machine in unison, the spirit of Carrera lives on vividly, long after all is at rest and the machinery cold. The 911 3.2 Carrera really is a great car, in emotion and in engineering, a real place of combined business and pleasure. Long live the 911 Carrera!

1987 Targa.

1988 Coupé.

911 Carrera

1986 Cabriolet.

CHAPTER 31

TECHNICAL OVERVIEW

The 911 3.2 Carrera was manufactured from 1984 to 1989, and included Coupé, Targa, Cabriolet, and Turbo-Look (Supersport) body variations. This was the last of the 911 line to be designated as such by the factory, and manufactured under that number. Providing a nice blend of the classic and new, it was also the last car to carry the distinctive, and somewhat characterful, 'impact bumpers'.

With a flat-six 3164cc powerplant, the factory figures show a power output for the European specification of 231bhp, with 0 to 62.5mph (100kmh) coming up in 6.1 seconds, and a top speed of 152mph. For the two American specification engines, the factory figures show power outputs of 207 and 217bhp, with 0 to 60mph coming up in 6.3 and 6.1 seconds respectively, and top speeds of 146 and 149mph. With an unladen weight of 1210kg, the 3.2 Sport equiped Carrera has an excellent power to weight ratio: 191bhp/tonne for Europe; 171 and 179bhp/tonne for America. It can return anything up to 41mpg if driven with care.

The 3.2 Carrera stands as one of the Porsche fans' favourites. It has no electronic driving aids, no ABS, no power steering, and no traction control. In fact, it's driving in its purest form; a great combination of driver and car. Driven through the rear wheels only, maximum power comes at 6520rpm, with maximum torque at 4800rpm.

The engine is a 6-cylinder, 4-stroke, horizontally-opposed (flat or boxer) air-cooled unit, comprising a light alloy two-piece crankcase, forged steel crankshaft, forged steel con rods, forged light alloy pistons, light alloy separate cylinders (barrels), and light alloy cylinder heads. The valve arrangement is an overhead V-pattern, and consists of single intake and exhaust valves operated by a single, chain-driven, overhead, cast steel camshaft per bank.

The engine is air-cooled, the air being forced around the engine by a belt-driven, multi-blade fan, situated at the rear. The crankshaft fan ratio is 1:1.67, and the air flow rate is 1500 litres/second at 6000rpm.

Lubrication is via a dry sump with separate oil reservoir configuration. The oil, which also assists in engine cooling, is passed through a thermostatically-controlled cooler on the crankcase, within the fan air stream, and onto an

1984 Carrera engine bay.

oil cooler radiator situated at the front of the car, under the front right fender. From 1987 onwards, the front-mounted radiator was fan-assisted. Oil pressure at 5000rpm is 3.5 bar at 90 degrees C, and a pressure indicator gauge and lamp is located on the dashboard. Oil capacity is 13 litres and consumption is generally up to 1.5 litres/1000km.

The standard factory exhaust system consists of a single pipe system, with a junction outside of the heat exchanger, with primary and main silencers (mufflers). A catalytic converter in place of the primary silencer was standard fitment in America, and optional in Germany. The heat exchangers, which are attached to the main exhaust pipes, are located at the front of the engine, and direct warm air to the passenger cabin via electronic blowers and an automatic temperature control.

The fuel system is of the DME type (Digital Motor Electronics) and is the Bosch Motronic system. Fuel is pumped via an electric roller cell pump. Fuel tank Fuel tank capacity is 80 and 85 litres, for 1984 and post 1984 cars, of which 8 litres is the reserve.

The electrical system is a 12 volt system, fed from an outboard located battery. The ignition is electronic (breakerless), and the firing order is 1-6-2-4-3-5.

Earlier cars came with the 915 specification gearbox and cable-operated clutch, whereas cars from 1987 onwards had a G50 specification gearbox and hydraulically-operated clutch. Five forward gears and one reverse through single dry plate clutch, spiral bevel differential, rear double universal joint halfshaft axles. Final drive ratio is 3.875:1 for the 915 and 3.44:1 for the G50 gearboxes.

The front suspension set-up comprises independent wishbones turning on torsion bars fixed to vertical MacPherson struts. At the rear, the system comprises independent semi-trailing arms turning on torsion bars also fixed to vertical MacPherson struts. Anti-roll bars to the front and the rear.

With no springs, the car is weighted on the torsion bars and loaded on the dampers and, apart from increasing the diameter or stiffness of the torsion bars, the dampers provide the optimum adjustment for the car's handling.

The braking system is a servo assisted, hydraulic, dual circuit system, with internally ventilated discs on all four wheels.

The chassis is a rigid floorpan monocoque, making it extremely stiff.

The body design is a 2-door, 2+2 coupé, made from hot-dip galvanised sheet steel, with optional front and rear spoilers.

Dimensions	
Length	4291mm
Width	1652mm (Sport Equipment) 1775mm (Turbo-Look / Supersport Equipment)
Height	1320mm
Wheelbase	2272mm
Track variation caused by various wheel widths	
6in front wheels	1372mm
7in front wheels	1398mm
6in rear wheels	1354mm
7in rear wheels	1380mm
8in rear wheels	1405mm
9in rear wheels	1492mm
Ground clearance	120mm
Overhang angle	Front 15.5° Rear 17°
Weights (Sport equipped cars)	
Front curb weight	490kg
Rear curb weight	720kg
Total curb weight	1210kg

Capacities	
Engine oil	13 litres
Fuel	85 litres
Brake fluid	0.2 litres
Screen fluid	8 litres

Carrera Colour Codes : (Official factory codes)	
1984	908, 027,700, 32Z, 182, 956, 655, 20C, 661, 662, 811, 810 and 966
1985/86	908, 027, 700, 673, 536, 347, 492, 822, 33P, 33X, 33N, 539, 936, 20C and 961
1987/88	908, 700, 347, 80F, 10W, 499, 21M, 80K, 980, 35Y, 699, 40B, 697, 40D, 35V, 35U and 80D
1989	908, 700, 347, 80K, 60M, 548, 22C, 980, 697, 37B, 693, 22D, 81L, 550, 22E, 40L, 81K, 37B and 22E

Despite many owners believing that they have a Guards Red car, the 3.2 Carrera was never painted in Guards Red. The colour name is actually India Red (Code 027) later changed to Indian Red (Code 80K).

The wheels came in two designs. The aluminium alloy forged Fuchs wheels in 15 and 16 inch diameter and the light alloy pressure cast Teledial wheels in 15 inch diameter.

Body Type	Year	Chassis Number (all start WPO...)	Engine Type	Gearbox Type
Coupé EUR	1984 1985 1986 1987 1988 1989	ZZZ 91 ES10 0001 – 5000 ZZZ 91 FS10 0001 – 5000 ZZZ 91 GS10 0001 – 5000 ZZZ 91 HS10 0001 – 5000 ZZZ 91 JS10 0001 – 5000 ZZZ 91 KS10 0001 – 5000	930.20 930.20/26 930.20/26 930.20/26 930.20/26 930.20/26	915.67 915.72 915.72 G50 G50 G50
Club Sport EUR	1987 1988 1989	ZZZ 91 HS10 5000 – 6000 ZZZ 91 JS10 5000 – 6000 ZZZ 91 KS10 0001 – 5000	930.20/26 930.20/26 930.20/26	G50 G50 G50
Club Sport USA	1987 1988 1989	ABO 91 HS12 5000 – 6000 ABO 91 JS12 5000 – 6000 ABO 91 KS12 0001 – 5000	930.25 930.25 930.25	G50.01 G50.01 G50.01
Coupé JAP	1984 1985 1986 1987 1988 1989	ZZZ 91 ES10 9500 - 10000 ZZZ 91 FS10 9500 - 10000 ZZZ 91 GS10 9500 - 10000 ZZZ 91 HS10 9500 - 10000 ZZZ 91 JS10 9500 - 10000 ZZZ 91 KS10 9500 - 10000	930.21 930.21 930.21 930.25 930.25 930.25	915.67 915.67 915.67 G50.01 G50.01 G50.01
Coupé USA	1984 1985 1986 1987 1988 1989	ABO 91 ES12 0001 – 5000 ABO 91 FS12 0001 – 5000 ABO 91 GS12 0001 – 5000 ABO 91 HS12 0001 – 5000 ABO 91 JS12 0001 – 5000 ABO 91 KS12 0001 – 5000	930.21 930.21 930.21 930.25 930.25 930.25	915.67 915.67 915.67 G50.01 G50.01 G50.01
Targa EUR	1984 1985 1986	ZZZ 91 ES14 0001 – 5000 ZZZ 91 FS14 0001 – 5000 ZZZ 91 GS14 0001 – 5000	930.20 930.20/26 930.20/26	915.67 915.72 915.72

Body Type	Year	Chassis Number (all start WPO...)	Engine Type	Gearbox Type
Targa EUR	1987 1988 1989	ZZZ 91 HS14 0001 – 5000 ZZ 91 JS14 0001 – 5000 ZZZ 91 KS14 0001 – 5000	930.20/26 930.20/26 930.20/26	G50 G50 G50
Targa JAP	1984 1985 1986 1987 1988 1989	ZZZ 91 ES14 9500 - 10000 ZZZ 91 FS14 9500 - 10000 ZZZ 91 GS14 9500 - 10000 ZZZ 91 HS14 9500 - 10000 ZZZ 91 JS14 9500 - 10000 ZZZ 91 KS14 9500 - 10000	930.21 930.21 930.21 930.25 930.25 930.25	915.67 915.72 915.72 G50.01 G50.01 G50.01
Targa USA	1984 1985 1986 1987 1988 1989	EBO 91 ES16 0001 – 5000 EBO 91 FS16 0001 – 5000 EBO 91 GS16 0001 – 5000 EBO 91 HS16 0001 – 5000 EBO 91 JS16 0001 – 5000 EBO 91 KS16 0001 – 5000	930.21 930.21 930.21 930.25 930.25 930.25	915.67 915.72 915.72 G50.01 G50.01 G50.01
Cabriolet EUR	1984 1985 1986 1987 1988 1989	ZZZ 91 ES15 0001 – 5000 ZZZ 91 FS15 0001 – 5000 ZZZ 91 GS15 0001 – 5000 ZZZ 91 HS15 0001 – 5000 ZZZ 91 JS15 0001 – 5000 ZZZ 91 KS15 0001 – 5000	930.20 930.20/26 930.20/26 930.20/26 930.20/26 930.20/26	915.67 915.72 915.72 G50.01 G50.01 G50.01
Cabriolet JAP	1984 1985 1986 1987 1988 1989	ZZZ 91 ES15 9500 - 10000 ZZZ 91 FS15 9500 - 10000 ZZZ 91 GS15 9500 - 10000 ZZZ 91 HS15 9500 - 10000 ZZZ 91 JS15 9500 - 10000 ZZZ 91 KS15 9500 - 10000	930.21 930.21 930.21 930.25 930.25 930.25	915.67 915.72 915.72 G50.01 G50.01 G50.01
Cabriolet USA	1984 1985 1986 1987 1988 1989	EBO 91 ES17 0001 – 5000 EBO 91 FS17 0001 – 5000 EBO 91 GS17 0001 – 5000 EBO 91 HS17 0001 – 5000 EBO 91 JS17 0001 – 5000 EBO 91 KS17 0001 – 5000	930.21 930.21 930.21 930.25 930.25 930.25	915.67 915.72 915.72 G50.01 G50.01 G50.01
Speedster EUR	1989	ZZZ 91 KS15 5000 – 6000	930.20/26	G50
Speedster USA	1989	EBO 91 KS17 5000 – 6000	930.25	G50.01

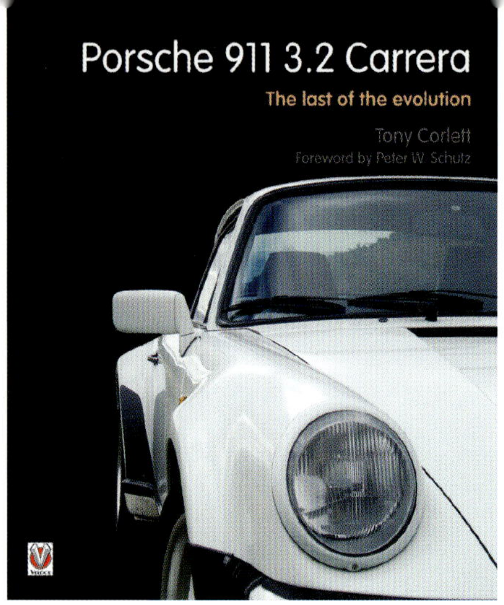

Chapter 32

Technical data

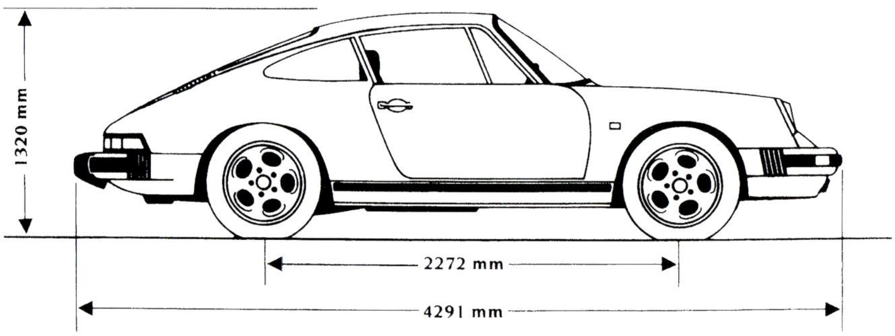

Engine				
Type	930/20 930/21 930/25 930/26	3164cc - 231 bhp - ROW 3164cc - 207 bhp – Catalyst - USA 3164cc - 217 bhp – Catalyst - USA 3164cc - 231 bhp - SW		1984 - 1989 1984 - 1986 1987 - 1989 1985 - 1989
Number of cylinders	6	Horizontally opposed (flat or Boxer)		
Bore	95mm	(3.74in)		
Stroke	74.4mm	(2.93in)		
Displacement	3164cc	(193.1 cu in)		
Compression ratio	10.3:1	9.5:1 (USA)		
Maximum power	231 bhp 207 bhp 217 bhp	170 kW 152 kW 160 kW	5900rpm 5900rpm 5900rpm	ROW USA USA
Maximum torque	210 ftlb 193 ftlb 195 ftlb	284 Nm 262 Nm 265 Nm	4800rpm 4800rpm 4800rpm	ROW USA USA
Maximum engine speed	6520 rpm			
Dry engine weight	219kg (483lbs)			
Crankcase	Two piece die-cast silicon aluminium alloy			
Crankshaft	Forged steel on 8 main bearings			
Connecting rods	Forged steel			
Pistons	Forged light alloy			

Cylinders	Light alloy Nicasil lined separate barrels			
Cylinder heads	Light alloy			
	Cross-flow hemispherical combustion chambers			
Camshaft	Cast steel			
	Single overhead per bank			
	Chain driven			
Valve arrangement	'V' pattern	1 intake	1 exhaust	
Valve guides	Brass	Press-fit		
Valve clearance	0.10mm	(intake and exhaust - cold)		
Cooling	Air-cooled			
Fan drive	Belt driven from crankshaft			
Crankshaft/fan ratio	1 to 1.67			
Air flow rate	1500 litres / second @ 6000rpm			
Lubrication	Dry sump lubrication with separate oil tank			
Oil cooling	Thermostatically controlled oil cooler on crankcase in fan stream plus front oil radiator under front right fender			1984 - 1989
	Above plus fan to front radiator			1987 - 1989
Oil filter	Full flow			
Oil pressure	3.5 bar minimum @ 5000rpm			
Oil temperature	90 °C (190 °F)			
Oil consumption	Up to 1.5 litres / 1000 kms			
Exhaust system	Single pipe system	Heat exchangers	Primary silencer muffler	Main silencer muffler
Catalytic converter	3-way catalyst in place of primary silencer/ muffler with oxygen sensor		USA	930/21 and 25
Fuel system type	Injection	Bosch L-Jetronic with Digital Motor Electronics DME		
Fuel delivery	1 electric roller cell pump			
Battery voltage	12V			
Battery capacity	66amp/h			
Alternator output	90amp / 1260W			
Ignition	Electronic (breakerless) digital transistorised			
Spark plugs	Bosch WR 4 DPO			
Firing order	1 - 6 - 2 - 4 - 3 - 5			
Suspension				
Front	Independent with wishbones and McPherson struts with torsion bars and anti-roll bars.			
Rear	Independent semi-trailing arms with torsion bars and anti-roll bar			
	Torsion bars Turbo-Look Turbo-Look	front/rear 18.8mm/24mm 18.8mm/25mm 18.8mm/26mm 18.8mm/27mm	 1984/1985 1986/1989 1984/1986 1987/1989	

	Anti-roll bars Turbo-Look	front/rear 20mm/18mm 22mm/21mm 22mm/20mm	 1984/1985 1986/1989 1984/1989	
Shock absorbers	Front and rear hydraulic double-acting gas pressure dampers			
Steering	Rack and pinion			
Transmission				
Type	915 G50	915-72 / 915-67 / 915-69 915-73 / 915-68 / 915-70 G50-00 / Europe and rest of world G50-01 / USA, Canada and Japan G50-02 / Switzerland		1984 - 1986 1984 - 1986 1987 - 1989 1987 - 1989 1987 - 1989
Housing	Die-cast aluminium			
Gears	5 forward + 1 reverse			
Clutch	Single dry plate	Cable-operation Hydraulic-operation	1984 - 1986 1987 - 1989	
Body				
Type	2 door 2 + 2 coupé All sheet steel Hot-dip galvanised Optional front and rear spoilers Optional wide-body		Sport Turbo-Look	1984 - 1989 1984 - 1989
Brakes				
Type	Hydraulic dual circuit – Servo-assisted			
Discs	Standard Turbo-Look	Ventilated discs all round Cross drilled discs		
Callipers	Standard Turbo-Look	Cast iron to front and rear Cast aluminium to front and rear		
Wheels				
Type	Forged Fuchs light alloy Cast Teledial light alloy			
Size	6J x 15 7J x 15 8J x 15 6J x 16 7J x 16 8J x 16 9J x 16	Fuchs and Teledial Fuchs and Teledial Fuchs only Fuchs only Fuchs only Fuchs only Fuchs only	Turbo-Look	1986/1989
Tyres	Size	195 / 65 VR 15 and 215 / 60 VR 15 205 / 55 VR 16 and 225 / 50 VR 16 205 / 55 VR 16 and 245 / 45 VR 16		Turbo-Look
Capacities				
Engine oil	13 litres			
Gearbox oil	3 litres			
Fuel tank	80 litres 85 litres	Including 8 reserve Including 8 reserve	1984 1985 - 1989	
Brake fluid	0.2 litres			

Screenwash	8 litres			
Intensive wash	0.6 litres			
Dimensions				
Wheelbase	2272mm	89.45in		
Track - front	1372mm 1398mm	54.02in 55.04in	6in wide rims 7in wide rims	
Track - rear	1380mm 1405mm 1492mm	54.29in 55.34in 58.70in	7in wide rims 8in wide rims 9in wide rims	
Length	4291mm	168.94in		
Width	1652mm 1775mm	65.04in 69.88in	Standard Turbo-Look	
Height (unladen)	1320mm	51.97in		
Ground clearance	120mm	4.72in		
Turning circle	10.95m	35.93ft		
Overhang angle	Front Rear	15.5 deg 17 deg		
Weights (Sport equipped cars)				
Front curb weight	490kg	1080lb		
Rear curb weight	720kg	1558lb		
Total curb weight	1210kg	2668lb		
Max permitted	1530kg	3374lb		
Max front axle load	680kg	1499lb		
Max Rear axle load	940kg	2073lb		
Max roof load	35kg	77lb		
Performance				
Maximum speed	152mph (245kmh) 152mph (245kmh) 146mph (235kmh) 149mph (240kmh) 149mph (240kmh)	930/20 930/20 930/21 930/25 930/25	ROW ROW USA USA USA	 Club Sport Club Sport
Acceleration				
0-62.5mph	6.1 seconds	930/20	ROW	
0-60mph	6.3 seconds 6.1 seconds 5.1 seconds 5.6 seconds	930/21 930/25 930/20 930/25	USA USA ROW USA	 Club Sport Club Sport
Standing kilometre	26.1 seconds	930/20	ROW	
Standing $^{1}/_{4}$ mile	14.7 seconds 14.4 seconds	930/21 930/25	USA USA	
Fuel consumption	41.4mpg 31.4mpg 20.8 mpg	@ constant 56mph @ constant 75mph Urban cycle		
All technical data as published by Porsche A.G.				

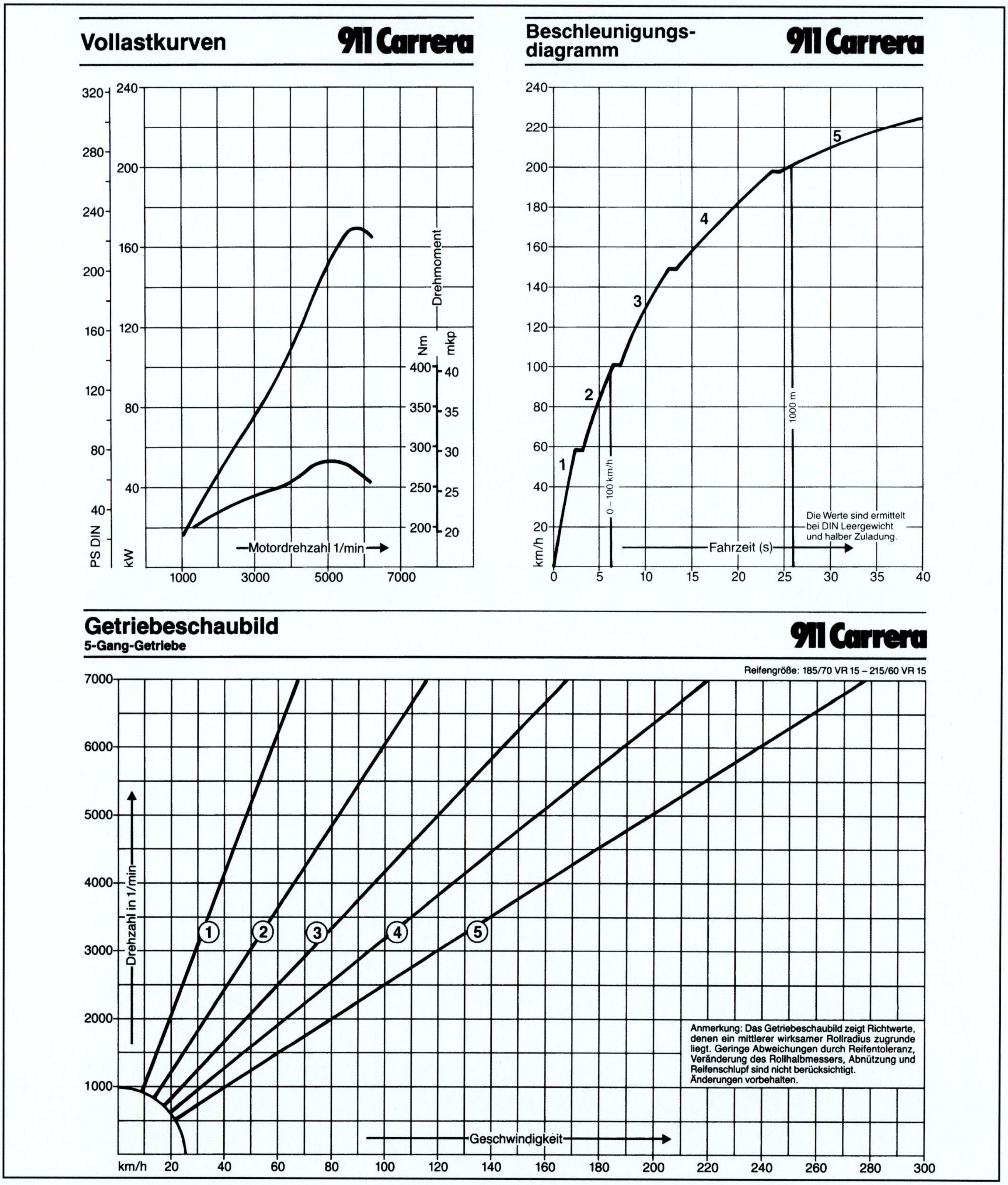

911 Carrera power charts.

Also from Veloce Publishing ...

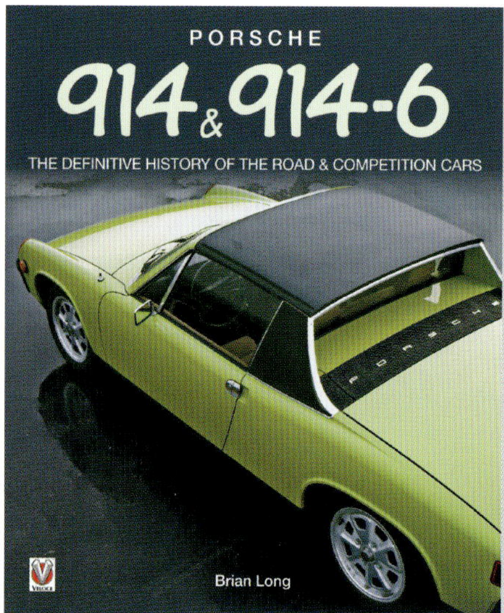

ISBN: 978-1-845840-14-3 £29.99

ISBN: 978-1-903706-02-2, £29.99

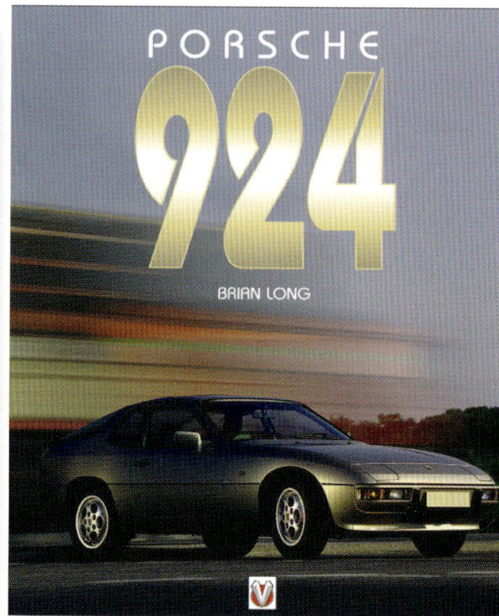

ISBN: 978-1-901295-85-6, £29.99

ISBN: 978-1-845844-03-5, £35

ISBN: 978-1-903706-34-3, £34.99

For full details visit us on the web at www.veloce.co.uk/www.velocebooks.com

Porsche 928

This book covers the full history of the Porsche 928, looking at the variants sold on the domestic, American, British, Australian and Japanese markets, from the time the car was launched in 1977 until the last one was built in 1995. In line with the policy established by the author in his other Porsche titles, contemporary material – supplied almost exclusively by the factory – has been used to illustrate the book for authenticity, and to help owners pinpoint what is and what is not correct for any specific year in any given country. Advertising and brochures are also reproduced, giving the reader a feel for the era and

ISBN: 978-1-903706-30-5, £34.99

Porsche 908 – The long distance runner

The most famous racing drivers drove it, and, for a long time, it was a guaranteed winner for Porsche: Now, finally, the first comprehensive work about the 908 has been published in the English language. The authors portray the fascinating history of the Porsche 908 racing car, and clearly explain its complex technology. Racing history is fully documented, and detailed statistics enable the reader to quickly look up all of the racing data. In addition, there are little-known anecdotes and contemporary reports from eye-witnesses and drivers. A wealth of contemporary, previously unreleased images evoke the fascinating atmosphere and excitement of the great seventies racing era.

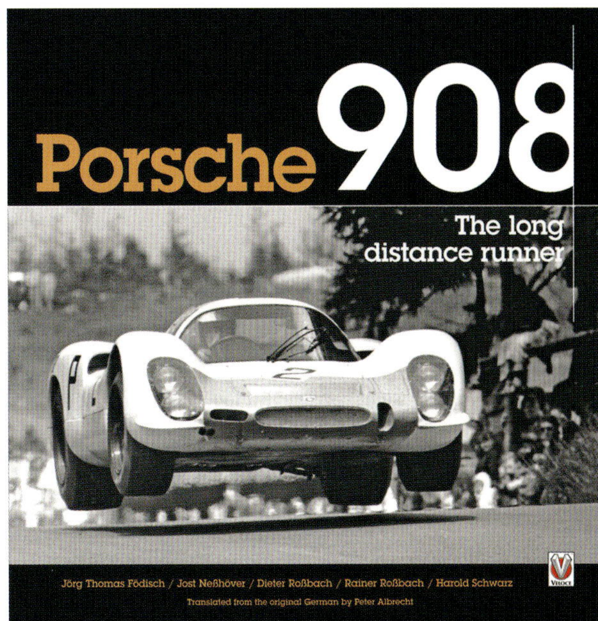

ISBN: 978-1-84584-201-7, £45.00

Porsche 911 3.2 Carrera
The last of the evolution
Tony Corlett
Foreword by Peter W. Schutz

INDEX

JOLLEN SEGELN

Inhalt

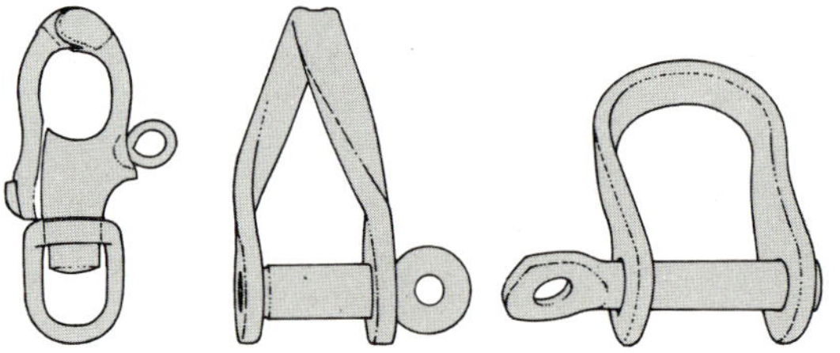

Titel der englischen Originalausgabe
Bond/Sleight DINGHY SAILING
First published in Great Britain 1983

Deutsche Bearbeitung: Ramon Gliewe

ISBN 3-7688-0418-6
Die Rechte für die deutsche Ausgabe liegen beim
Verlag Delius Klasing & Co, Bielefeld

Printed in Italy 1983
by A. Mondadori, Verona

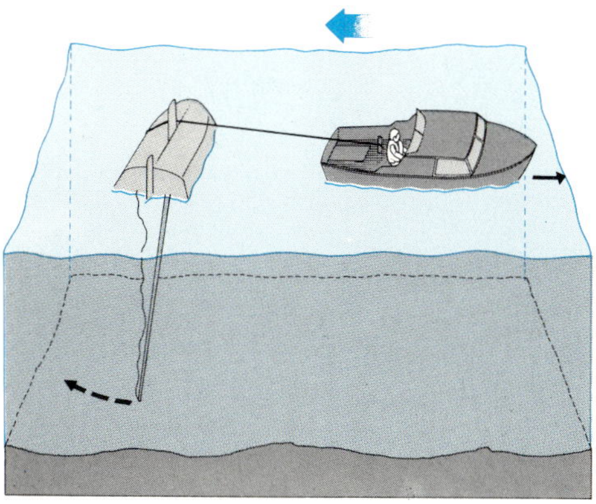

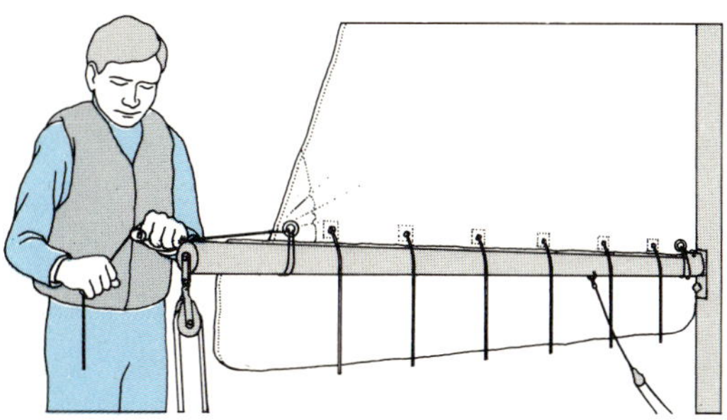

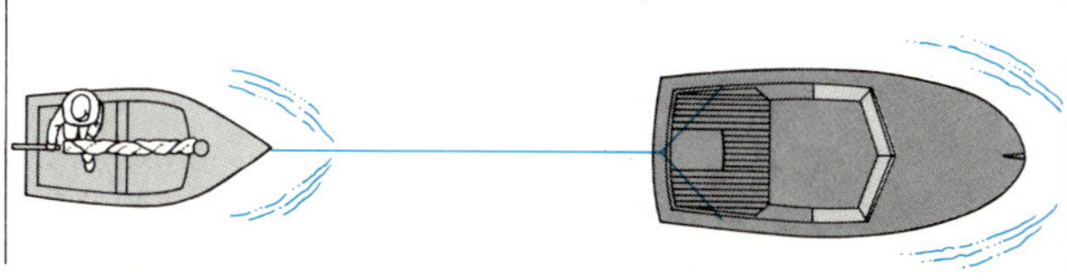

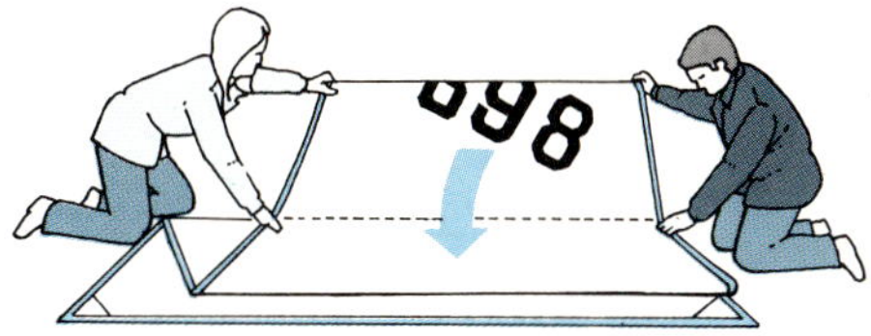

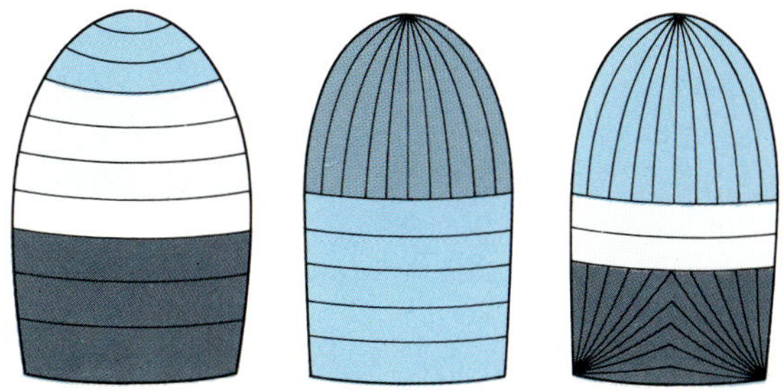

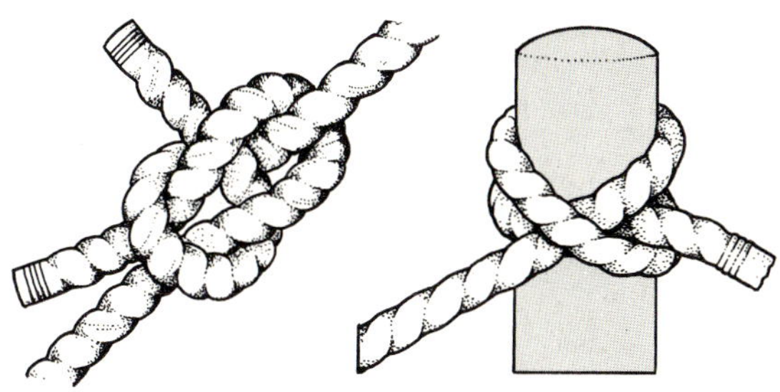

Ein Wort voraus

Nicht jeder, der mit dem Segeln beginnt, will auch gleich ein Weltmeister werden, aber der Wunsch der meisten ist es doch, ein Segler zu werden, der sein Boot in allen Lagen sicher beherrscht.

Bei der Planung dieses Buches konnten wir auf einen beträchtlichen Erfahrungsschatz zurückgreifen. Erfahrungen, die auf dem weiten Gebiet des Segelsports gesammelt wurden. Angefangen bei Segelkursen bis hin zur Ausrichtung von Regattaveranstaltungen. Wir hoffen nicht nur ein leicht verständliches Lehrbuch für Segelanfänger geschrieben zu haben, sondern auch ein praktisches Handbuch für den erfahrenen Segler, mit dem er seine Segeltechnik noch verbessern und sich vervollkommen kann.

Wir haben zahlreiche Illustrationen verwendet, um den Text so anschaulich wie möglich zu machen, und wir sind Schritt für Schritt vorgegangen, so daß ein Segelneuling ohne alle seglerische Vorkenntnisse dieses Buch verstehen und danach lernen kann. Es führt ihn bis ans Rennsegeln heran.

Seit frühen Jahren sind wir beide begeisterte Segler und wir hoffen, daß etwas von unserer großen Begeisterung für unseren Sport in diesem Buch seinen Niederschlag gefunden hat. Weiterhin hoffen wir aber auch, hierdurch eine neue Generation für das Jollensegeln zu motivieren und ihnen eine solide seemännische Grundlage für ihren Sport vermitteln zu können.

Mast- und Schotbruch!

Bob Bond
Steve Sleight

Die Entwicklung der Segelschiffahrt

Segeln hat sich zu einer Freizeitbeschäftigung entwickelt, die überall in der Welt ihre begeisterten Anhänger hat. Es ist eine verhältnismäßig junge Sportart. Begonnen hatte es im 18. und 19. Jahrhundert mehr als ein exklusiver Zeitvertreib der feinen Gesellschaft. Man ließ segeln. Seine Popularität erlangte der Segelsport so recht erst nach dem Zweiten Weltkrieg mit dem preiswerten Kunststoff-Serienbau von Booten.

Natürlich hat die See die Menschheit bereits seit Jahrtausenden fasziniert, und der erfinderische menschliche Geist fühlte sich durch sie herausgefordert. So kam er aufs Boot. Flüsse und Seen bildeten nicht nur eine reiche Nahrungsquelle für den frühen Menschen, sondern sie waren auch Verkehrswege, Verbindungen zwischen oft anders unzugänglichen Regionen. Ziemlich sicher ist, daß die ersten „Boote" nur für die Binnenfahrt gedacht waren und nicht für die offene See. Der Mensch besaß noch keine navigatorischen Kenntnisse, und die unbekannte Weite des Meeres erfüllte ihn mit Furcht.

Die frühesten „Boote" waren wohl sicher nichts weiter als simple Baumstämme, die von der Strömung mitgenommen wurden. Was lag dann näher, als mehrere zu einem Floß zusammenzulaschen, das mit Stakstangen dirigiert werden konnte. Wo es kein Holz gab, band man statt dessen Schilfbündel zusammen. Solche archaischen Schilfboote gibt es heute noch am Nil und auf dem Titicacasee in den Anden. Als man gelernt hatte, das Feuer zu beherrschen und scharfe steinerne Werkzeuge herzustellen, wurde der Baumstamm zum Einbaum ausgehöhlt und mit hölzernen Paddeln fortbewegt. Solche Einbäume findet man noch heute in Teilen Afrikas, Südamerikas und der Südsee.

Der Segel-Antrieb

In der Bronzezeit entstand das über ein Spantenskelett gebaute Plankenschiff, und man entdeckte den Wind als Antriebskraft. 1906 wurde in einem ägyptischen Grab das Modell eines Segelschiffes aus der Zeit um 2400 v. Chr. gefunden. Es trägt ein einfaches Rahsegel an einem kurzen mittschiffs stehenden Mast. Gesteuert wurde mit einem großen paddelförmigen Ruder, das am Heck befestigt war. Solche ursprünglich ägyptischen Rahsegel entdeckt man noch in malaiischen Gewässern. Auch das Lateinersegel gilt als eine ägyptische Erfindung. Es revolutionierte die Segelschiffahrt, ermöglichte es doch, weitaus höher am Wind zu segeln als mit einem Rahsegel. Auf Fischerbooten im Mittelmeer und arabischen Daus hat es bis heute überlebt. Eine stärker dem Rahsegel angeglichene Segelform, aber mit guten Am-Wind-Eigenschaften, entwickelten die Chinesen: das Dschunkenrigg. Es war den europäischen Takelagen der Entdeckerzeit eindeutig überlegen. Neuerdings sieht man es gelegentlich auch auf modernen Yachten.

Viele Prinzipien der alten Handelsschiffahrt finden sich auch im Konzept der modernen Sportsegelei wieder. Damals wie heute war es das Ziel, schnelle

Traditionelle Riggs von Arbeitsbooten aus aller Welt.

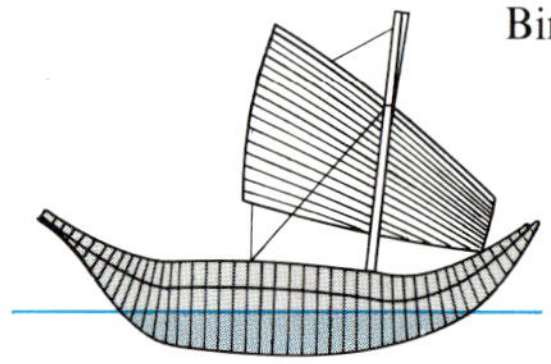
Binsenboot

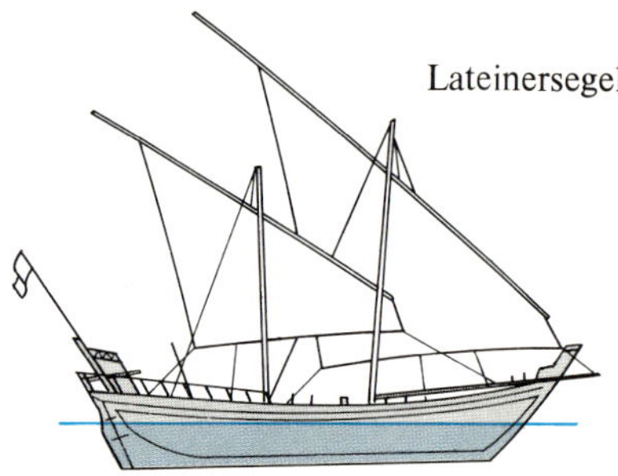
Lateinersegel

Chinesisches Dschunkenrigg

Schiffe zu bauen. Man wußte, daß der Wirkungsgrad der Segel im proportionalen Verhältnis zur Bootsgröße stand. Je größer die Segel, die ein Schiff tragen konnte, um so schneller war es. Der Größe eines Segels aber waren Grenzen gesetzt, dort, wo es nicht mehr zu bedienen war oder zu vieler Arbeitskräfte bedurfte, um es noch zu bedienen. Europäische Bootsbauer versuchten das Problem zu lösen, indem sie die Segelfläche in handigere Größen unterteilten und auf mehrere Masten verteilten. Die Schiffe der Entdeckungsreisenden, die neue Seewege und Kontinente erschlossen, waren nach diesem Prinzip getakelt. Aber auch die Schiffe, die später fast vier Jahrhunderte lang den Welthandel über die Ozeane abwickelten. Und die großen Schulschiffe, die uns Heutige als Windjammer begeistern, sind es noch immer.

In der Küstenfahrt dagegen, und besonders in der nordeuropäischen, entwickelten sich spezielle Riggs, die den örtlichen Gegebenheiten angepaßt waren. Während die Rahsegler hervorragend geeignet waren, die beständig wehenden Winde auf ihren Ozeanrouten voll zu nutzen, brauchten die Küstensegler Riggs für häufig wechselnde Windverhältnisse. Man kombinierte auf die verschiedensten Weisen Rah- mit Schratsegeln, die besser für vorliche Winde und Kreuzkurse geeignet waren. So entstand eine Fülle charakteristischer Schiffstypen wie Barken, Barkentinen, Briggs, Brigantinen, Schoner und Ketschen.

Verschiedene Variationen des Gaffelriggs, der traditionellen Takelung der meisten west- und nordeuropäischen Arbeitsboote bis zum Beginn der Dampfschiffahrt.

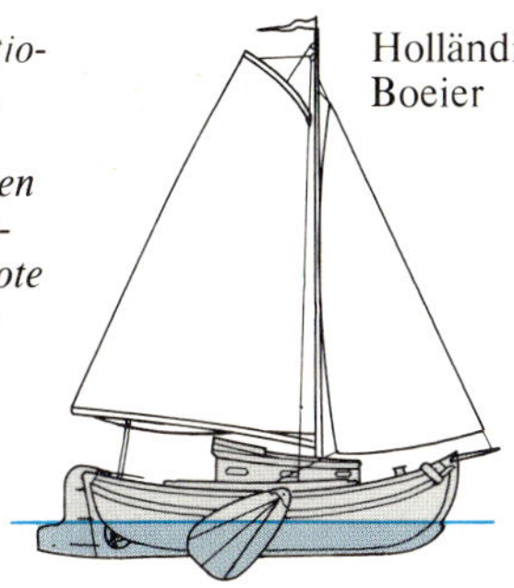

Holländischer Boeier

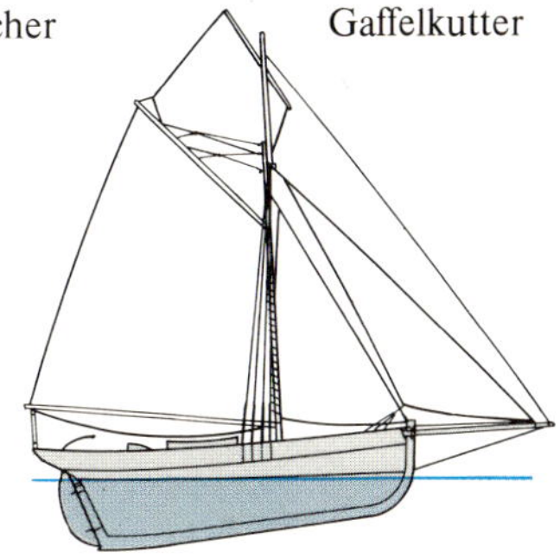

Gaffelkutter

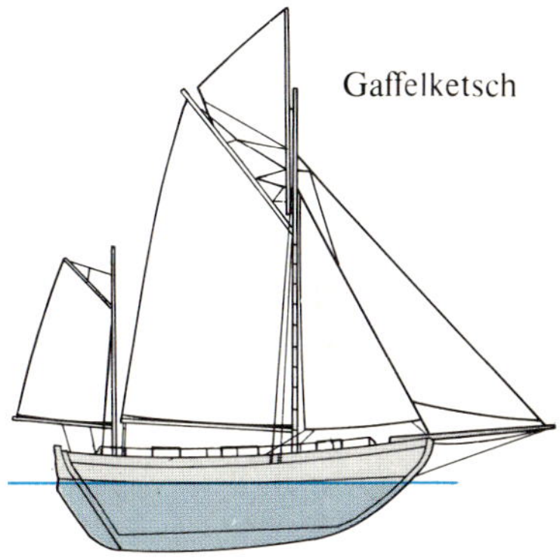

Gaffelketsch

Das Bermudarigg, uns als Hochsegel geläufiger, löste das Gaffelrigg ab und ist heute die übliche Yachttakelung.

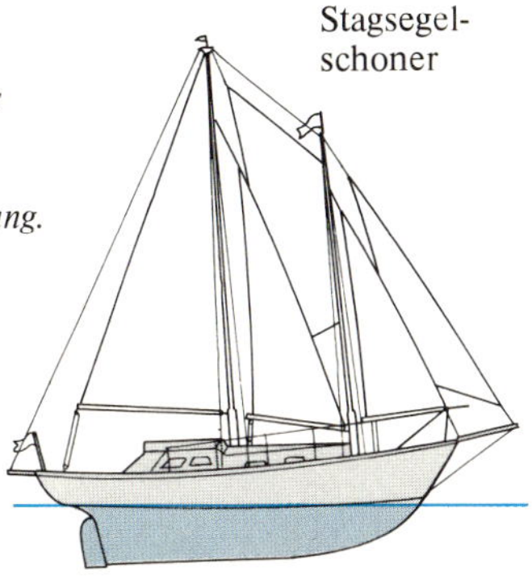

Stagsegelschoner

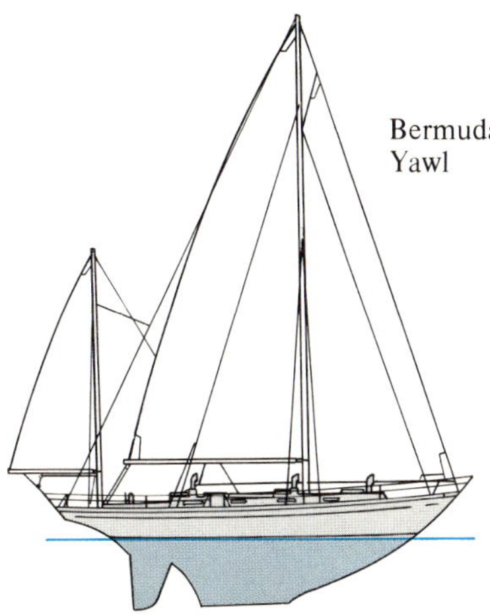

Bermuda-Yawl

Bermuda-Slup

Im 19. Jahrhundert erreichten die großen Handelssegler den höchsten Grad ihrer Vollendung. Regelrechte Rennen, die sich die Kapitäne auf den Routen in den Fernen Osten und nach Australien untereinander lieferten, führten zu immer effektiveren Schiffen und Takelagen. Als geradezu sensationell galten die in den USA entwickelten Klipper. Ein klassisches Beispiel für diese schnellen Segler ist die 1845 gebaute *Rainbow*. Stolz erklärte der Kapitän: „Es wird kein Schiff geben, das sie je schlagen kann!" Fast ein halbes Jahrhundert lang sollte er recht behalten. Die Klipper verkürzten die bisherigen Segelzeiten fast um die Hälfte. Ihre Konstruktion basierte auf den Chesapeake-Frachtseglern. Sie hatten einen scharfen Bug, einen stromlinienförmigen Rumpf und eine Kombination von Rah- und Schratsegeln.

Mit Beginn der Industrialisierung tauchten erste Versuche auf, Schiffe mit einer Dampfmaschine anzutreiben. Doch diese ersten Dampfer waren gegenüber den schnellen Seglern überhaupt nicht konkurrenzfähig. Das änderte sich aber bald, und die Dampfschiffe dominierten nun in der Fracht- und Passagierschiffahrt. Segler wurden fast nur noch in der näheren Küstenfahrt beschäftigt.

Zu Anfang des 20. Jahrhunderts hatten die Dampfmaschinen die Segel überflüssig gemacht. Doch die Menschen hatten inzwischen begonnen, das Segeln als Freizeitvergnügen zu entdecken. Viele der in der Frachtschiffahrt arbeitslos gewordenen Küstensegler wurden zu Yachten umfunktioniert. Das Gros der frühen Yachten, gerade in Deutschland, aber auch in anderen europäischen Ländern, waren Frachtschiffe und Fischereifahrzeuge. Die Segelschiffahrt wurde zur Domäne von begeisterten Amateuren. Seitdem hat sich der Yachtbau zu einem wichtigen Zweig des Schiffbaus entwickelt, entstanden die verschiedensten Konstruktionen und Typen von Yachten. Die modernen Sportboote sind nicht nur sicherer und schneller geworden, sie sind auch weitaus leichter zu handhaben.

Eine Idee von Abenteuer und Freiheit ist es, was so viele Menschen am Yachtsport so ungeheuer fasziniert – wenn sie sich in kleinen Booten mit den Elementen und Kräften der Natur messen. Ganz besonders auch beim Jollensegeln.

In Handikap-(Yardstick-)Regatten können die verschiedensten Bootsklassen gegeneinander segeln. Hier im Bild ein Internationales Kanu, eine Hornet und ein Fireball an einer Wendemarke.

Links: Das englische Mirror Dinghy ist eine sehr erfolgreiche Jollenklasse mit starker Verbreitung (außer bei uns). Sie wird von Kindern gesegelt und ist auch bei Anfängern beliebt.

Der Cherub ist eine sogenannte Konstruktionsklasse, die dem Eigner freistellt, mit Rumpf und Rigg zu experimentieren. Die einzelnen Boote können dementsprechend erheblich voneinander abweichen (wird bei uns nicht gesegelt).

Das Jollensegeln

Das Angebot an Jollentypen und Jollenklassen ist selbst für Experten unüberschaubar geworden. In fast jedem Land gibt es eine Fülle von nationalen Klassen, die schon im Nachbarland kaum bekannt oder verbreitet sind.

Als echte Jollenvorläufer kann man die bereits um 1875 in den USA gebauten Scharpies bezeichnen. Offene, völlig flachbödige Arbeitsboote mit einem schmalen, sehr langen Mittelschwert, wie es erst für die modernen Gleitjollen wiederentdeckt wurde. 1887 entstand in Irland die erste speziell zum Freizeitsegeln konstruierte Einheitsklasse. Es war die Water Wag, 14 Fuß, 3 Inch (4,33 m) lang. Sie wurde eifrig auf der Bucht von Dublin gesegelt. Und es gibt diesen Bootstyp auch heute noch, fast 100 Jahre später.

Die erste Jolle, in der verhältnismäßig regelmäßig internationale Regatten ausgetragen wurden, war das englische 14-Fuß-Dinghy. Eine sogenannte Grenzmaßklasse, in der man konstruktiv experimentieren kann. Sie wurde in Großbritannien zwar erst 1923 zur nationalen Klasse erhoben – 1927 zur internationalen –, war aber schon vor dem Ersten Weltkrieg entstanden. Allerdings blieb sie im wesentlichen auf Großbritannien und die USA beschränkt. In Deutschland wurde sie überhaupt nicht gesegelt. Das berühmteste 14-Fuß-Dinghy war die von Uffa Fox konstruierte *Avenger*. In 57 Wettfahrten des Jahres 1928 belegte sie 52mal den 1. Platz. Die steigenden Kosten in dieser Klasse führten schon bald zu dem kleineren 12-Fuß-Dinghy, das es dreimal – 1920, 1924 und 1928 – zu olympischen Ehren brachte.

Die eigentliche Wiege des mitteleuropäischen Jollenbaus aber stand an der Spree. Dort entstanden zu Anfang dieses Jahrhunderts verschiedene Typen von Binnenjollen. Von dort führte der Weg zu den Wander- und H-Jollen und den Jollenkreuzern für Binnenfahrtensegler und zu den schnellen Rennjollen. Zu den 10- und 20-m^2-Rennjollen und den 22-m^2-Nationalen Jollen.

Es waren rassige schmale lange Renner, die noch heute als das Nonplusultra im Jollenbau gelten. Man fand sie vom Platten- bis zum Gardasee auf nahezu allen größeren Binnenrevieren. Die 20-m^2-Rennjolle beispielsweise war 7,70 m lang. Obwohl aus schwerem Vollholz gebaut, kamen diese Rennjollen unter günstigen Voraussetzungen bereits ins Gleiten. Ihre Geschwindigkeiten blieben unerreicht, bis Anfang der 50er Jahre die modernen Leichtbaujollen auftauchten.

Dagegen war die 1931 von William Crosby im Auftrag der amerikanischen Bootszeitschrift „Rudder" konstruierte 4,72 m lange Snipe ein ausgesprochen schwerfälliges und häßliches Boot. Dennoch brachte sie es durch starken Rückhalt im amerikanischen Mutterland bis zum Anfang der 50er Jahre auf die

Cadet-Jollen im Rennen, ein internationales Zweimann-Jugendboot, das bei uns jedoch nicht gesegelt wird.

Rechts: Eine traditionelle britische Binnenjolle, karweel aus Holz gebaut und mit Gaffelsegel, ein typisches Familien- oder Wanderboot.

größte Jollenklassen-Flotte der Welt. Nur in Deutschland beziehungsweise der Bundesrepublik und einigen anderen europäischen Ländern konnte sie nie Fuß fassen.
1938 entstand in dem berühmten amerikanischen Konstruktionsbüro Sparkman & Stephens die 5,80 m lange Knickspantjolle Lightning. Auch sie fand starke Verbreitung, wird aber bei uns auch nicht gesegelt. In Deutschland war von Carl Martens die 5,00 m lange Piratenjolle konstruiert worden, als preiswert herzustellendes Jugendboot, das sich schnell in Österreich und der Schweiz, in Ungarn, Dänemark und Schweden durchsetzte.
Die große Revolution im Jollenbau wurde Anfang der 50er Jahre durch die aus Sperrholz und später Kunststoff gebauten Gleitjollen eingeleitet. Am Anfang steht die von dem Engländer John Westell 1953 gezeichnete 5,05 m lange 505er-Jolle. Sie stand zusammen mit dem holländischen Flying Dutchman zur Diskussion als Olympiaklasse, verlor dann aber gegen die holländische Jollenkonstruktion. In einem kompetenten Urteil hieß es seinerzeit über den 505er: „Man kann diesen geradezu revolutionären Entwurf nur uneingeschränkt bewundern." Alle seitdem entstandenen Gleitjollen-Konstruktionen sind mehr oder minder stark vom 505er beeinflußt worden, weit stärker als vom Flying Dutchman.
In den 60er Jahren stammte fast die Hälfte aller neuen Jollen-Konstruktionen aus Frankreich. Manche von ihnen errangen den internationalen Status. So der 470er, der olympische Klasse wurde.
Um 1960 tauchten auch die ersten Katamarane – Doppelrumpfboote – auf den Jollenrevieren auf und mischten kräftig mit. Erste Einheitsklasse wurde der von den englischen Brüdern Prout konstruierte Shearwater, ein 5,03 m langer Rennkatamaran. Mit dem Tornado kam ein Katamaran zu olympischen Ehren. Obwohl einige Jollensegler anderer Auffassung sind, zählen auch die Rennkatamarane zu den Jollen. Durch sie wurde die Jollenszene erheblich bereichert.

Links: Die Ex-Weltmeister im 505er, Peter White und John Davis, demonstrieren ihr Können auf dieser anspruchsvollen Hochleistungsjolle.

Die ungewöhnlich große Segelfläche der Bermuda-Einheitsjolle verlangt eine sehr erfahrene Crew.

Bootsbau

Jahrhundertelang war das einzige Bootsbaumaterial Holz. Heute hingegen kann auf verschiedene Materialien zurückgegriffen werden. Die meisten Serienboote werden aus glasfaserverstärktem Kunststoff (GFK) gebaut, einem recht neuen Bootsbaumaterial. Erste Versuche damit wurden Anfang der 40er Jahre in den USA gemacht. Im Yachtbau fand der Kunststoff erst Ende der 50er Jahre Eingang, in Deutschland sogar noch später. Er ermöglichte den modernen relativ preiswerten Serienbau und trug wesentlich zu der lawinenartigen Ausbreitung des Segelsports bei. Das traditionelle Vollholz wird nur noch in Liebhaberbauten (zu Liebhaberpreisen) verarbeitet. Zweifellos hat es seine Vorzüge. Sorgfältig gebaute Vollholzschiffe haben eine sehr hohe Lebenserwartung.

Klinker und Karweel

Es gibt zwei Arten der Beplankung von Vollholzschiffen: die Klinker- und die Karweelbauweise. Die Klinkerbauweise ist die ältere. Sie geht auf die Wikingerschiffe zurück, wenn nicht gar auf noch frühere Zeiten. Die Planken überlappen dachziegelartig. Früher wurden sie mit den Spanten durch Holzdübel verbunden, später mit Kupfernieten. Da es an der Überlappung der Planken Dopplungen gibt, sind klinkergebaute Schiffe relativ schwer, auch wenn sie mit weniger Spanten auskommen als karweelgebaute. Für schnelle Hochleistungsyachten war diese Bauweise deshalb nicht geeignet. Allerdings ergibt sie äußerst robuste Rümpfe von hoher Lebensdauer.

Die traditionelle Klinkerbauweise sieht man heute nur noch bei schweren Arbeitsbooten. Rechts eine Spantsektion mit den überlappenden Plankengängen.

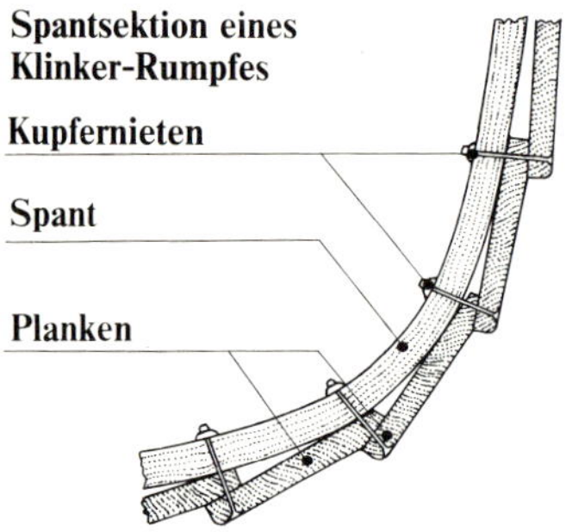

Bei der Karweelbauweise stoßen die Planken plan aneinander. Sie ergibt ebenfalls starke, aber etwas leichtere Rümpfe und eine glatte strömungsgünstigere Außenhaut. Zwischen die Stoßkanten kommt ein flexibles Füllmaterial, früher aus geteerter Baumwolle, heute aus Synthetik. Innen werden die Stoßnähte manchmal durch sogenannte Nahtspanten abgedeckt. Beide Bauweisen haben den Nachteil, daß die Rümpfe undicht werden, wenn sie stärker austrocknen.

Bootsbausperrholz

Die Entwicklung des Bootsbausperrholzes revolutionierte den Holzbootsbau. Es besteht aus wasser- und kochfest verleimten Holzfurnieren und kann kaum schrumpfen, schwellen oder sich verziehen. Eine sorgfältig gebaute Sperrholzbootshaut bleibt immer dicht. Aus Sperrholz kann man ebenso steife und solide Rümpfe wie aus Vollholz bauen, aber sie sind wesentlich leichter. Erst der Sperrholzbau ermöglichte die Konstruktion leichter moderner Gleitjollen.

Die ersten Sperrholzboote wurden noch recht konventionell gebaut. Im Grunde war es eine Karweelbeplankung, nur daß die Außenhaut aus größeren Platten bestand, die zusätzlich durch Preßdruck mit den Spanten verleimt wurden. Ein Problem gab es allerdings dabei: die Sperrholzplatten ließen sich nur in einer Richtung krümmen. Wurden sie also in ihrer Länge gekrümmt, um die Kurven des Vor-und Hinterschiffs zu erhalten, konnten sie nicht mehr in der Breite verformt werden, um dem Boot die erwünschte runde Rumpfform geben zu können. So entstand eine neue Konstruktion: die Knickspantbauweise. Der Rumpf – Seitenteile und Boden – bestand aus mehreren Platten, die in verschiedenen Winkeln (Knicken) gegeneinanderstießen. So erhielt er eine, je nach Bootstyp, mehr oder minder,

Obwohl neuer, hat auch die Karweelbauweise für den Yachtbau fast nur noch historischen Wert. Rechts im Bild ein kleiner sogenannter Doppelender, unten ein alter Yachtrumpf, karweel geplankt, und eine alte Wanderjolle (ganz rechts).

Spantsektion eines karweelgebauten Rumpfes

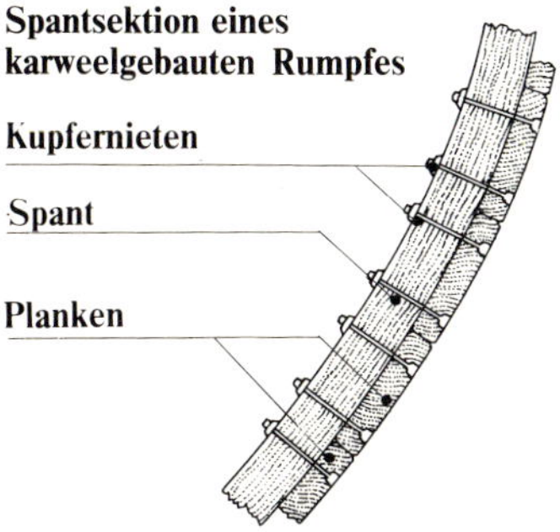

einmal oder mehrfach geknickte Querschnittsform. Da Knickspanter eine größere Formstabilität haben als vergleichbare Rundspanter, war diese Bauweise besonders bei Familien-Jollen beliebt. Man behielt diese Spantform vereinzelt auch später im Kunststoff-Bootsbau bei.

Auch die Klinkerbauweise wurde gelegentlich mit Sperrholz praktiziert, indem die Platten in schmalere Bänder geschnitten wurden, die wiederum ermöglichten, dem Rumpf eine Rundspantform zu geben.

Ein weiterer Schritt in der Entwicklung des modernen Bootsbaus waren die formverleimten Sperrholzrümpfe. Die Außenhaut besteht aus diagonal gegeneinander versetzten Schichten dünner geschälter oder gemesserter Furniere, die miteinander verleimt werden. Je dünner die Furniere sind, um so mehr Schichten und Leimfugen sind notwendig, und um so fester und steifer wird die Bootsform. Spanten sind kaum noch erforderlich, um genügend Querfestigkeit zu erreichen. Die Furniere wiederum eignen sich nur für rundspantige Rumpfformen. Um ihnen die gewünschte Form geben zu können, ist ein festes Blockmodell, auch Baukern genannt, notwendig. Um den hohen Anpreß- und Leimdruck zu erzeugen, gibt es verschiedene Verfahren: vom Nageln bis zu Druckkammern aus Stahlblech.

Baukästen

Da Sperrholz auch von Bootsbau-Amateuren verhältnismäßig leicht zu verarbeiten ist, wurden denn auch bald Jollenbaukästen für Selbstbauer angeboten. Besonders in England wurden sie ein großer Erfolg. In Deutschland hingegen haben sie nie eine Rolle gespielt. Eine der größten englischen Jollenklassen, die Mirror, verdankt ihre enorme Verbreitung überwiegend den Hobby-Bootsbauern.

Knickspant-Sperrholz-Bauweise, sie ermöglichte erst die Konstruktion leichter Gleitjollen wie den Fireball (rechts unten). Eine verhältnismäßig preiswerte und auch von Amateuren leicht zu bewerkstelligende Bauart.

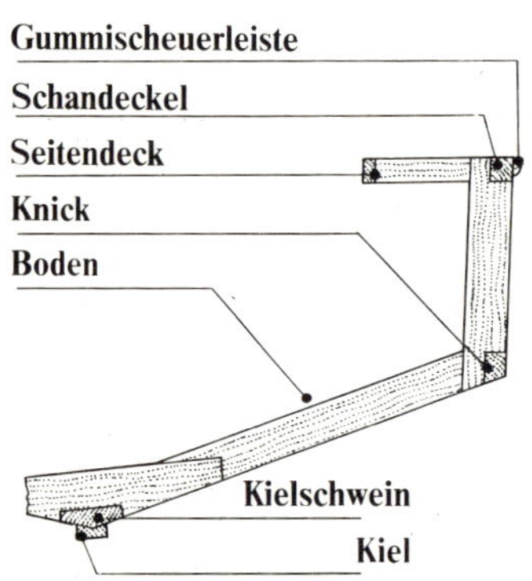

Die Rümpfe wurden oder werden zum Teil „genäht". Die zusammenstoßenden Bauteile – Boden, Seitenteile, Deck, Schwertkasten – sind an ihren Kanten, auf Paß, mit Löchern versehen. Durch Kupferdraht werden sie miteinander verbunden. So erhält der Rumpf seine Form und Steifigkeit. Anschließend werden die Nähte mit synthetischer Dichtungsmasse wasserdicht versiegelt.

Der Kunststoff-Bootsbau

Heute werden Jollen fast nur noch, und auch der größte Teil der Yachten, aus Kunststoff gebaut. Ein Material, das fast beliebig verformbar ist, so daß sich jedes Bauteil daraus herstellen läßt. Die Boote werden überwiegend in einer Hohlform oder Matritze und nur selten über einen Kern, die Patritze, gebaut. Für die Herstellung dieser Arbeitsform ist zunächst ein Modell erforderlich, meistens aus Holz. Die Kunststoffrümpfe, man spricht von Schalen, werden entweder im Handauflegeverfahren oder im Spritzverfahren hergestellt. Beide Verfahren eignen sich für jede Formgröße. Zunächst wird die Hohlform mit einem Trennmittel präpariert, um später das Entformen der Schale zu ermöglichen. Dann trägt man mit Pinsel, Lammfellwalze oder Spritzpistole die äußere Deckschicht aus Harz auf, das sogenannte Gelcoat. Ist es ausgehärtet, kommt darauf eine Harzschicht, in die die erste Glasfasereinlage eingebettet wird. Darüber kommt wieder eine Harzschicht. So wird eine Lage nach der anderen eingebracht und mit Harz durchtränkt, bis die vorgesehene Wandstärke erreicht ist.

Beim Spritzverfahren hat man eine Harzspritzanlage, die mit einem Schneidwerk kombiniert ist, das die von Spulen zugeführten Glasfaserstränge zu Glasseidenstapeln verschiedener Länge schneidet. Sie werden dann gleichzeitig mit dem Harz unter hohem Druck in die Form gespritzt.

Bei kleineren Booten arbeitet man mit einer einteiligen Rumpfform (Schale), bei größeren Yachten oft mit zweiteiligen. In jeder Form entsteht eine Bootshälfte, die später in der Mitschiffsebene zur kompletten Schale verbunden werden. Deck und Aufbauten bilden fast immer eine gesonderte Form. Wie beim formverleimten Sperrholzbau kommt man auch beim Kunststoffbau mit wenigen Versteifungen des Bootskörpers aus, die nachträglich hineingeklebt – einlaminiert – werden.

Kunststoff (GFK) ist heute das hauptsächliche Baumaterial für Jollen, wie auch für diese 505er. Es ermöglicht, Boote leicht, aber von gleicher Festigkeit wie Holzboote herzustellen und erlaubt einen rationellen Serienbau.

Bootstypen

Das Angebot, gerade an Jollen, ist so riesig und unübersichtlich, daß es einen künftigen Bootskäufer vollständig verwirren muß. Man müßte schon ziemlich genau wissen, für welchen Zweck man sein Boot einsetzen will: zum Fahrtensegeln, allein oder mit Familienangehörigen, oder zum sportlichen Segeln. Wer diesbezügliche Ambitionen hat, muß wiederum nach einer Regattaklasse Ausschau halten, die auf seinem Revier – oder von seinem Club – gesegelt wird. Überhaupt spielt auch das künftige Revier bei der Kaufentscheidung eine Rolle. Ist es ein sehr flaches oder tiefes Gewässer? Ein windarmes oder ein windreiches Revier?
Wer ein Gebrauchtboot kaufen möchte, muß sehr genau auf den Umfang der zusätzlichen Ausrüstung achten. Sie kann sich gewaltig im Preis niederschlagen. Wer sein erstes Boot kauft, sollte sich unbedingt von einem erfahrenen Segler beraten lassen oder sogar einen Sachverständigen hinzuziehen.

Ein Mirror Dinghy – der Briten liebstes Kinderboot.

Familien-Jollen

Es gibt ausgesprochen stabile Jollen, die vornehmlich als Wander- oder Fahrtenboote gedacht sind und denen es nicht viel ausmacht, wenn man ihnen einige Kilo Gepäck einlädt. Die 5 m lange Conger-Jolle ist beispielsweise so ein Boot, für zwei Erwachsene und ein Kind. Sie hat eine kleine Schlupfkajüte, in der man auch mal übernachten kann. Sportlich ambitionierte Familien können im Conger auch Regatten bestreiten. Als reines Familien- und Wanderboot war ursprünglich auch der 5,80 m lange Zugvogel konzipiert. Im Laufe der Jahre mauserte er sich jedoch immer mehr zu einem Regattaboot. Die ursprünglichen Vorzüge, geräumiges Cockpit für bis zu vier Personen, und hohe Stabilität aber sind erhalten geblieben. Da die Bauvorschriften die Cockpiteinrichtung freistellen, gibt es Konstruktionen, die mehr in die eine oder andere Richtung ausgelegt sind. Noch größere Sicherheit für das Familiensegeln bietet die Kielversion des Zugvogel, gedacht auch für Wanderfahrten auf Küstengewässern. Sie ist kentersicher und ebenfalls Regattaklasse. Größere Verbreitung als Familien-Wanderboot hat die 4,80 m lange holländische VB-Jolle gefunden, ein relativ steifes Boot. Zwei Schläfer haben unter der Zeltkajüte bequem Platz.

Zugvogel

Rennjollen

Die meisten Jollen fallen unter diese Kategorie. Aber da gibt es viele Spielarten. Sie stellen recht unterschiedliche Anforderungen an das seglerische Können und die körperlichen Kräfte des einzelnen. Jüngere und leichtgewichtigere Segler sind mit dem 420er sicher gut beraten. Diese internationale Jollenklasse ist weit verbreitet und wird mit Trapez – zum Ausreiten des Bootes – und Spinnaker gesegelt.

Der 420er ist ein interessantes und noch relativ leichtes Boot, das regatta-ambitionierten Jungseglern und -seglerinnen viele Möglichkeiten bietet, in Meisterschaften ihr Können unter Beweis zu stellen. Der 470er ist gewissermaßen der größere Bruder des 420er. Er ist olympische Klasse und dementsprechend noch stärker international verbreitet, stellt aber auch höhere seglerische Ansprüche. Eine geradezu explosionsartige Verbreitung fand der Laser, eine Einmann-Jolle. Innerhalb von elf Jahren wurden über 100 000 Boote gebaut. Er erfreut sich, besonders unter jugendlichen Seglern großer Beliebtheit. Obwohl simpel zu bedienen - es gibt kein Vorsegel und keine komplizierten Beschläge -, verlangt er große körperliche Gewandtheit und ausgefuchste Segeltechnik. Der Laser II ist die größere Zweimann-Version für leichtgewichtige Segler und ein guter Einstieg in die Regattaszene. Für Fortgeschrittene bietet sich der Flying Dutchman an, seit 1960 olympische Klasse. Noch anspruchsvoller und schwieriger zu segeln ist der 505er, gewissermaßen das Nonplusultra einer Rennjolle.

Laser

505er

Kinderjollen

Wer für seinen jüngsten Seglernachwuchs eine Jolle sucht, ist sicher mit der amerikanischen Kinderjolle Optimist gut beraten. Das nur 2,30 m lange kastenförmige Boot hat eine unwahrscheinlich schnelle Verbreitung in aller Welt gefunden. Wer damit richtig umzugehen gelernt hat, der kann segeln – so sagt man. Bereits 6jährige tummeln sich im Opti, denn die nur 3,50 m^2 große Segelfläche können sie schon gut beherrschen. Fortgeschrittenen bieten sich im Opti viele Möglichkeiten, Regatten zu segeln. Sogar internationale Meisterschaften gibt es. Der Enthusiasmus und das seglerische Geschick, das die kleinen Regattahasen dabei entwickeln, zwingt den Großen oft genug alle Achtung ab. Es gibt auch noch andere Kinderjollen wie etwa das in England sehr verbreitete Mirror Dinghy, aber keine kann es an Popularität mit dem Opti aufnehmen.

Ein Aufsteigerboot für Optisegler ist die 3,66 m lange Jugendjolle Filius, mit 8 m^2 Segelfläche und zu zweit zu segeln.

Optimist

Was man vorher wissen muß

Weshalb so viele Menschen segeln und dem Segelsport über Jahre, meist ein ganzes Leben lang treu bleiben, dafür gibt es verschiedene Erklärungen: Freizeitspaß, körperliche Fitneß, ein Hauch von Freiheit und Abenteuer oder auch sportlicher Ehrgeiz. Segeln ist eine Freizeitbeschäftigung für jeden, ob noch voller jugendlichen Tatendrangs oder schon reifer an Jahren, und auch für fast jeden Geldbeutel. Man muß nur für seine Zwecke und sein seglerisches Können das geeignete Boot herausfinden.

Grundsätzlich ist zwischen zwei Konstruktionsprinzipien zu unterscheiden: den offenen Jollen – sie sind das Thema dieses Buches – und den größeren eingedeckten Kajütbooten. Es ist sicher richtig, auf einer Jolle segeln zu lernen. Man bekommt da viel schneller das richtige Gefühl für das Verhalten eines Bootes, weil eine Jolle viel unmittelbarer reagiert als ein schwerfälliges Kajütboot. So unterrichten denn auch die meisten Segelschulen auf Jollen. Niemand sollte sich einfach in ein Boot setzen, um irgendwie loszusegeln. Ohne gründliche praktische Ausbildung geht es nicht. Dazu sind die Gewässer viel zu befahren, gibt es zu viele genau zu beachtende Verkehrsvorschriften. Man würde nur sich und andere in Gefahr bringen. Am besten, man besucht eine Segelschule. Das Studium dieses Buches ist eine hervorragende Vorbereitung auf solch einen praktischen Segelkursus. Ich habe versucht, die Segeltechnik durch Illustrationen so klar und allgemeinverständlich wie möglich darzustellen. Wenn man alles genau befolgt, kann man daraus eine Menge lernen – oder erkennen, was man falsch gemacht hat. Vermitteln möchte ich hier vor allem die Grundkenntnisse des Jollensegelns, aber auch einiges für Fortgeschrittene, wie das Spinnaker- und Trapezsegeln.

Um praktische Segelerfahrungen zu sammeln, ist es nicht notwendig, selbst ein Boot zu besitzen. Im Gegenteil, es ist sogar sinnvoller und besser, zunächst als Vorschoter mit einem erfahrenen Steuermann zu segeln. Erst wenn man sich absolut sicher und allen Situationen gewachsen fühlt, sollte man an den Kauf eines eigenen Bootes denken. Denn Segeln zählt zu jenen Beschäftigungen, in denen die Erfahrungen erst allmählich aus der eigenen Praxis erwachsen und man vielleicht am meisten aus seinen anfänglichen Fehlern lernt.

Segeln ist einfach eine Sache, die viel Spaß macht. Es bedarf dazu keiner außerordentlichen körperlichen Kräfte, nur einer gesunden Konstitution und eines aufgeweckten Geistes. Man lernt dabei, ein gesundes Selbstvertrauen zu entwickeln, seine angeborene Intelligenz zu gebrauchen und wird für die Elemente Wind und Wasser sensibilisiert. Viele werden bald herausfinden – so wie auch ich seinerzeit –, daß Segeln zu einem großartigen Lebensinhalt werden kann.

Ein Mirror Dinghy unter Spinnaker und eine Lark-Jolle.

Einmann-Jollen vom Typ Topper während einer Clubregatta.

6729
21657
8015
9359

Bekleidung und Sicherheitsausrüstung

Die Bekleidung hängt vom Boot ab, das man segelt, vom Wetter und der Gegend, in der man segelt. Da die Temperatur auf dem Wasser stets niedriger ist als an Land, muß die Bekleidung warmhalten und außerdem soll sie wasserdicht sein. Jollensegler, die fast ständig Spritzwasser ausgesetzt sind, tragen meistens einen wasserdichten Overall und darunter einen Naßbiber genannten Neoprenanzug. Außerdem sollte man stets ein oder zwei wasserdicht verpackte dicke Pullover dabei haben. Eine Schwimmweste oder, besser noch, eine Rettungsweste sollte an Bord einer Jolle ständig getragen werden.

Der Steuermann trägt einen wasserdichten Overall und eine Schwimmweste darüber.

Ölzeug und Naßtaucheranzug

Die wind- und wasserdichte Oberbekleidung, Ölzeug genannt, ist verschieden in Schnitt, Qualität, Material und Farbe. Es gibt sie als Overalls, oder Hose und Jacke getrennt. Leicht aus dünnem Nylon oder sehr derb aus mit PVC-beschichteten Textilien, oft mit einem Innenfutter, um die starke Schwitzwasserbildung darunter zu reduzieren. Alle Nähte müssen verschweißt sein, um wirklich wasserdicht zu sein. Zweiteiliges Ölzeug ist nie so vollständig wasserdicht wie ein Overall, dafür aber kann man die Stücke, je nach Bedarf, auch einzeln tragen. Öljacken sind angenehmer als Ölblusen, weil man sie auch offen tragen kann und nicht so stark darin schwitzt. Sie sind aber auch nicht so wasserdicht wie Blusen. Die Ärmel sollten unbedingt eine enganliegende Gummimanschette haben, damit einem nicht pausenlos Wasser reinläuft.

Ein doppelter Verschluß der „Knopfleiste" hält Nässe fern.

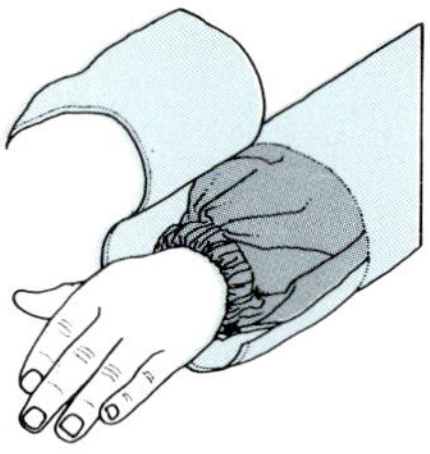

Elastische Gummizüge in den Ärmeln gegen eindringendes Wasser.

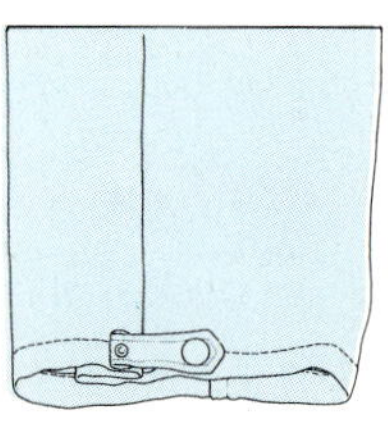

Verschlüsse unten am Hosenbein dienen dem gleichen Zweck.

Wärmeschutz

Jollensegler, vor allem die Regattasegler unter ihnen, müssen damit rechnen, zu kentern und ins Wasser zu fallen. Das kann zu einem plötzlichen und erheblichen Wärmeverlust des Körpers führen. Der beste Schutz dagegen ist ein Neopren-Naßtaucheranzug, als Naßbiber bekannter. Zwischen Haut und Naßbiber bildet sich ein durch die Körpertemperatur erwärmter Wasserfilm. Er verhindert eine schnelle Auskühlung durch Wärmeaustausch mit dem umgebenden kalten Wasser. Der ärmellose „Long John" ist unter Seglern deshalb beliebt, weil er die Bewegungsfreiheit nicht allzu sehr einschränkt. Gewöhnlich wird eine Bolero genannte Überjacke darüber getragen.
Man kann ferner zum Warmhalten mehrere Kleidungsstücke übereinanderziehen, wie Wollhemden und Pullover. Man sollte nicht glauben, daß ein dicker Pullover mehr wärmt, als zwei übereinandergezogene dünnere. Das Gegenteil ist der Fall. Auch gibt es Spezialunterwäsche, die die Körperwärme in ihrer flauschigen Innenstruktur festhält und zudem noch sehr schnell trocknet.

Schwimm- und Rettungswesten

Jeder Jollensegler sollte ständig eine Schwimm- oder Rettungsweste tragen. Das Angebot ist groß, und man muß deutlich zwischen den unterschiedlichen Funktionen unterscheiden. Im Gegensatz zur Schwimmweste, die nur als Schwimmhilfe dient, ist die Rettungsweste ohnmachtssicher. Das heißt, sie dreht einen Bewußtlosen in eine stabile Rückenlage und hält sein Gesicht über Wasser. Bewußtlosigkeit kann schnell durch Unterkühlung eintreten. Viele Jollensegler und Segler auf kleineren Binnengewässern ziehen Schwimmwesten vor, auf See aber gehören, aus Sicherheitsgründen, grundsätzlich Rettungswesten. Sie müssen den Richtlinien des Bundesverkehrsministeriums entsprechen und ein amtliches Prüfsiegel tragen. Schwimmwesten sind durchweg Feststoffwesten, gefüllt mit geschlossen-zelligem Schaumstoff. Rettungswesten dagegen sind fast ausschließlich luftgefüllt. Es gibt verschiedene Aufblassysteme: Entweder wird eine CO_2-Patrone durch Seewasser aktiviert oder mit einer Reißleine ausgelöst oder aber die Weste wird mit dem Mund aufgeblasen. Westen mit Patronenfüllung müssen jährlich gewartet werden. Leib- und Schrittgurte verhindern, daß sich die Weste hoch- oder gar über den Kopf schiebt.

Feststoff-Schwimmweste

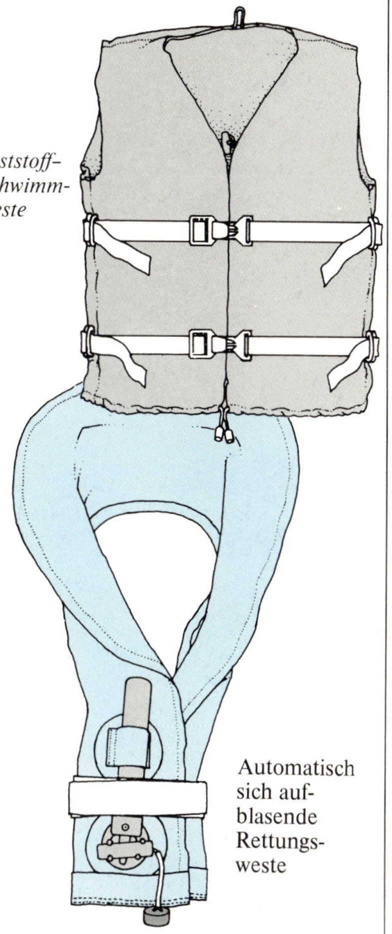

Automatisch sich aufblasende Rettungsweste

Dieser Laser-Steuermann trägt eine Schwimmweste, wie sie auf Binnenrevieren fast ausschließlich von Jollenseglern getragen werden. Sie sind nur Schwimmhilfen.

Schuhzeug

Auf einer Jolle stets Stiefel oder Schuhe tragen. Niemals barfuß segeln, denn allzu leicht kann man auf dem nassen Boden ausrutschen oder sich die Füße an Beschlägen verletzen. Seglerschuhzeug wird aus verschiedenen Materialien hergestellt. Wichtig ist eine griffige, gut profilierte Sohle.

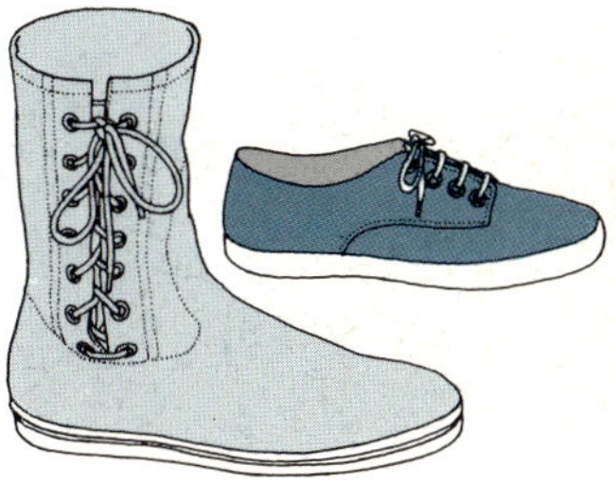

Weitere Dinge

Vom Schotenreißen bekommt man schnell Blasen in den Händen. Deshalb sind spezielle Segelhandschuhe empfehlenswert. Bei kühleren Temperaturen unbedingt eine enganliegende Wollmütze und einen Wollschal tragen, um die kälteempfindlichen Nackenpartien zu schützen. Bei sonnigem Wetter mit einer breiten Schirmmütze das Gesicht vor Sonnenbrand schützen. Brille oder Sonnenbrille mit einem Band um den Nacken sichern, damit sie nicht außenbords fallen. Auf längeren Fahrten unbedingt trockene Kleidung zum Wechseln mitnehmen. Alles in wasserdichte Plastikbehälter verstauen und sicher festzurren.

Begriffe rund ums Boot

Jedes Boot, ob klein oder groß, hat die gleichen Bestandteile: Einen Rumpf, einen Mast, ein Segel, einen Kiel – auf der Jolle ersetzt ihn ein aufholbares Schwert – und ein Ruder. Der Rumpf dient dazu, die Besatzung aufzunehmen und Mast und Segel zu tragen, die man als Rigg bezeichnet. Die Form des Rumpfes ist ganz entscheidend für das Fahrverhalten eines Bootes. In ihm zeigt sich das Können des Konstrukteurs. Einen idealen Rumpf für alle Wind-und Seegangsverhältnisse gibt es nicht. Jeder ist ein mehr oder minder gut gelungener Kompromiß. Das Vorschiff wird als Bug, das Hinter- oder Achterschiff als Heck bezeichnet.
Als Segelform hat sich das Hoch- und Bermudasegel allgemein durchgesetzt. Größe und Schnitt der Segel sind abhängig von der Größe des Bootes und dem Zweck, für den es konstruiert wurde. Rennjollen beispielsweise tragen auf einem leichten Rumpf eine relativ große Segelfläche, die das Boot zwar schnell macht, aber auch stärker krängt. Deshalb muß es von der Mannschaft „ausgeritten" werden. Auf den meisten Booten werden die Masten von Drahtseilen gehalten: den Wanten, die am Seitendeck angreifen, und dem Vor- und Achterstag, die zu den Bootsenden führen. Diese Verstagung bezeichnet man als stehendes Gut. Das laufende Gut umfaßt alle beweglichen Leinen und Drähte, mit denen etwas bewegt wird: die Fallen zum Hochziehen der Segel, die Schoten, mit denen die Segelstellung zum Wind reguliert wird, Auf-, Nieder- und Achterholer und Streckertaljen. Am Fuß des Großsegels ist ein sogenannter Baum üblich, der das Segel in Form hält. Der Baumniederholer verhindert ein Steigen.
Die Segel sind aus einzelnen Bahnen zusammengenäht. Als Segeltuch wird überwiegend das aus Polyester entwickelte Dacron verwendet.
Gesteuert wird mit dem Ruder am Heck. Es wirkt mit seiner Unterwasserfläche aber auch der seitlichen Abdrift entgegen, die durch den Winddruck auf die Segelfläche hervorgerufen wird. Hauptsächlich jedoch verhindert das Schwert die Abdrift.

Segelbezeichnungen

Üblich auf Yachten ist als Großsegel das dreieckige Hochsegel, auch als Bermudasegel bezeichnet. Es hat das frühere Gaffelsegel seit der Mitte der 30er Jahre nach und nach verdrängt. Das Gaffelrigg findet man heute eigentlich nur noch auf Oldtimern und in England. Das Großsegel wird im oberen Bereich durch die um den Mast schwenkbare Gaffel ausgespreizt. Noch seltener ist das Luggersegel, bei dem eine ursprüngliche Rah zu einer Gaffel verkürzt ist, die allerdings nach vorne über den Mast hinausragt, ebenso wie meist auch der Baum. Das Segel wird nämlich nicht mit dem Baum am Mast angeschlagen, sondern mit der Gaffel am Mast aufgehängt. Das Sprietsegel ist ein viereckiges, durch eine diagonale Spreize ausgesteiftes Segel. Es ist die charakteristische Besegelung der Kinderjolle Optimist. Hoch- und Gaffelsegel werden meistens mit einem Vorsegel – der Fock oder Genua – kombiniert. Führt ein Boot nur ein Großsegel an einem weit vorne stehenden Mast, spricht man von einer Kattakelung. Fast alle Einmann-Jollen sind solche Katboote.

Jollendetails

Die Illustration zeigt eine 4,20 m lange Jolle mit Hochtakelung für zwei Mann. Sie enthält fast alle typischen Details eines Bootes, das keine allzu hohen seglerischen Anforderungen stellt. Sehr untypisch ist allerdings die englische Heckschotführung. Sie ist bei uns nahezu unbekannt und recht unpraktisch im Gegensatz zu der üblichen Mittelschotführung, wie sie das Bild rechts oben zeigt. Etwas ungewöhnlich ist auch die Ducht.

Mittelschotführung

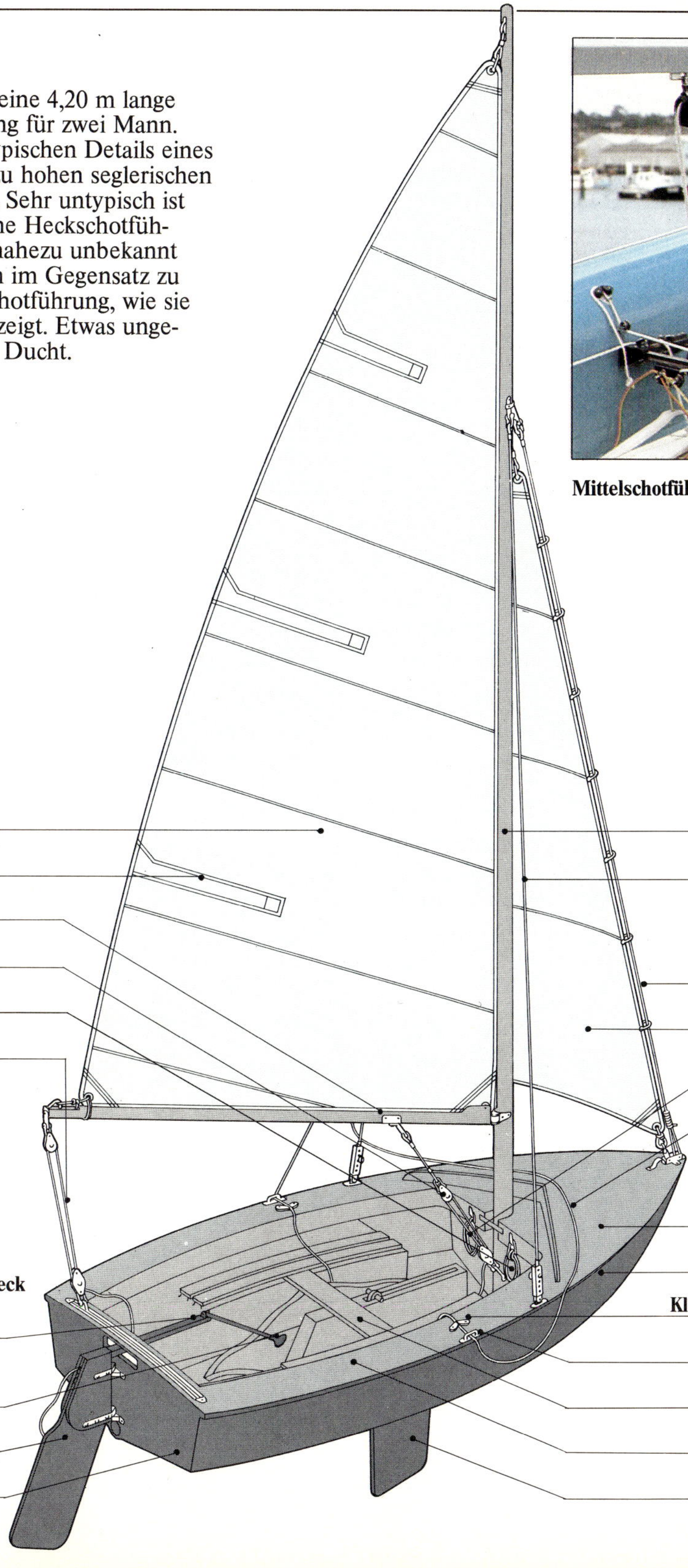

Eindeckung und Sitzgelegenheiten

Fast alle Jollen sind teilweise eingedeckt, um Spritzwasser und überkommendes Wasser, so weit wie möglich, dem Cockpit fernzuhalten. Aber Umfang und Form der Eindeckung sind bei den einzelnen Klassen sehr unterschiedlich. Üblich ist fast immer eine Eindeckung des Vorschiffs bis zum Mast. Nur wenige Typen sind bis zur Bugspitze vollständig offen. Auf manchen Jollen, vornehmlich solchen für Wanderfahrten, ist auch das Hinterschiff eingedeckt. Üblich sind mehr oder weniger breite Seitendecks, die bis an den Spiegel – den hinteren Abschluß des Cockpits – heranreichen. Sie dienen gleichzeitig der Crew als Sitzfläche. Manche Boote haben auch Seitenbänke und/oder eine Ducht – eine Querbank – im Cockpit. Eine solche Querducht ist stets dann erforderlich, wenn das Boot gleichzeitig als Ruderdingi gedacht ist.

Fußgurte

Fußgurte, auch als Ausreit- oder Trimmgurte bezeichnet, sind auf einer Rennjolle unerläßlich. Es sind breite Gewebebänder, die von einem Punkt nahe am Spiegel bis zu einem Punkt in der Nähe des Mastes über den Boden des Cockpits laufen. Nur mit ihrer Hilfe ist es möglich, eine Jolle optimal auszureiten, indem die Mannschaft sich mit dem Fußrist einhängt. Selbstverständlich müssen die Gurte sehr sicher befestigt sein. Reißt einer, führt das unweigerlich zu einem Sturz über Bord. Außerdem sollten sie für Steuermann und Vorschoter unterteilt und in der Länge verstellbar sein. Bändsel oder Gummistropps halten sie hoch, damit man sie jederzeit sofort mit den Fußspitzen angeln kann.

Nylon-Fußgurte, von einem Querstropp angeliftet.

Das Schwert

Mittschiffs in einem wasserdichten Kasten steckt auf einer Jolle ein einziehbares Schwert, entweder aus Holz, Kunststoff oder Metall. Es wirkt der seitlichen Abdrift entgegen. Deshalb muß es auf Kursen am Wind – da ist die seitliche Abdrift am größten – ganz hinuntergelassen werden. Auf Vorm-Wind-Kursen ohne Abdrift dagegen kann man es vollständig aufholen. Es gibt Senk- und Steckschwerter. Das Ein- und Ausfahren eines Senkschwertes geschieht mit dem Schwertfall, das in jeder beliebigen Position in einer Klemme fixiert werden kann. Das Steckschwert beansprucht weniger Platz und wird deshalb vornehmlich auf sehr kleinen Jollen verwendet. Es wird senkrecht in den Schwertkasten hineingesteckt und von einem Gummistropp in Position gehalten. Bei vollständig aufgeholtem Schwert kann es passieren, daß der Baum dagegen schlägt.

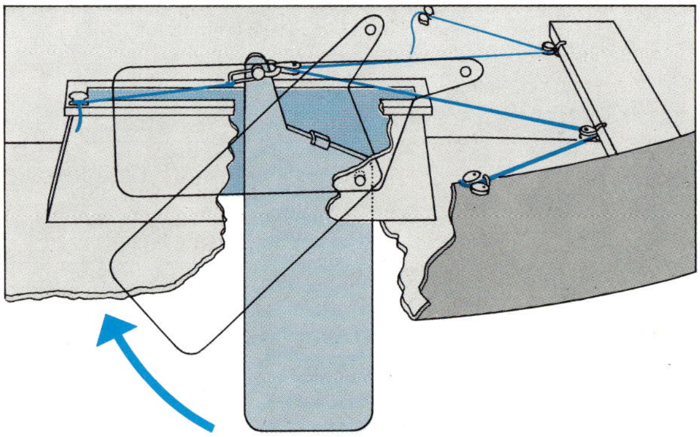

Klapp- oder Senkschwert mit Schwertfall, es hängt an einem Drehbolzen im Schwertkasten.

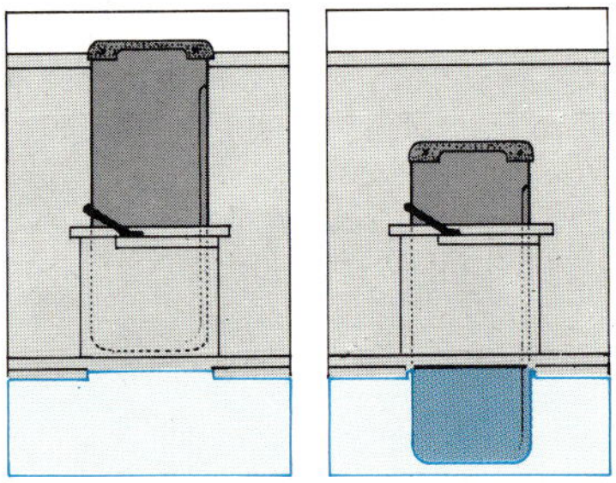

Ein einfaches Steckschwert, aufgeholt und halb gefiert, mit einem Gummistropp arretiert.

Ruder, Pinne und Pinnenausleger

Auf allen Jollen kann man das Ruder abnehmen. Es hängt an Zapfen oder Fingern in entsprechenden Beschlägen am Spiegel. Die meisten Jollen haben ein zwischen zwei Ruderbacken drehbares Ruderblatt, das der Wassertiefe entsprechend, mit einem Ruderfall, aufgeholt oder abgesenkt werden kann. Im Ruderkopf steckt die Pinne, mit der gesteuert wird. Üblich ist heute ein Pinnenausleger. Nur er ermöglicht dem Steuermann, sich beim Ausreiten auf dem Seitendeck weit außenbords zu hängen. Diese Pinnenverlängerung sitzt meist in einem Kardangelenk auf der Pinne und kann daher in alle Richtungen geschwenkt oder geklappt werden. Sie sollte eingeklappt unbedingt eine Arretierungsmöglichkeit haben.

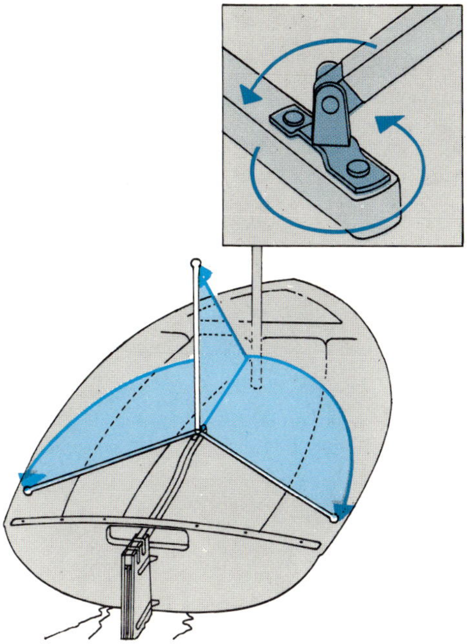

Die Verbindung von Pinnenausleger und Pinne. Die Zeichnung unten veranschaulicht, wie der Pinnenausleger geklappt und gedreht werden kann.

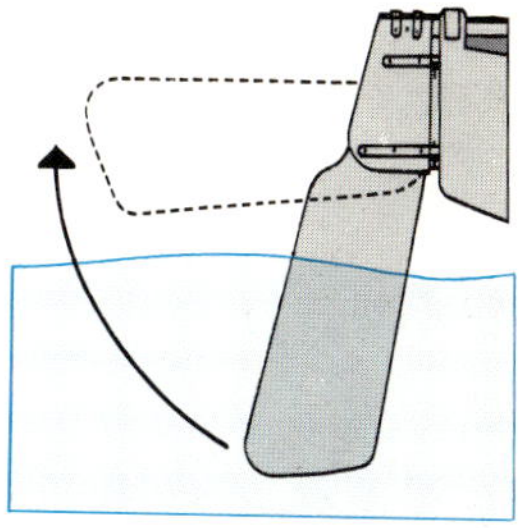

Das schwenkbare Ruderblatt, es wird mit dem Ruderfall aufgeholt, mit einem Niederholer abgesenkt.

Auftriebskörper

Alle Jollen müssen genügend Auftriebskörper besitzen, um das voll Wasser geschlagene Boot und seine Besatzung über Wasser zu halten. Mit anderen Worten: es muß absolut unsinkbar sein. Art und Anbringung der Auftriebskörper kann sehr unterschiedlich sein. Zum Teil wird sie von der Klassenvorschrift für den entsprechenden Jollentyp festgelegt. Bei vielen Jollen ist der Auftrieb in Form von Lufttanks, die zusätzlich noch ausgeschäumt sein können, gleich in die Decksschale integriert. Die Inspektionsluken sollten gelegentlich zur Belüftung der Tanks geöffnet werden. Auf anderen Booten besteht der Auftrieb aus Schaumstoffblöcken oder aufgeblasenen Luftsäcken unter Vor- und Seitendeck. Sie sind leichter zu kontrollieren, können aber auch leichter beschädigt werden. Auf jeden Fall müssen Luftsäcke gleichmäßig aufgeblasen sein, um einheitlichen Auftrieb zu ergeben. Er ist so zu bemessen, daß bei einer Kenterung das Schwert klar über der Wasseroberfläche bleibt. Auch sollte sich das Boot nach dem Aufrichten von seiner Besatzung wieder leersegeln lassen.

Luftsäcke als Auftriebskörper, üblicherweise sind sie unter den Seitendecks und dem Vordeck verzurrt.

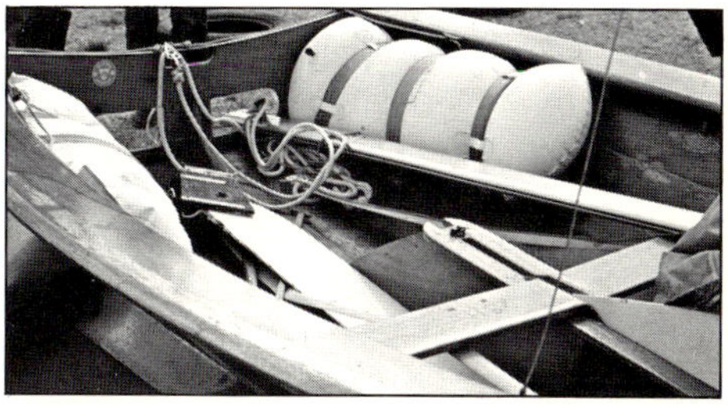

Die meisten modernen Rennjollen haben in Vor- und Seitendeck integrierte Lufttanks, oft auch ausgeschäumt. Auf dem Bild deutlich zu erkennen vorne die Inspektionsluken.

Der Mast

Der Mast trägt das oder die Segel. Die meisten Masten sind aus eloxiertem Aluminium. Hohlverleimte Holzmasten sind sehr selten geworden. Das Hochsegel wird direkt am Mast gefahren. Die Vorderkante des Segels, sein Vorliek, wird in eine Nut an der Rückseite des Mastes eingeführt und darin hochgezogen. Der Mast kann abgenommen werden. Er steht entweder auf dem Kiel oder in einer Mastspur an Deck, auf Jollen häufig in einer Kerb- oder Lochschiene. Sie erlaubt, den Mast zum Trimmen um mehrere Zentimeter nach vorn oder hinten zu versetzen. Kleine Boote, wie Einmann-Jollen, die nur ein Großsegel führen, haben einen unverstagt im Deck steckenden Mast. Das heißt, auf Wanten und Vorstag wird verzichtet. Boote mit einem Vorsegel dagegen kommen ohne Verstagung nicht aus.

Mast und stehendes Gut, typisch für eine kleine Jolle.

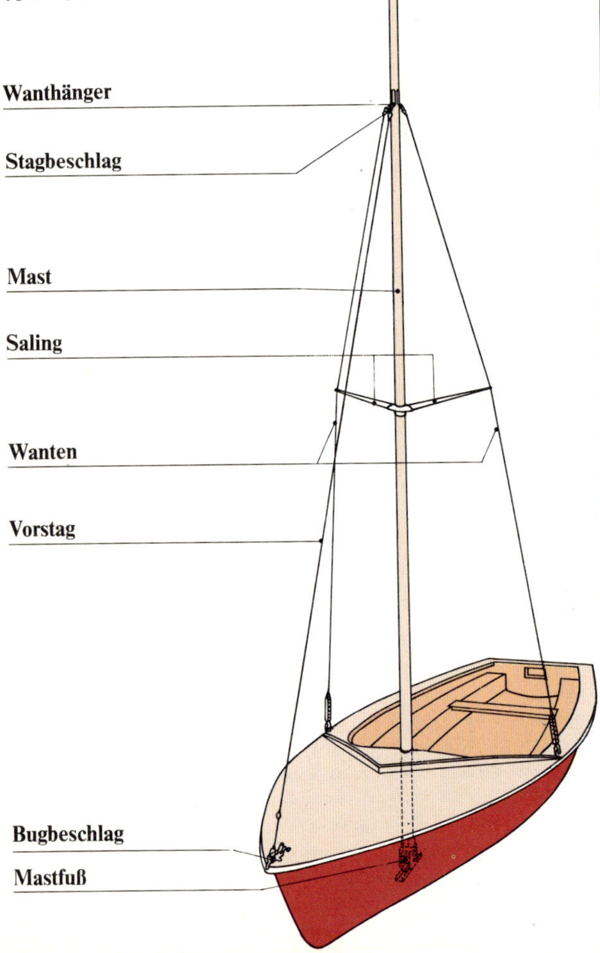

Mastbeschläge

Es gibt eine Reihe von Beschlägen, die dazu dienen, den Mast aufzustellen und zu fixieren und die Verstagung am Mast anzubringen. Unterschiedliche Bootstypen haben auch unterschiedliche Beschläge, entsprechend den seglerischen Anforderungen, die an sie gestellt werden. Auf einer anspruchsvollen Rennjolle beispielsweise ist der Mast ein kompliziertes Instrument zum Segeltrimm unter verschiedenen Segelbedingungen (mehr darüber auf Seite 143). Entsprechend umfangreich ist auch die Bestückung mit Beschlägen. Doch eins gilt für alle Arten von Mastbeschlägen: sie müssen erstklassig befestigt sein. Beim Segeln treten an den Beschlägen ständig wechselnde Belastungen auf, deshalb sollten sie vor jedem Törn auf Schwachstellen hin kontrolliert werden.

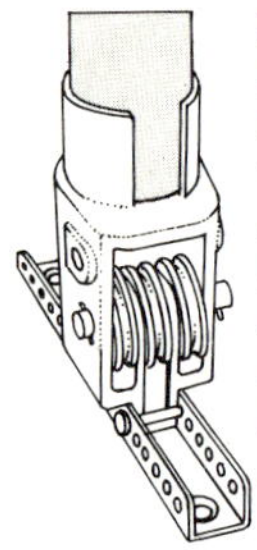

Mastfuß
Die Mastspur hält den Mastfuß in der gewünschten Position. Er kann nach vorne und hinten verstellt werden. Die drei Rollen sind Führungsrollen für Fock-, Großsegel- und Spinnakerfall.

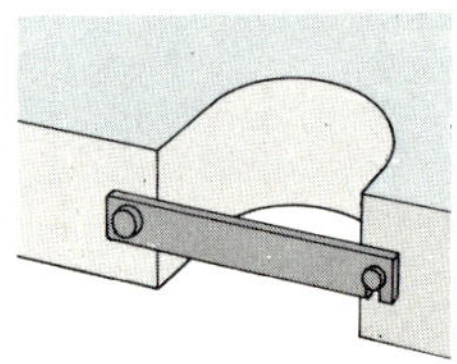

Mastdurchlaß
Masten, die auf dem Kiel stehen, erfahren eine zusätzliche Abstützung durch den Durchlaß. Eine Falle verschließt ihn.

Püttings
So werden die fest mit dem Rumpf verbundenen Stahlplatten bezeichnet, an denen die Wanten sitzen.

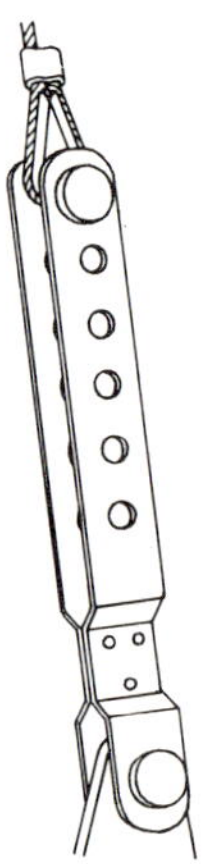

Lochbandbeschlag
Die Wanten können auch direkt mit den Püttings verbunden werden, aber dazwischen gesetzte Lochbänder oder Spannschrauben ermöglichen einen besseren Masttrimm.

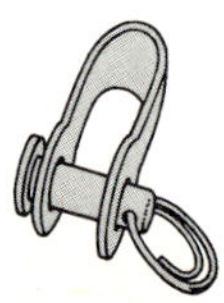

Steckverbindung
Sie dient dazu, die Wanten mit dem Lochband oder Pütting, beziehungsweise mit dem Wanthänger am Mast zu verbinden.

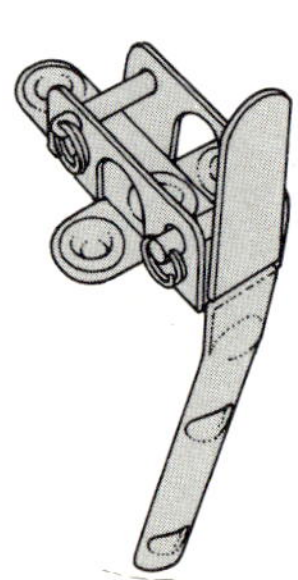

Bugbeschlag
Am Bugbeschlag werden Vorstag, Fockhals und die Vorleine angeschlagen. Da große Zugkräfte auftreten, muß er gut mit dem Deck verbolzt sein. Manchmal ist er – wie hier – mit einer Metallplatte als Stevenschutz verbunden.

Mastsetzen

Zu Beginn der Segelsaison oder – wenn man sein Boot trailert – vor jedem Start muß der Mast gesetzt werden. Das kann man durchaus alleine machen, denn die meisten Jollenmasten sind leicht und handlich, besser aber geht es natürlich zu zweit. Vor dem Aufrichten vergewissert man sich, daß keine Hindernisse, wie etwa elektrische Freileitungen, im Wege sind. Eine Berührung mit dem Alumast kann tödlich sein. Nun legt man den Mast parallel zum Boot, die Mastspitze zum Heck, und klariert die Wanten und das Vorstag. Hat das Boot eine Decksspur, werden die Wanten an ihren Püttings an Deck befestigt, der Mast aufrecht gestellt und aufrecht in seine Spur eingesetzt. Jetzt neigt man ihn, etwas unter Zug, nach vorne und befestigt das Vorstag. Haben die Wanten nicht genügend Spiel, um den Mast neben das Boot zu stellen, wird er längs übers Cockpit gelegt, sein Fuß in die Spur eingeführt und der Mast dann am Vorstag in die Vertikale aufgerichtet. Hat das Boot eine Kielspur und eine Decksdurchführung, zunächst den Mast in seine Spur einsetzen. Falls es eine Decksöffnung mit Falle ist, erst die Falle schließen, damit der Mast nicht nach hinten hinauskippen kann. Danach dann Wanten und Vorstag mit ihren Steck- oder Schraubverbindungen an den Decksbeschlägen anschlagen.

Aufriggen des auf dem Kiel stehenden Mastes eines Fireball.

Decksmastspur

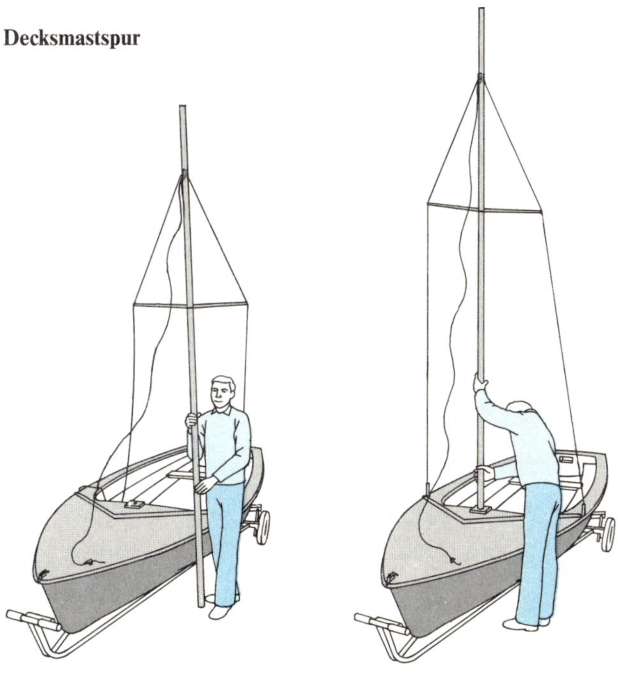

1 *Die Wanten sind an ihren Püttings befestigt, der Mast wird aufgestellt ...*

2 *... und in seine Spur an Deck gesetzt und nach vorne geholt, um das Vorstag am Bugbeschlag zu befestigen.*

Der Baum und seine Beschläge

Der Baum ist üblicherweise aus demselben Material wie der Mast, überwiegend also aus Aluminium. Er kann ein rundes, ovales oder rechteckiges Profil haben. Auf der Oberseite befindet sich eine Nut, in die das Fuß- oder Unterliek des Großsegels eingezogen wird. Am vorderen Ende des Baumes gibt es meistens einen Beschlag, an dem der Segelhals – die vordere untere Ecke des Segels – mit einem Schäkel oder Splintbolzen fixiert wird. An einem anderen Beschlag am hinteren Ende des Baumes wird das Schothorn – die hintere untere Ecke des Segels – ausgeholt und befestigt. Die Verbindung zwischen Baum und Mast nennt sich Lümmelbeschlag. Der Lümmel, der von einem Lümmellager aufgenommen wird, kann am Baum, aber auch am Mast sitzen. Es kann ein einfacher Haken, ein rundum schwenkbarer Zapfen, eine Steckbolzenverbindung oder ein Schlitten sein, der auf einer Schiene am Mast auf- und niederfährt. Der Baumniederholer ist eine Talje, die das unerwünschte Steigen des Baumes auf Vorm-Wind-Kursen verhindert. Sie greift auf der Unterseite des Baumes auf etwa einem Viertel der Länge an. Das andere Ende führt zum Mastfuß. Die Zeichnung rechts zeigt einen einfachen Baumniederholer. Auf hochgestochenen Rennjollen handelt es sich um ein raffiniertes System, das dem Trimm von Mast und Segeln dient.

Ein fester Lümmelbeschlag in viereckiger Zapfenform. Der Baum kann nicht gedreht werden.

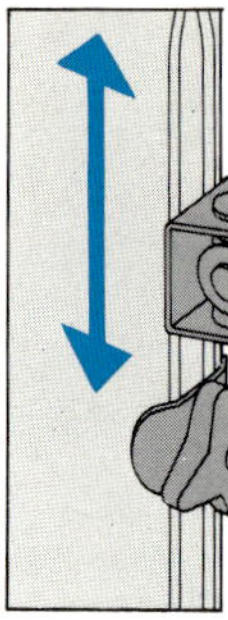

Auf einer Schiene gleitender Lümmelbeschlag mit ebenfalls gleitender Arretierungsschraube.

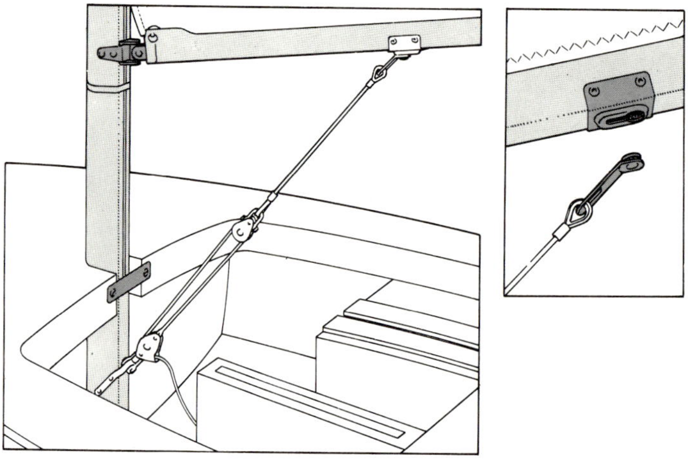

Baumniederholer mit einfacher Talje. Das obere Ende wird in die Platte mit Langloch an der Unterseite des Baumes eingepickt.

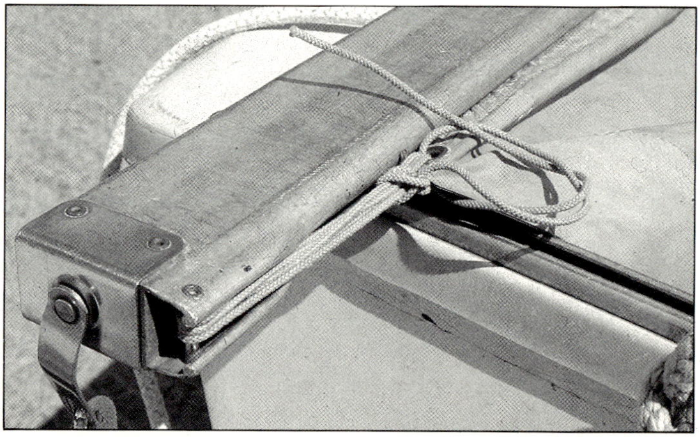

Es gibt verschiedene Systeme, das Schothorn auszuholen. Hier geschieht es mit einem einfachen Bändsel, das über einen Bolzen gezogen wird.

Die Segel

Das Rigg, beziehungsweise die Takelage, bestimmt die Anzahl der Segel. Außer den Einmann-Booten haben fast alle Jollen ein Großsegel und ein Vorsegel (Fock oder Genua). Bis zur Erfindung der Kunstfaser waren Yachtsegel aus Baumwolle. Heute wird fast nur noch das aus Polyester entwickelte Dacron verwendet. Es dehnt sich nicht, hat eine hohe Zerreißfestigkeit und ist wasserabweisend und verrottungsfest. Es leidet allerdings unter ultravioletter Sonnenbestrahlung und ist empfindlich gegen Scheuern und Knicken. Das Tuch wird in verschiedenen Stärken zu Leicht- und Schwerwettersegeln verarbeitet. Einige Boote haben mehrere Satz Segel für unterschiedliche Windverhältnisse. Bei leichtem Wind wird meistens statt der kleinen Fock eine große Genua gefahren. Die Ecken der Segel – als Hals, Kopf und Schothorn bezeichnet – sind verstärkt. Vor- und Fußliek des Großsegels sind mit einem Tau eingefaßt, weil sie in die Nut von Mast und Baum eingezogen werden. Segellatten aus Holz oder Kunststoff in den Lattentaschen am Achterliek des Großsegels dienen der besseren Formgebung und sollen ein Flattern des Achterlieks verhindern. Fock oder Genua werden mit Stagreitern auf das Vorstag gesetzt, auf modernen Rennjollen häufig jedoch auch ohne Stagreiter gefahren. Die Segelstellung wird mit den Schoten reguliert, die entsprechend Vor- und Großschot heißen.

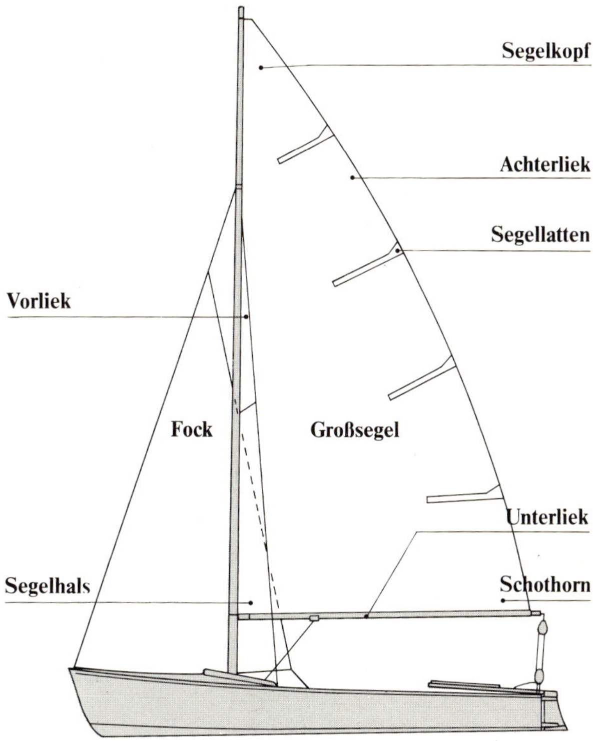

Blöcke

Blöcke sind Gehäuse mit gekehlten Rollen (Scheiben), über die eine Leine läuft. Ein Block kann nur eine Scheibe haben oder aus einer Kombination von Scheiben bestehen. Entsprechend der Art ihrer Verwendung haben Blöcke am Fuß oder am Kopf die unterschiedlichsten Beschläge. Es gibt sie in allen möglichen Größen und aus verschiedenen Materialien. Sie dienen dem Umlenken einer Zugrichtung oder an Taljen, wie beispielsweise der Großschot, der Kraftersparnis.

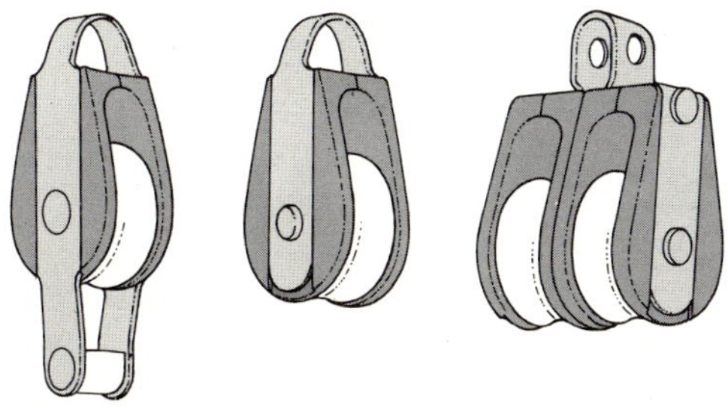

Block mit Auge und Hundsfott — **Block mit Auge** — **Zweischeibiger Block**

Schäkel

Schäkel sind kleine Bügel, heute meistens aus nichtrostendem Stahl, die dazu dienen, alles Mögliche an Bord miteinander zu verbinden. Es gibt sie in verschiedenen Größen und Stärken und verschiedenen Ausführungen für spezielle Verwendungszwecke. Der „klassische" Schäkel ist der D-förmige Schraubschäkel. Daneben gibt es Schlüsselschäkel. Ihr Schäkelbolzen kann nicht heraus- und über Bord fallen, wie es Schraubbolzen gerne tun. Eine andere Spielart sind Schnappschäkel, die ein Federbolzen verschließt. Stets sollte man reichlich Ersatz an Schäkeln bei sich haben.

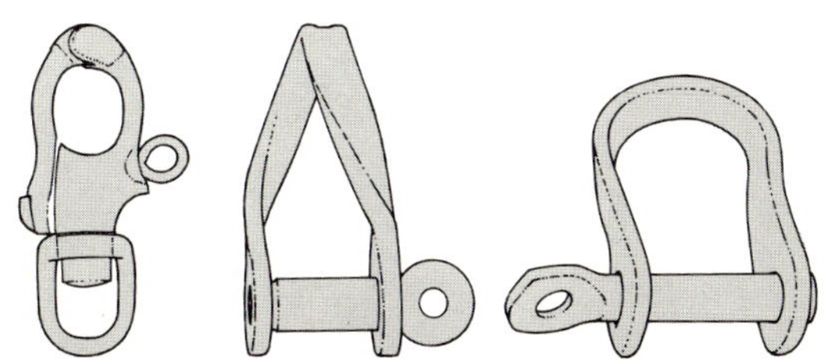

Schnappschäkel — **Schraubschäkel gedreht** — **Schraubschäkel geschweift**

Das Großsegelfall

Das Großsegelfall ist eine Leine, häufig mit einem Drahtvorläufer. Seltener ist es vollständig aus Draht. Es wird am Kopf des Großsegels angeschäkelt, um das Segel zu setzen. Es läuft zu einer Umlenkrolle in der Rückseite der Mastspitze, dann durch den Mast und tritt im unteren Teil des Mastes über eine weitere Umlenkrolle wieder aus. Üblicherweise an der rechten (Steuerbord-) Seite. Das Fall wird auf einer Klampe am Mast belegt und das Ende, sauber aufgeschossen, dahintergesteckt. Auf älteren Booten läuft das Fall nicht durch den (hohlen) Mast, sondern außen entlang. Ein Drahtfall wird mit einer Schlinge, seemännisch als Auge bezeichnet, über einen Haken gehängt.

Das Fockfall

Es dient zum Setzen des Vorsegels. Es wird ebenfalls am Segelkopf angeschäkelt und besteht meistens aus einer Leine mit einem Drahtvorläufer. Die Führung im Mast ist ähnlich wie beim Großsegelfall, nur tritt es oben an der Vorderseite und unten an der Backbordseite (links) aus. Belegt wird es ebenfalls auf einer Klampe. Auf Hochleistungsjollen allerdings sitzt das Fall häufig auf einem Hebelstrecker (rechts). Er ermöglicht, die gewünschte extreme Spannung auf das Vorliek des Segels zu bringen.

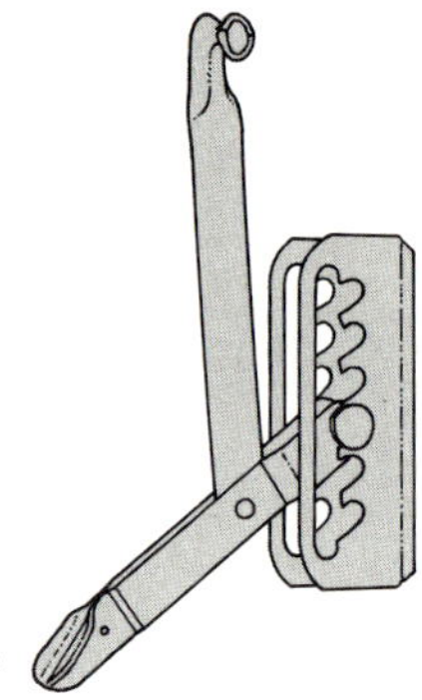

Hebelstrecker oder -spanner für das Fockfall, wie man ihn auf hochgezüchteten Rennjollen findet.

Die Großschot

Die Großschot ist eine geflochtene griffige Leine, mit der das Großsegel bedient wird. Üblich ist auf Jollen die Mittelschotführung. Die Schot sitzt etwa auf der Mitte des Baumes und der Fußblock ebenfalls etwa in der Mitte des Cockpits. Einige ältere und ausländische Jollen, besonders in England, haben eine Heckschotführung. Die Schot greift an der Hinterkante des Bootes, am Spiegel, an. Die Bedienung ist umständlicher. Alle Großschoten sind als Taljen durch Blöcke geschoren, die eine Kraftersparnis von 3:1 bis 4:1 ergeben. Der Fußblock der Mittelschot sitzt häufig auf einem sogenannten Traveller, einer quer übers Cockpit verlaufenden Schiene oder Stange mit einem oft rollengelagerten Schlitten. Der Traveller erlaubt dem Steuermann, die Großschot mehr zur einen oder anderen Seite hin zu fahren, was einen nicht unerheblichen Einfluß auf den Trimm des Segels hat (s. Seite 144). Alle Rennjollen, bei denen es auf solche Feinheiten ankommt, haben Traveller. Auf einigen Booten wird die Großschot ständig aus der Hand gefahren, auf anderen kann sie in Schotklemmen festgesetzt werden.

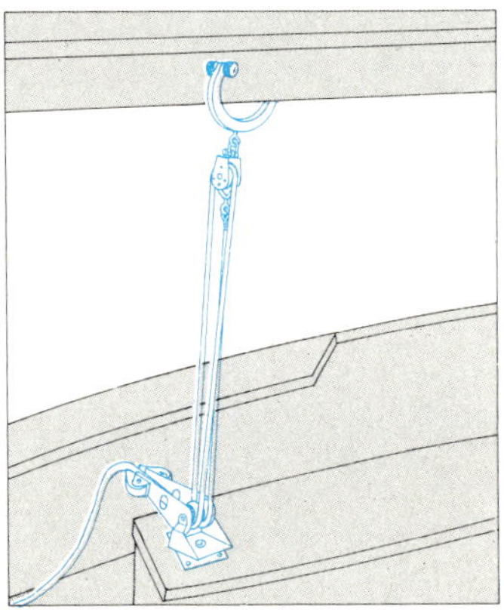

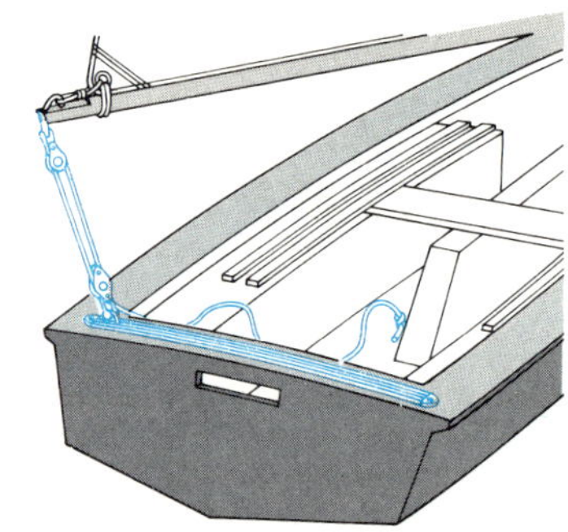

Oben: Heckschotführung mit Traveller, der Fußblock gleitet mit einem Schlitten auf einer Schiene. (Nur noch auf älteren, besonders englischen Jollen zu finden.)

Oben links: Mittelschotführung mit festem Fußblock und Schotring. Er ermöglicht das Großsegel zu reffen (auf den Baum aufzurollen).

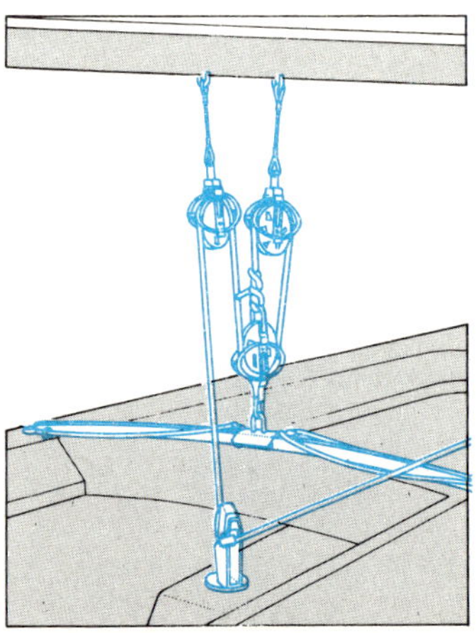

Mittelschotführung mit Traveller und festem Fußblock, wie sie auf allen modernen und internationalen Rennjollen üblich ist.

Die Fockschoten

Das Vorsegel – Fock oder Genua – wird mit zwei Schoten bedient. Sie werden entweder ans Schothorn angeschäkelt oder mit einem Knoten (Palstek) angesteckt. Knoten ist besser, denn der Metallschäkel an einer im Wind schlagenden Fock kann eher Verletzungen verursachen. Ob die Schot besser aus zwei Leinen besteht oder aus einer langen, in der Mitte halbierten, ist Ansichtssache. Man nimmt die beiden Schotenden auf jeder Seite außen um die Wanten herum, fädelt sie durch ihre Leitösen und sichert sie mit einem Achtknoten (s. Seite 146), damit sie nicht ausrauschen können. Die Leitösen sind entweder fast auf dem Seitendeck montierte Ringe oder Bügel, sogenannte Augen, oder sie sitzen verstellbar auf einer Fockschot-Leitschiene – meist einem Lochband mit Federstift.

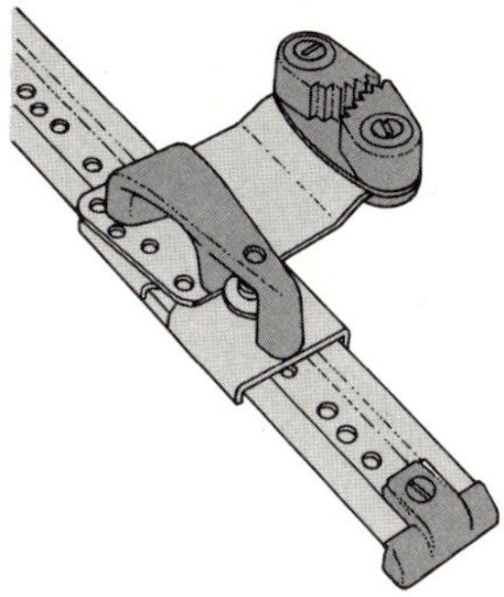

Fockschotleitschiene mit Schlitten, auf dem eine Curryklemme sitzt.

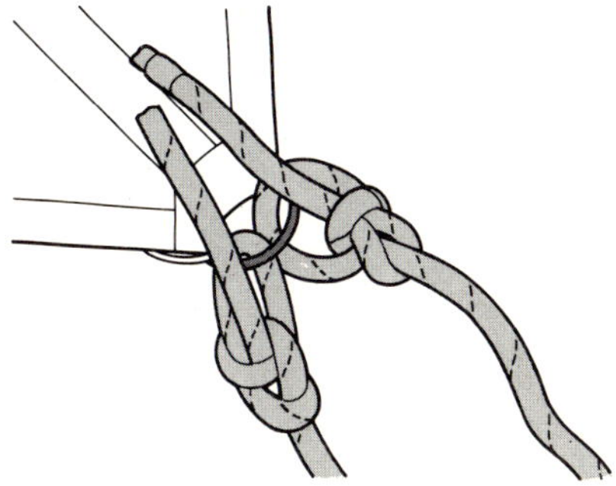

Zwei getrennte Fockschoten, mit je einem Palsteck am Schothorn angesteckt.

Klemmen

Es gibt eine Vielzahl von Klemmvorrichtungen aus unterschiedlichen Materialien. Sie dienen alle dem gleichen Zweck: eine unter Zug stehende Leine sicher zu bekneifen und sich blitzschnell lösen zu lassen. Ursprünglich kannte man nur Klampen (unten rechts), doppelarmige Knaggen aus Holz oder Metall, neuerdings auch aus Kunststoff, um die das Tauende achtförmig herumgelegt wurde und sich auf diese Weise bekniff. Zu den eigentlichen Klemmen zählt die Klampe nicht. Wohl am meisten verbreitet ist die nach ihrem Erfinder benannte Curryklemme (unten links, kombiniert mit einer Leitöse). Sie hat zwei bewegliche gezahnte Backen, die sich unter Gegenzug öffnen. Sie wird vorwiegend zum Festsetzen von Schoten und Streckern verwendet. Gleiche Funktion hat die Kammklemme, auch englisch als Clamcleat bezeichnet. Sie bekneift in einem sich verjüngenden geriffelten Spalt. Man findet sie häufig am Schwert- und Ruderfall.

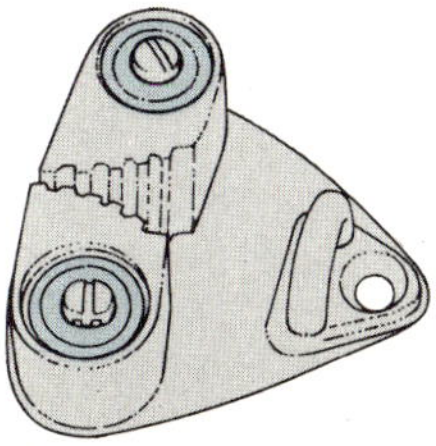

Leitöse mit Curryklemme

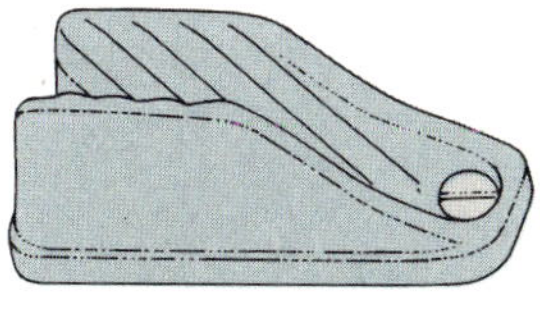

Kammklemme

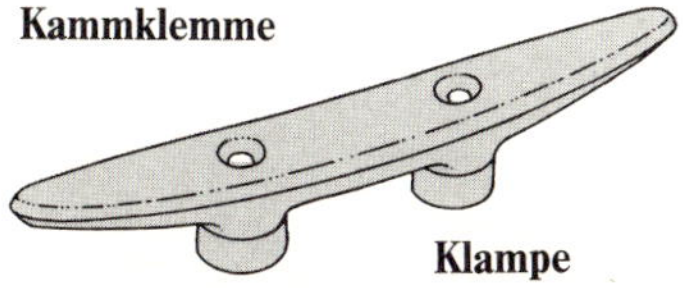

Klampe

Zusätzliche Ausrüstung

Abgesehen von der Ausrüstung, die fest mit dem Boot verbunden ist, braucht man einige zusätzliche Dinge, ohne die man niemals lossegeln sollte. Dazu zählen ein Leichtgewichtanker mit mindestens 20 Meter Leine, zwei Festmacheleinen, zwei Stechpaddel oder Ruder (wenn das Boot zum Rudern eingerichtet ist), Pütz und Schwamm, Reservelenzstopfen, Reserveschäkel und ein Bordmesser mit einem Dorn, um festgefressene Schäkelbolzen zu lösen. Und selbstverständlich gehört für jedes Besatzungsmitglied eine Rettungsweste an Bord. Alle Ausrüstungsgegenstände müssen so – am besten unter dem Vor- oder Seitendeck – gestaut werden, daß sie nicht verloren gehen, falls das Boot kentert. Auszuschließen ist das mit einer Jolle nie.

Lenzeinrichtungen

Eigentlich sollten alle Jollen automatische Lenzeinrichtungen besitzen. Entweder Selbstlenzer im Boden, die das Wasser aus dem Boot saugen, sobald es genügend Fahrt macht, oder aber Lenzöffnungen im Spiegel. Sie können mit Klappen, Stopfen oder ähnlichem verschlossen sein. Manche öffnen automatisch, andere müssen von Hand geöffnet und geschlossen werden.

Weshalb ein Boot segelt

Um segeln zu können, ist es nicht unbedingt erforderlich, die Theorie des Segelns zu kennen. Es gibt sogar sehr erfolgreiche Segler, die sich nie um die Theorie gekümmert haben. Aber es ist schon hilfreich, wenn man eine ungefähre Vorstellung davon hat, welche Kräfte wie auf Boot und Segel einwirken und was sie bewirken. Tatsache aber ist leider auch, daß Anfänger häufig mit sehr viel theoretischem Ballast konfrontiert und dadurch eher verunsichert oder sogar abgeschreckt werden. Besser läßt man sie zunächst einmal selbst herausfinden, was ein Segelboot kann und nicht kann und aus ihren eigenen Beobachtungen lernen. Kinder führen uns vor, wie gut sich diese Methode in der Praxis bewährt. Man lernt schnell, ein Boot allein nach „Gefühl" zu segeln. Und mancher mag sich vielleicht damit zufrieden geben.
Wer jedoch nach mehr Perfektionismus strebt oder nach Regatta-Lorbeeren, der wird ohne Verständnis der Theorie, der aero- und hydrodynamischen Vorgänge am Boot, kaum auskommen.

Wie das Segel arbeitet

Daß Rückenwind schiebt, ist eine jedermann bekannte Tatsache. Nach diesem Prinzip segelt ein Boot vor dem Wind. Das Segel setzt dem Wind einen Widerstand entgegen. Die Luftströmung wird abgebremst. Je größer die Widerstandsfläche ist, umso mehr Luftmasse wird abgebremst und umso größer ist der Schub, der gleichbedeutend mit Vortrieb ist.
Auf andere Art entsteht der Vortrieb beim Segeln im Am-Wind-Bereich. Die Luftmasse wird nicht mehr abgebremst, sondern durch ein flaches, als aerodynamisches Profil geschnittenes Segel störungsfrei abgelenkt – zumindest dann, wenn das Segel richtig geschnitten ist und richtig steht. Die Luftströmung wird dabei gleichzeitig in Luv (der dem Wind zugekehrten Seite) verzögert und in Lee (der Rückseite) beschleunigt. Dabei entsteht ein Überdruck in Luv, und – durch die Beschleunigung der Luftströmung – ein erheblich größerer Unterdruck in Lee. Beide Kräfte – Über- und Unterdruck – wirken als Gesamtkraft in die gleiche Richtung, fast senkrecht zur Richtung des einfallenden Windes. Das Segel arbeitet nach demselben Prinzip wie die Tragfläche eines Flugzeuges. Aus der Aerodynamik stammt denn auch die Bezeichnung „Auftrieb". Er ist nicht mit Vortrieb gleichzusetzen. Der Wind liefert dem Boot überhaupt keinen nach vorn gerichteten Vortrieb, sondern nur einen quer zur Windrichtung orientierten Auftrieb. Wäre das Boot ein flach auf dem Wasser liegendes Brett, würde es einfach seitwärts „segeln". Aber die Lateralfläche – gebildet aus dem Unterwasserschiff, einschließlich Schwert und Ruderblatt – setzt dem seitlichen Abtreiben Widerstand entgegen. Dieser Lateralwiderstand verwandelt einen Teil der quergerichteten Gesamtkraft des durch den Wind erzeugten Auftriebs in Vortrieb. Das heißt, in Fahrt voraus. Je spitzer der Wind von vorne kommt, um so geringer wird der aus der quergerichteten Kraft gewonnene Vortrieb. Schließlich hört er vollständig auf.
Damit der Wind das Segel optimal anströmen kann, spielt der richtige Anstellwinkel des Segels zum Wind eine große Rolle.
Die Zeichnung rechts veranschaulicht, wie sich die Gesamtkraft (durchgezogene blaue Linie) in Vortrieb (= Fahrt voraus) und Querkraft aufteilt. Je seitlicher der Wind einfällt, umso mehr nimmt der Vortrieb zu und die Querkraft ab. Kommt der Wind von hinten, erzeugt er nur noch Vortrieb, die Querkraft hört auf.

Das Segel spaltet die Luftströmung, dabei entsteht ein Überdruck in Luv und ein Unterdruck in Lee.

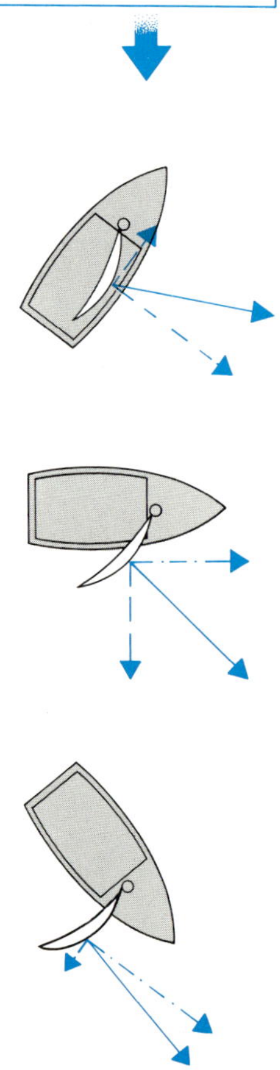

Die Gesamtkraft (durchgezogene blaue Linie) wirkt auf allen Kursen rechtwinklig zum Segel. Die Querkraft nimmt ab, je mehr das Boot vom Wind abfällt.

Wie das Schwert arbeitet

Auf einer Jolle ist es hauptsächlich das Schwert, das der seitlichen Abdrift entgegenwirkt. Je länger es ist, umso wirksamer ist es. Doch es kann auf Am-Wind-Kursen nicht verhindern, daß das Boot unter dem Winddruck auf das Segel stets etwas in Querrichtung ausweicht. Dieser Winkel zwischen dem gesteuerten und dem tatsächlich gesegelten Kurs wird als Abdrift oder Leeweg bezeichnet. Da die seitliche Abdrift am Wind am größten ist, muß das Schwert auf einem Am-Wind-Kurs vollständig hinuntergelassen werden. Je mehr man auf einen Vorm-Wind-Kurs geht, umso mehr kann das Schwert aufgeholt werden. Wird es auf einem Am-Wind-Kurs aufgeholt, rutscht das Boot zwar zur Seite weg, aber die Krängung – die seitliche Neigung – wird geringer, weil dem Winddruck auf die Segel nur ein sehr geringer Gegendruck der Lateralfläche gegenübersteht. Daraus ergibt sich die Feststellung: Je stärker die Abdrift, desto geringer ist die Krängung.
Aber auch bei starker Krängung verringert sich die Lateralfläche durch die starke Neigung des nur noch teilweise eingetauchten Schwertes und Ruderblattes. Deshalb vergrößert sich bei starker Krängung ebenfalls die seitliche Abdrift. Deshalb ist es so wichtig, eine Jolle so aufrecht wie möglich zu segeln, will man gute Fahrt voraus machen. Das wird erreicht, indem die Mannschaft ihr Gewicht so weit wie möglich nach Luv bringt.

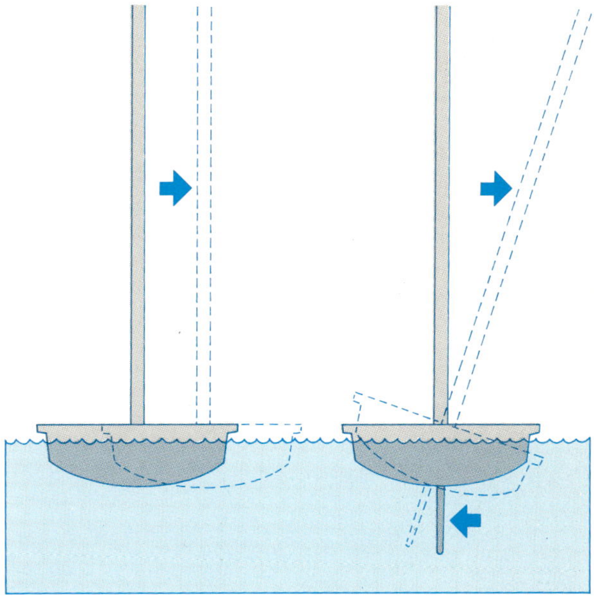

Ein Boot mit aufgeholtem Schwert bietet dem Wind wenig seitlichen Widerstand. Es rutscht zur Seite weg.

Mit dem Schwert unten bildet es unter Wasser einen erheblichen seitlichen Widerstand. Die seitwärts gerichtete Kraft wandelt sich teilweise in eine krängende Kraft um.

Wie das Ruder arbeitet

Das Ruder soll erstens die Lateralfläche vergrößern und so der seitlichen Abdrift entgegenwirken und zweitens ist es das Steuer eines Bootes. Seine Wirkung beruht auf dem Staudruck, der vor dem Ruderblatt entsteht, wenn es gegen das anströmende Wasser angestellt wird. Schlägt man das Ruderblatt beispielsweise nach Steuerbord (rechts) ein, drückt der Staudruck das Bootsheck zur gegenüberliegenden Seite. Die Spitze des Bootes, der Bug, dreht nach Steuerbord. Genau betrachtet ist es das Heck, das man steuert, nicht der Bug. Die Drehachse liegt vor der Bootsmitte, deshalb vollführt das Heck immer einen größeren Bogen als der Bug. Ein Boot dreht stets in die Richtung, in die das Ruderblatt zeigt, auch beim Rückwärtssegeln. Die Pinne jedoch, mit der das Ruder gelegt wird, zeigt in die entgegengesetzte Richtung. Also bei Steuerbord-Ruder, wenn das Boot nach Steuerbord (rechts) dreht, muß die Pinne nach Backbord (links) gelegt werden. Das irritiert Anfänger manchmal zunächst etwas, geht einem aber schnell in Fleisch und Blut über.
Wird das Ruder zu stark eingeschlagen, verliert es seine Wirkung. Das quergestellte Ruderblatt bildet einen so großen Widerstand im Wasser, daß es nur noch als Bremse wirkt, mit der man tatsächlich zu viel Fahrt abstoppen kann. Auch kleinere Ruderausschläge haben stets eine, wenn auch sehr geringfügige Bremswirkung. Deshalb sollte man, um gut und schnell zu segeln, bei Geradeausfahrt so wenig wie möglich mit dem Ruder arbeiten.

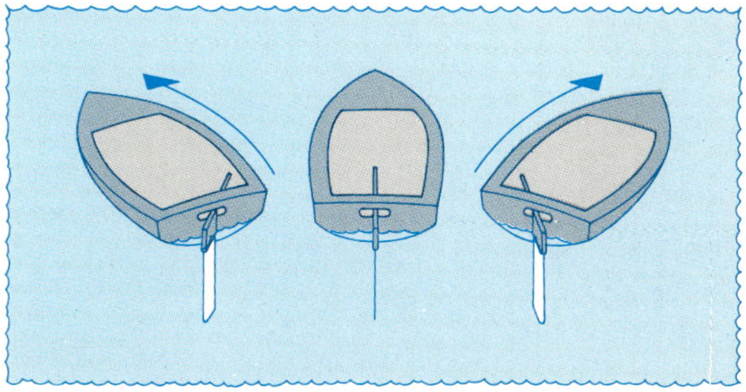

Wird das Ruder nach Backbord gelegt (links), dreht das Heck nach Steuerbord (rechts) und umgekehrt.

Kurse zum Wind

Direkt gegen den Wind ansegeln kann kein Boot. Für jedes gibt es einen unterschiedlich großen Sektor zum Wind, in dem es nicht mehr voraus segelt, sondern sogar rückwärts treibt. Im allgemeinen beträgt dieser tote Sektor 90°, jeweils 45° rechts und links von der Windrichtung. Das macht schon deutlich, wie wichtig es für einen Segler ist, die genaue Windrichtung zu kennen. Da der Wind jedoch nicht zu sehen ist, muß man sich an sichtbare Merkmale halten. Hat man einen Windanzeiger an Bord, einen Verklicker oder Windfäden am Want, wird gerade einem Anfänger die Sache erheblich erleichtert. Der erfahrene Segler hingegen hat ein ziemlich sicheres „Gefühl" für den Wind.

Gesegelt werden kann nur mit dem scheinbaren Wind, der sich aus dem tatsächlich wehenden Wind und dem vom Boot verursachten Fahrtwind zusammensetzt.

Zwischen dem nicht mehr zu befahrenden Sektor am Wind und dem Segeln, „platt vorm Laken", das heißt, mit dem Wind genau von hinten, liegen mehrere Kurse. Sie haben ihre eigenen Bezeichnungen und erfordern jeweils eine andere Segelstellung, teilweise auch einen anderen Trimm des Bootes durch die Mannschaft. Auf diesen verschiedenen Kursen zum Wind immer den richtigen Anstellwinkel der Segel zu finden, macht dem Anfänger die meisten Schwierigkeiten. Doch mit zunehmender Praxis bekommt er fast automatisch das richtige Gespür dafür. Er lernt, Windschwankungen rechtzeitig zu erkennen und auszunutzen, und wie er auf Böen reagieren muß.

Alle Kurse zum Wind können über die rechte Bootsseite (Steuerbord) oder die linke Bootsseite (Backbord) gesegelt werden. Ihre Bezeichnung bleibt jeweils gleich.

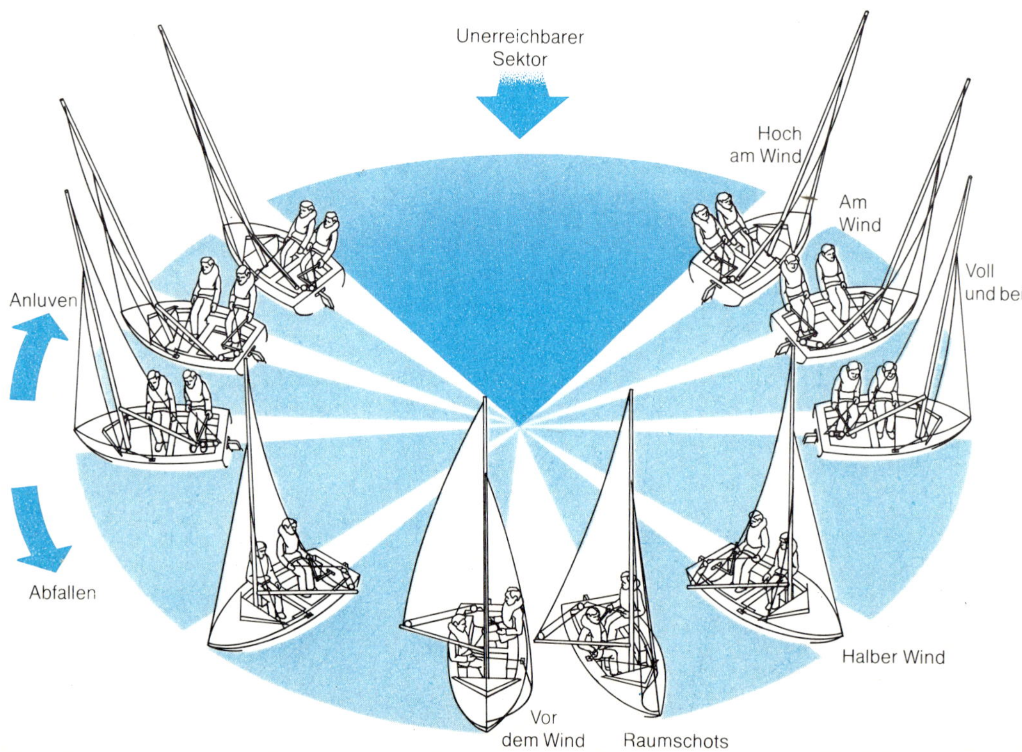

Der unerreichbare Sektor

Es gibt also einen Sektor von 0° (Vorausrichtung) bis zu etwa 45° nach beiden Seiten, in dem ein Boot nicht mehr voraus segelt, sondern entweder mit killenden (flatternden) Segeln stehen bleibt oder sogar rückwärts treibt. Segelt man zu dicht an der Grenze dieses Sektors, beginnt die Fock zu killen und das Boot verliert spürbar an Fahrt. In diesem Fall muß der Steuermann sofort die Pinne zu sich heranziehen und so weit abfallen, bis das oder die Segel wieder voll stehen.

Hoch am Wind

Ein Kurs hart an der Grenze des unerreichbaren Sektors, auf dem das Boot noch Fahrt macht, aber Krängung und Abdrift am größten sind. Die Segel sind so dicht wie möglich geholt, das Schwert ist vollständig unten. Man nennt solches Segeln auch kneifen. Die Mannschaft muß stark ausreiten.

Halber Wind

Das Boot segelt etwa 90° zum scheinbaren Wind. Das Schwert ist ungefähr halb oder noch etwas mehr aufgeholt, die Segel sind so weit gefiert, daß sie gut voll stehen. Auf diesem Kurs erreichen alle Segelboote ihre größte Geschwindigkeit, besonders aber die leichten Gleitjollen.

Am Wind

Auf diesem Kurs läuft ein Boot seine optimale Höhe. Das heißt, man kommt so am besten zu einem Ziel, das in Luv liegt. Krängung und Abdrift werden etwas geringer, die Geschwindigkeit nimmt merklich zu. Wahrscheinlich wird man die Schoten auf diesem Kurs leicht fieren – etwas schricken – müssen.

Raumschots

Ein Kurs raumer als Halbwind, das heißt, mehr vom Wind weg. Das Großsegel ist bis an die Wanten aufgefiert, der Vorschotmann rutscht zur Bootsmitte, das Schwert wird fast vollständig aufgeholt. Raum nennt man jedoch verallgemeinernd auch alle Kurse zwischen „am Wind" und „vorm Wind".

Voll und bei

Das Boot fällt noch weiter ab, das heißt, es dreht weiter vom Wind weg, die Schoten werden etwas mehr gefiert. Krängung und Abdrift nehmen weiter ab, die Geschwindigkeit nimmt zu. Das Schwert kann etwas aufgeholt werden.

Vorm Wind

Der Wind kommt genau von hinten. Da die Fock jetzt vom Großsegel abgedeckt wird, nimmt man sie auf die andere Seite und fährt sie als „Schmetterling". Die Mannschaft sitzt zum Ausbalancieren auf der rechten und linken Bootsseite. Ein schwieriger Kurs.

Windanzeiger

Es ist für einen Segler wichtig zu wissen, woher der Wind weht. Erfahrene spüren das an ihrem Gesicht, nicht so Erfahrene sollten nach anderen Indikatoren Ausschau halten: In strömungsfreien Gewässern drehen sich Boote vor Anker mit dem Bug in den Wind. Rauch und Flaggen wehen in Zugrichtung des Windes. Auch aus den Wellen lassen sich gewisse Rückschlüsse ziehen, doch erfordert das einiges an Erfahrung, denn sie laufen oft nicht in der gleichen Richtung wie der Wind. Die besten Windanzeiger sind ein sogenannter Verklicker – ein ausgesteifter Wimpel – im Masttopp und Windfäden an den Wanten. Auch stellt sich das Großsegel in Windrichtung, wenn man die Schot los gibt.

Natürliche Windanzeiger

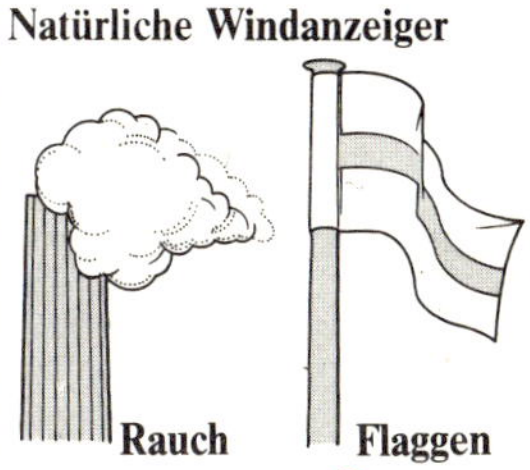

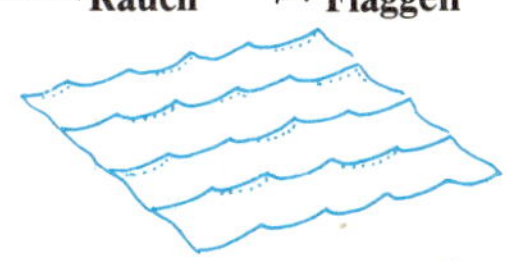

Künstliche Windanzeiger

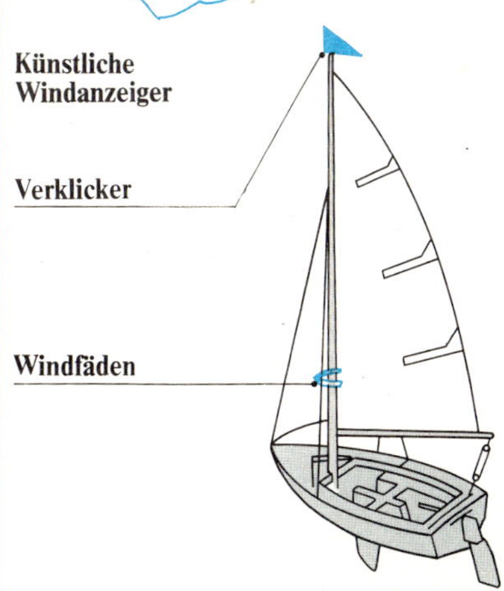

Bootsbedienung

Bevor jemand mit einer Jolle zu segeln beginnt, muß er sich eingehend damit vertraut machen, wie die verschiedenen Einrichtungen an Bord funktionieren, wie sie zu bedienen sind und was man mit ihnen bewirken kann. Obwohl sie, entsprechend der Bootskonstruktion, recht unterschiedlich sein können, funktionieren sie doch nach dem gleichen Prinzip. Steuermann und Vorschoter müssen lernen und wissen, wie sie damit das Beste aus ihrem Boot herausholen.

Bei einer Kursänderung müssen auch Segel- und Schwertstellung, Schot- und Ruderführung und die Sitzposition der Mannschaft geändert werden.

Einsatz der Segel

Abgesehen von der Antriebskraft, die die Segel liefern, haben sie auch größeren Einfluß auf das Kursverhalten eines Bootes. Ein Segel, das sich vor dem Schwert befindet, verleiht dem Bug eine Drehtendenz vom Wind weg. Entsprechend versucht ein hinter dem Schwert gesetztes Segel, das Heck zum Abfallen zu bringen. Stehen die Segel einwandfrei, sind also die Kräfte von Vor- und Großsegel genau ausbalanciert, muß das Boot geradeaus segeln, wenn man die Pinne losläßt. Sind die Segel nicht richtig geschotet, kann es schwierig werden, Kurs zu halten. Wenn man beispielsweise nur die Großschot anholt oder sie wesentlich dichter fährt als die Fockschot, wird das Boot luvgierig (Drehtendenz zum Wind). Holt man dagegen nur die Fockschot dicht, wird das Boot leegierig (Drehtendenz vom Wind weg).

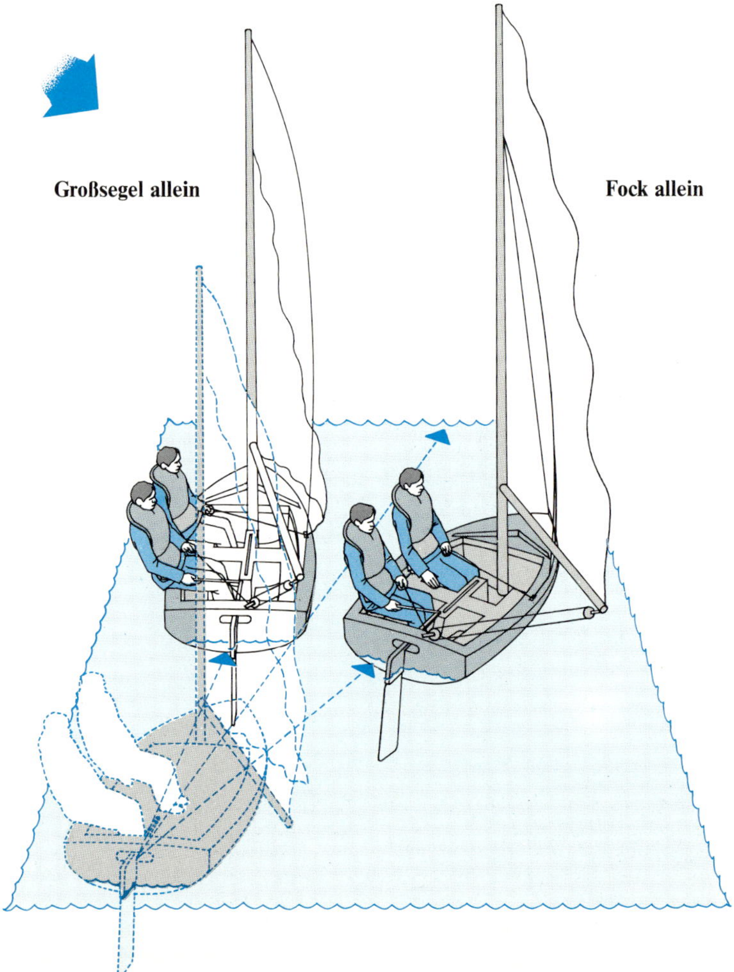

Das Boot liegt mit flatternden (killenden) Segeln in einer Am-Wind-Position. Das Ruder liegt mittschiffs. Läßt man die Fock weiter killen und holt nur das Großsegel dicht, nimmt das Boot Fahrt auf und luvt an (es dreht nach Luv). Holt man in derselben Ausgangssituation nur das Vorsegel dicht und läßt das Großsegel weiter killen, nimmt das Boot ebenfalls langsam Fahrt auf, es fällt aber ab (es dreht nach Lee).

Einsatz des Ruders

Das Ruder wird vom Steuermann mit der Pinne bedient, die häufig einen Pinnenausleger hat. Der Ausschlag des Ruders bewirkt eine Kursänderung des Bootes. Ein nach Luv eingeschlagenes Ruderblatt (Luv-Ruder) dreht das Boot nach Luv, ein nach Lee eingeschlagenes (Lee-Ruder) nach Lee. Die Pinne zeigt stets in die entgegengesetzte Richtung. Beim Anluven drückt der Steuermann die Pinne von sich weg, beim Abfallen zieht er sie zu sich heran. Wegen der starken Bremswirkung sollte das Ruder niemals hart gelegt werden. Bei allen mit dem Ruder eingeleiteten Kursänderungen müssen gleichzeitig die Segel entsprechend bedient werden.

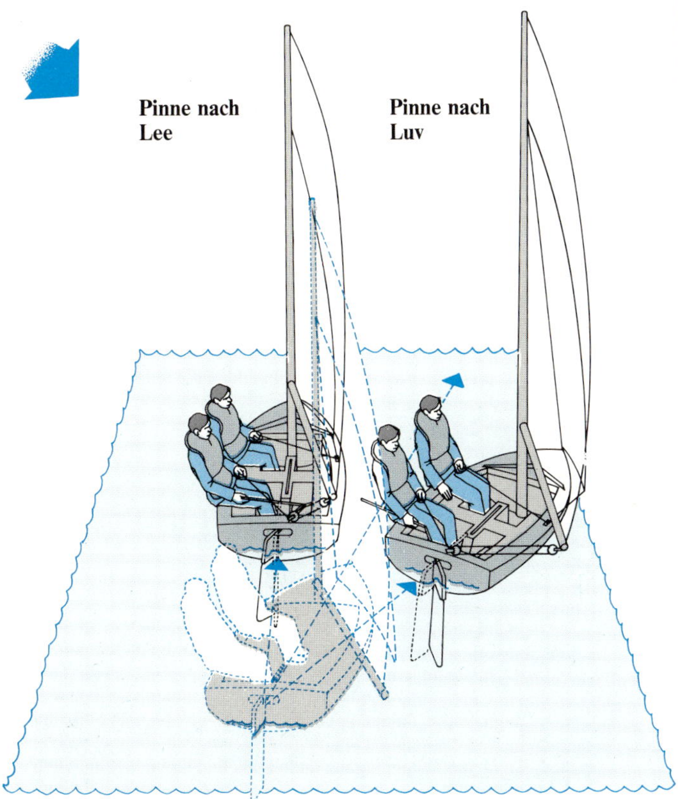

Schiebt der Rudergänger die Pinne von sich weg (nach Lee), luvt das Boot an. Werden die Schoten nicht entsprechend angeholt, fangen die Segel an zu killen. Das Boot kommt zum Stillstand, wenn es vollständig in den Wind gedreht wird. Zieht der Rudergänger die Pinne zu sich heran (nach Luv), fällt das Boot ab. Die Schoten müssen entsprechend gefiert werden, das Boot nimmt mehr Fahrt auf.

Einsatz des Schwertes

Als Anfänger mag es einem schon mal passieren, daß man vergißt, das Schwert hinunterzulassen. Luvt das Boot nicht wie erwartet an, sondern schiebt es sich zur Seite weg, zunächst die Schwertstellung kontrollieren. Mit dem Schwert läßt sich unter Umständen aber auch der Kurs stabilisieren. Ist das Boot leicht luvgierig, genügt es manchmal, das Schwert etwas aufzuholen. Ist das Boot etwas leegierig, mag es genügen, das Schwert vollständig hinunterzulassen.

Bootstrimm

Als Bootstrimm bezeichnet man alle Maßnahmen, die dazu dienen, daß ein Boot besser und schneller segelt. Ist ein Boot so getrimmt, daß es auf „ebenem Kiel" schwimmt, hat es den richtigen Wasserlinienverlauf und es segelt geradeaus. Sitzt die Besatzung zu weit vorne, wird das Boot buglastig. Der Bug taucht zu tief ein, die Wasserlinie verkürzt sich, das Boot wird langsamer und luvgierig. Sitzt die Besatzung zu weit hinten, wird das Boot hecklastig. Die Wasserlinie verkürzt sich ebenfalls, das Heck saugt sich fest, das Boot wird langsamer und leegierig. Wird es stark zu einer Seite gekrängt, dreht es nach der anderen.

Die Mannschaft sitzt zu weit vorne

Die Mannschaft sitzt zu weit hinten

Segelklar machen

Nur recht kleine und leichte Boote wird man von Hand zu Wasser tragen können. Für etwas größere braucht man Bootsrollen, aus Kunststoff oder aufblasbar, oder einen Trolley, einen Bootskarren. Für Sandböden sollte er möglichst breite Räder haben, die nicht so tief einsinken.
Die Abdeckplane (Persenning) wird abgenommen und die bewegliche Ausrüstung ins Boot gepackt. Dabei ist darauf zu achten, daß die Lenzstopfen drinnen sind. Üblich ist es, das Boot bereits auf dem Bootskarren aufzuriggen und die Segel anzuschlagen, aber noch nicht zu setzen, sondern beizubändseln, damit sie nicht auswehen.

Jollen werden bei leichtem Wind an Land für eine Regatta aufgeriggt.

Bootstransport

Ob man die Segel bereits auf dem Stellplatz setzt oder erst am Slip, mag jedem freigestellt bleiben. Auf überfüllten Stellplätzen kann es jedoch Probleme geben. Üblicherweise liegt das Boot auf seinem Stellplatz so auf seinem Trolley, daß es für den Transport weiter hinausgeschoben werden muß. Dazu hebt einer den Bug an, während der andere den Wagen weiter unterschiebt. Aufpassen dabei, daß man nicht versehentlich die Deichsel an den Kopf bekommt. Um das Heck vor rauhem Bodenkontakt zu bewahren, packt man währenddem am besten einen alten Autoreifen drunter. Liegt das Boot richtig auf dem Trolley, kann man den Handgriff der Deichsel mühelos anheben. Die Vorleine vorsichtshalber am Handgriff belegen, damit das Boot nicht vom Wagen fällt, falls man während des Transportes gegen ein Hindernis stößt. Nicht am Boot selbst schieben oder ziehen, sondern nur an der Wagendeichsel. Selbstverständlich achtet man auf Löcher, Steine oder andere Unebenheiten des Bodens. Ist eine Rinne zu queren, geht man sie schräg an und überfährt sie jeweils nur mit einem Rad. Wird das Boot auf einem Slip zu Wasser gelassen, läßt man es mit dem Heck voraus abrollen.
Auf Bootsrollen, die immer wieder hinter dem Heck weggenommen und vor den Bug gelegt werden müssen, ist der Transport etwas mühseliger, aber es geht natürlich auch.

Das Boot liegt gut ausbalanciert für den Transport auf dem Trolley (Slip- oder Bootswagen).

Der Bootswagen wird an der Deichsel gezogen, die Vorleine ist daran befestigt.

Anschlagen des Großsegels am Baum

Das Segel wird aus seinem Sack genommen und mit seinem Unter- oder Fußliek in die Nut auf der Oberseite des Baumes eingezogen. Am besten macht man das zu zweit. Einer führt das Liek ein, der andere zieht das Schothorn bis ans Ende des Baumes. Dann den Segelhals mit seiner Kausch am Baum festsetzen und das Segel mit dem Nockbändsel am Schothorn straff nach hinten ziehen und das Nockbändsel am entsprechenden Beschlag am Ende des Baumes festbinden. Nun die Segellatten in ihre Taschen am Achterliek stecken. Um gleich die richtigen zu finden, sollte man sie sich numerieren. Kontrollieren, ob die Großschot klar durch ihre Blöcke läuft, und dann den Baum als Beschwerung oben auf das Segel legen, damit es nicht ausweht.

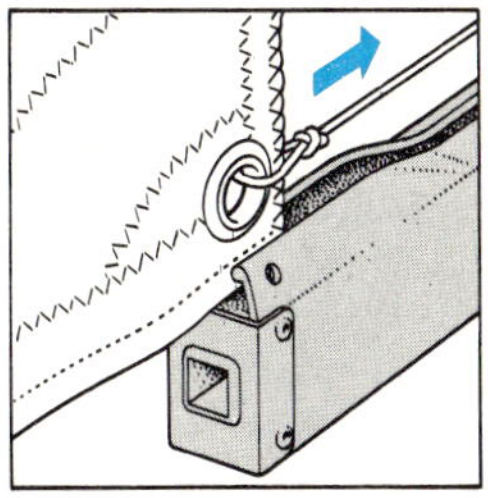

1 *Das Unterliek in die Nut des Baums einführen.*

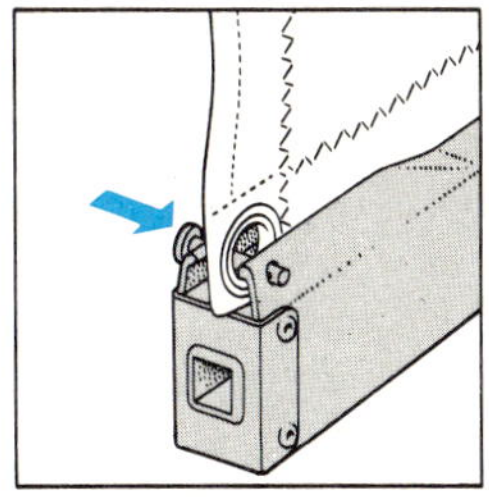

2 *Den Splintbolzen durch den Segelhals stecken.*

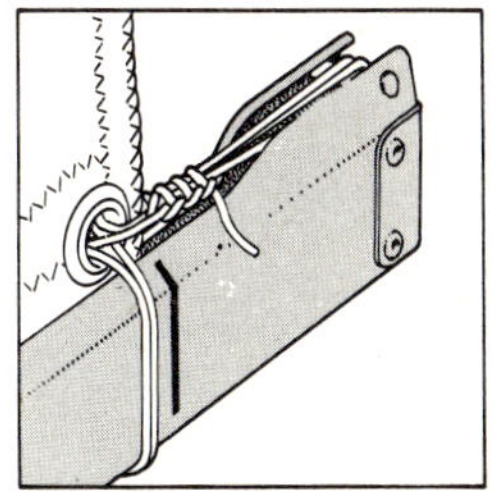

3 *Das Schothorn mit dem Nockbändsel durchsetzen.*

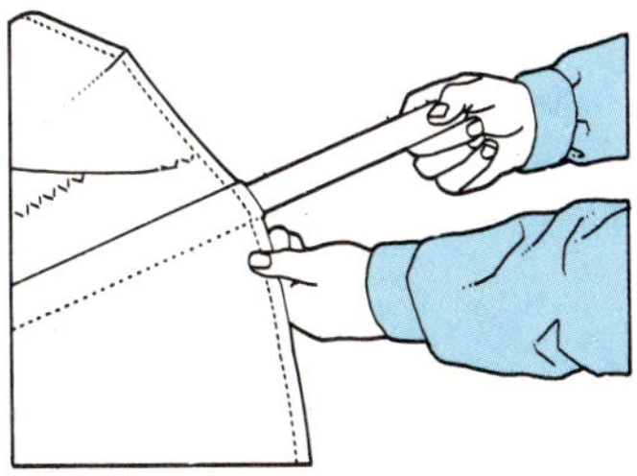

4 *Die Segellatten in die Lattentaschen stecken.*

5 *Ist das Großsegel angeschlagen, den Baum aufs Segel legen, damit es vom Wind nicht weggeweht wird.*

Anschlagen der Fock

Die Fock wird aus ihrem Sack geholt und aufs Vordeck gelegt. Die Ecke mit dem Segelhals heraussuchen und ihn am Bugbeschlag anschäkeln. Dann werden die Stagreiter auf das Vorstag gesetzt, und zwar von unten nach oben. Danach das Fockfall an den Segelkopf schäkeln und die Fockschot ans Schothorn schäkeln oder knoten. Die Fockschoten außerhalb der Wanten zu ihren Leitösen führen und auf die Enden einen Achtknoten setzen. Mit dem Fall oder auch der Fockschot das Segel am Vorstag so beibinden, daß der Wind es nicht auswehen kann.

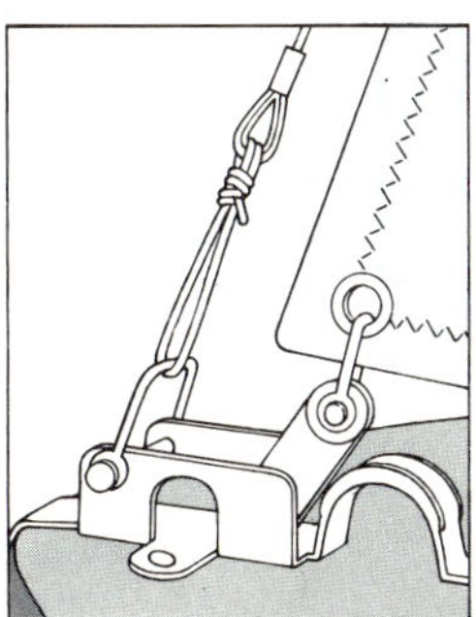

1 *Den Segelhals am Bugbeschlag anschäkeln.*

2 *Die Stagreiter aufs Vorstag setzen.*

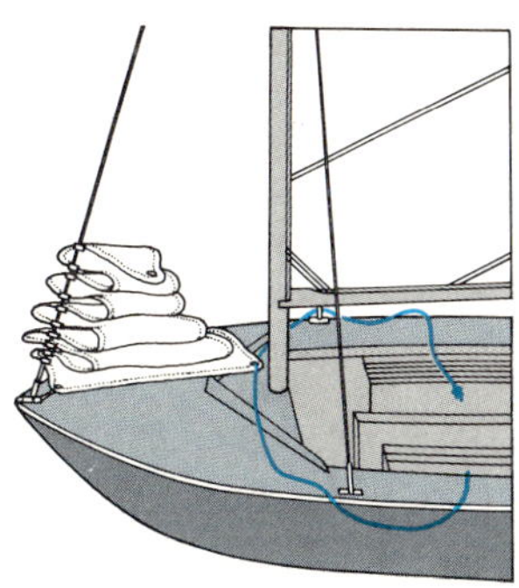

3 *Die Schoten anstecken und durch die Leitösen ziehen.*

4 *Fock- und Großsegelfall am Segelkopf anschäkeln.*

Leinen los

Sowohl in den Segelclubs, die Kurse durchführen, als auch auf den Segelschulen wird der Anfänger seine ersten Schläge unter den wachsamen Augen eines erfahrenen Ausbilders absolvieren und sich nach dessen Anweisungen richten. Das ist in jedem Fall der beste Weg. Natürlich kann man sich das Segeln auch alleine beibringen. Dann sollte man sich aber bemühen, einen erfahrenen Jollensegler zu finden und ihn bitten, bei den ersten Versuchen mitzusegeln.

Unbedingt sollte ein Segelneuling nur bei leichten Winden starten, bei Windstärken bis allerhöchstens 3. Und auf einem geeigneten und ruhigen Revier. Einem Revier also, ohne starke Strömungen, unberechenbare Fallböen oder regen Schiffsverkehr. Wenn man das Revier selbst nicht kennt, sollte man unbedingt vorher genaue Erkundigungen einziehen. Auch schon deshalb, weil es manchmal Sperrungen gibt oder Schutzzonen, die nicht befahren werden dürfen.

Bevor die Leinen endgültig losgeworfen werden können, gilt ein letzter gründlicher Check dem Boot und seiner Ausrüstung. Befindet sich alles in einwandfreiem Zustand? Hat man nichts vergessen? Ist tatsächlich alles an Bord, was man für die Fahrt braucht (s. Seite 35)? Und es ist auch sicher verstaut? Hat man warme Kleidung dabei, wenn es kühler wird oder man länger als geplant braucht, um wieder an Land zu kommen?

Hat man seine Segel bereits an Land angeschlagen, kann es nicht schaden, das Boot auf dem Bootswagen mit der Nase in den Wind zu drehen und Fock und Großsegel einmal hochzuziehen, um zu sehen, ob nichts verhakt oder „vertörnt" ist, sondern alles klar läuft. Ist es an dem, werden die Segel wieder heruntergeholt und gesichert, damit sie nicht auswehen.

Bringt man sein Boot in einem überfüllten Hafen oder an einem betriebsamen Strand zu Wasser, ist es besser, an einen ruhigen Platz zu paddeln und dort, ohne alle Nervosität, seine Segel zu setzen. Ideal ist es, wenn man dazu eine freie Boje findet, an der man mit dem Bug festmachen kann, so daß sich das Boot in Windrichtung legt. Bei Wind, der auf das Ufer oder den Steg zu weht, muß man sich zum Segelsetzen entsprechend weit entfernen. Denn das Boot wird in der ersten Phase, nach dem Loswerfen der Leine, bevor es Fahrt aufnimmt, erheblich achteraus getrieben.

Hat man später erst genügend Segelerfahrung, ist es meist, mit ein paar kleinen Tricks, kein Problem, auch bei auflandigem Wind, direkt vom Slip, Steg oder Strand loszusegeln.

Mit einer Einmann-Jolle ist manches schwieriger, auch wenn nur ein Segel zu bedienen ist. Man hat keinen Zweiten, der einem bei Zuwasserlassen, beim Segelsetzen und vor allem auch beim Ausbalancieren des Bootes hilfreich zur Hand gehen kann. Da Einmann-Jollen im allgemeinen auch eine geringere Stabilität als ein Zweimann-Boot haben, also leichter kentern können, und ein schnelleres Reaktionsvermögen verlangen, sind sie für einen Einstieg in die Segelei nicht unbedingt das Richtige.

Fortgeschrittene setzen die Segel häufig bereits an Land, Anfänger sollten sie besser erst draußen im freien Wasser setzen.

Zu Wasser lassen

Einen Slip – eine Bootsrampe – sollte man sich sehr genau ansehen, bevor man mit seinem mit dem Boot beladenen Trolley rauf rollt: Wie steil er ist, wie glitschig, und ob er nicht abrupt endet, so daß man ins tiefe Wasser fallen kann. Ist es sehr steil und schlüpfrig, sollte man den Trolley mit einer langen, an einem festen Punkt oberhalb des Slips belegten Leine sichern, damit er sich nicht selbständig machen kann. Die Vorleine des Bootes bleibt so lange am Handgriff des Wagens belegt, bis er das Wasser erreicht. Nun dirigiert einer den Trolley so weit ins Wasser, bis das Boot aufschwimmt. Während der Trolley-Lenker den Wagen aus dem Wasser zieht und wegbringt, holt der andere das Boot an der Vorleine seitlich an den Slip, um den Slip für andere freizumachen, die (meistens) schon warten. Dann klettern beide ins Boot. Wer zuerst drin ist, stabilisiert es für den anderen, der gibt dem Boot beim Einsteigen einen kräftigen Stoß, und dann wird zu der Stelle hinausgepaddelt, wo man seine Segel setzen will.

Links außen: Lösen der Vorleine von der Wagendeichsel bevor der Wagen ins Wasser gerollt wird. Daneben: Das Boot schwimmt auf, einer hält es an der Vorleine, der andere zieht den Wagen drunter weg.

An Land holen

Wenn sich das Boot dem Slip nähert, muß einer raus, bevor es mit dem Boden auf den Slip aufsetzt. Dabei muß er aufpassen, nicht danebenzutreten und ins tiefe Wasser zu fallen. Er hält das Boot so lange neben dem Slip fest, bis der andere mit dem Trolley heran ist. Den Wagen so tief ins Wasser schieben, daß das Boot eingeschwommen werden kann. Niemals das Boot mit Gewalt auf den nicht tief genug abgetauchten Trolley zerren. Zu leicht kann der Wagen dabei beschädigt werden. Nun die Vorleine am Handgriff des Wagens belegen und das Gespann den Slip heraufziehen. Ist er steil und sehr schlüpfrig, wieder eine längere Sicherungsleine an Land ausbringen, damit der Trolley einem nicht entgleitet oder man selbst mitsamt dem Gespann ins Wasser schliddert.

Sowie das Boot richtig auf dem Wagen sitzt, die Vorleine an der Wagendeichsel festmachen und dann erst den Trolley herausziehen.

Rudern

Um sein Boot zum Segelsetzen an einen bestimmten Platz zu bringen oder bei Flaute überhaupt nach Hause zu kommen, muß es gepaddelt oder gerudert – seemännisch gepullt – werden. Gepullt wird mit den Riemen. Sie lagern in Dollen (Drehgabeln). Man sitzt mit dem Rücken nach vorne auf der Ducht (Ruderbank). Beim Ausholen des Riemens sind die Arme nicht ganz ausgestreckt, der Oberkörper wird leicht vorgebeugt. Beide Riemen werden gleichzeitig eingetaucht und durch ruckartiges Beugen der Arme und kurzes Zurückreißen des Oberkörpers aus dem Kreuz heraus durchs Wasser geholt. Werden die Ruderblätter von vorn nach hinten durchs Wasser geholt, macht das Boot Fahrt voraus. Bei einseitigem Pullen mit nur einem Riemen dreht das Boot nach der Seite, auf der nicht gepullt wird. Durch gleichzeitiges Eintauchen des anderen Riemens wird die Drehbewegung noch beschleunigt. Die meisten Jollen haben jedoch keine Einrichtung (Dollen und Ducht) zum Rudern. Außerdem lassen sich die langen Riemen schlecht im Boot unterbringen.

Entweder rudert einer mit beiden Riemen, während der andere steuert, oder beide rudern mit je einem Riemen (rechts). Nur bei exakt gleichzeitigen Aktionen der beiden Ruderer bleibt das Boot auf (Geradeaus-) Kurs.

Paddeln

Man sitzt mit dem Paddel in Fahrtrichtung. Die Hand zur Wasserseite umfaßt den Schaft, die andere Hand den Aufgriff des Paddels. Das Blatt wird fast senkecht ins Wasser gestoßen und nach hinten gerissen. Die Hand auf dem Aufgriff übt dabei einen leichten Gegendruck aus. Der Oberkörper folgt der Bewegung mit einer kleinen ruckartigen Beugung nach vorne. Wird nur auf einer Seite gepaddelt, dreht das Boot zur anderen und der Steuermann muß ständig mit dem Ruder gegenanhalten. Ist man allein, mal auf der einen, mal auf der anderen Seite paddeln, um die Drehbewegung jeweils sofort wieder aufzuheben. Oder man wriggt. Beim Wriggen wird das Paddel mit einem Anstellwinkel von etwa 45° hinter dem Heck von rechts nach links bewegt oder umgekehrt. Am Ende des Weges dreht man das Paddel um 90°, so daß es jetzt in einem entgegengesetzten Anstellwinkel zum Wasser steht, dann wird es von links nach rechts oder umgekehrt bewegt und so fort.

Links außen: Wriggen mit dem Paddel über Heck. Daneben: Paddeln zu zweit über die Seite.

Segelsetzen auf dem Wasser

Um dem Wind beim Setzen der Segel keine Angriffsfläche zu bieten, muß das Boot mit dem Bug im Wind liegen. Deshalb ist es gut, wenn man mit dem Bug an einer Boje oder ähnlichem festmachen kann. Dann stellt sich das Boot, ähnlich einer Wetterfahne, selbst in den Wind. Das Großsegel wird zuerst gesetzt oder geheißt (nicht gehißt!). Dazu muß die Großschot los sein. Wenn bisher noch nicht geschehen, wird das Fall am Großsegelkopf angeschäkelt und das Segel, Hand über Hand, hochgezogen. Zum Schluß wird das Fall in einer Bucht um die Klampe genommen und mit der rechten Hand in das unter Zug stehende Stück des Falls – die sogenannte feste Part – eingefallen, um genügend Spannung auf das Vorliek zu bekommen. Eventuell hebt man den Baum etwas an, um das Fall steifer durchsetzen zu können. Dann das Fall auf der Klampe belegen und das Ende aufschießen und über die Klampe hängen (s. Seite 153). Hat der Baum am Lümmelbeschlag eine Streckertalje, diese ebenfalls steif durchsetzen. Danach, wenn vorhanden, den Baumniederholer am Baum einpicken und durchsetzen.
Vorm Vorsegelsetzen schnell noch ein kontrollierender Blick, ob alle Stagreiter angeschlagen und nicht miteinander verhakt sind, ob die Schoten durch ihre Leitösen gezogen und mit einem Achtknoten gesichert sind. Das Fall wird so steif durchgesetzt, daß das Vorstag gerade anfängt lose zu kommen. Es geht leichter, wenn man mit einer Hand ins Vorstag einfällt. Dann das Fall auf der Klampe belegen, das Ende aufschießen und über die Klampe hängen. Alle Vorsegelfallen kommen stets an die Backbordseite des Mastes, das Großsegelfall wird an Steuerbord belegt. Hat das Fockfall zum Durchsetzen einen Hebelstrecker, das Drahtauge im Fall über den Haken hängen und den Streckerhebel umlegen.

Mit dem Boot an einer Mooring liegend, wird zunächst die Fock...

... und dann das Großsegel gesetzt. (Bei uns ist die Reihenfolge grundsätzlich genau umgekehrt.)

Erste Segelerfahrungen

Nachdem nun also die Segel gesetzt worden sind, kann endlich losgesegelt werden. Eigentlich sollte man wenigstens auf dieser ersten Ausfahrt einen erfahrenen Segler mit an Bord haben, sofern man sich nicht in der Obhut eines Segellehrers befindet. Um erstmal etwas sicherer im Umfang mit Schot und Pinne zu werden, sollte man zunächst das Wenden üben (s. Seite 53). Ideal ist es, wenn man irgendwo zwei Bojen oder ähnliche Schwimmkörper hat, um die man in 8-Form herumkurven kann. Auf jeden Fall hält man sich bei seinen ersten Segelversuchen stets in Landnähe. Gerät man in irgendwelche Schwierigkeiten, einfach in den Wind drehen und die Schoten loswerfen. Das Boot bleibt dann fast auf der Stelle liegen, und man kann überlegen, was zu tun ist. – Und schließlich muß man auch wieder an Land. Zum Segelbergen macht man dort wieder fest, wo man seine Segel gesetzt hat und paddelt dann zurück zum Slip, Strand oder Steg.

Um die Fahrt aus dem Boot zu nehmen, einfach auf einem Kurs „voll und bei" die Schoten loswerfen und die Segel auswehen lassen.

Schot und Pinne

Zunächst geht es darum, daß Steuermann und Vorschoter richtig sitzen. Der Steuermann üblicherweise auf dem Seitendeck, gut klar vom Ausschlag des Pinnenendes. Er steuert mit der hinteren Hand und hält in der vorderen die Großschot. Pinnen ohne Pinnenausleger gibt es kaum noch. Man hält den Pinnenausleger in der Hand mit dem Daumen oben drauf, oder zwischen Daumen und Zeigefinger. Die zweite Methode ist günstiger, wenn man sich beim Ausreiten weit hinaushängen muß. Immer darauf achten, daß sich das Ende der Großschot nicht irgendwo verhakt, und sei es zwischen den eigenen Füßen. Um die vordere Hand zum Holen der Großschot freizubekommen, klemmt man sich die Schot entweder zwischen die Knie oder bekneift sie zwischen Pinne und Pinnenhand. Beim Auffieren läßt man sie durch die Hand laufen. - Der Vorschoter muß jeweils dort sitzen, wo er mit seinem Gewicht das Boot am besten ausbalancieren kann, damit es aufrecht segelt.

Mit Schot und Pinne so lange jonglieren, bis man ein Gefühl für die Reaktionen des Bootes bekommt.

Lossegeln voll und bei

Sobald die Besatzung ihre Positionen eingenommen hat, kann es losgehen. Der Vorschoter holt die Leeschot, der Steuermann die Großschot an, damit das Boot allmählich in Fahrt kommt. Das Schwert ist gut halb gefiert (hinuntergelassen). Der Steuermann zieht die Pinne etwas zu sich heran, bis der Verklicker im Masttopp einen Winkel von nicht ganz 80° erreicht, der anzeigt, daß das Boot voll und bei segelt. Nun die Pinne mittschiffs legen und Vor- und Großschot so einregulieren, daß das Vorliek der Segel nicht killt. Auf diesem Kurs zum Wind lernt man wohl am besten das richtige Gespür für Kurs und Segeltrimm. Bewegt man die Pinne leicht hin und her, kann man die Kursänderungen an den Bewegungen des Bugs gegenüber dem Horizont sofort erkennen. Und man merkt auch, wie das Boot schneller oder langsamer wird. Jetzt sucht man sich einen festen Punkt an Land und steuert ihn an, um korrektes Kurshalten zu lernen. Hat man damit keine Schwierigkeiten mehr, kann man sich auf den richtigen Trimm der Segel konzentrieren. Damit beginnt man bei jedem Segel einzeln. Die Schot wird jeweils so weit gefiert, bis das Vorliek anfängt zu killen. Dann wird sie wieder so weit dichtgeholt, bis das Killen gerade verschwindet. So stehen die Segel für diesen Kurs optimal. Windfäden an den Segeln können eine große Hilfe sein. Da der Wind niemals konstant aus einer Richtung weht, muß man den Stand der Segel häufiger auf die beschriebene Weise korrigieren. - Das Gewicht der Besatzung muß so verteilt werden, daß das Boot aufrecht segelt. Krängt es nach Lee, muß die Mannschaft auf der hohen Luvkante ausreiten. Krängt es nach Luv, muß sie sofort ins Boot zurückrutschen.

Für den ersten Törn gutes Wetter und leichten Wind wählen, wenn auch andere Boote draußen sind.

Anluven

Beim Anluven gilt es, alle Kräfte zu nutzen, die eine Luvtendenz des Bootes fördern, und alle auszuschalten, die ihr hinderlich sind. Will man anluven, das heißt, höher an den Wind herangehen, wird zunächst die Großschot dichter genommen, danach erst die Fockschot. Auch das Schwert wird vorher gefiert. Dann schiebt der Steuermann die Pinne gleichmäßig von sich fort. Zwar ist es im Prinzip günstig, wenn das Boot zum Anluven nach Lee krängt, doch möglicherweise luvt es dadurch schneller und höher an den Wind als der Besatzung lieb ist. Sie hält sich bereit, sofort mehr auszureiten, um der zunehmenden Krängung entgegenzuwirken, die durchs Anluven entsteht. Sowie der neue Kurs anliegt, werden die Segel wieder richtig eingestellt.

1 *Anluven aus einem Kurs voll und bei. Das Schwert vollständig fieren.*

2 *Luv-Ruder legen (Pinne nach Lee) und die Schoten entsprechend anholen.*

3 *Das Boot ist auf einem Am-Wind-Kurs angeluvt, es krängt mehr, die Crew muß entsprechend stärker ausreiten, die Schoten sind dichtgeholt.*

Abfallen

Beim Abfallen (vom Wind) muß das Boot unbedingt aufrecht segeln. Allenfalls kann es etwas nach Luv krängen. Krängt es nach Lee, erhält es eine heftige Tendenz zum Anluven. Sie kann so stark sein, daß es unmöglich ist, gegenanzusteuern. Zumal, wenn man gerade eine Bö erwischt und die – nun zu dicht gefahrene – Großschot festsitzt. Wenn man vorher das Schwert etwas aufholt, hilft das dem Boot erheblich. Segelt es aufrecht, zum Abfallen zunächst die Großschot auffieren, dann erst Ruder legen, indem man die Pinne zu sich heranzieht. Dieses sollte man sich zum Prinzip machen, um instinktiv richtig zu reagieren, wenn man sehr plötzlich abfallen muß, etwa um einem unvorhergesehenen Hindernis auszuweichen. Liegt der neue Kurs an, werden die Segel entsprechend geschotet.

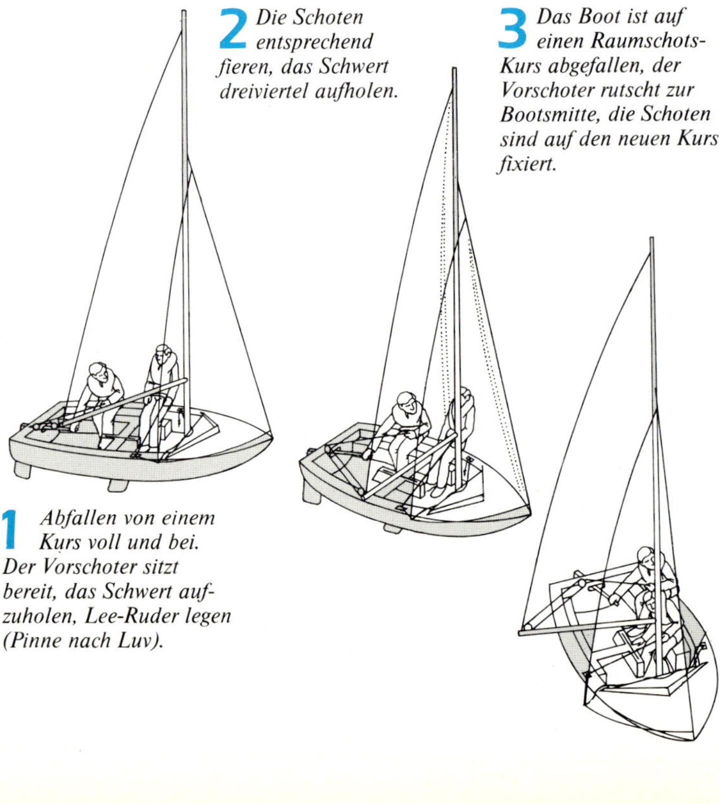

1 *Abfallen von einem Kurs voll und bei. Der Vorschoter sitzt bereit, das Schwert aufzuholen, Lee-Ruder legen (Pinne nach Luv).*

2 *Die Schoten entsprechend fieren, das Schwert dreiviertel aufholen.*

3 *Das Boot ist auf einen Raumschots-Kurs abgefallen, der Vorschoter rutscht zur Bootsmitte, die Schoten sind auf den neuen Kurs fixiert.*

Beidrehen

Um ein Boot vorübergehend zum Stehen zu bringen, kann man entweder auf einem Am-Wind-Kurs in den Wind schießen, das heißt, den Bug genau in den Wind drehen, oder auf einem Halb-Wind-Kurs anluven und die Schoten fieren (einen Nahezu-Aufschießer fahren). In beiden Fällen wird das Boot nicht lange so liegen bleiben, sondern rückwärts treiben, wenden oder abfallen und wieder Fahrt aufnehmen, also ein unkontrolliertes Eigenleben entwickeln. Nicht so beim Beidrehen. Die übliche Methode beizudrehen sieht so aus: Wenden, aber die Fockschot nicht loswerfen, so daß die Fock - in Luv - backsteht. Nun die Großschot fieren und die Pinne nach Lee drücken und dort gegebenenfalls festsetzen. Der Fock, die das Boot nach Lee rumdrücken will, wirkt das gefierte Großsegel und das Luv-Ruder entgegen, so daß sich die beiden Drehmomente weitgehend aufheben. Das Boot treibt nur minimal nach Lee und liegt relativ ruhig, und man hat Zeit, irgendwelche Dinge zu klarieren. Das Schwert sollte dabei viertel bis halb aufgeholt sein. Das muß man ausprobieren. Wie man überhaupt ausprobieren muß, ob und wie sich das eigene Boot beidrehen läßt. Viele Jollentypen lassen sich nämlich gar nicht beidrehen. Um aus beigedreht wieder loszusegeln, braucht man nichts weiter zu tun, als die Fock in Luv loszuwerfen, auf die andere Seite zu nehmen und die Großschot anzuholen.

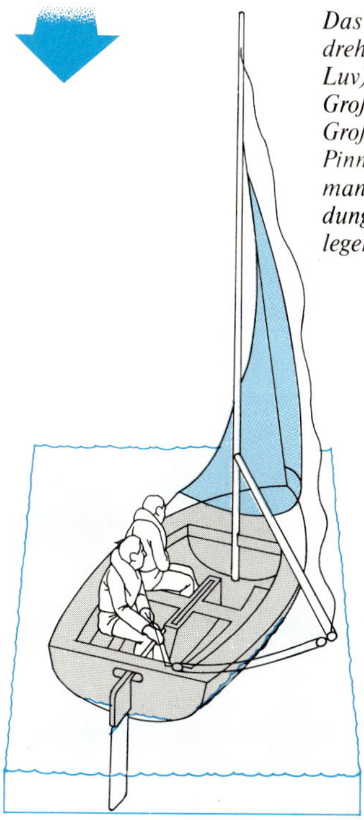

Das Boot liegt beigedreht. Die Fock ist (in Luv) backgesetzt, die Großschot gefiert, das Großsegel weht aus, die Pinne muß der Steuermann (auf dieser Abbildung) noch nach Lee legen.

Wollfäden

Die Segel sind richtig getrimmt, wenn die Lieken nicht mehr killen. Eine große Hilfe für den korrekten Trimm sind feine Wollfäden, die etwa zwei Handbreit hinter dem Vorliek aufgesetzt sind. Diese feinen Fäden, auf beiden Seiten am Segel befestigt, liegen bei richtiger Segelstellung glatt an, ohne zu flattern. Die Abbildungen zeigen zwar nur die Befestigung der Fäden an der Fock, jedoch kann man ebenso mit dem Großsegel verfahren.

Kontrolle des Segeltrimms

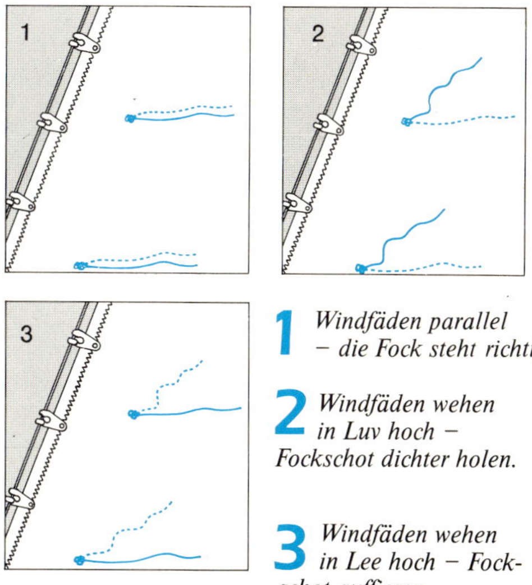

1 *Windfäden parallel – die Fock steht richtig.*

2 *Windfäden wehen in Luv hoch – Fockschot dichter holen.*

3 *Windfäden wehen in Lee hoch – Fockschot auffieren.*

Wenden

Häufig wird schon kurz nach dem Ablegen vom Steg oder von der Boje das erste Wendemanöver fällig. Wenden heißt, mit dem Bug durch den Wind gehen, so daß der Wind nach dem Manöver von der anderen Seite einfällt. Im Bordalltag wird das Wenden oft auch als über Stag gehen bezeichnet. Wie bei allen Manövern müssen auch beim Wenden Steuermann und Vorschoter gut aufeinander eingespielt sein. Zur Verständigung von Steuermann und Vorschoter dienen sogenannte Kommandos. Sie werden vom Steuermann gegeben.
Für manchen Anfänger ist das Wenden zuerst recht verwirrend, weil er dabei leicht die Orientierung auf dem Wasser verliert. Doch das gibt sich schnell. (Die praktische Erfahrung widerspricht der unten vertretenen Ansicht des Autors. Gerade Segelneulinge schaffen die Wende häufig nicht, wenn sie aus einem Kurs voll und bei oder gar halber Wind andrehen. – Bearbeiter)

Für einen Anfänger ist es leichter, aus einem Kurs voll und bei zu wenden (links). Der zu durchmessende Kreisbogen beträgt etwa 180°. Die Crew braucht nichts zu überstürzen, sondern hat mehr Zeit zum Überlegen. Schneller wendet man natürlich aus einem Am-Wind-Kurs (rechts).

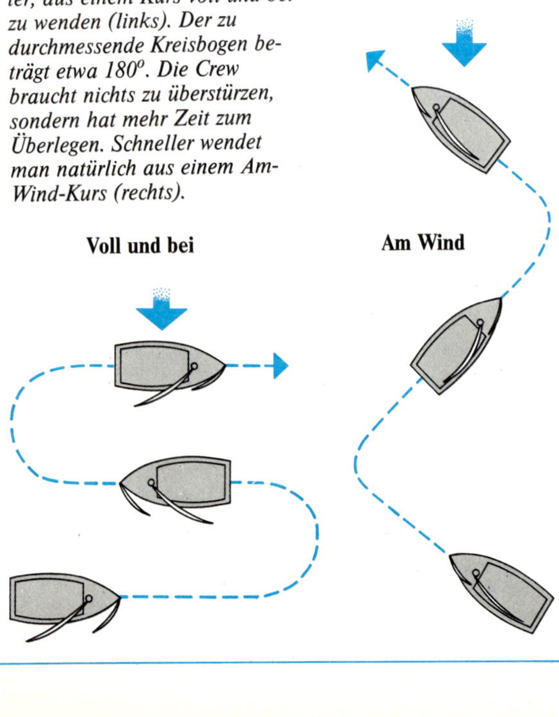

So wird gewendet

Wichtig beim Wenden ist, daß das Boot während des ganzen Manövers genügend Fahrt behält und nicht mit dem Bug im Wind stehen bleibt, rückwärts treibt oder auf den alten Bug zurückfällt. Mit Jollen ist deshalb vor dem Wenden von einem raumen Kurs aus unbedingt auf einen Am-Wind-Kurs zu gehen. So vermeidet man, daß sich das Boot während der langen Drehphase totläuft. Um Fahrt im Boot zu behalten, darf auch das Ruder nicht ruckartig und hart eingeschlagen werden. Es wird langsam und weich gelegt. Sonst liegt das Ruderblatt schon quer, bevor das Boot überhaupt andrehen konnte, und stoppt gleich zu Anfang die Fahrt ganz erheblich. Die Ruderlage muß sich dem Drehmoment des Bootes anpassen und darf ihm nicht vorauseilen. Ist das Boot auf die neue Leeseite abgefallen, wird sanft Gegenruder gelegt, um das Drehmoment aufzuheben. Geht ein Boot schwer durch den Wind – wie beispielsweise leichte Katamarane –, läßt man die Vorschot belegt. Die Fock kommt dann nach einiger Zeit auf dem neuen Bug back und unterstützt dadurch die Drehung. Erst auf das Kommando „Über vorn!" wird die Fock losgeworfen und rübergenommen. Üblicherweise wirft der Vorschoter die Fockschot los, sowie das Vorsegel während des Drehens an zu killen fängt. Sobald es auf die neue Leeseite übergegangen ist, holt er die Fockschot dicht. Dieser Augenblick muß genau abgepaßt werden. Holt nämlich der Vorschoter die neue Lee-Fockschot zu früh dicht, kann sich die Fock backstellen und das Boot auf den alten Bug zurückfallen lassen. Hat sie aber erst einmal voll Wind gefangen, ist sie, ohne Winsch, selbst auf kleineren Booten kaum noch dicht zu bekommen. Die Großschot fährt man auf Jollen aus der Hand. Durch Mittschiffsholen des Großbaums kann man das Wendemanöver unterstützen. Die Mannschaft wechselt in dem Augenblick auf die andere Seite, da das Boot im Wind liegt und der Baum mittschiffs kommt.
Anfängern wird es immer mal passieren, daß ihnen das Boot beim Wenden im Wind liegenbleibt. Das Ruder hat nun keine Wirkung mehr. Es muß langsam auf Rückwärtsgang gelegt werden, weil das Boot allmählich achteraus zu treiben beginnt. Der Vorschoter hält nun die Fock mit der Hand back. Er darf sie jedoch nicht zu weit nach Luv hinaushalten, denn dann wirkt sie nicht auf Drehung, sondern unterstützt nur die Achterausfahrt. Das auf Achterausfahrt gelegte Ruder und die backgehaltene Fock werden den Bug meistens doch noch zum Abfallen bringen. Sobald der Wind gut von der neuen Seite ins Segel fällt, wird die Fock übergenommen und das Ruder auf Vorausfahrt gelegt. Sollte das Boot auf den alten Bug zurückfallen, muß man zunächst

WEITER AUF SEITE 54

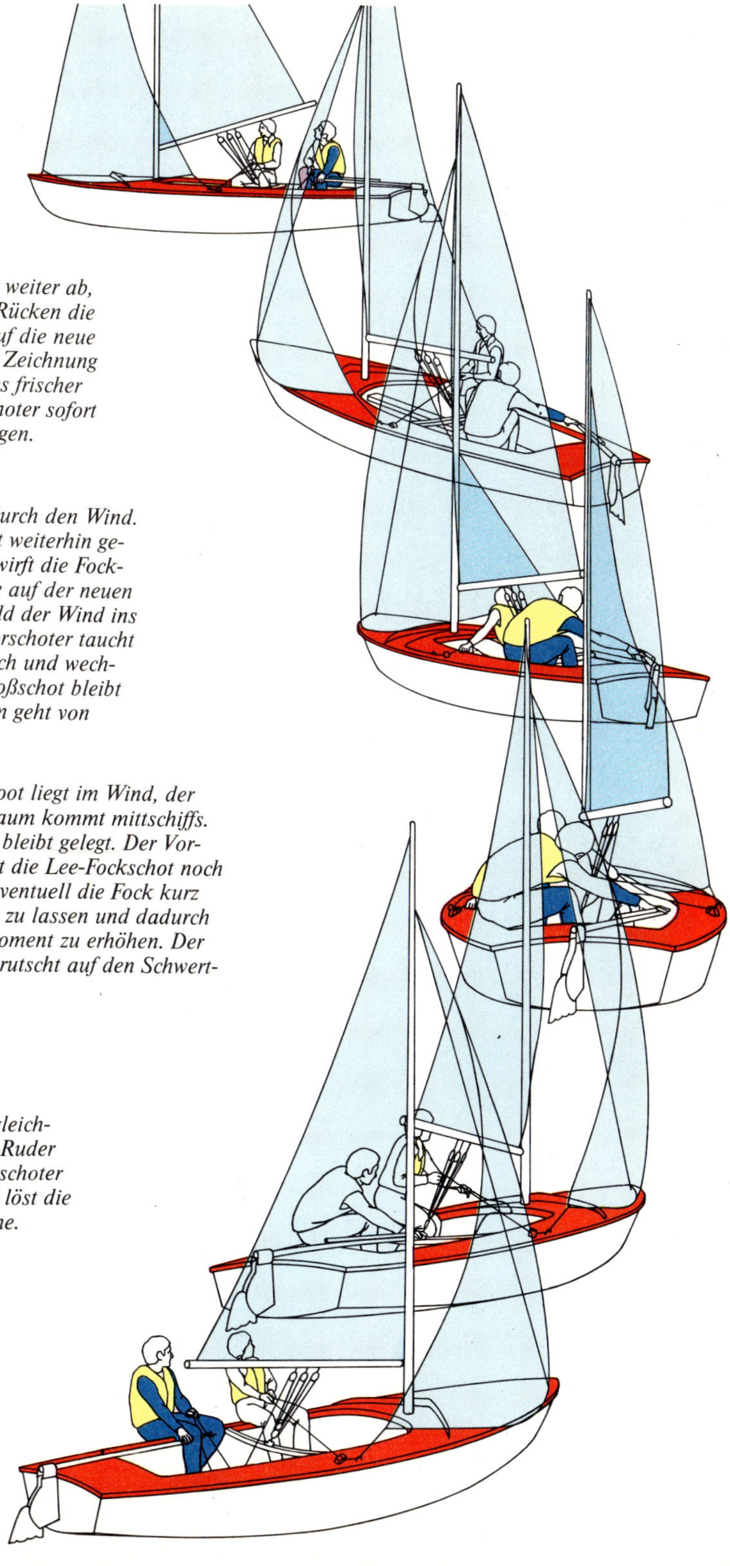

6 *Der Steuermann legt leicht Gegenruder, um die eingeleitete Drehtendenz rechtzeitig aufzuheben. Das Boot läuft auf Backbord-Bug ab. Das Wenden ist beendet. Jetzt kann gegebenenfalls die Feineinstellung von Groß- und Fockschot erfolgen.*

5 *Der Steuermann fällt weiter ab, wechselt hinter dem Rücken die Ruderhand und rutscht auf die neue Luvseite hinüber (auf der Zeichnung nicht dargestellt). Wenn es frischer weht, muß sich der Vorschoter sofort zum Ausreiten hinaushängen.*

4 *Das Heck geht durch den Wind. Das Ruder bleibt weiterhin gelegt. Der Vorschoter wirft die Fockschot los und holt sie auf der neuen Lee-Seite dicht, sobald der Wind ins Segel einfällt. Der Vorschoter taucht unter dem Baum durch und wechselt die Seite. Die Großschot bleibt dichtgeholt, der Baum geht von selbst über.*

3 *Das Boot liegt im Wind, der Großbaum kommt mittschiffs. Das Ruder bleibt gelegt. Der Vorschoter hält die Lee-Fockschot noch dicht, um eventuell die Fock kurz backstehen zu lassen und dadurch das Drehmoment zu erhöhen. Der Vorschoter rutscht auf den Schwertkasten.*

2 *Der Steuermann legt gleichmäßig und weich Luv-Ruder (Pinne nach Lee). Der Vorschoter klariert die Luv-Schot und löst die Lee-Schoot aus der Klemme.*

1 *Anlaufen (hier auf der Zeichnung) auf Steuerbord-Bug. Der Steuermann gibt das Kommando: „Klar zum Wenden!" Rückmeldung des Vorschoters: „Ist klar!"*

weiter abfallen, um erneut Fahrt aufzunehmen, um das Wendemanöver wiederholen zu können.
Die Gründe für ein mißglücktes Wendemanöver noch einmal zusammengefaßt: 1. Das Andrehen zum Wenden aus einem zu raumen Kurs. Wenn nicht gleichzeitig die Schoten dichtgeholt werden, verliert man bei dem langen Andrehen zu viel Fahrt. Aus dem Wenden wird ein Aufschießer. 2. Das Boot segelt vor dem Wenden mit zu wenig Fahrt zu hoch am Wind, deshalb verhungert es in der Wende. 3. Durch ruckartiges hartes Ruderlegen ist das Boot zu stark abgebremst worden. 4. Die Fockschot ist zu früh losgeworfen worden.
Ein weiterer Fehler, der von Anfängern häufiger gemacht wird: Sie fallen nach dem Wenden auf dem neuen Bug zu weit ab, obwohl sie auf einem Am-Wind-Kurs weiterlaufen wollten. Die Schoten aber sind nun für den raumeren Kurs zu dichtgeholt, und das Boot läuft nicht mehr. Um wieder in Fahrt zu kommen, müssen die Schoten zunächst gefiert werden, und dann wird langsam auf den Am-Wind-Kurs angeluvt.

Wenden mit der Trapez-Jolle

Die meisten anspruchsvolleren Zweimann-Jollen können oder müssen sogar mit Trapez gesegelt werden. Das Wendemanöver eines solchen Bootes ist natürlich im Prinzip nicht anders als das eines Bootes ohne Trapez. Neu hinzu kommt hier nur, daß der Vorschoter zum Wenden ins Boot zurückkommen, den Trapezgurt aus- und wieder einhaken und auf der neuen Luvseite wieder ins Trapez einsteigen muß. Bei alledem darf er nicht vergessen, seine Fockschot zu bedienen.

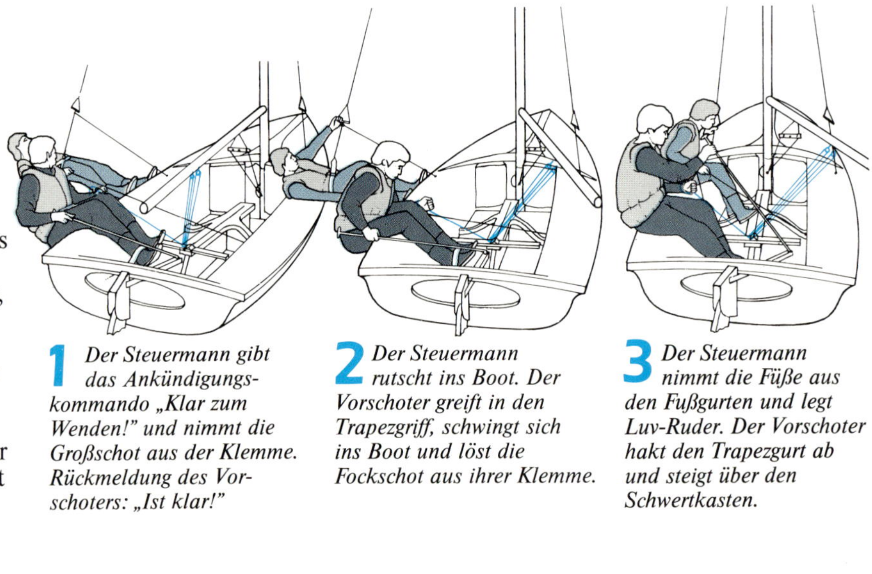

1 *Der Steuermann gibt das Ankündigungskommando „Klar zum Wenden!" und nimmt die Großschot aus der Klemme. Rückmeldung des Vorschoters: „Ist klar!"*

2 *Der Steuermann rutscht ins Boot. Der Vorschoter greift in den Trapezgriff, schwingt sich ins Boot und löst die Fockschot aus ihrer Klemme.*

3 *Der Steuermann nimmt die Füße aus den Fußgurten und legt Luv-Ruder. Der Vorschoter hakt den Trapezgurt ab und steigt über den Schwertkasten.*

Wenden mit der Einmann-Jolle

Da Einmann-Jollen sehr sensible Boote sind und sofort auf Veränderungen im Gewichtstrimm reagieren, müssen alle Bewegungen beim Wenden schnell, aber geschmeidig und fließend ausgeführt werden.

1 *Das Boot segelt fast aufrecht. Der Steuermann legt die Pinne.*

2 *Der Baum kommt mittschiffs, der Steuermann bückt sich und taucht unter ihm durch.*

Das Wenden sollte man üben, bis man die einzelnen Handgriffe ganz automatisch tut, bei jedem Wind und Wetter.

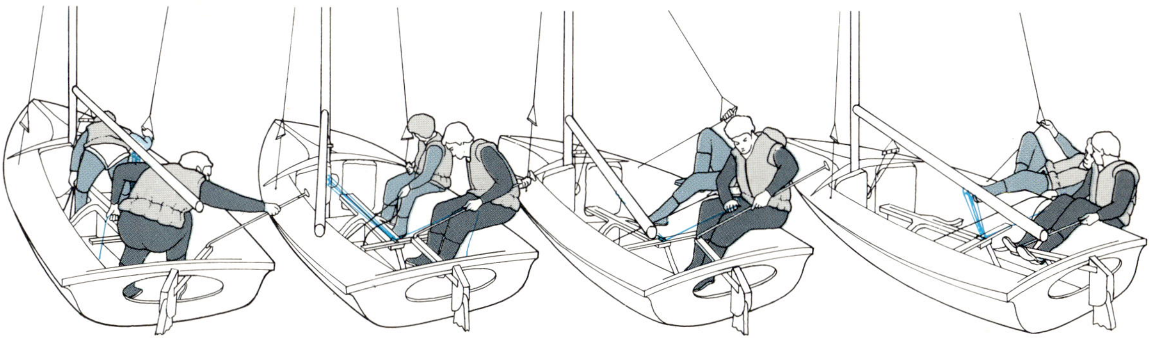

4 *Die Crew taucht unter dem übergehenden Baum durch. Der Steuermann klappt den Pinnenausleger zur anderen rum. Der Vorschoter wirft die Fockschot los.*

5 *Das Boot ist über Stag gegangen. Die Mannschaft hat die Seite gewechselt, der Steuermann Schot- und Pinnenhand. Der Vorschoter holt die Fockschot und hakt seinen Trapezgurt ein.*

6 *Der Steuermann holt die Großschot für den neuen Am-Wind-Kurs dicht und angelt sich die Fußgurte. Der Vorschoter greift sich den Trapezgriff und beginnt, ins Trapez zu steigen.*

7 *Das Boot liegt auf Kurs. Steuermann und Vorschoter reiten aus. Die Schoten sind in ihren Klemmen arretiert (sofern sie nicht aus der Hand gefahren werden).*

3 *Der Bug ist durch den Wind. Der Steuermann holt hinter dem Rücken die Pinne wieder mittschiffs.*

4 *Der Steuermann setzt sich auf die neue Luvseite und wechselt Schot- und Pinnenhand.*

5 *Der Steuerman trimmt das Segel auf dem neuen Bug und reitet gegebenenfalls aus.*

Halsen

Halsen ist der Wechsel der Windseite vor dem Wind, also das Mit-dem-Heck-durch-den-Wind-drehen. Dieses Manöver erfordert schon etwas Übung. Auf einer Jolle sollte man sich zunächst nur bei leichtem Wind daran versuchen. Aber selbst für eine geübte Crew kann das Halsen bei viel Wind gefährlich werden. Die meisten Kenterungen passieren beim Halsen.

Zunächst muß soweit abgefallen werden, bis das Boot genau vor dem Wind segelt. Der Steuermann fiert die Großschot entsprechend auf. Dann holt er die Schot schnell, aber gleichmäßig dicht, bis der Großbaum mittschiffs steht. Nun wird das Ruder langsam und leicht so weit gelegt, daß der Großbaum von selbst übergeht. Man nennt dieses Herumschwenken des Baumes von der einen auf die andere Seite schiften. Jetzt wird die Großschot blitzschnell Hand über Hand gefiert, damit es nicht zu einem harten Einrucksen des Großbaums in die noch dichtgeholte Schot kommt. Sie muß sofort nachgeben können, wenn Kraft darauf kommt. Das Boot muß unbedingt so lange vor dem Wind gehalten werden, bis die Großschot auf der neuen Leeseite bis in die Vorm-Wind-Stellung aufgefiert worden ist. Erst danach kann wieder angeluvt, die Großschot entsprechend angeholt und auf den gewünschten Kurs gegangen werden.

Achtung: Der Steuermann muß darauf gefaßt sein, daß in dem Moment, da das Großsegel übergeht, das Boot schlagartig eine scharfe Drehtendenz zur neuen Luvseite hin erhält. Wenn er in diesem Augenblick nicht Gegenruder – auch Stützruder genannt – gibt, sondern das Boot anluven läßt, gerät es gleich darauf mit der noch angeholten Großschot quer zum Wind. Die nach außen gerichtete Zentrifugalkraft kommt hinzu, und das Boot kann kentern. Das Fieren der Großschot nützt dann kaum noch etwas, weil das Boot bereits so stark gekrängt ist, daß das Baumende ins Wasser taucht und der Baum dadurch wieder nach hinten gedrückt wird. Die meisten Kenterungen beim Halsen werden durch diesen Fehler verursacht.

Die richtige Dosierung des Stützruders verlangt Erfahrung und etwas Fingerspitzengefühl vom Steuermann. Wird nämlich zu stark Gegen- oder Stützruder gelegt, schlägt der Baum wieder auf die alte Seite zurück. Das kann ebenfalls zu einer Kenterung führen und sogar zu Bruch in der Takelage. Da das Halsen schneller und vehementer vonstatten geht als das Wenden, muß auch die Besatzung entsprechend schneller reagieren. Wenn er nicht schon vorher dort hockte, setzt sich der Vorschoter bei dem Vorbereitungskommando „Klar zum Halsen!" auf den Schwertkasten. Der Steuermann wechselt auf die neue Luvseite, wenn der Baum überkommt. Beim Halsen muß die Crew ganz besonders auf den übergehenden Baum achten, damit sie ihn nicht an den Kopf bekommt. Da das Boot vor dem Wind liegt, kann die Fock bereits vorher auf die künftige Leeseite rübergenommen werden. Sonst geschieht es, während der Großbaum überkommt.

Hier noch einmal die Fehler zusammengefaßt, die einem Anfänger beim Halsen unterlaufen und dazu führen können, daß das Manöver mißglückt: 1. Die Großschot wird zu früh dichtgeholt, nämlich, wenn das Boot noch nicht vor dem Wind liegt. Das Großsegel geht nicht über, und es entsteht eine starke und gefährliche Drehtendenz des Bootes nach Luv. 2. Beim Übergehen des Baumes wird kein Stütz- oder Gegenruder gelegt. Das kann, bei einer stärkeren Brise, zu einer Kenterung führen. 3. Es wird zu hart und lange Stützruder gelegt. Das Boot fällt auf den alten Bug zurück. Der Großbaum schlägt mit Wucht ebenfalls zurück.

Noch ein weiterer Punkt ist beim Halsen mit einer Jolle zu beachten: Das Schwert sollte niemals vollständig gefiert sein, sondern mindestens zur Hälfte aufgeholt werden. Das gefierte Schwert bildet sozusagen einen Stolperfuß, über den eine Jolle beim Halsen kentern kann.

Die hier beschriebene sogenannte Blockhalse muß jeder Anfänger sicher beherrschen, dann kann er an die Regattahalse herangehen (S. 58).

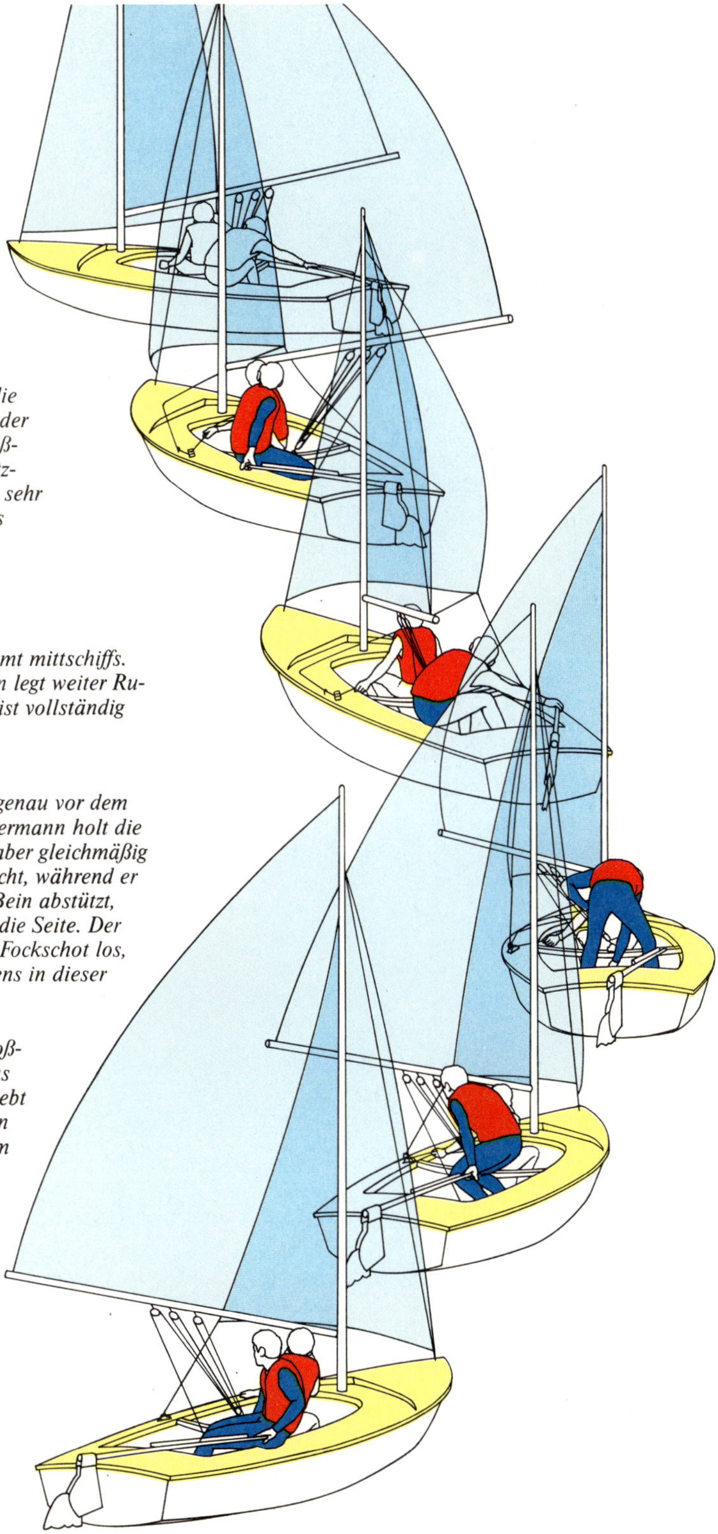

6 Ist das Boot wieder ins Gleichgewicht gekommen, luvt der Steuermann auf einen Raumschots-Kurs an. Groß- und Fockschot werden entsprechend angeholt, das Boot läuft (in diesem Fall) auf Steuerbord-Bug ab. Das Halsen ist beendet. Der Vorschoter hat während des gesamten Manöverablaufs seinen Platz auf dem Schwertkasten nicht verlassen.

5 Sobald der Großbaum auf die andere Seite übergeht, muß der Steuermann blitzschnell die Großschot fieren und gleichzeitig Stütz- oder Gegenruder legen, um dem sehr starken Drehmoment des Bootes nach Luv entgegenzuwirken.

4 Der Baum kommt mittschiffs. Der Steuermann legt weiter Ruder. Die Großschot ist vollständig dichtgeholt.

3 Das Boot liegt genau vor dem Wind. Der Steuermann holt die Großschot schnell, aber gleichmäßig Hand über Hand dicht, während er die Pinne mit dem Bein abstützt, und wechselt dabei die Seite. Der Vorschoter wirft die Fockschot los, die Fock geht meistens in dieser Phase bereits über.

2 Der Steuermann fiert die Großschot vollständig und legt das Boot direkt vor den Wind. Er erhebt sich und klemmt sich die Pinne in die Kniekehle, um die Hände zum Dichtholen der Großschot freizuhaben.

1 Boot läuft (hier auf der Zeichnung) auf Backbord-Bug auf einem Raumschots-Kurs an. Der Steuermann gibt das Vorbereitungskommando „Klar zum Halsen!" Der Vorschoter meldet: „Ist klar!" Der Steuermann legt Lee-Ruder (Pinne nach Luv), um auf einen Vorm-Wind-Kurs abzufallen. Er sitzt in Luv, der Vorschoter mittschiffs auf dem Schwertkasten.

Schiften

Schiften bedeutet – auf einem Kurs vor dem Wind – das Übernehmen der Segel von einer Seite auf die andere. Beispielsweise beim Halsen. Es ist sogar die entscheidende Phase bei dem ganzen Halsemanöver. Deshalb sollte das Schiften - zunächst bei leichten Winden - so lange geübt werden, bis man es souverän beherrscht. Geschiftet wird aber nicht nur beim Halsen. Es kann auch aus einem anderen Grund auf einem Vorm-Wind-Kurs notwendig werden. Beispielsweise bei einer leichten Winddrehung. Oder aus Gründen des besseren Trimms, denn nicht jedes Boot liegt auf jedem Bug gleich gut auf dem Ruder. Beim Regattasegeln muß man manchmal schiften, um eine Bahnmarke auf der richtigen Seite runden zu können, oder aber, um sich Wegerecht zu verschaffen. Beim Schiften werden Steuerbord-Bug und Backbord-Bug gewechselt. Backbord-Bug aber hat Wegerecht vor Steuerbord-Bug (s. Seite 106).

Die Regattahalse

An der Regattahalse sollten sich Anfänger nur bei leichtem Wind versuchen. Sie ist etwas für erfahrene Jollensegler. Sie unterscheidet sich vom üblichen Halsen (der sogenannten Blockhalse) insofern, als die Großschot beim Schiften nicht dichtgeholt wird. Der Steuermann greift oben um die Schot und nimmt das Segel von Hand, mit etwas Schwung, auf die andere Seite rüber.

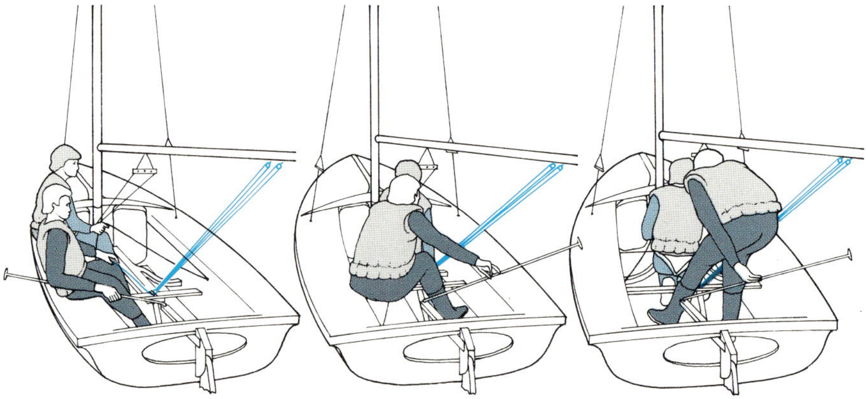

1 *Der Steuermann gibt das Ankündigungskommando: „Klar zum Halsen!" und arretiert die Großschot.*

2 *Die Crew verlagert ihr Gewicht zur Bootsmitte hin. Der Steuermann klappt den Pinnenausleger zur künftigen Luvseite herum.*

3 *Der Steuermann legt leicht Ruder, wechselt hinter dem Rücken die Pinnenhand und umfaßt die Großschot. Der Vorschoter sitzt auf dem Schwertkasten und legt die neue Lee-Schot klar.*

Halsen mit der Einmann-Jolle

Das Prinzip ist natürlich das gleiche wie auf einer Zweimann-Jolle, nur muß der Steuermann das Boot alleine ausbalancieren. Das Boot muß vor dem Schiften aufrecht oder sogar etwas nach Luv gekrängt segeln. (Auf der nebenstehenden Bildserie wird mit lose hängender Schot gehalst. Das ist bedenklich und nur bei leichtem Wind möglich.)

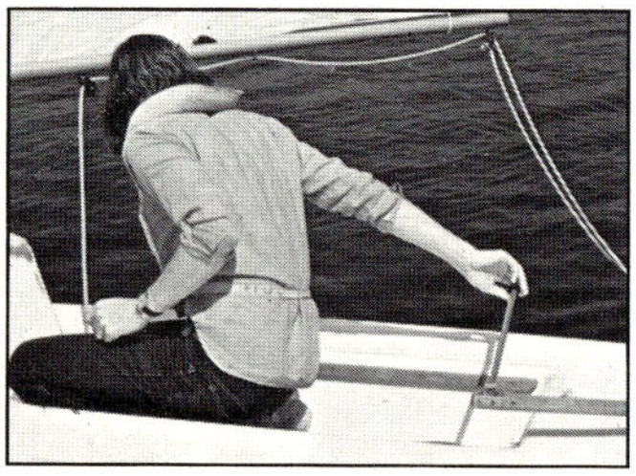

1 *Das Boot wird genau vor den Wind gebracht, der Steuermann sitzt mittschiffs.*

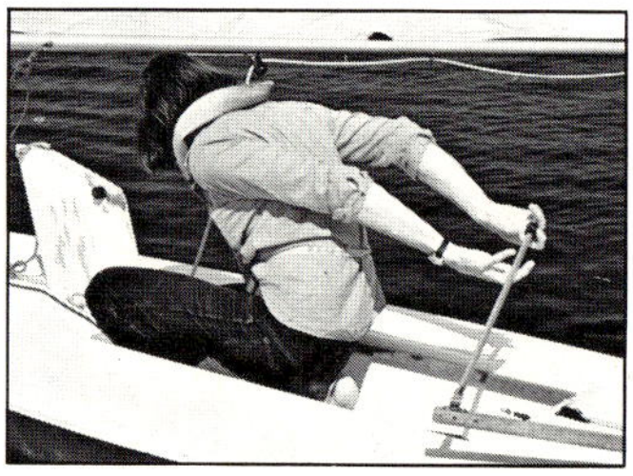

2 *Der Steuermann wechselt die Pinnenhand . . .*

Einmann-Rennjollen, wie das olympische Finn-Dinghy hier im Bild, sind schwieriger zu halsen als übliche Jollen und erfordern viel seglerische Erfahrung.

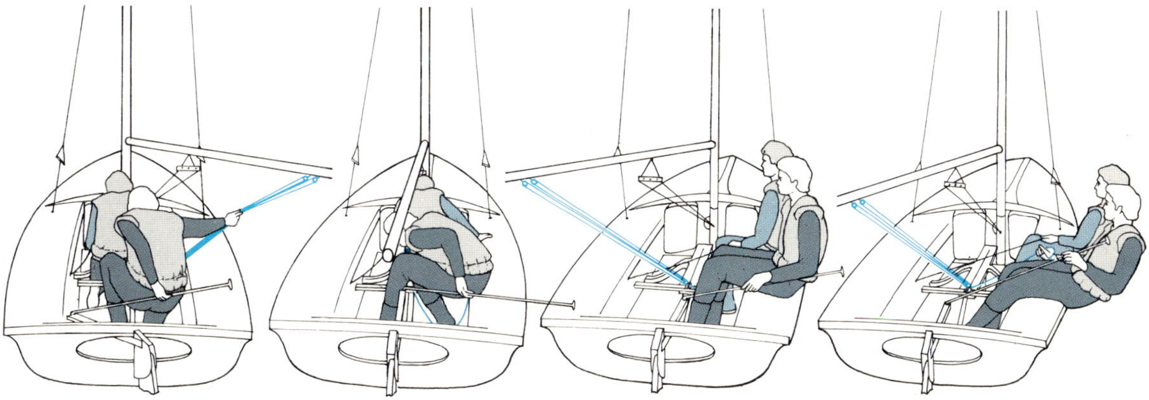

4 *Der Steuermann legt weiter Ruder und holt den Großbaum an der Großschot mittschiffs.*

5 *Die Crew taucht unter dem übergehenden Baum durch, der Steuermann gibt ihn von Hand an der Schot zur anderen Seite hinüber. Dann legt er Gegenruder.*

6 *Die Crew hat die Seite gewechselt. Das Ruder liegt wieder mittschiffs. Der Steuermann nimmt die Großschot aus der Klemme, der Vorschoter trimmt die Fockschot.*

7 *Das Halsen ist beendet. Der Steuermann hat wieder auf einen Raumschots-Kurs angeluvt.*

3 *. . . und legt Ruder, während er sein Gewicht gleichzeitig nach Luv verlagert.*

4 *Der Baum geht über, der Steuermann gibt Stützruder und wechselt auf die neue Luvseite.*

5 *Das Halsen ist beendet. Die Schot wurde nicht bedient (kann bei stärkerem Wind zur Kenterung führen).*

Richtig segeln auf allen Kursen

Als Manöver bezeichnet man im Segelsport alle Tätigkeiten, die irgendwelche Veränderungen in der Bootsführung bewirken. So auch das Wenden, Halsen oder Aufschießen. Nachdem diese Basismanöver hinlänglich geübt worden sind und sitzen, kann man sich auf die richtige Segeltechnik auf den verschiedenen Kursen zum Wind konzentrieren. Dazu zählt die richtige Ruderführung, die richtige Stellung der Segel und der für den jeweiligen Kurs richtige Trimm des Bootes durch die Besatzung. Die größte Aufmerksamkeit erfordern die Kurse hoch am Wind und direkt vorm Wind. Am Wind wird leicht übersteuert, und das Boot macht keine Fahrt mehr. Vorm Wind besteht immer die Gefahr einer sogenannten Patenthalse, bei der der Baum unbeabsichtigt zur anderen Seite rüberschlägt. Die Kurse voll und bei bis raumschots sind verhältnismäßig problemlos.

Segeln am Wind

Der Am-Wind-Kurs erfordert ein hohes Maß an seglerischem Fingerspitzengefühl. Die richtige Segelstellung muß ausprobiert werden. Man holt den Großbaum so weit dicht, daß sein Ende etwa über Ecke Heck steht. Jetzt kneift man sich vorsichtig so hoch an den Wind heran, bis das Vorliek des Großsegels zu killen beginnt – in diesem Fall leicht nach Luv beutelt. Dann fällt man gerade so weit ab, daß diese Erscheinung wieder verschwindet. Nun gilt es, den Stand von Vor- und Großsegel miteinander in Einklang zu bringen. Das Vorsegel wird so dicht geholt, daß der Abwind das Großsegel im Vorliekbereich nach Luv beutelt. Nun die Vorschot vorsichtig fieren, bis die Falten oder Beutel wieder verschwinden. So sind die Segel für den Am-Wind-Kurs optimal getrimmt. Hat man die ideale Einstellung von Groß- und Vorsegel zueinander gefunden, möglichst nicht mehr so viel mit den Schoten arbeiten, sondern kleine Richtungsänderungen des Windes mit leichten Kurskorrekturen durch das Ruder parieren. Diese Windschwankungen sind auch der Grund, wenn die Segel eben noch einwandfrei standen, plötzlich aber das Vorliek des Vorsegels zu killen beginnt, ohne daß man seinen Kurs geändert hätte. Der Wind hat geschralt. Das heißt, er fällt mehr von vorne ein. Man muß sofort entschlossen abfallen, bis die Segel erneut voll stehen. Kaum bemerkt wird jedoch von einem nicht so erfahrenen Steuermann, wenn er zu weit abfällt. Das Boot läuft dann auch nicht mehr richtig, weil jetzt die Segel zu dicht stehen. Sie werden nicht mehr optimal vom Wind angeströmt. Es kommt sogar zu einer fahrthemmenden Verwirbelung der Luftströmung am Segel. Eine gute Orientierungshilfe ist, wie immer, der Verklicker im Masttopp. Er muß stets parallel zum Kopfbrett des Großsegels stehen.

Die Jolle segelt auf einem Am-Wind-Kurs und wird von ihrer Mannschaft auf der hohen Kante ausgeritten.

Am Wind ist die seitliche Abdrift am größten. Deshalb muß das Schwert vollständig abgesenkt (gefiert) sein. Wie bereits auf Seite 37 dargestellt, rutscht das Boot zur Seite weg, wenn das Schwert aufgeholt wird, aber die Krängung nimmt ab. Man kann eventuell also, um die Krängung zu verringern, das Schwert etwas aufholen, muß dann dafür aber eine geringere Fahrt in Vorausrichtung und eine höhere Abdrift in Kauf nehmen. Jede Jolle muß von ihrer Mannschaft ausgeritten werden. Bei kräftiger Brise, indem sie sich weit hinaushängt oder der Vorschoter ins Trapez steigt. Die richtige Sitzposition der Crew hängt von den Windverhältnissen ab. Bei leichtem Wind konzentriert sie ihr Gewicht zur Bootsmitte hin, bei kräftigerem Wind ungefähr am Ende des zweiten Drittels der Bootslänge.

Segeln mit raumem Wind und vorm Wind

Auch auf dem Halb-Wind-Kurs weht raumer Wind, denn das Boot läuft einen Kurs in einem Winkel von etwa 120° zum wahren Wind. Groß- und Vorsegel werden so weit gefiert, daß das Vorliek gerade noch nicht killt. Es ist dies der Kurs, auf dem alle Segelboote ihre Höchstgeschwindigkeit erreichen.
Raumschots-Kurs bedeutet, noch weiter über den Halb-Wind-Kurs hinaus abzufallen. Meist beginnt das Boot hier schon wieder langsamer zu werden. Auf diesen Kursen steigt der Baum, und das Großsegel verwindet sich. Ein verwundenes Segel aber büßt erheblich an Wirksamkeit ein. Deshalb muß spätestens jetzt der Baumniederholer steif durchgesetzt werden. Schralen und Raumen des Windes wird auf diesen Kursen nicht mehr mit dem Ruder ausgeglichen, weil man seinen anliegenden Kurs unbeirrt durchhalten kann, sondern mit den Schoten. Der Verklicker ist eine verläßliche Orientierungshilfe für die Stellung des Großsegels. Je raumer der Wind kommt, um so geringer wird die Abdrift. Entsprechend kann das Schwert aufgeholt werden, gut bis zur Hälfte. In Böen wird eine Jolle auch auf diesen Kursen noch von der Mannschaft auf der hohen Kante ausgeritten werden müssen. Bei leichten Winden bringt der Vorschoter sein Gewicht mehr zur Bootsmitte hin. Eventuell auf den Schwertkasten.
Beim Vorm-Wind-Segeln kommt der Wind genau von hinten. Das Großsegel ist vollständig aufgefiert. Da das Vorsegel jetzt vom Großsegel abgedeckt wird, fällt es ein. Es kann vom Vorschoter zum Schmetterlingssegeln auf die andere Seite, nach Luv, genommen und dort eventuell mit dem Bootshaken oder Paddel ausgebaumt werden. Vom Steuermann verlangt dieser Kurs angespannte Aufmerksamkeit, denn allzu leicht kann ihm das Boot aus dem Ruder laufen und mit einer Patenthalse das Großsegel auf die andere Seite herumschlagen. Das kann zu einer Kenterung führen. Außerdem ist die Gefahr für die Mannschaft groß, den Baum beim Übergehen gegen den Kopf geschlagen zu bekommen. Ein noch unsicherer Steuermann sollte deshalb bei mehr Wind lieber einen etwas raumeren Kurs steuern, auf dem nicht ständig die Gefahr einer Patenthalse droht. Krängung braucht auf diesem Kurs kaum noch ausgeglichen zu werden. Deshalb verteilt sich die Mannschaft zum Ausbalancieren auf die beiden Bootsseiten. Der Steuermann am besten in Luv, von wo er das Großsegel besser beobachten kann, der Vorschoter vorne in Lee, sicherheitshalber mit einer Hand am Großbaum.

Einen Kurs absegeln und kreuzen

Um in der Bootsführung sicherer, im Umgang mit Schot und Pinne noch vertrauter zu werden, sollte man sich als nächstes vornehmen, konsequent einen bestimmten Kurs abzusegeln, der um einige Wendemarken - Bojen, vor Anker liegende Boote oder ähnliches - herumführt. Dabei kann man vorzüglich das Wenden und Halsen und alle Kurse zum Wind üben. Man sollte sich unbedingt auch ein Ziel wählen, das genau dort liegt, wo der Wind her weht. Gegen den Wind ansegeln kann man bekanntlich nicht. Man muß also eine andere Taktik anwenden und gegen den Wind aufkreuzen: Man nähert sich, abwechselnd über Steuerbord-Bug und Backbord-Bug segelnd, im Zick-Zack-Kurs seinem Ziel. Den jeweils auf einem Bug zurückgelegten Weg bezeichnet man als Schlag. Im allgemeinen gilt fürs Kreuzen, die einzelnen Schläge möglichst hoch am Wind zu segeln und so wenig Weg wie möglich nach Lee - vom Ziel weg - zu verschenken. Doch ist das nicht unbedingt immer die schnellste Art und Weise, um ans Ziel zu kommen. Nicht selten erreicht man es auf einem etwas raumeren Kurs schneller, obwohl das Boot einen längeren Weg zurückzulegen hat, weil auf diesem raumeren Kurs die Geschwindigkeit größer und die seitliche Abdrift geringer ist. Man spricht in diesem Fall von der optimalen Höhe, die ein Boot läuft. Auf den einzelnen Schlägen wird dann gewendet, wenn man das Ziel querab hat. Nur vor dem letzten Schlag direkt auf das Ziel zu, sollte man es achterlich als querab haben. Sonst wird man es unter Umständen noch nicht anliegen können, weil das Boot beim Wenden etwas zurückgefallen ist oder aber weil Abdrift durch Strömung oder Wind stärker waren als man geglaubt hatte.

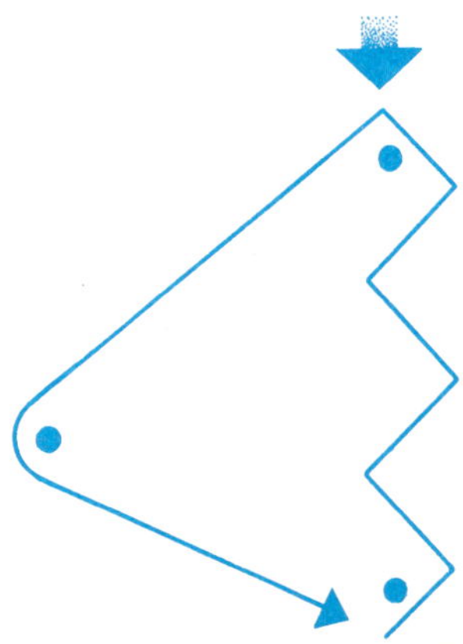

Ein Dreieckskurs um nicht zu weit auseinanderliegende Bojen ist vorzüglich geeignet, sich in der praktischen Bootsführung zu vervollkommnen und auch das Kreuzen zu üben.

Der Leeweg

Obwohl es Aufgabe des Schwertes ist, der seitlichen Abdrift entgegenzuwirken, läßt sich ein gewisser Grad von Abdrift nicht vermeiden. Sie trifft besonders stark auf Am-Wind-Kursen auf. Der Winkel zwischen dem gesteuerten und dem wirklich gesegelten Kurs wird als Leeweg bezeichnet. Er führt in Lee an einem angesteuerten Ziel vorbei. Deshalb muß man auf Am-Wind-Kursen stets in Luv von seinem Ziel halten. Wie groß der Vorhaltewinkel, der gleichbedeutend mit dem Leeweg ist, sein muß, das lehrt allein die Erfahrung. Er ist unabhängig von der Höhe am Wind, die das Boot läuft, von der Windstärke und auch vom Bootstyp. Lediglich auf einem Kurs vor achterlichem oder nahezu achterlichem Wind kann der Leeweg vergessen werden.

Scheinbarer Wind

Wenn vom Wind gesprochen wird, muß unterschieden werden zwischen wahrem und scheinbarem Wind (s. auch Seite 38). Richtung und Stärke des wahren Windes kann man nur an einem festen Punkt feststellen. Sobald ein Boot Fahrt aufnimmt, werden Richtung und Stärke durch den Fahrtwind beeinflußt. Der wahre Wind wandelt sich zum scheinbaren Wind. Nur dieser ist an Bord spürbar und maßgeblich für die Kurse. Der scheinbare Wind fällt stets vorlicher ein als der wahre Wind. Die Zeichnungen veranschaulichen, wie man Richtung und Stärke des scheinbaren Windes ermitteln kann.

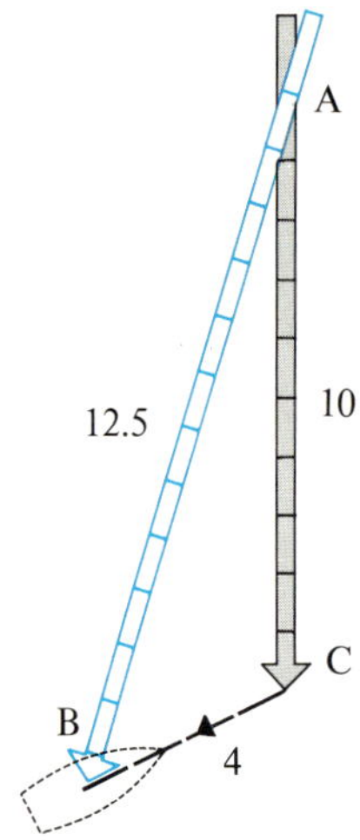

Die Verbindung der Punkte A-C gibt Richtung und Geschwindigkeit des wahren Windes an. Auf einem Am-Wind-Kurs (oben rechts) ist der wahre Wind schwächer als der scheinbare. Auf einem Raumschots-Kurs (rechts unten) ist der wahre Wind stärker als der scheinbare Wind.

Wahrer Wind

Scheinbarer Wind

Fahrtwind (abhängig von der Bootsgeschwindigkeit)

Geschwindigkeit in Knoten

0 1 2 3 4 5

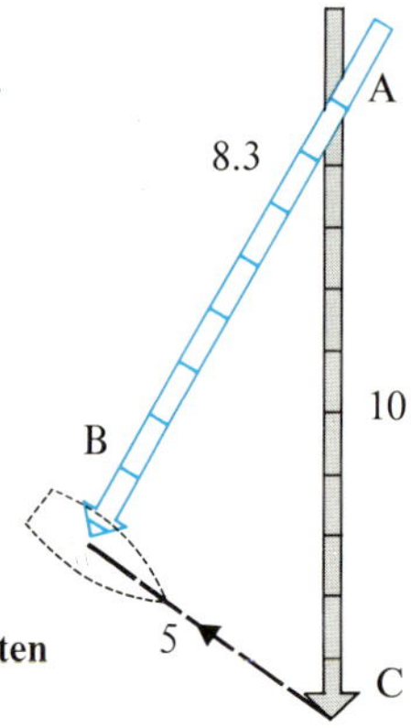

Winddrehungen

Der Wind wechselt häufig Richtung und Stärke. Nur wer die kleinste Veränderung bemerkt und die entsprechenden Korrekturen vornimmt, holt das Beste aus seinem Boot heraus. Ein gutes Training ist, am Wind ein Ziel anzusteuern, das schon fast im unerreichbaren Sektor liegt. Jede kleinste Winddrehung wirkt sich dann zum Vorteil oder Nachteil aus, je nachdem ob der Wind schralt oder raumt. Ein „Schraler" ist ein Wind, der mehr von vorn kommt und zum Abfallen zwingt, Beim „Raumer", der seitlich einfällt, kann man anluven. Schralt der Wind, bedeutet das also, daß man weiter abfallen muß und womöglich noch einen Kreuzschlag zu segeln hat.
Raumt der Wind, kann ein zuvor vielleicht nicht erreichbares Ziel direkt angelaufen werden.

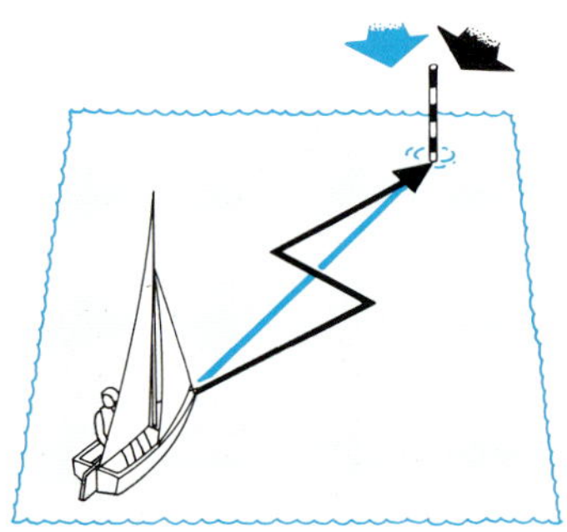

Schraler
Bei einem Schraler auf einem Am-Wind-Kurs kann das Boot sein Ziel nur mit einem Kreuzschlag erreichen.

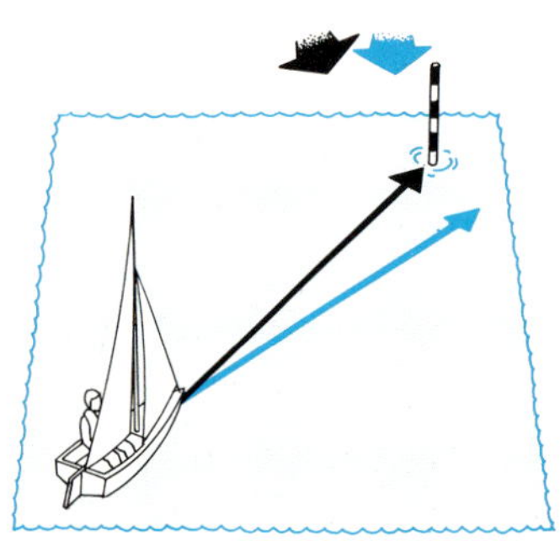

Raumer
Mit einem Raumer hat das Boot keine Probleme, das Ziel auf direktem Kurs zu erreichen, selbst wenn es vorher nicht erreichbar war.

Wenden und Halsen ohne Ruder - Rückwärtssegeln

Typisch für Anfänger ist, daß sie viel zu hart Ruder legen. Beim Wenden kann das Boot dadurch so stark abgebremst werden, daß es gar nicht mehr durch den Wind geht. Deshalb sollte man sich stets vergegenwärtigen, daß Kursänderungen auch durch Trimm-Maßnahmen erreicht werden können, wie bereits auf Seite 50 beschrieben. Noch einmal kurz zusammengefaßt: Zum Abfallen zuerst das Großsegel fieren und das Boot leicht nach Luv krängen, dann erst Ruder legen. Die Fockschot bleibt zunächst angeholt. Der Druck aufs Vorsegel erleichtert das Abfallen. Zum Anluven erst das Großsegel dichter nehmen, das Boot nach Lee krängen und die Fockschot etwas fieren. Die Wirkung dieser Trimmveränderungen an Boot und Segel läßt sich am besten erproben, wenn man einfach mal das Ruder aushängt. Der Schwert bleibt halb gefiert, damit man sich ganz auf den Gewichts- und Segeltrimm konzentrieren kann. Eine halbe Stunde wenden und halsen um zwei Bojen, ohne Ruderhilfe, bringt mehr Erkenntnisse über den wirkungsvollen Einsatz von Trimm-Maßnahmen, als wochenlanges normales Segeln. Selbst wenn man zunächst nur Schnörkel zu segeln schafft.

Man muß auch üben, unter Vor- und unter Großsegel allein zu segeln und zu manövrieren. Man braucht das gelegentlich, um beispielsweise an einem Steg oder einer Mooring anzulegen. Manchmal ist es sogar notwendig, rückwärts zu segeln. Zunächst schießt man in den Wind, dann drückt der Vorschoter den Baum des Großsegels bis an die Wanten heraus. Der Wind fällt nun von vorne ein und schiebt das Boot achteraus. Das Ruderblatt in die Richtung legen, in die das Boot rückwärts segeln soll.

Bei sehr leichtem Wind kann es sinnvoll sein, das Boot etwas nach Lee zu krängen, damit die Segel besser stehen. Auch sollte dann die Crew möglichst tief im Boot sitzen, um wenig Luftwiderstand zu erzeugen. Bei leichtem Wind sitzt sie weiter vorne, nimmt der Wind zu, etwa auf Mitte Cockpit. Auf Raumschots-Kursen, wenn das Boot gleitet, rutscht sie ziemlich weit nach hinten. Will man wissen, ob sein Boot in der Längsschiffsachse richtig getrimmt ist, genügt ein Blick ins Heckwasser: Ist es stark verwirbelt, muß das Gewicht weiter nach vorne.

Rückwärtssegeln

1 Das Boot liegt im Wind, der Vorschoter drückt den Baum nach vorn - das Großsegel wird backgehalten –, das Boot nimmt Fahrt achteraus auf.

2 Das Ruder auf Achterausfahrt legen - das Ruderblatt in die Richtung, in die das Boot drehen soll. Crewgewicht nach vorne.

Unten: Segeln ohne Ruder. Mit etwas Übung gelingt sogar das Halsen.

Kentern

In der Regel kentert ein Boot aus zwei Gründen: Entweder ist der Wind zu stark, so daß die Besatzung die Krängung nicht mehr ausgleichen kann, dann kentert das Boot nach Lee. Oder aber die Besatzung macht grundsätzliche Fehler. Das geschieht vielfach auf Raumschots-Kursen, wenn das Boot aus dem Ruder läuft und dann nach Luv kentert. Allerdings sind die meisten Jollen gutartig und lassen manchen Fehler zu, ohne daß es zur Kenterung kommt. Rennboote dagegen sind erheblich sensibler, weil sie meistens extrem leicht sind und mehr Segelfläche tragen.
Die Gefahr des Kenterns besteht bei allen Schwertbooten, und daher ist wichtig zu wissen, wie man sich bei einer Kenterung verhält und wie man ein Boot wieder aufrichtet. Das zu üben, sollte zur Grundausbildung jedes Jollenseglers gehören. Am besten fängt man damit an, das Boot bei ruhigem Wetter selbst zu kentern und dann zu lernen, wie man es am besten wieder auf die Beine stellt. Dabei gewinnt man nicht nur Erfahrung, sondern auch Selbstsicherheit.
Da alle Jollen zusätzlich Auftrieb haben, besteht keine Gefahr, daß sie sinken. Man sollte nicht vergessen, die Auftriebskörper von Zeit zu Zeit zu überprüfen. Wichtig ist das richtige Auftriebsvolumen, denn zu viel des Guten führt dazu, daß das hoch aufschwemmende Boot zu schnell abgetrieben wird, oder daß man nicht auf das Schwert steigen kann. Die Methode des Aufrichtens hängt von den jeweiligen Umständen (Kenterung nach Luv oder Lee) und vom Bootstyp ab.
Was auch immer zu einer Kenterung geführt hat, auf jeden Fall muß die Besatzung beim Boot bleiben, weil sie mit dem Boot zusammen leichter gefunden wird und am Boot einigermaßen sicher ist. Lebensgefährlich ist es, zu versuchen, an Land zu schwimmen, weil die Entfernungen immer unterschätzt und die eigenen Kräfte überschätzt werden, auch von guten Schwimmern.

Die „Hineinschaufel"-Methode

Nach dieser Methode wird der Vorschoter beim Aufrichten sozusagen ins Boot geschaufelt. Dazu steigt der Steuermann aufs Schwert und richtet das Boot durch sein Gewicht und Zug an der Fockschot auf. Der Vorschoter hängt sich an die Ausreitgurte. Da er beim Aufrichten gleich mit ins Boot kommt, kann er das Boot, dessen Cockpit voll Wasser ist, austrimmen und verhin-

1 *Der Vorschoter prüft, ob das Schwert voll ausgefahren ist. Dann löst er die Großschot, falls sie in einer Klemme festsaß. Der Steuermann schwimmt zum Heck und kontrolliert, ob das Ruder noch in seinem Beschlag sitzt.*

4 *Der Vorschoter hält sich an den Ausreitgurten, beziehungsweise am Schwertkasten fest, während der Steuermann auf das Schwert klettert und sich an der Fockschot hochzieht.*

dern, daß es gleich wieder kentert. Und er kann auch dem Steuermann behilflich sein, ins Boot zu kommen. Natürlich müssen Steuermann und Vorschoter ihre Aktionen genau koordinieren. Der Vorschoter darf sich beispielsweise nicht ins Cockpit hängen, bevor der Steuermann auf dem Schwert steht, sonst würde er mit seinem Gewicht das Boot kieloben drehen (durchkentern). (Dies ist eine spezielle, vom englischen Autor Anfängern gelehrte Methode. Sie funktioniert nur bei leichteren Winden - die Bildserie zeigt Flaute - und nicht mit allen Jollen und darüber hinaus nur dann, wenn der ins Cockpit zu Schaufelnde nicht gerade ein Schwergewicht ist. Die übliche Methode finden Sie auf der nächsten Seite beschrieben. – Bearbeiter)

2 *Der Vorschoter hält das Heck fest, während der Steuermann die Großschot über das Heck nimmt und mit ihr, als Sicherheitsleine, in der Hand zum Schwert herumschwimmt.*

3 *Während der Steuermann das Schwert erreicht, ist der Vorschoter zum Cockpit geschwommen, hat dort die Luv-Fockschot klariert und wirft sie, über das Seitendeck, dem Steuermann zu.*

5 *Der Steuermann steht auf dem Schwert, und nachdem er sich überzeugt hat, daß der Vorschoter klar ist, hängt er sich voll in die Fockschot und beginnt, das Boot aufzurichten.*

6 *Der Vorschoter liegt bereits mit dem Oberkörper im Cockpit, der Steuermann klettert schließlich über das Seitendeck ins Boot. Die Besatzung macht sich klar, das Boot sofort lenzzusegeln.*

Kentern nach Luv

Kentert eine Jolle nach Luv, zeigt der auf der Wasseroberfläche liegende Masttopp in Windrichtung. Beginnt nun die Besatzung mit dem Aufrichten, kann passieren, daß der Wind unter das Segel faßt und das Boot plötzlich hochschnellt und der Mannschaft auf den Kopf kippt. Oder aber, daß es gleich zur nächsten Seite kentert. Deshalb muß vor dem Aufrichten der Bug in den Wind gedreht werden. Dann stellt oder stemmt sich die Crew aufs Schwert und drückt – eventuell durch Wippen – das Boot hoch. Dies ist auch die übliche Methode bei einer Kenterung nach Lee. Sobald sich die Jolle in der Horizontalen befindet, ziehen sich Steuermann und Vorschoter von je einer Seite – dadurch das Boot stabilisierend – zugleich ins Cockpit. Das ist, besonders mit vollgesogener Kleidung nicht immer ganz leicht. Meistens wird man jedoch einen Fußgurt oder den Traveller erreichen und sich dann von einer kräftigen Beinschere unterstützt, ins Cockpit halb ziehen und halb wälzen können.

Das Boot ist gerade im Begriff nach Luv zu kentern, eine versierte Crew hätte es davor bewahren können.

Aufrichten eines durchgekenterten Bootes

Reagiert die Besatzung nicht schnell genug, kann eine Jolle leicht durchkentern. Befindet man sich unter dem Boot – keine Panik. Man greift nach Scheuerleiste oder Spiegel und taucht unter durch. Echt schwierig wird das Aufrichten dann, wenn das Schwert in den Schwertkasten zurückgerutscht ist. Man fischt sich ein Schotende, holt es über den Bootsboden, stemmt sich auf der gegenüberliegenden Seite mit den Fußspitzen gegen die Scheuerleiste und zieht kräftig. Befindet sich das Boot erst in der 90°-Lage, schwimmt einer zum Mast und drückt ihn hoch. In diesem Fall muß der Masttopp in Windrichtung zeigen, damit der Wind unter das Segel fassen und das Aufrichten unterstützen kann. Dabei ein Schotende fest in der Hand behalten, damit das Boot nicht allein davonsegelt, nachdem es sich aufgerichtet hat. Einfacher geht es, wenn das aus dem Boden herausragende Schwert von der Besatzung als Hebel benutzt werden kann. Das Aufrichten aus der 90°- Lage erfolgt dann, wie oben beschrieben.

1 *Die Mannschaft steht oder kniet auf Scheuerleiste oder Bootsboden und hängt sich mit ganzer Kraft ans Schwert, beziehungsweise die Fockschot.*

2 *Allmählich richtet sich das Boot auf. Der Mann am Schwert kann sich jetzt mit seinem ganzen Körpergewicht ranhängen und hebeln.*

Aufrichten einer Einmann-Jolle

Im Prinzip unterscheidet es sich in nichts vom Aufrichten einer Zweimann-Jolle, außer in einem Punkt: daß man allein ist und allein auch wieder ins Boot muß. Deshalb sollte man versuchen, das Boot erst gar nicht zu verlassen. Kenterungen nach Lee vollziehen sich manchmal nahezu im Zeitlupentempo, so daß man nicht ins Wasser katapultiert wird, sondern auf der Bordwand sitzen oder bäuchlings kleben bleibt. Man braucht sich manchmal nur an die Bordkante zu hängen, um das Boot wieder in die Senkrechte zu hebeln. Oder man rutscht übers Seitendeck aufs Schwert, und kurz bevor das Boot in die Horizontale herumschlägt, zieht man sich übers Seitendeck zurück ins Cockpit. Dabei muß man nur höllisch aufpassen, daß man den herumschwingenden Baum nicht gegen den Kopf bekommt.

1 *Sowie das Segel durchs Wasser schleift, zieht sich der Steuermann an der Scheuerleiste hoch, sein Gewicht so weit wie möglich aufs Seitendeck verlagernd.*

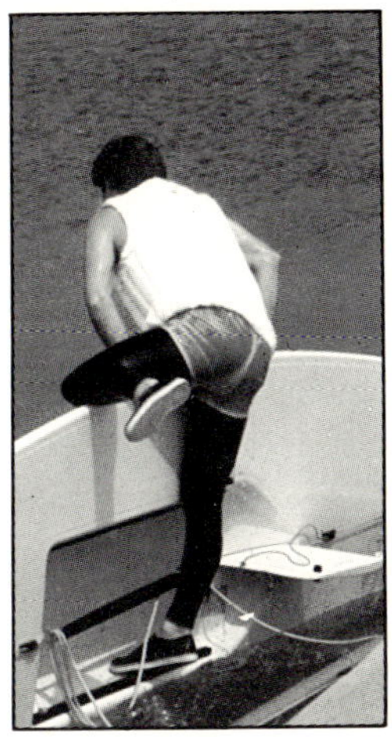

2 *Dann steigt er über aufs Schwert und wippt das Boot wieder in die Horizontale.*

Lenzsegeln

Manche Jollen schaufeln sich beim Aufrichten viel Wasser ins Cockpit, andere dagegen bleiben fast trocken. Hat das Boot Selbstlenzer, segelt man es über die Lenzer auf einem Raumschots-Kurs leer. Dabei muß es möglichst waagerecht gehalten werden. Krängt es, läuft das Wasser über das Lee-Deck ab. Das macht das Boot äußerst instabil, so daß die Gefahr einer erneuten Kenterung besteht. Wer keine Selbstlenzer hat oder wenn so viel Wasser im Cockpit verblieben ist, daß sie es nicht schaffen, muß von Hand Wasser geschöpft – geöst – werden. Dazu wird das Boot beigedreht. Und während es ein Mann durch entsprechende Gewichtsverlagerung gut ausbalanciert – denn es ist in diesem Zustand hochgradig instabil –, schöpft der andere. Wenn er die Pütz wie eine Schaufel benutzt, schafft das sehr schnell das Wasser außenbords.

Mast im Grund

Kentert eine Jolle im flachen Wasser durch, kann es natürlich geschehen, daß sich ihr Mast in den Grund bohrt. In diesem Fall ist es nicht sinnvoll zum Aufrichten auf den Bootsboden zu steigen. Das zusätzliche Gewicht würde den Mast nur tiefer in den Schlick drücken. Meist wird es der Mannschaft nicht gelingen, ihr Boot von Hand aufzurichten. Man muß die Hilfe eines zugkräftigen Motorbootes in Anspruch nehmen. Eine starke Schleppleine wird sicher am Want befestigt, über den Boden hinweg- und am Schwert vorbei- und auf die Heckklampe des Schleppers genommen. Das Motorboot muß langsam im rechten Winkel zur Kiellinie der Jolle anschleppen und wenn möglich in Windrichtung ziehen.

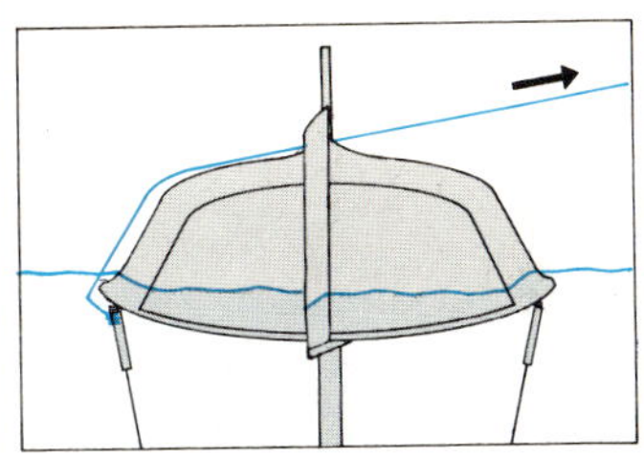

1 *Die Leine über den Bootsboden führen und möglichst am Leewant befestigen, so daß das Segel in Lee hoch kommt.*

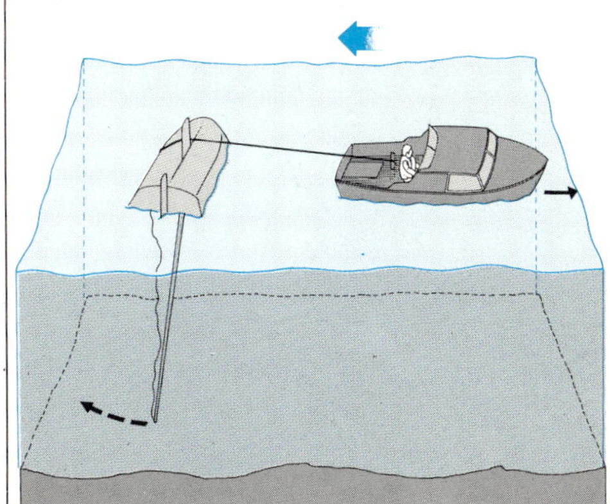

2 *Im rechten Winkel zum gekenterten Boot anschleppen und möglichst auch in Richtung gegen den Wind.*

Mann über Bord

Nicht nur auf einer seegehenden Yacht bedeutet „Mann über Bord" äußerste Lebensgefahr. Auch auf einer Jolle, auf einem geschützten Binnenrevier, kann es gefährlich werden, wenn das Wasser sehr kalt ist oder der über Bord Gefallene, aber auch der im Boot Zurückgebliebene in Panik gerät. Jemand kann leicht „zu Bach" gehen, wenn beispielsweise die Fußgurte reißen. Es ist wichtig, daß nicht nur der Steuermann, sondern auch der Vorschoter genau weiß, was zu tun ist, wenn der andere außenbords geht. Wie er, plötzlich allein, das Boot zu ihm zurück bringt und wie er ihn wieder an Bord kriegt. Das Manöver muß absolut sitzen und kann deshalb nicht oft genug geübt werden. Dabei genügt es nicht, nur mit einer Boje oder irgendeinem Schwimmkörper zu üben. Denn wenn da plötzlich ein Mensch im Wasser schwimmt, sieht alles ganz anders aus und – die größte Schwierigkeit besteht darin, ihn überhaupt wieder ins Boot zu bekommen.

Die sicherste Methode, um zurückzukehren, ist, das Boot sofort auf Halb-Wind-Kurs zu bringen, abzulaufen und eine sogenannte Kuhwende zu fahren. Auch wenn es mit Halsen womöglich schneller geht, sollte man das – besonders als Anfänger – besser lassen, zumal man sehr wahrscheinlich nur noch alleine im Boot sitzt.

Der Fußgurt ist gerissen, der Vorschoter schießt rücklings ins Wasser.

Mann im Wasser

Wer unvorbereitet außenbords geht, zumal wenn das Wasser ziemlich kalt ist, erhält schon einen gehörigen Schock. Dann ist es gut, sich sofort klarzumachen, daß man ja von seiner Rettungsweste getragen wird und nicht befürchten muß, unterzugehen. War die Rettungsweste beim Fall ins Wasser nicht aufgeblasen, sofort die Gaspatrone auslösen. Ist sie nur von Mund aufzublasen, sollte man sie unbedingt zumindest halbaufgeblasen tragen. Es ist nämlich viel schwieriger als man glaubt, eine Rettunsweste im Wasser vollständig aufzublasen, besonders, wenn das Wasser kalt ist und Panik oder Schock den Atem kurz werden lassen. Sobald man dazu in der Lage ist, den Arm über dem Kopf schwenken, damit man von Bord aus besser gesehen wird. Rettungswesten haben eine Trillerpfeife, mit der man sich akustisch bemerkbar machen kann. Wenn das Boot nicht in unmittelbarer Nähe hält, nicht versuchen, hinzuschwimmen. Das bringt nichts in der schweren Segelbekleidung und mit der Rettungsweste. Man vergeudet nur nutzlos seine Kräfte, die man nachher womöglich dringend braucht, um wieder ins Boot zu gelangen.

Der Mann im Wasser schwenkt seinen Arm überm Kopf, damit er von Bord aus besser zu sehen ist.

Zurücksegeln

Wenn auf einer Jolle jemand außenbords geht, wird sie augenblicklich krängen und aus dem Ruder laufen, weil ein Trimmgewicht fehlt. Deshalb muß der an Bord Gebliebene zunächst das Boot wieder ausbalancieren und auf Kurs bringen. Ist es der Vorschoter, läßt er die Fock fliegen und rutscht nach hinten und übernimmt Großschot und Pinne. Sofort auf einen Halb-Wind-Kurs gehen, gleichgültig, ob man auf einem Am-Wind- oder einem Vorm-Wind-Kurs gesegelt ist. Gleichzeitig ein orientierender Blick zurück, wo genau sich der Mann im Wasser befindet. Dann eine Kuhwende fahren und wieder auf Halb-Wind-Kurs gehen und neben dem Schwimmer einen Nahezu-Aufschießer fahren. Zum Nahezu-Aufschießer wird angeluvt, etwa drei Bootslängen bevor man seinen Mann querab hat. Wichtig ist es, das Boot unmittelbar neben ihm zum Stehen zu bringen. (Darüber, ob man den Nahezu-Aufschießer in Luv oder Lee des außenbords Gegangenen fährt, gibt es unterschiedliche Auffassungen. Während Autor Bond den Aufschießer in Lee propagiert, wird auf den meisten deutschen Segelschulen ein Aufschießer in Luv erwartet. Beide Manöver haben Vor- und Nachteile. – Bearbeiter)

Beim Nahezu-Aufschießer neben dem Schwimmer segelt das Boot auf einem Am-Wind-Kurs.

1 *Ist jemand über Bord gefallen, kurz die Lage überdenken und sich das Manöver genau überlegen. Seinen Mann dabei nicht aus dem Auge verlieren.*

2 *Auf Halb-Wind-Kurs abfallen und, sofern man allein ist, die Fockschot loswerfen, um sich auf Ruder und Großschot konzentrieren zu können. (Ein erfahrener Segler schafft auch noch die Fock dazu.)*

3 *Anluven und eine Kuhwende fahren, dabei seinen Mann im Auge behalten.*

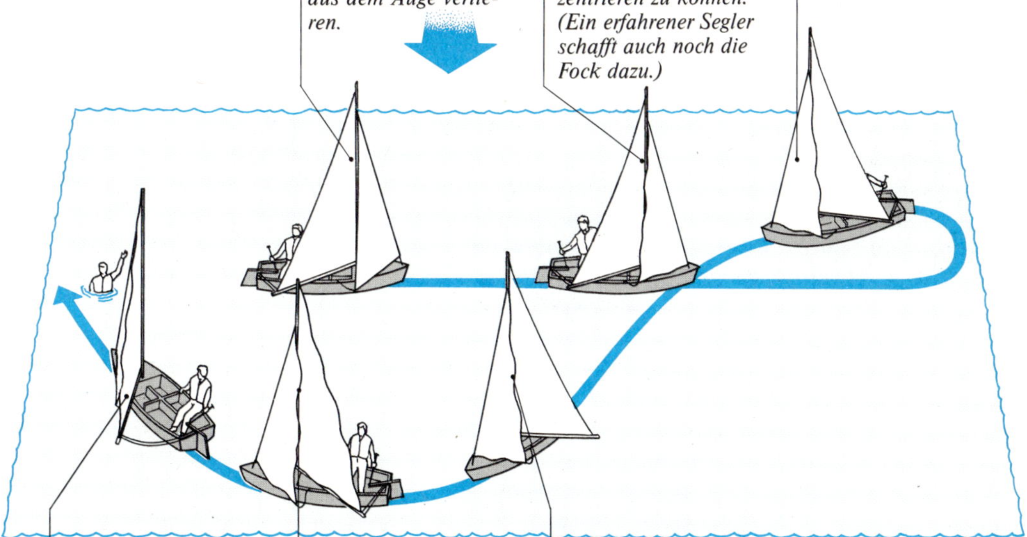

6 *Großschot los und das Boot in Lee des Mannes auslaufen lassen, so daß man ihn etwa in Höhe des Cockpits hat.*

5 *Anluven zum Nahezu-Aufschießer, wenn sich der Mann etwa in Verlängerung des Großbaums befindet.*

4 *Wieder abfallen und auf Halb-Wind-Kurs gehen. Der Mann im Wasser bleibt in Luv.*

Mann an Bord

Sobald man sein Boot in Lee des über Bord Gefallenen zum Stehen gebracht hat, muß man ihn so schnell wie möglich zu fassen bekommen. Ist er in Reichweite, die Pinne kräftig nach Luv drücken und loslassen. Dann rutscht man bis zu den Wanten nach vorne und packt seinen Mann. Er wirkt wie eine Art Treibanker, der das Boot nach Luv herumdreht. Doch das Lee-Ruder wirkt diesem Drehmoment entgegen, so daß sich das Boot nicht mit dem Bug in den Wind legt oder Fahrt aufnimmt. Es liegt beigedreht. Ist der Schwimmer kräftig und in guter Verfassung, wird er sich ohne große Hilfe über das Seitendeck ins Cockpit ziehen können. Aber schwere nasse Kleidung schränkt seine Bewegungsfreiheit doch ziemlich ein. Wenn gar noch Auskühlung oder Schock hinzukommen, wird er es ohne fremde Hilfe nicht schaffen. Gibt es Schwierigkeiten, sollte man ihn zunächst mit einer unter den Armen hindurchgenommenen Leine sichern. Wenn irgend etwas schief läuft, verliert er so wenigstens nicht den Kontakt mit dem Boot. Er sollte immer über das Seitendeck aufgefischt werden, nicht übers Heck. Bei der Übernahme übers Heck nimmt das Boot wieder Fahrt auf und wird dabei äußerst unstabil*. Die einzige Ausnahme von dieser Regel besteht dann, wenn der über Bord Gefallene hilflos und die Jolle so instabil ist, daß sie bei einer Übernahme seitwärts kentern würde. Nun krängt man dem Schwimmer das Boot so weit wie möglich entgegen. So wird er in der Lage sein, sich mit dem Oberkörper übers Seitendeck zu legen, und es ist ein Leichtes, ihm unter die Arme zu packen und ihn vollends ins Cockpit zu ziehen. Falls das Schwierigkeiten bereitet, gibt es noch eine andere Methode: Man holt den Mann auf dem Rücken der Länge nach längsseits, den Kopf dicht hinter den Wanten, die Füße zum Heck hin. Dann hält er sich mit der bootsseitigen Hand am Want fest und versucht, einen oder beide Füße aufs Seitendeck zu legen. Dann packt man ihn am Gurt der Rettungsweste oder am Hosenbund, während er gleichzeitig das Kreuz durchdrückt, und rollt ihn ins Cockpit.

1 *Der Steuermann krängt das Boot...*

2 *...und zieht seinen Mann übers Seitendeck rein.*

* Auf den meisten deutschen Segelschulen ist man da anderer Auffassung. Sie lehren die Übernahme übers Heck, bei der es üblicherweise keine Probleme gibt, zumal noch das Ende der Großschot als hilfreiche Handreichung gegeben werden kann. Das Boot wird dabei nicht unstabiler als bei einer Übernahme über die Seite. Im Gegenteil, mit leichten Jollen besteht bei seitlicher Übernahme stets die Gefahr einer Kenterung. Auch nimmt das Boot dabei keineswegs Fahrt auf. Es sei denn, die Schoten haben sich verhakt, so daß die Segel nicht frei auswehen können, sondern Wind fangen. Wird allerdings über das Seitendeck aufgenommen, muß der Nahezu-Aufschießer in jedem Fall in Lee des Schwimmers erfolgen. Würde das Boot in Luv liegen, würden Baum und Großschot und die in Lee peitschende Fockschot die Übernahme stark behindern, wenn nicht gar unmöglich machen. Außerdem ist die Gefahr einer Kenterung in dem Fall noch größer. Bei der Übernahme in Luv muß sich der Helfer im Cockpit nur vor dem möglicherweise herumschlagenden Baum in Acht nehmen, besonders dann, wenn er – der Empfehlung entsprechend – das Boot stark krängt.
– Bearbeiter

Reffen

Je mehr der Wind zunimmt, um so schwieriger wird es für die Besatzung, eine Jolle auszureiten. Bis dann der Punkt kommt, an dem die Kräfte nicht mehr ausreichen. Eine erfahrene Crew weiß zwar mit allerlei Trimmtricks diesen Zeitpunkt länger hinauszuzögern, aber irgendwann riskiert jeder eine Kenterung, wenn er seine Segelfläche nicht verkleinert.
Da gibt es zwei Möglichkeiten: Entweder man wechselt seine Segel gegen kleinere aus, oder man verringert die Fläche seiner gesetzten Segel, ein Vorgang, den man als reffen bezeichnet. Wer sie sich leisten kann, ist mit kleineren Starkwindsegeln besser bedient, weil ein gerefftes Segel nie so gut steht und deshalb auch nicht so wirkungsvoll ist. Es gibt verschiedene Methoden zu reffen: Einbinden des überschüssigen Tuches (Bindereff) oder aufwickeln des Segels auf den Baum oder Mast (Rollreff). Rennjollen allerdings lassen sich meistens gar nicht reffen. Wieviel Segelfläche eingerefft werden muß, ist reine Erfahrungssache. Wie weit man ein Segel überhaupt reffen kann, hängt beim Bindereff von der Anzahl der Reffreihen ab. Mit dem Rollreff kann das Segel beliebig verkleinert werden. Bei unsicherer Wetterlage ist es ratsam und vor allem einfacher, schon vor dem Ablegen zu reffen. Befindet man sich auf dem Wasser, wird zum Reffen oder Ausreffen beigedreht.

Das Bindereff

Die traditionelle Art, ein Segel zu reffen, ist mit dem Bindereff, wie es ähnlich schon die Rahschiffe hatten. Man kommt heute mehr und mehr auf diese Reffart wieder zurück, weil ein so gerefftes Segel besser steht.
Für jede Reffposition befindet sich eine Reihe Reffbändsel im Segel. Diese Reffbändsel steigen in einer Kurve zum Mast leicht an, damit man auch den Segelbauch glatt und straff einbinden kann. Im Vorliek und Achterliek des Segels sind am Ende jeder Reffreihe starke Kauschen eingeschlagen, mit denen das Segel an Hals und Schothorn durchgesetzt und festgemacht wird. Die Reffbändsel dienen zum Auftuchen und Festmachen des eingerefften Segeltuchs.

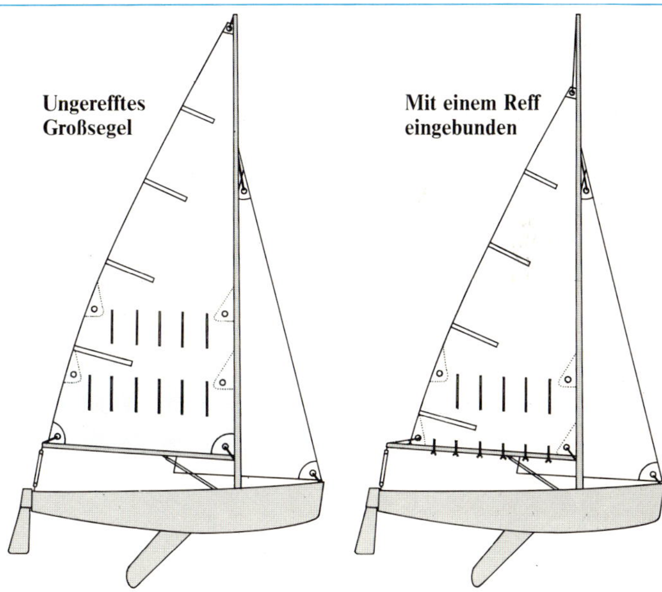

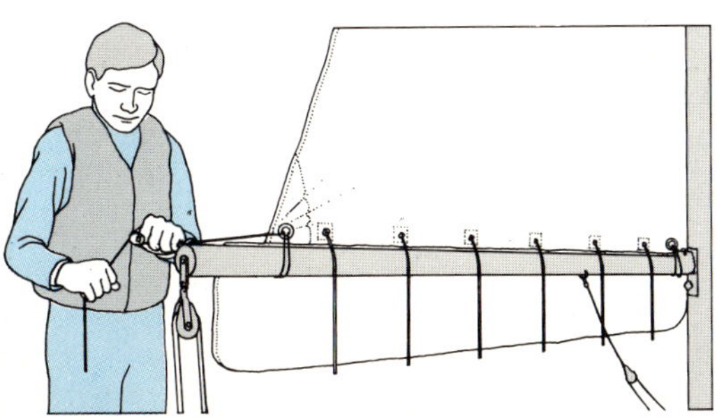
Ausholen der Reffkausch zur Baumnock

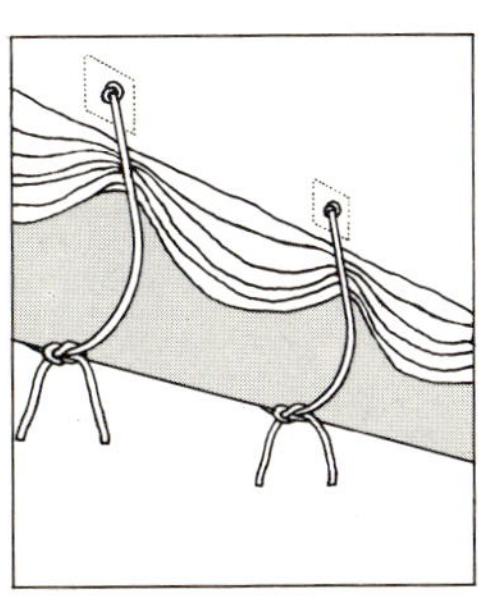
Reffbändsel mit Kreuzknoten

Baumniederholer und Großsegelfall los und das Großsegel so weit fieren, daß die Reffkausch auf den Baum kommt. Dann das Segel wieder durchsetzen und das Fall belegen. Mit dem sogenannten Schmeerreep, einem starken Bändsel, die hintere Reffkausch auf den Baum herunter- und nach hinten ausholen. Dann das Tuch am Baum aufrollen und mit den Reffbändseln festbinden. Danach den Baumniederholer durchsetzen.

Das Rollreff

Diese Art zu reffen ist nur dann möglich, wenn die Großschotblöcke nicht fest am Baum sitzen, sondern an einem Schotring oder einem drehbaren Beschlag an der Baumnock. Ansonsten ist es die simpelste Reffmethode: Der Baum wird aus seinem Lümmelbeschlag genommen und das Segel von Hand aufgerollt. Hat der Baum einen Niederholer, hilft man sich mit einem Segelsack, so, wie rechts unten gezeigt. Wichtig ist, das Achterliek in Falten auf den Baum zu legen, bevor mit dem Aufrollen begonnen wird. Sonst sitzt der Baum nicht waagerecht, wenn das gereffte Segel wieder durchgesetzt wird.

1 *Vorm Einrollen des Segels eine Falte von etwa 15 cm ins Achterliek schlagen und auf dem Baum auftuchen, damit sich das Segel glatt aufrollt.*

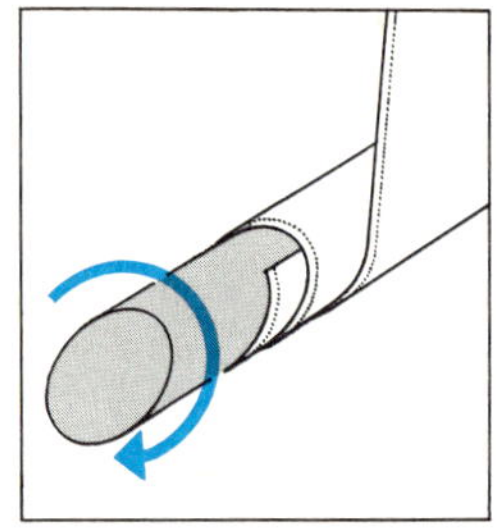

2 *Den Baum drehen und dabei das Segel an Vor- und Achterliek straffziehen.*

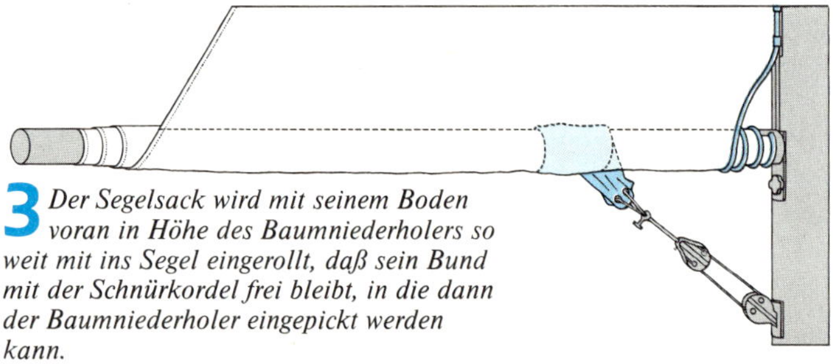

3 *Der Segelsack wird mit seinem Boden voran in Höhe des Baumniederholers so weit mit ins Segel eingerollt, daß sein Bund mit der Schnürkordel frei bleibt, in die dann der Baumniederholer eingepickt werden kann.*

Reffen um den Mast

Manche Boote, bei denen das Segel mit einer Tasche am Mast befestigt ist, können gerefft werden, indem das Segel um den Mast gerollt wird. Auch wenn der Reffvorgang manchmal unterschiedlich ist, das Prinzip ist gleich. Um den Mast drehen zu können, muß der Baum abgenommen werden. In beiden Fällen müssen Halsstrecker und Schothornstrecker gelöst und nach dem Reffen wieder festgesetzt werden.

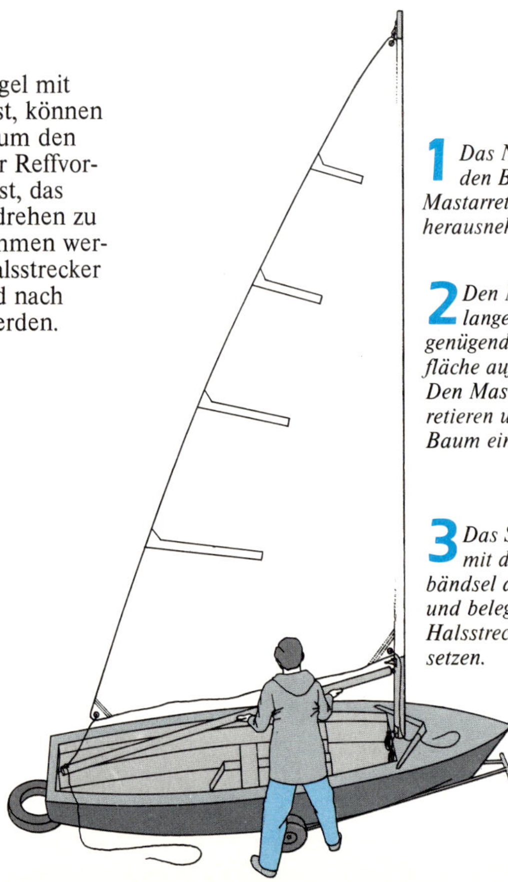

1 *Das Nockbändsel am Schothorn lösen, den Baum auspicken, Halsstrecker und Mastarretierung lösen, eventuell Segellatten herausnehmen.*

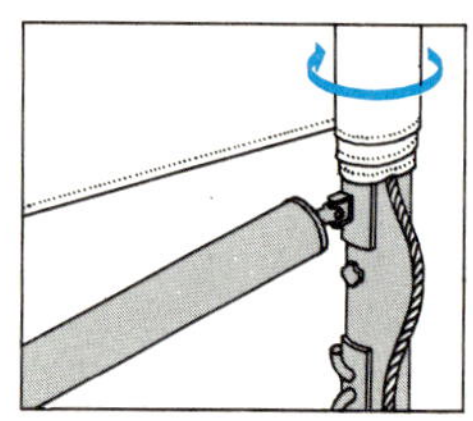

2 *Den Mast so lange drehen, bis genügend Segelfläche aufgerollt ist. Den Mast wieder arretieren und den Baum einhängen.*

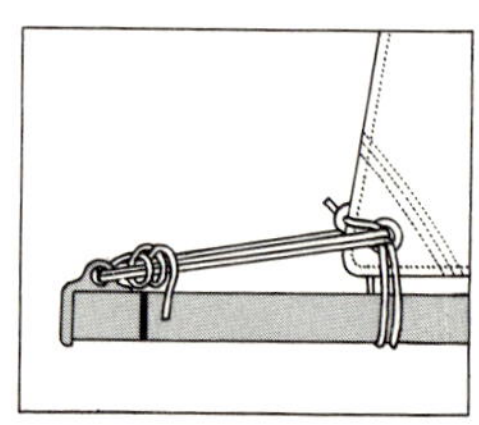

3 *Das Schothorn mit dem Nockbändsel ausholen und belegen, den Halsstrecker durchsetzen.*

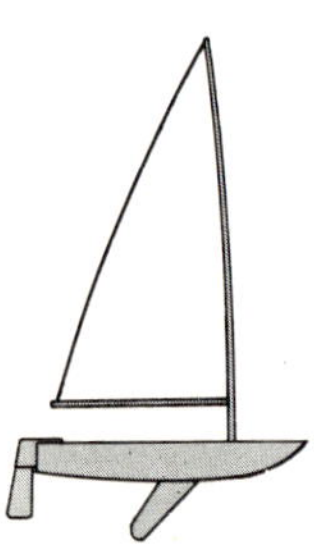

Ungerefft

Gerefft

Reffen der Fock

Hat man das Großsegel gerefft und die Fock nicht verkleinert, wird man schnell feststellen, daß das Boot schwieriger zu segeln ist, weil sich die Segelfläche gewissermaßen nicht mehr im Gleichgewicht befindet. Manche Jollen haben denn auch eine große Genua für leichten Wind und eine kleinere Fock für Starkwind. Wer kein kleineres Vorsegel zum Auswechseln hat, kann seine Fock verkleinern, indem er sie aufs Vorstag aufrollt. Die Fockschot wird abgeschlagen und das Segel einige Male stramm um das Vorstag gewickelt, ohne das Fall zu fieren. Erscheint einem die übriggebliebene Segelfläche klein genug, wird die Schot wieder angepickt oder -geknotet. Manche Jollen haben auch einen fest mit dem Vorstag verbundenen Fockroller, der vom Cockpit aus bedient wird. Das Vorsegel wird auf eine Spindel aufgerollt und kann so stufenlos verkleinert werden.

Durch Aufrollen aufs Vorstag ist die Segelfläche der Fock verkleinert worden.

Reffen auf dem Wasser

Mit einem Bändselreff ist es kein Problem, auch draußen auf dem Wasser zu reffen, sobald man merkt, daß es zu stark bläst. Man überzeugt sich vorher, ob man genügend freien Seeraum hat, denn während des Reffens ist man weitgehend manövrierunfähig. Dann dreht man das Boot bei und holt das Schwert zur Hälfte hoch. Es dauert einige Zeit, bis man mit dem Einbinden des Reffs fertig ist, und man wird erstaunt sein, wie weit das Boot währenddem getrieben ist. Der Steuermann drückt die Pinne mit dem Bein oder Fuß nach Lee, um die Hände zum Arbeiten freizuhaben. Gerefft wird, wie auf Seite 71 beschrieben. Auch mit dem Rollreff kann man auf dem Wasser die Segelfläche verkleinern. Wenn die Crew gut eingespielt ist, geht es sogar schneller.

Am Steg gereffte Boote vorm Auslaufen bei frischer Brise.

Eine Jolle liegt zum Reffen des Großsegels auf dem Wasser beigedreht.

Start und Landung am Ufer

Obschon die meisten Jollen direkt vom Ufer aus zu Wasser gebracht werden können, sind damit einige Schwierigkeiten verbunden. Abgesehen von der Frage des Zugangs zum Ufer von der Straße oder dem Parkplatz aus, können die Uferbeschaffenheit – Sand oder Schilf –, die Frage, ob Hoch- oder Niedrigwasser herrscht, Probleme bereiten. Sofern es möglich ist, sollte man sich das betreffende Ufer bei Niedrigwasser ansehen, um festzustellen, ob und wo es Unterwasserhindernisse gibt, wie der Böschungswinkel des Ufers ist etc. Ist das nicht möglich, kann man aus dem Charakter des Ufers Rückschlüsse ziehen. Sandige Uferbereiche lassen auf einen allmählich abfallenden Grund schließen, steinige Ufer fallen meistens sehr schnell auf größere Tiefen ab, Schilfgürtel versprechen Flachwasser.

In Tidengewässern sollte man vor dem Absegeln berechnen, wie der Wasserstand bei der Rückkehr sein wird. Zweckmäßigerweise sollte man zwei Stunden vor oder nach Hochwasser abfahren oder zurückkehren. Von überfüllten Ufern oder Ufern mit modrigem Untergrund paddelt man am besten ein Stück weg, bevor man die Segel setzt.

Eine große Rolle spielt auch, ob es sich um eine Luv- oder Leeküste handelt. An einer Luvküste weht ablandiger Wind. Hier ist es ziemlich einfach vom Ufer wegzukommen, zurückzukommen ist dagegen schwieriger. An einer Leeküste weht auflandiger Wind. Er macht das Wegsegeln vom Ufer schwierig oder bei Brandung gar unmöglich. Das Boot wird immer wieder ans Ufer zurückgeworfen oder von der Brandung vollgeschlagen.

Bei ablandigem Wind wird, gerade von einem Anfänger, nur allzu leicht die Windstärke unterschätzt, weil er sich beim Lossegeln unter der Landabdeckung befindet. Er ist dann vielleicht nicht auf das vorbereitet, was wirklich „draußen" los ist. Deshalb muß man sich vor dem Start alle nur zugänglichen Wetterinformationen beschaffen. Wer alleine segelt muß jemand die Zeit seiner Rückkunft mitteilen und sich - wenn irgend möglich - auch daran halten.

Meistens ist die Rückkehr ans Ufer unproblematischer als der Start, es sei denn, das Ufer ist einem fremd. Nähert man sich dem Ufer, müssen die Fallen klarliegen, damit die Segel auch schnell geborgen werden können. Ebenso wichtig ist es, auf die abnehmende Wassertiefe zu achten, um Schwert und Ruderblatt rechtzeitig entsprechend aufzuholen.

(In England spielt sich die Jollensegelei teilweise vor der Küste ab. Deshalb findet das Küstensegeln hier eine recht ausführliche Würdigung. Für uns hingegen gilt: Jollen gehören grundsätzlich nicht auf die See, weil das zu risikoreich ist. Es sei denn im Rahmen von Hochleistungsregatten, die unter entsprechenden Sicherheitsvorkehrungen durchgeführt werden. - Bearbeiter)

Ein Laser kehrt bei starkem Wind und Brandung an eine Leeküste zurück. Der Steuermann läßt das Boot höchste Geschwindigkeit laufen, um zu vermeiden, daß die Wellen überm Heck brechen und einsteigen. Bei einer Brandung wie dieser ist es wahrscheinlich kaum möglich, in den Wind zu schießen, um die Fahrt abzustoppen. Da kann man nur direkt auf den Strand zulaufen, in allerletzter Minute rausspringen und das Boot schnell aus der Brandung ziehen.

Rechts: Diese Segelschüler haben es leicht. Der Wind weht parallel zur Küste, sie können ihre Boote direkt vom Ufer weg- und zurücksegeln.

Start von einer Luvküste

Es macht keinen grundlegenden Unterschied, ob man flaches oder tiefes Wasser hat, aber es gibt zwei Möglichkeiten, um vom Ufer wegzukommen. Die erste Methode ist einfacher, aber auch weniger kontrolliert im Ablauf. Die zweite empfiehlt sich für eine versierte Mannschaft und wenn wenig Platz zur Verfügung steht.

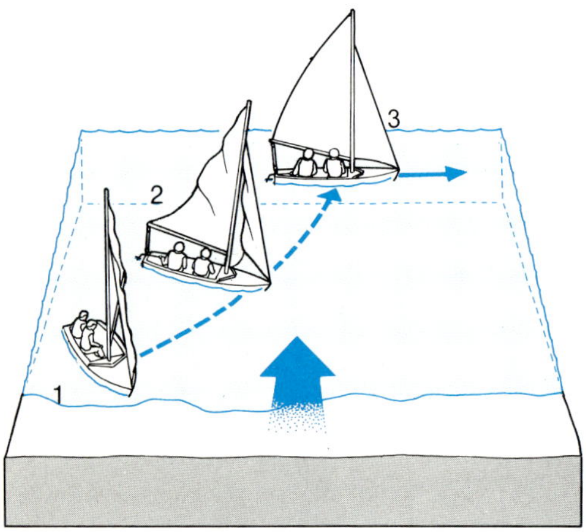

Methode 1
Das Boot wird mit dem Bug in den Wind gelegt, die Segel werden gesetzt, der Besatzung steigt ein (1) und wartet, bis das Boot genügend abgedriftet ist (2) und geht dann auf Kurs (3).

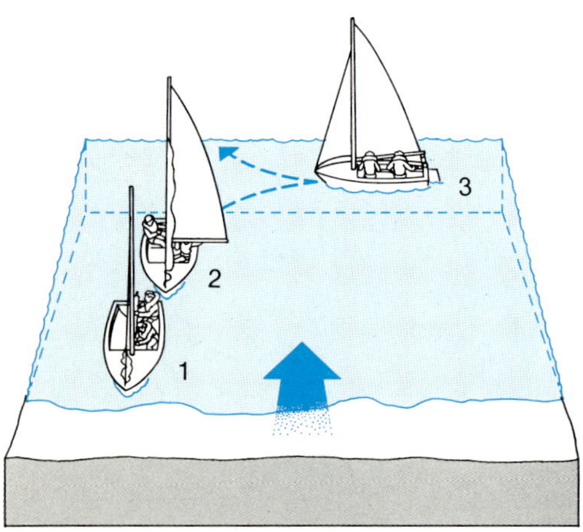

Methode 2
Das Boot liegt mit dem Bug im Wind, die Segel sind gesetzt, die Mannschaft ist an Bord (1). Mit backgehaltenem Großsegel wird rückwärts gesegelt (2), die Pinne zu der Seite eingeschlagen, nach der man wegsegeln will. Ist das Wasser tief genug, Großsegel rüber, Fock anholen und auf Kurs gehen (3).

Start von einer Leeküste mit tiefem Wasser

Das Boot liegt, den Bug im Wind, mit dem Heck auf dem Strand. Die Segel sind gesetzt, das Ruder ist eingehängt. Die Mannschaft hält den Bug im Wind und beobachtet die Brandung (1). Sobald eine Welle unter dem Rumpf durchgelaufen ist, zieht sie das Boot blitzschnell ins Wasser, hechtet hinein und drückt dabei den Bug in Fahrtrichtung (2). Der Steuermann holt nun die Großschot dicht, der Vorschoter fiert das Schwert und holt die Fockschot dicht. Der Steuermann fällt etwas ab (3), damit das Boot mehr Fahrt aufnimmt. Dann wendet er, falls er zu dicht unters Ufer gekommen ist. Sonst hält er Kurs. Sofern das Boot in der Brandung Wasser übergenommen hat, wird mit dem Lenzen gewartet, bis das Boot frei von der Brandungszone ist.

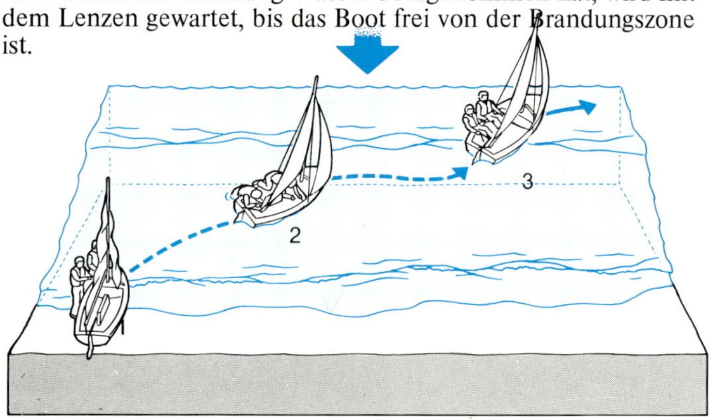

Start von einer Leeküste mit flachem Wasser

Die Segel sind gesetzt (1), die Besatzung schiebt das Boot bis in etwa brusthohes Wasser und fiert entsprechend das Schwert. Der Steuermann steigt ein (2), der Vorschoter drückt den Bug nach Lee und steigt ebenfalls ein. Der Rudergänger holt die Großschot an, legt etwas Ruder (3), damit das Boot Fahrt aufnimmt, und versucht, sich vom flachen Wasser freizusegeln. Sobald es die Wassertiefe erlaubt, wird das Schwert vollständig gefiert. Die Fock wird angeholt, sobald das Boot Fahrt voraus macht und nicht mehr nach Lee treibt (Position 3 oder 4).

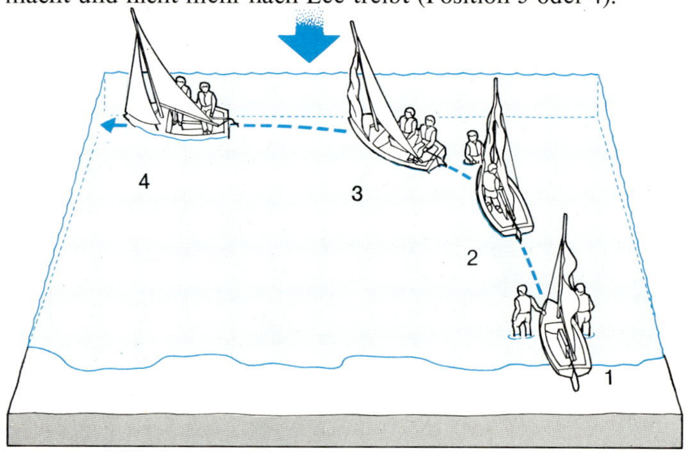

Der Start vom Ufer eines Binnensees ist meistens völlig unproblematisch. Sind womöglich Stege vorhanden, macht das die Sache noch einfacher: die Crew kann trockenen Fußes an Bord und vom Boot wieder an Land steigen.

Oben: Start von einer Leeküste. Der Steuermann dieses Sunfish sitzt bereits drin, klariert Schot, Ruder und Schwert, während der zweite Mann das Boot, Bug zum Wind, ins tiefe Wasser zieht.

Steht vor einer Leeküste Brandung, müssen die Boote ziemlich weit hinausgezogen werden, bevor man lossegeln kann. Wem es nicht gelingt, schnell genug ins Boot zu hechten und die Schoten dichtzuholen, der wird unweigerlich wieder zurückgeworfen.

Landen an der Luvküste

Weht der Wind ablandig vom Ufer weg, kann man nicht direkt auf die Küste zusegeln, sondern muß aufkreuzen. Dabei kann man beobachten, daß der Wind nur ganz selten rechtwinklig vom Ufer herweht. Bei sorgfältiger Überlegung wird man so auch den günstigen Kurs zum Ufer finden. Ist das Boot schon dicht unterhalb des Ufers, hält sich der Vorschoter bereit, um ins Wasser zu springen und das Boot festzuhalten, damit es nicht wieder zurücktreibt.

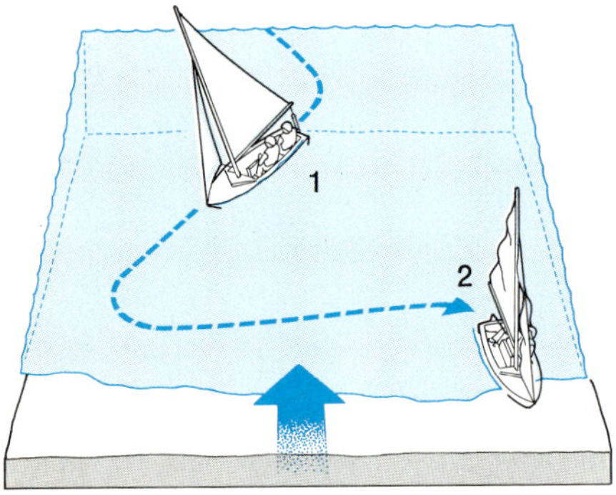

Landen auf tiefem Wasser
Man kreuzt gegen das Ufer auf, bis man dicht unter Land ist (1). Der letzte Kreuzschlag wird parallel zum Ufer so angelegt, daß man das Boot mit einem Aufschießer am gewünschten Landeplatz zum Stillstand bringt (2).

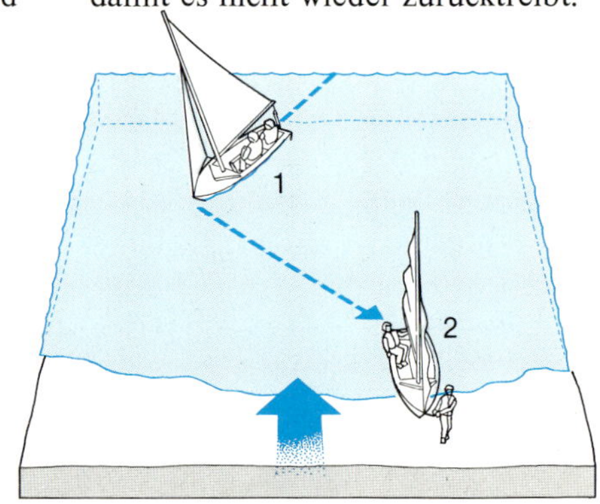

Landen auf flachem Wasser
Man kreuzt gegen das Ufer auf, bis man in flachem Wasser ist (1). Schwert und Ruderblatt werden der Wassertiefe entsprechend aufgeholt, der letzte Kreuzschlag wird gegen das Ufer gesegelt. Der Steuermann schießt gegen das Ufer auf, der Vorschoter springt mit der Vorleine an Land (2).

Landen an der Leeküste

Da man mit achterlichem Wind segelt, ist die Landung ziemlich einfach. Gefahr droht jedoch von der Brandung bei steilen brechenden Wellen. Unter solchen Umständen sollte man mit möglichst hoher Fahrt auf das Ufer zulaufen, damit die Wellen nicht über das Heck ins Boot einsteigen. Im flachen Wasser springt die Besatzung über Bord, stoppt das Boot von Hand ab und dreht es mit dem Bug in den Wind. Keinesfalls sollte man nach Lee aus dem Boot springen, da die Gefahr besteht, dabei unter das von einem Brecher zur Seite geschleuderte Boot zu geraten.

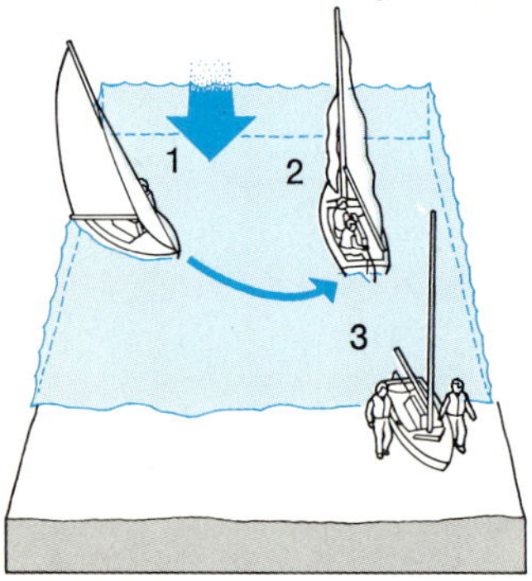

Flaches Wasser
Auf Halb-Wind-Kurs anlaufen (1), in hüfthohem Wasser aufschießen (2) und die Segel bergen, aussteigen und das Boot, Bug voran, an Land ziehen (3).

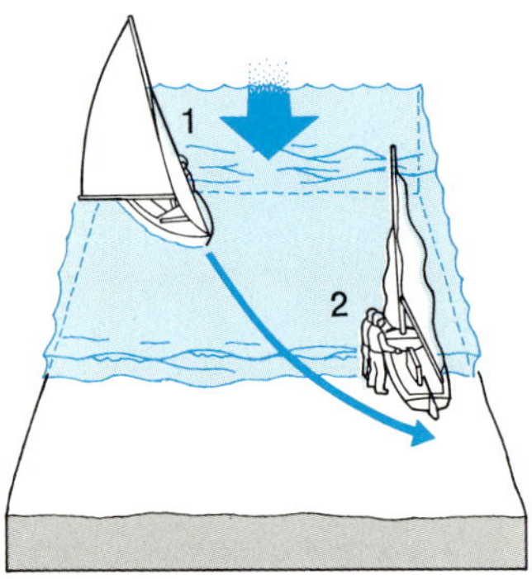

Tiefes Wasser und Brandung
Anlaufen auf Raumschots-Kurs (1). Kurz bevor das Boot auf Grund läuft, springt die Crew in Luv über Bord und dreht den Bug in den Wind (2).

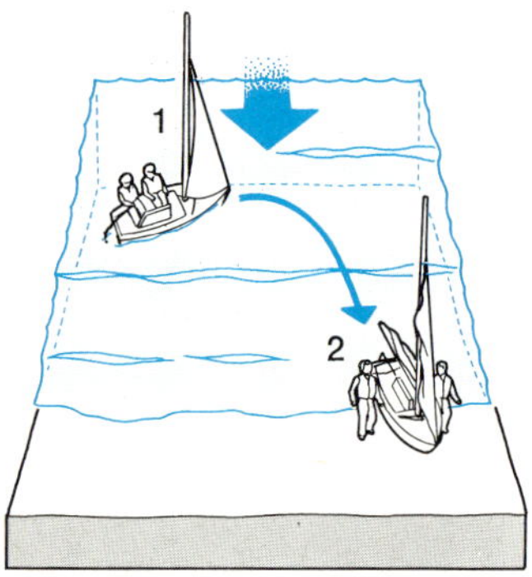

Tiefes Wasser ohne Brandung
In den Wind schießen und das Großsegel bergen (1) und auf Halb-Wind-Kurs unter Fock aufs Ufer zulaufen, die Fock auswehen lassen, über Bord springen und das Boot an Land ziehen (2).

Ab- und Anlegen am Steg

In vielen Fällen muß vom Steg abgelegt werden. Manchmal ist er der einzige Zugang zum Wasser, von dem man auch das Boot zu Wasser bringen muß. Meistens befinden sich aber Slipanlagen in der Nähe, die ein bequemes Slippen ermöglichen. An- und Ablegen am und vom Steg hat den Vorteil, daß das Boot stets manövrierfähig ist. Man kann es dort zum Segelsetzen festmachen und auch vorübergehend liegenlassen, ohne daß etwas passiert. Schwimmstege oder Pontons in Gezeitengewässern haben den Vorzug, daß sie wasserstandsunabhängig sind und man keine Probleme mit den Festmacherleinen hat. Der Nachteil ist nur, daß eine quersetzende starke Strömung ein längsseits liegendes Boot heftig gegen den Ponton drückt oder sogar darunter, was zu Beschädigungen führen kann.
Da Pontons und Stege an beliebten Segelplätzen meist belegt sind von festgemachten oder an- und ablegenden Booten, ist beim Näherkommen mit dem eigenen Boot besondere Vorsicht geboten. Der Anlaufkurs muß gut überlegt sein, damit Kollisionen mit anderen Booten vermieden werden. In strömenden Gewässern kann es zusätzliche Schwierigkeiten geben, wenn der Strom gegen Wind steht. Ideal ist es natürlich, wenn man das Boot gegen den Wind elegant zum Stillstand bringen kann. Dabei sollte der Anlaufkurs möglichst immer so eingerichtet werden, daß man notfalls auch wieder abdrehen kann. Weht der Wind in einem Winkel auf den Steg zu, legt man in strömungsfreiem Gewässer an der Leeseite des Steges an. Dabei stellt sich die Besatzung darauf ein, sich am Steg festzuhalten, damit das Boot nicht abtreibt. Sobald das Boot steht, springt der Vorschoter mit der Vorleine in der Hand an Land und belegt sie, wo es am zweckmäßigsten ist. Bleibt das Boot längere Zeit am Steg liegen, werden die Segel heruntergenommen und beigebändselt. Auch wird das Boot mit einer Achterleine festgemacht, notfalls mit der Großschot.

Längsseits gehen am Steg bei ablandigem Wind. Der Vorschoter hält das Boot am Steg fest, damit es nicht wieder abtreibt, in der anderen Hand hat er die Vorleine, mit der er gleich auf den Steg übersteigen wird. Der Steuermann balanciert die Jolle aus.

Ablegen bei ablandigem Wind

Das Boot liegt im Wind, das Schwert ist gefiert, die Segel sind gesetzt. Nun ist zu überlegen, wie man sich am besten vom Steg freisegelt. Hat man genügend Freiraum hinter dem Heck, wird wie auf der linken Abbildung verfahren. Andernfalls muß man so oder ähnlich, wie auf der rechten Abbildung dargestellt, ablegen.

Rechts: Nichts ist leichter, als bei ablandigem Wind von einem Steg abzulegen. Man braucht das Boot nur abzudrücken.

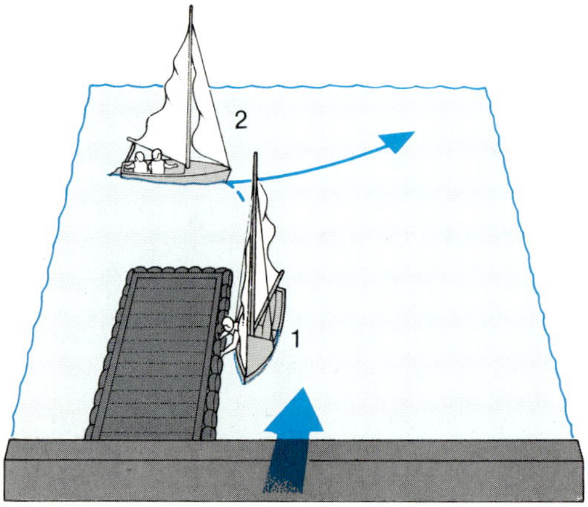

Freier Raum achteraus
Der Vorschoter macht die Vorleine vom Steg los, schiebt das Boot kräftig achteraus (1) und hält die Fock back. Der Steuermann legt die Pinne auf Rückwärtsfahrt und läßt das Boot so weit abfallen, daß die Schoten für einen Kurs voll und bei angeholt werden können (2). Der Vorschoter läßt die Fock übergehen und holt die Fockschot dicht. Das Boot fällt ab und nimmt Fahrt auf.

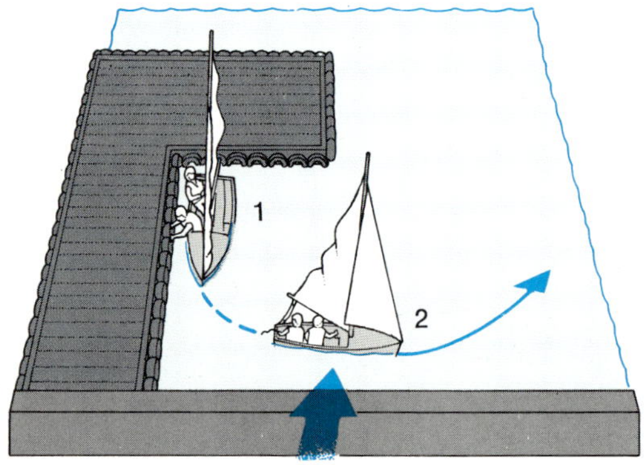

Kein freier Raum achteraus
Der Steuermann sitzt an der Pinne. Der Vorschoter macht die Vorleine los, schiebt das Boot kräftig voraus, während der Steuermann Lee-Ruder legt. Der Vorschoter nimmt die Fock auf der Seite zum Steg back, bis das Boot genügend abgefallen ist (2). Dann werden die Schoten angeholt – das Boot nimmt Fahrt auf und segelt sich frei.

Ablegen bei auflandigem Wind

Das Boot wird von Hand an den Stegkopf verholt (1). Der Steuermann setzt die Segel (Großsegel zuerst) und fiert das Schwert (2). Ist das Boot segelklar, drückt der Vorschoter den Bug vom Steg ab und gibt dem Boot einen kräftigen Pull voraus. Der Steuermann legt leicht Lee-Ruder, die Schoten werden dichtgeholt, und das Boot läuft auf Am-Wind-Kurs ab (3).

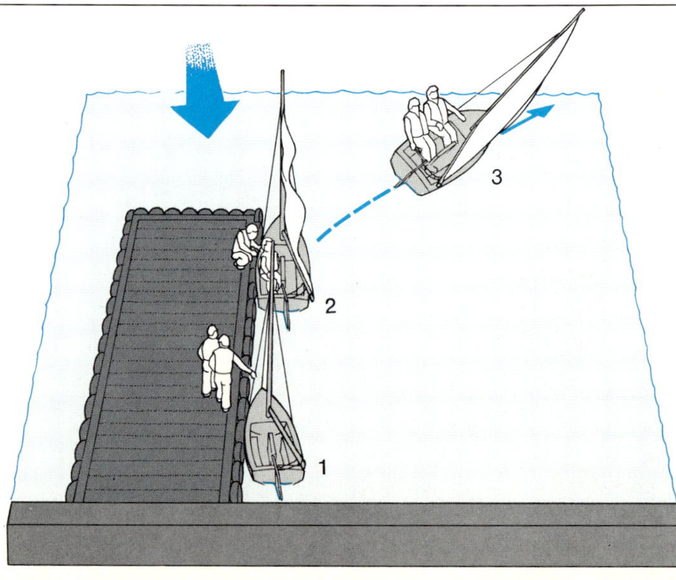

Anlegen bei ablandigem Wind

Zum Anlegen an einem Steg bei ablandigem Wind läuft man möglichst dicht unter Land, parallel zum Ufer, an. Der Aufschießer zum Steg wird so gefahren, daß man notfalls wenden und wieder ablaufen kann. Ist man am Steg, sollte das Boot mit losen Schoten kaum noch Fahrt machen, damit die Besatzung sich am Steg festhalten kann. Liegt das Boot längsseits, springt der Vorschoter mit der Vorleine an Land und macht sie fest.

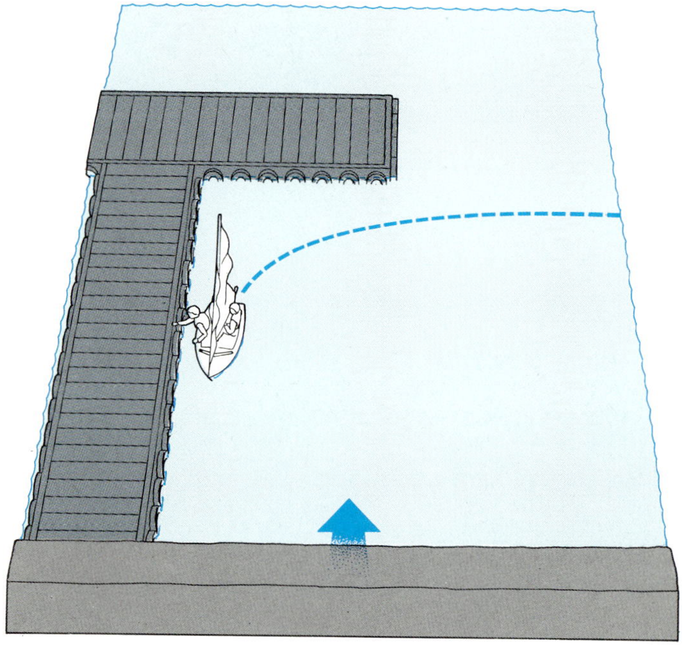

Je nach Windrichtung raumschots oder mit halbem Wind den Steg anlaufen und dicht daneben aufschießen. Der Vorschoter hält das Boot am Steg fest und belegt die Vorleine so schnell wie möglich.

Anlegen bei auflandigem Wind

Nähert man sich einem Steg bei auflandigem Wind, wählt man den Kurs möglichst dicht entlang des Steges, bevor man das Boot mit einem Aufschießer zum Halten bringt. Wichtig dabei ist, daß man genügend Raum für den Aufschießer vor dem Steg zur Verfügung hat und das Boot nicht den Steg rammt. Andererseits ist der Aufschießer nicht zu spät zu fahren, sonst läuft das Boot über das Stegende hinaus. Liegt der Steg parallel zum Ufer, also nicht im rechten Winkel, wird das Großsegel vorher geborgen und nur unter der Fock angelegt.

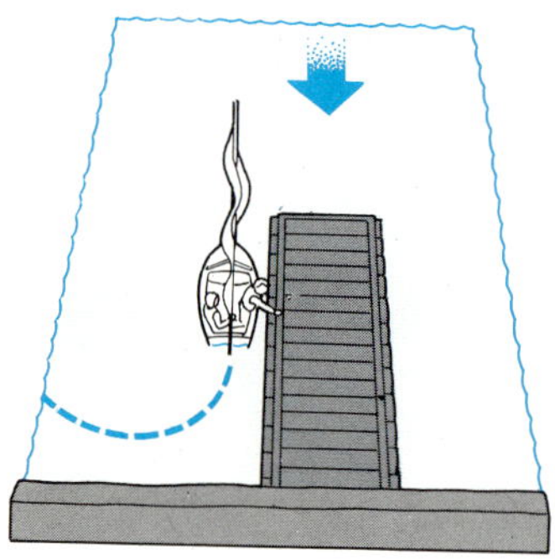

Steg im rechten Winkel zum Ufer
Angelaufen wird mit Halbwind auf das Ufer zu, dann wird ein Aufschießer parallel zum Steg gefahren, damit das Boot längsseits zum Stillstand kommt.

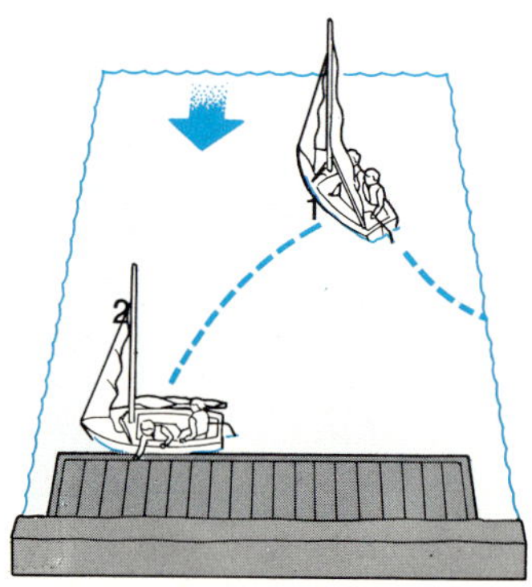

Steg parallel zum Ufer
Angelaufen wird auf Am-Wind-Kurs, aufschießen (1), das Großsegel bergen, abfallen und unter Fock zum Steg laufen. Kurz vorher die Fockschot loswerfen, anluven und parallel zum Steg zum Stehen kommen (2).

Ablegen in strömendem Gewässer

Das Ablegen vom Steg in strömendem Gewässer hängt davon ab, ob der Wind oder die Strömung stärker ist. Ist die Strömung stärker als der Wind, entscheidet ihre Richtung, von wo aus abgelegt wird. Als Regel gilt, immer von der Seite abzulegen, die sich in Lee des stärkeren Elementes befindet. Besondere Aufmerksamkeit ist dann geboten, wenn ein kräftiger Wind gegen den Strom bläst. Dabei entsteht ein unangenehmer kurzer Seegang auf der Strom-Leeseite von Schwimmstegen.

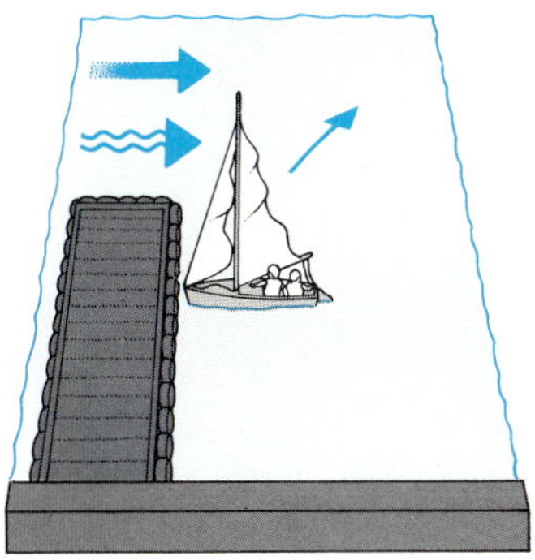

Wind und Strom gleiche Richtung
Das Boot wird zum Stegende mit dem Bug gegen Strom und Wind festgemacht. Der Vorschoter nimmt die Vorleine auf Slip, steigt ein, hält die Fock back und läßt die Vorleine ausrauschen. Der Steuermann legt die Pinne auf Rückwärtsfahrt und läßt das Boot abfallen, bis die Segel Wind fangen und die Schoten angeholt werden können.

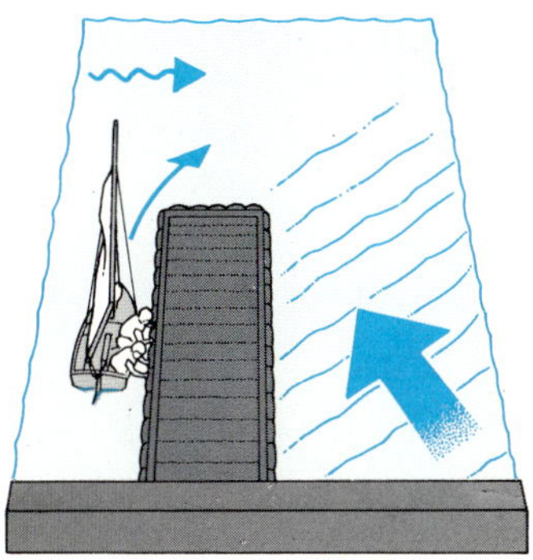

Wind gegen schwächeren Strom
Das Boot liegt zum Segelsetzen an der Wind-Leeseite des Steges. Die Mannschaft verholt es von Hand zum Ende des Steges, drückt es kräftig so weit wie möglich vom Steg ab und holt die Schoten dicht auf Halbwind-Kurs. Wichtig ist es, so schnell wie möglich Fahrt aufzunehmen, um nicht vom Strom auf den Steg gesetzt zu werden.

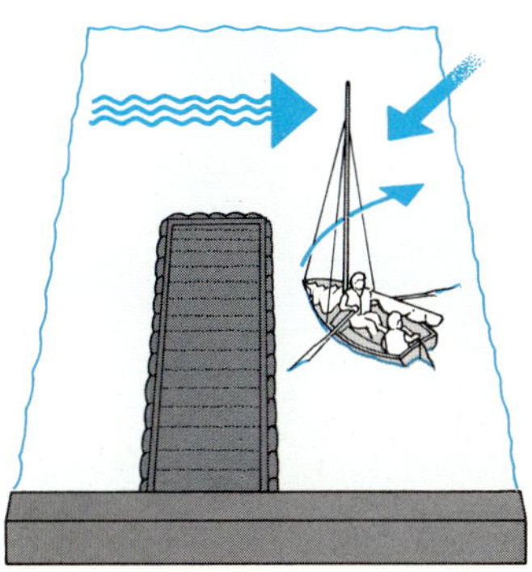

Starker Strom gegen leichten Wind
Das Boot liegt an der Strom-Leeseite des Ponton, Bug in Richtung gegen den Strom. Die Besatzung paddelt oder rudert das Boot mit dem Strom vom Steg frei. Befindet sich das Boot in freiem Wasser, wird es in den Wind gedreht, das Schwert gefiert, und die Segel werden gesetzt.

Anlegen in strömendem Gewässer

Auf strömenden Gewässern sollte, wenn irgend möglich, immer gegen das jeweils stärkere Element - Wind oder Strom - angelegt werden. Das muß vor dem Anlagemanöver ermittelt werden. Am einfachsten ist es natürlich, wenn Wind und Strom aus der gleichen Richtung kommen. Dabei darf aber nicht vergessen werden, daß das Boot auch ohne Segel mit dem Strom weitertreibt. Am schwierigsten ist das Anlegemanöver, wenn Wind gegen Strom steht. Treffen Wind und Strom etwa gleichstark im rechten Winkel aufeinander, hat man zuweilen die Wahl, gegen den Wind oder den Strom aufzuschießen.

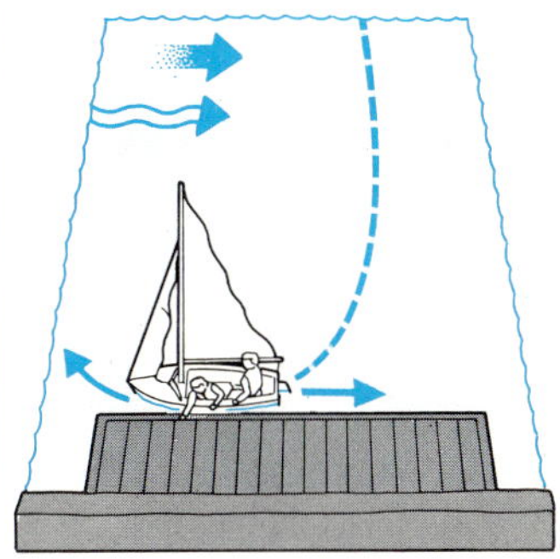

Wind und Strom aus der gleichen Richtung
Anlaufen mit halbem Wind und kurz vor dem Steg aufschießen. Auf Raum achteraus achten, denn das Boot wird nach dem Auslaufen rückwärts treiben, so lange bis die Leinen fest sind.

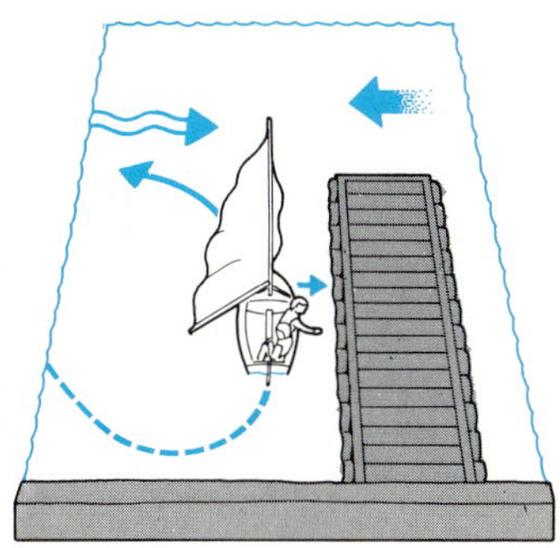

Wind gegen Strom
Angelaufen wird die Wind-Leeseite des Stegs, die gleichzeitig Strom-Luvseite ist. Vor dem Steg wird gewendet und das Boot mit aufgefierten Schoten neben dem Steg zum Stehen gebracht.

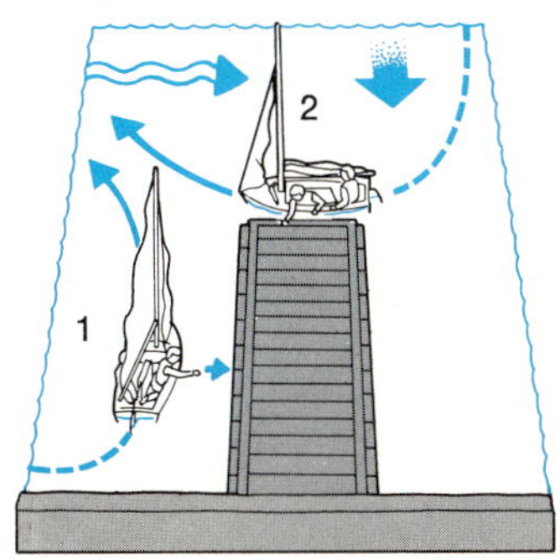

Wind und Strom im rechten Winkel
Will man an der Strom-Luvseite festmachen, läuft man mit Am-Wind-Kurs an und läßt das Boot gegen den Wind auslaufen (1). Will man am Stegende anlegen, wird das Großsegel geborgen und unter Fock zum Steg gesegelt (2).

Ab- und Anlegen an der Mooring-Boje

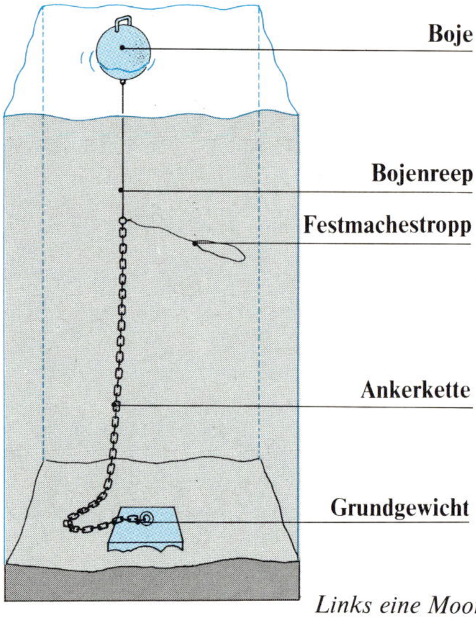

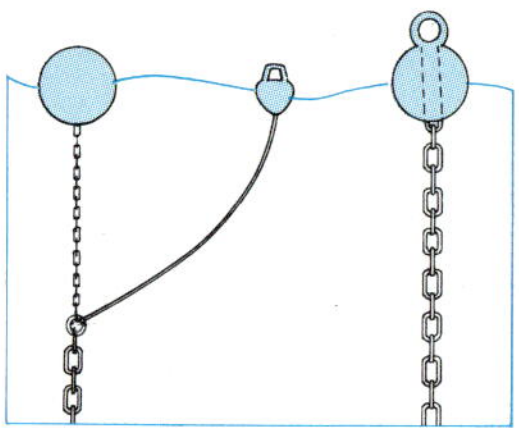

Links eine Mooringboje mit einer kleinen Fangboje zum Aufnehmen des unter Wasser schwimmenden Festmachestropps, der unterhalb der Bojereeps an der Kette sitzt. Rechts eine einfache Festmacheboje mit einem Ring oder Auge oben, durch das die Festmacheleine geschoren wird.

Eine Mooring besteht aus einem Grundgewicht - meist einem Betonklotz - oder einem Anker oder einer im Grund verankerten schweren Kette, einer Bojenkette und einer Boje. Sie dient zum ständigen Festmachen meist größerer Kielyachten, wenn keine oder nicht genügend Hafen- oder Stegliegeplätze vorhanden sind. Seltener liegen Jollen während der Segelsaison an einer Mooring-Boje. Aber fast jeder Jollensegler wird gelegentlich mal an einer Boje festmachen müssen oder wollen, beispielsweise um Segel zu setzen oder zu bergen.

Durch die Länge der Ankerkette kann eine Mooring leicht unterschiedlichen Wasserständen angepaßt werden. Es gibt verschiedene Arten von Moorings, aber das Boot ist immer mit einer Leine am Ring der Boje oder mit einem Stropp an der Bojenkette festgemacht.

Häufig liegen die einzelnen Bojenplätze so dicht nebeneinander, daß man beim An- und Ablegen äußerst vorsichtig sein muß. Zum Bojenplatz kommt man entweder mit einem kleinen Dingi oder mit einem Versetzboot. Bevor man ablegt, muß das Boot natürlich segelklar gemacht werden, das Ruder wird eingehängt, das Schwert gefiert, und die Segel werden gesetzt. Zum Ablegen von der Boje wird die Vorleine auf Slip gelegt, das heißt, das freie Ende der Vorleine wird durch das Bojenauge genommen und an Deck belegt. Dann wird die Vorleine geslipt, nachdem alles klar ist und der Ablaufkurs festliegt.

Bevor man seine Mooring anläuft, sollte man die Lage der anderen Boote zu Wind und Strom beobachten, weil das eigene Boot später die gleiche Lage einnehmen wird. Der Kurs muß immer so eingerichtet werden, daß man gegen das stärkere Element - Wind oder Strom - aufschießen kann. Läuft Strom, geht man besser hinter verankerten Bojen herum, damit man nicht vom Strom gegen sie getrieben wird. Hat man die Boje gefaßt, gleich die Vorleine festmachen, denn bei starkem Strom kann man das Boot nicht lange von Hand an der Boje halten. Dann werden die Segel geborgen, aufgetucht oder abgeschlagen, wird das Boot gelenzt und aufgeklart. Bleibt es einige Zeit an der Boje liegen, werden die Segel und alle losen Ausrüstungsgegenstände von Bord genommen, Schwert und Ruderblatt aufgeholt, damit das Boot frei um die Boje schwojen kann. Oder man hängt das Ruder überhaupt aus. Sinnvoll ist es auch, zumindest das Cockpit mit einer Plane (Persennig) abzudecken, um Schmutz und Regen fernzuhalten. Die Auftriebskörper sollten in jedem Fall in Ordnung sein, damit das vom Regen eventuell doch vollgeschlagene Boot nicht womöglich auf Tauchstation geht.

Ein Nahezu-Aufschießer in Lee der Boje. Präzisionsarbeit wäre es, wenn der Vorschoter die Boje in Höhe des Wants fischen könnte, ohne solche Verrenkungen übers Vordeck anstellen zu müssen.

Ablegen von der Boje

Vor dem Ablegen in strömungsfreien Gewässern wird zunächst das Schwert gefiert und die Vorleine auf Slip genommen. Nachdem die Segel gesetzt sind, holt sich der Vorschoter an die Boje heran und nimmt sie auf die Seite, die zur Luvseite werden soll. Dann wird die Vorleine losgeworfen und sich an der Boje so weit wie möglich voraus verholt. Je weiter, um so besser fällt das Boot ab.

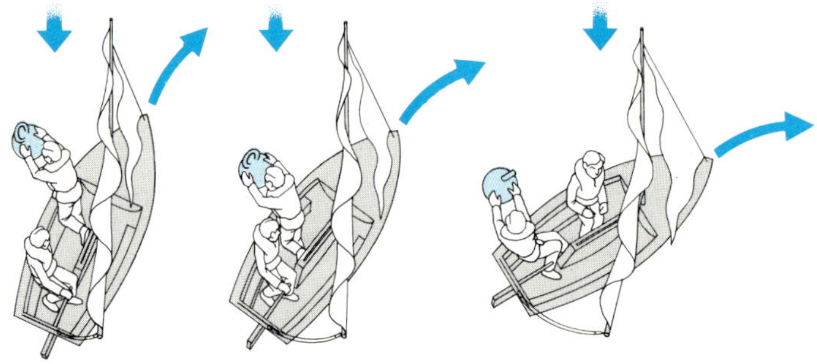

Boje los am Bug
Die Fock muß noch backgenommen werden, um weiter abzufallen.

Boje los mittschiffs
Das Boot ist schon so weit abgefallen, daß man wohl direkt lossegeln kann.

Boje los achtern
Es brauchen nur noch die Schoten angeholt zu werden, um ablaufen zu können.

Anlegen in stehendem Gewässer

Der Aufschießer neben der Boje muß so bemessen werden, daß der Vorschoter sie gut zu fassen bekommt. Wenn irgend möglich, wählt man deshalb einen Am-Wind-Kurs und macht einen Nahezu-Aufschießer in Lee der Boje, so daß sie sich kurz hinter dem Luv-Want befindet und mühelos vom Vorschoter vom Cockpit aus gefischt werden kann. Der Steuermann hält derweil das Boot im Gleichgewicht.

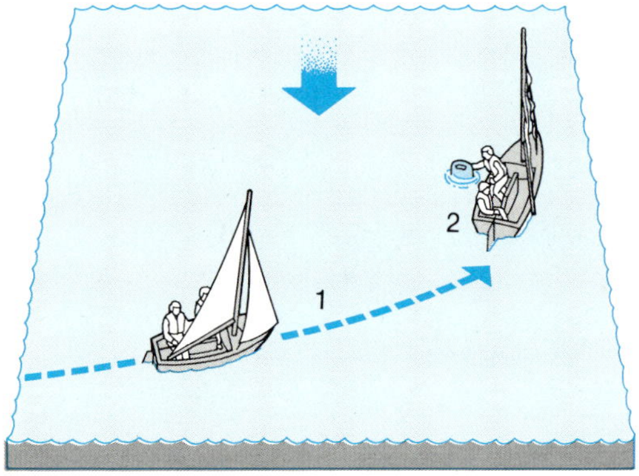

Der Anlauf erfolgt auf Am-Wind-Kurs (1). Neben der Boje aufschießen und die Boje fischen (2).

Festmachen an der Boje

Die Mooringboje muß so angelaufen werden, daß der Vorschoter sie in Luv fassen kann. Dann fischt er sich den Festmachestropp aus dem Wasser, führt ihn durch die Buglippe und belegt ihn auf der Bugklampe oder am Bugbeschlag. Dann werden die Segel geborgen. Hat die Boje keinen extra Festmachestropp, wird die Vorleine am Auge der Boje eingepickt.

Der Vorschoter fischt die Boje.

Ablegen in strömenden Gewässern

Liegt das Boot in strömenden Gewässern an der Boje, wird es sich immer in die Richtung des stärkeren Elementes - Wind oder Strom - drehen. Liegt es mit dem Bug im Wind, überwiegt die Windstärke. Sind Wind und Strom gleich stark, liegt das Boot etwa quer zu beiden. Bei stärkerer Strömung dreht es sich mit dem Bug in Stromrichtung.

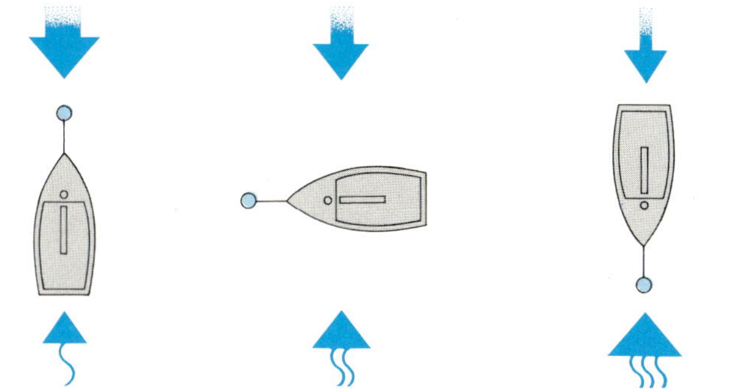

Wind stärker als Strom **Wind und Strom gleich stark** **Strom stärker als Wind**

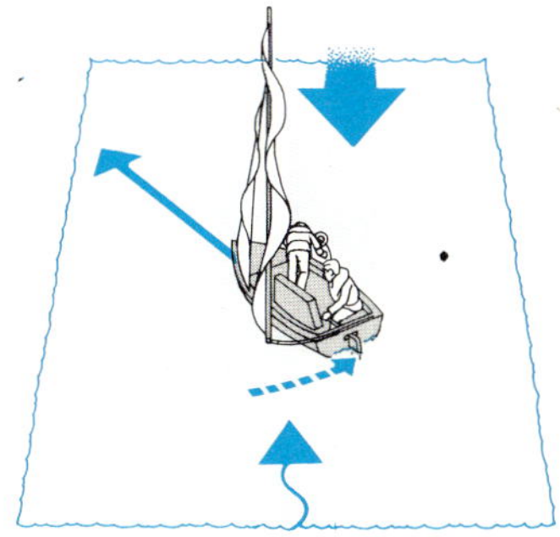

Ablegen – Wind stärker als Strom
Segel setzen, Schwert fieren. Die Boje auf die Seite nehmen, die Luv werden soll. Die Fock backhalten und die Vorleine loswerfen. Ist das Boot freigefallen von der Boje, Fock über und auf Kurs gehen.

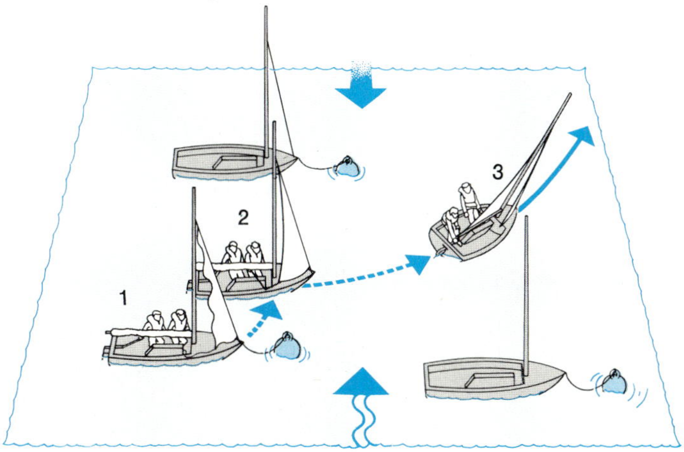

Ablegen – Wind und Strom gleich stark
Vorleine auf Slip legen und die Fock setzen (1). Die Boje in Stromluv nehmen, das Schwert fieren und Vorleine los. Fockschot dichtholen und sich von anderen Bojenliegern freisegeln (2). Dann anluven und das Großsegel setzen und auf Kurs gehen (3).

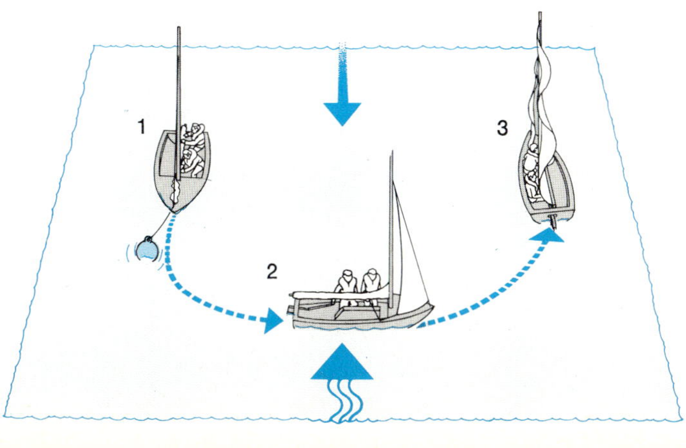

Ablegen – Strom stärker als Wind
Die Segel klar zum Setzen anschlagen. Das Schwert fieren, die Boje auf die Seite nehmen, die zur Leeseite werden soll. Fock hoch, Vorleine los und die Fockschot anholen (2) und zum Großsegelsetzen anluven (3).

Anlegen in strömendem Gewässer

Will man in strömendem Gewässer an eine Boje gehen, muß vorher Stärke und Richtung des Stroms in Relation zum Wind geprüft werden und wie sie den Kurs beeinflussen können. Die Stärke des Stroms kann man am besten an Tonnen oder ähnlichem beobachten, an ihrer „Bugwelle" und der Wirbelschleppe dahinter. Es kann für ein Gelingen des Manövers durchaus hilfreich sein, erst einen Probelauf zu unternehmen, bevor man tatsächlich an die Boje geht. Haben Wind und Strom die gleiche Richtung, kann man regulär neben der Boje aufschießen, muß aber berücksichtigen, daß das Boot sofort beginnt, achteraus zu treiben. Kreuzen Wind und Strom sich, schießt man in Stromluv neben der Boje auf. Steht Wind gegen Strom, muß einkalkuliert werden, daß das Boot nach dem Aufschießer nicht zum Stillstand kommt, sondern weitertreibt.

Vor der Tonne bildet sich eine „Bugwelle", dahinter eine Wirbelschleppe. Aus beiden kann man Schlüsse ziehen auf die Richtung des Stromes und – mit einiger Erfahrung – auch auf seine Stärke.

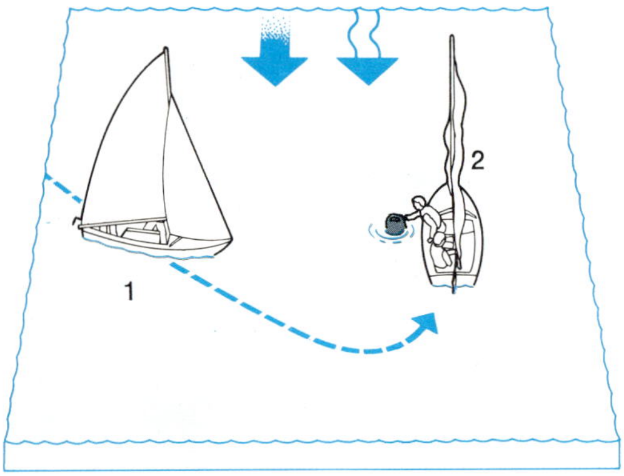

Wind und Strom aus der gleichen Richtung
Angelaufen wird raumschots oder mit halbem Wind. Wegen der Abdrift durch den Strom muß etwas vorgehalten werden (1). Der Aufschießer wird so bemessen, daß die Boje mittschiffs gefaßt werden kann (2).

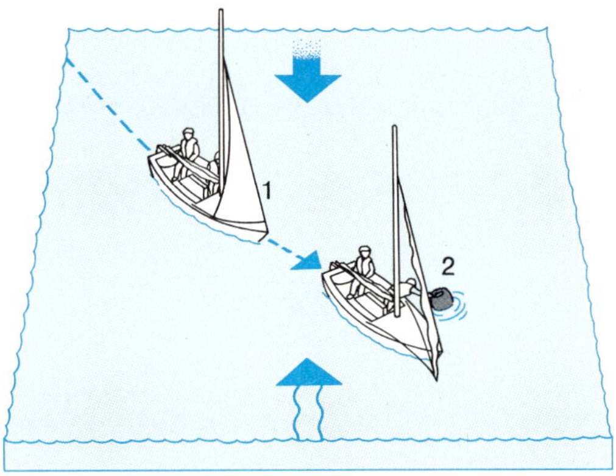

Wind gegen Strom
Ist der Wind stärker als der Strom, wird die Boje so angelaufen, wie auf Seite 86 für ein stehendes Gewässer beschrieben. Ist der Strom stärker, zunächst einen Aufschießer fahren und das Großsegel bergen. Dann abfallen und allein unter Fock die Boje anlaufen. Ist die Vorleine fest, Schwert hoch und Fock runter.

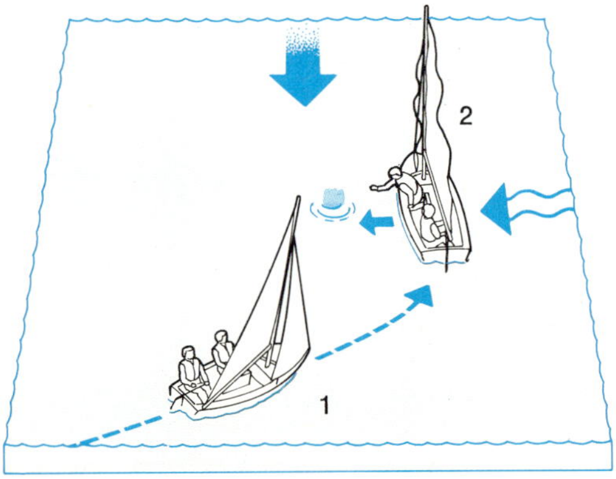

Wind und Strom kreuzen sich
Anlaufen auf einem Am-Wind-Kurs (1). Der Aufschießer erfolgt etwas in Stromluv der Boje, das Boot wird vom Strom seitlich auf die Boje zugetrieben (2).

Ankern

Ein Anker dient dazu, ein Boot sicher am Grund festzuhalten. Auch mit einer Jolle muß hin und wieder geankert werden. Beispielsweise um etwas an Bord zu reparieren, zu baden oder um bei Flaute nicht von einer starken Strömung davongetragen zu werden. Deshalb gehören Anker und Ankerleine einsatzbereit an Bord jeder Jolle, und man muß natürlich auch wissen, wie man mit ihnen umgeht. Es gibt verschiedene Ankertypen, die ihre Vor- und Nachteile haben. Einige kommen von Größe und Gewicht her für Jollen jedoch nicht in Frage.

Eine Jolle vor Anker.

Die Ausrüstung

Der Anker ist auf einer kleinen Jolle stets auch ein Platzproblem. Ein Anker mit großer Haltekraft ist der Danforth-Anker, der sich beigeklappt hervorragend stauen läßt. Allerdings hält er nicht so sehr gut auf stark verkrautetem oder steinigen Grund. Der Falt- oder Schirmdraggen ist ein kleinerer Anker. Die Arme lassen sich an den Schaft klappen und dort sichern. Er ist unter Jollenseglern beliebt wegen seines geringen Platzbedarfs. - Die Ankerleine sollte aus Polyamid sein - es verbindet hohe Bruchfestigkeit mit großer Elastizität - und unten am Anker einen Kettenvorlauf haben. Er zieht durch sein Eigengewicht den Ankerschaft herunter und verstärkt durch seine Haftreibung auf dem Grund die Haltekraft. Eine Leine muß am Anker angeschäkelt werden. Ein Knoten kann sich durch die Reibung leicht lösen. Auf dem Vordeck sollte sich möglichst eine Klampe befinden, um die Ankerleine zu belegen, und zumindest auf einer Seite des Vorstags eine Lippklampe. Sie ist wichtig, weil sie den Bug in Zugrichtung der Ankerleine hält. - Den Anker staut man unter dem Vordeck oder am Boden vor dem Schwertkasten. Dort muß er so verzurrt werden, daß er nicht hin- und herrutschen kann, sich aber schnell wieder lösen läßt. Der beste Platz für die Ankerleine ist ein Eimer unter dem Vordeck, in dem man sie sauber aufschießt, klar zum Auslaufen, mit dem Anker obendrauf. Selbstredend muß das Ende der Leine auf der Klampe oder am Mast fest belegt sein, damit Anker und Leine nicht auf Nimmerwiedersehen in der Tiefe verschwinden.

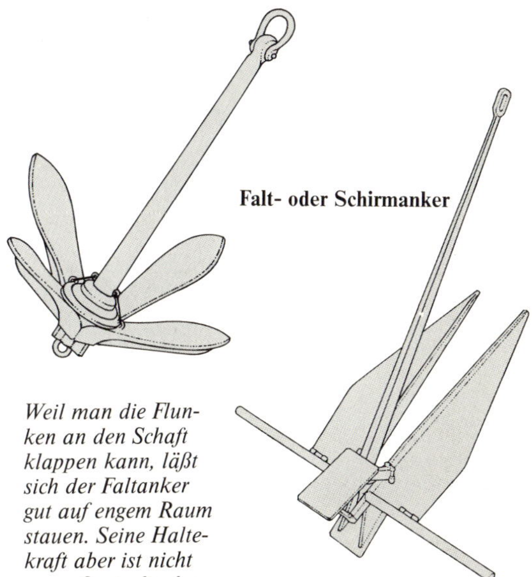

Weil man die Flunken an den Schaft klappen kann, läßt sich der Faltanker gut auf engem Raum stauen. Seine Haltekraft aber ist nicht so groß wie die des Danforth-Ankers.

Ankern in stehenden Gewässern

Hat man seinen Ankerplatz ins Auge gefaßt, dreht man sein Boot bei, um Anker und Ankerleine zu klarieren. Der Anker liegt auf dem Bootsboden, das Ende der Ankerleine wird vorne durch das Bugauge gezogen und wieder zurück zur Klampe geführt. Ist kein Bugauge vorhanden, muß die Ankerleine mit einem Tampen am Vorsteg beigebändselt werden. Das Auge in diesem Tampen muß so groß sein, daß sie glatt durchläuft. Aufpassen, daß sich die Leine nirgendwo verhakt und man nicht mit den Füßen drin steht. Meistens allerdings wird es kaum erforderlich sein, beizudrehen, um den Anker zu klarieren. Sinnvoller ist es, die Fock zu bergen, um das Vorschiff frei zu haben und nicht durch die Fockschoten behindert zu werden. Ist alles klar, am vorgesehenen Ankerplatz aufschießen und den Anker an der Leine Hand über Hand außenbords geben - nicht einfach über Bord werfen. Wenn man merkt, daß er den Grund erreicht hat, weiter so viel Leine ausgeben, daß ihre Länge mindestens der vierfachen Wassertiefe entspricht. Durch kurzes Festhalten der auslaufenden Leine kann man prüfen, ob der Anker auch tatsächlich gefaßt hat. Die beste Kontrolle, um festzustellen, ob das Boot nicht treibt, ist eine Seitenpeilung zu einem Objekt an Land. Das Großsegel wird nicht eher geborgen, um bei einem möglicherweise erforderlich werdenden zweiten Ankermanöver sofort manövrierfähig zu sein. Ein zweites Manöver muß dann gefahren werden, wenn der Anker nicht hält und Gefahr besteht, beispielsweise auf einen anderen Ankerlieger zu treiben.

Wenn keine Lippklampe vorhanden, wird die Ankerleine am Vorstag beigebändselt.

Die Ankerleine wird Hand über Hand ausgegeben bis der Anker den Grund erreicht hat.

Ankerlichten

Zunächst werden das Großsegel und die Fock gesetzt. Die Fock aber noch beigebändselt, damit sie beim Ankerholen nicht behindert. Dann wird die Ankerleine Hand über Hand eingeholt. Dabei holt man das Boot an den Anker heran. Steht die Ankerleine etwa senkrecht, den Anker mit einem kurzen Ruck aus dem Grund brechen, hochholen, abspülen und an Deck nehmen. Vorsicht, daß er nicht die Bordwand verkratzt oder beschädigt. Ähnlich wie beim Ablegen von der Boje holt man den Anker an der künftigen Luvseite ein. Die Fock wird ausgerissen und backgehalten und Lee-Ruder gelegt, bis der Bug weit genug abgefallen ist, um Fahrt voraus aufnehmen zu können.

Ausspülen des (schmutzigen) Ankers nach dem Aufholen.

Ankern in fließendem Gewässer

Zunächst ist festzustellen, wer den größeren Einfluß auf das Boot ausübt: der Wind oder der Strom. Man erkennt das an anderen Ankerliegern, ob sie mit dem Bug in Wind- oder Stromrichtung zeigen. Ist der Strom stärker, wird sich auch mein Boot mit dem Bug in Stromrichtung legen, sobald der Anker gefaßt hat. Steht Wind gegen Strom oder kommt der Wind in einem Winkel bis etwa querab zum Strom, ist es kaum oder gar nicht möglich, den Wind aus dem Großsegel zu bekommen, um es nach dem Ankern bergen zu können. In diesem Fall macht man vorher einen Aufschießer gegen den Wind, nimmt das Großsegel weg und läuft seinen gewählten Ankerplatz allein unter Fock an. Die Fock nachher zu bergen ist selbst bei achterlichem Wind kein Problem. - Beim Ankeraufgehen stellt sich das gleiche Problem. Zunächst muß man feststellen, woher der - schwächere - Wind weht. Kommt er aus dem vorderen Sektor, werden Großsegel und Fock gesetzt, und man holt den Anker ein, wie beschrieben. Kommt der Wind jedoch aus dem hinteren Sektor, kann man das Großsegel nicht, sondern nur die Fock setzen. Der Anker wird aufgenommen, und man läuft unter Fock ab, bis man genügend Raum hat, um so hoch an den Wind zu gehen, daß es möglich ist, das Großsegel zu setzen. Dann wird der Anker klariert, damit er sofort wieder einsatzbereit ist.

Anlaufen des Ankerplatzes allein unter Fock, gegen den Strom. Der Vorschoter ist gerade im Begriff, den Anker außenbords zu geben.

Schleppen

Wahrscheinlich wird man als Jollensegler selten in die Lage kommen, ein anderes Boot zu schleppen. Aber man sollte wenigstens wissen, wie es gemacht wird. Eher wird man selber der Geschleppte sein, etwa wenn der Wind einschläft oder auch nach einer Kenterung. Dann muß man wissen, wie man die Leine anzunehmen, zu belegen und sich zu verhalten hat. Normalerweise wird der Schlepper ein Motorboot sein. Üblich ist es, achteraus zu schleppen (Seite 94). Nur bei glattem Wasser und auf engem Raum kann es sinnvoller sein, längsseits zu schleppen. Manchmal - wenn beispielsweise ein ganzes Regattafeld in einer Flaute liegen bleibt - wird es notwendig, im Verband zu schleppen. Das erfordert eine besondere Schlepptechnik, die auf Seite 94 gezeigt und beschrieben wird.

Längsseits schleppen

Bei Wellengang kann man nicht längsseits schleppen. Die Boote würden heftig gegeneinander schlagen und könnten sich gegenseitig beschädigen. Bei glattem Wasser aber kann längsseits schleppen durchaus vorteilhaft sein, besonders in Schleusen und engen Fahrwassern. Man hat das Boot viel besser unter Kontrolle als ein nachgeschlepptes. Allerdings läßt sich das schleppende Motorboot schlechter manövrieren. - Auf der Jolle werden die Segel geborgen und weggestaut. Das Schwert wird vollständig aufgeholt und das Ruder ausgehängt. Zwischen beide Boote kommen kräftige Fender. Sie müssen erhebliche Druck- und Schubkräfte aufnehmen. Festgemacht wird mit einer Vor- und Achterleine und einer Spring vom Bug des Motorbootes zum Heck der Jolle. (Eine zweite Spring in umgekehrter Richtung wäre auch nicht schlecht für den Fall, daß auch mal Rückwärts manövriert werden muß.) Bleibt die Jollencrew bei sich an Bord, balanciert sie, etwa im hinteren Drittel sitzend, ihr Boot gut aus.

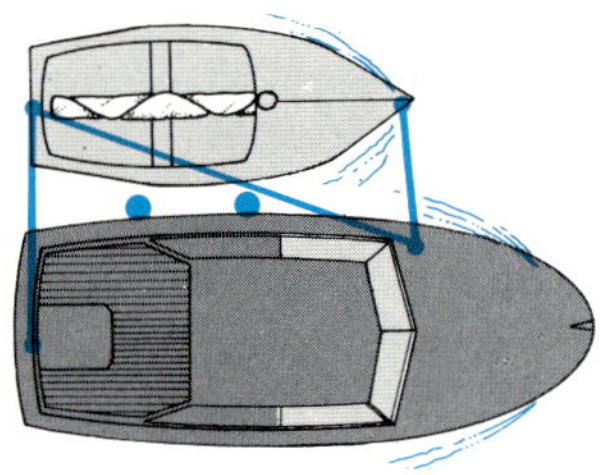

Oben und links: Eine Jolle wird längsseits geschleppt. Die Segel sind weggestaut, die Crew hält das Gleichgewicht. Abweichend von der Zeichnung, sollte die (kleinere) Jolle weiter vorne längsseits genommen werden, damit das Motorboot besser manövrieren kann.

Rechts: Ein Schleppverband. Besser sollten die Segel geborgen werden, wie auf den ersten Booten. Allerdings ist das bei den Topper-Jollen hinten nicht ganz so einfach, weil das Großsegel über den Mast gezogen ist. Aber es muß wenigstens frei auswehen können.

40

Achteraus schleppen

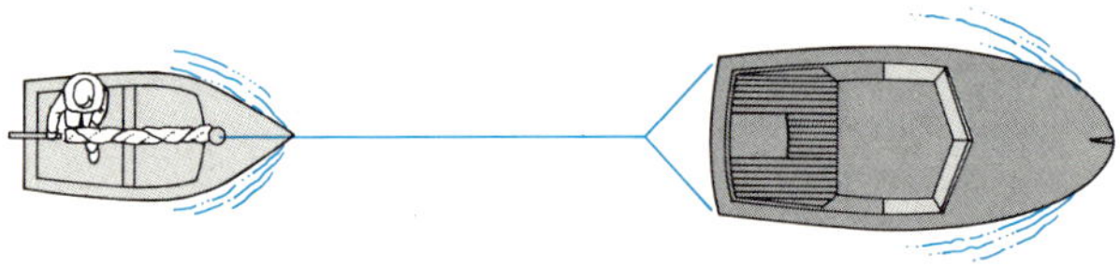

Auch hier gilt zunächst: die Segel bergen und das Schwert hochholen. Das Ruder jedoch wird nicht ausgehängt. Hat die Jolle eine Vorschiffsklampe, wird die Schleppleine zunächst nur mit einem Rundtörn belegt, um beim Anschleppen elastisch nachgeben zu können und ein hartes Einrucksen der Leine zu vermeiden. Dann wird das Ende der Schleppleine mit einem Slipstek am Mast belegt, um notfalls schnell loswerfen zu können. Gibt es keine Vorschiffsklampe, muß die Schleppleine am Vorstag beigebändselt werden. Das Motorboot nimmt die Schleppleine auf die Heckklampe. Sitzt sie nicht mittschiffs, empfiehlt es sich, die Leine über eine Hahnepot (s. Zeichnung) auf die beiden Heckklampen zu führen, damit der Anhang nicht fortwährend nach einer Seite zieht. Der Steuermann der Jolle sitzt weit hinten und hält sich im Kielwasser des Motorbootes.

Der Schleppverband

Sollen mehrere Boote geschleppt werden, auf allen die Segel bergen, das Schwert aufholen und die Schleppleinen klarlegen. Die Schleppleine des ersten Bootes wird auf der Heckklampe des Zugbootes belegt. Die Leinen der folgenden werden – in Ermangelung von Heckbefestigungsmöglichkeiten – an der Mittelducht oder den Fußgurten des Vorgängers festgemacht. Alle Boote, bis auf das letzte, hängen ihre Ruder aus. Die Crew plaziert sich weit hinten im Boot. Der Steuermann des letzten Bootes im Verband hält den ganzen Pulk auf Kurs im Kielwasser des Schleppers. Das erfordert Aufmerksamkeit und Geschick. Deshalb sollte der erfahrenste Steuermann in das letzte Boot gesetzt werden. Bei glattem Wasser kann der Verband auch verkürzt werden, indem man je einen Pulk auf die beiden Heckklampen des Zugbootes hängt (linke Abbildung). Der Mann im letzten Boot jedes Anhangs muß so steuern, daß die Boote nicht zusammenstoßen.
Nach einer anderen Methode schleppt das Zugboot eine starke Trosse nach, in die in einem Abstand von ungefähr 5 Metern Augen eingespleißt sind. Die Jollen brauchen sich dort mit ihren Vorleinen nur einzupicken. Oder – wenn die Trosse keine Augen hat – stecken sie ihre Schleppleine mit einem Stopperstek an. Und zwar rechts und links der Trosse auf Lücke. Nebeneinander festgemacht, würden sich die Bootskörper gegenseitig ansaugen. In diesem Fall darf die Schleppleine nicht am Vorstag beigebändselt werden. Sie darf auch nicht auf einer weit vorne sitzenden Vorschiffsklampe belegt werden, denn der Bug muß abscheren können, damit das Boot geradeaus läuft. Das Abscheren bewirkt die Ruderlage, jeweils von der Trosse weg. Festgemacht wird die Leine am Mast. Auch muß das Schwert etwas gefiert bleiben, um die Ruderwirkung zu verbessern.

Rechts: Die Boote sind an eine zentrale Schlepptrosse angesteckt. Allerdings sollten sich die Steuerleute besser im Auge behalten, anstatt sich den Rücken zuzukehren. Außerdem erhält das geschleppte Boot ohnehin ein krängendes Moment leineneinwärts.

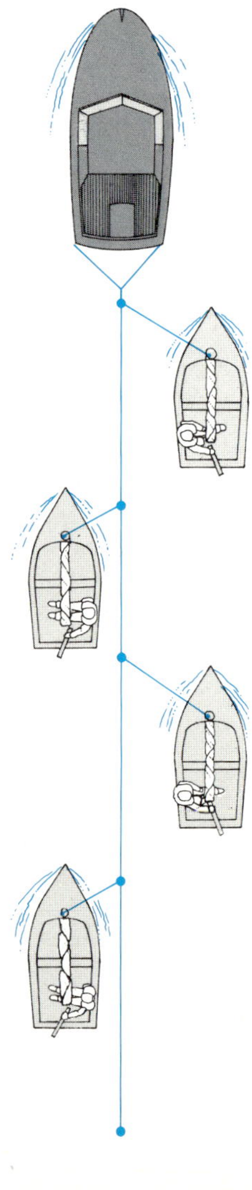

Unten: Nur bei glattem Wasser möglich. Der Mann im letzten Boot steuert den ganzen Pulk.

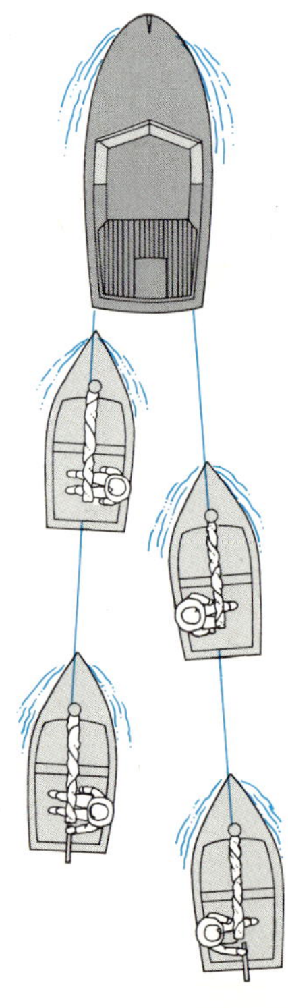

Auf dem Schlepper

Niemand sollte versuchen, ein Boot zu schleppen, so lange er nicht im Umgang mit seinem Motorboot hinlänglich vertraut ist. Und um einen Verband von mehreren Booten in rauhem Wasser zu schleppen, bedarf es schon einiger Erfahrung. Es sollten stets zwei an Bord sein: einer, der fährt, und einer, der den Schlepp beobachtet. Wenn man ein Boot im Seegang schleppt, muß die Leinenlänge so bemessen sein, daß sich beide Boote in der gleichen Wellenphase befinden, also gleichzeitig entweder auf dem Wellenkamm oder im Wellental. Werden mehrere Boote geschleppt, kann die Leine verkürzt werden. Bei achterlichem Wind und einem leichten Boot im Schlepp muß die Leine so weit verlängert werden, daß das Boot nicht auf der Heckwelle des Schleppers ins Surfen kommen kann und möglicherweise aufs Heck kracht. Das Motorboot darf nur so schnell fahren, daß die sogenannte Rumpfgeschwindigkeit eines kleinen Anhangs nicht überschritten wird, sonst besteht die Gefahr des Quer- und Umschlagens. Die Besatzung auf dem Anhang muß soweit wie möglich achtern sitzen, damit das Boot nicht giert, und das Schwert aufholen. Beim Loswerfen der Schleppleine am Ziel unbedingt darauf achten, daß sie nicht in den Propeller gerät.

Schleppen unter Segeln

Gelegentlich wird man auch als Jollensegler – beispielsweise bei einem Notfall – ein anderes Boot abschleppen müssen. Es ist recht schwierig, eine Schleppverbindung herzustellen, wenn sich beide Boote unter Segeln befinden. Deshalb ist es keine schlechte Entscheidung, wenn beide die Segel bergen und per Paddel Kontakt aufnehmen. In jedem Fall muß das zu schleppende Boot vorher die Segel bergen. Es behält das Schwert so lange unten, bis die Schleppleine festgemacht ist. Wird die Schleppverbindung unter Segeln hergestellt, nimmt der Schlepper die Leine in Luv über. Er läuft hoch am Wind an und braucht dann neben dem anderen Boot nur die Schoten zu fieren, um in Ruhe die Leine überzunehmen und bei sich auf der Heckklampe oder an den hinteren Fußgurten festzumachen. Dann die Schoten wieder dichtholen und langsam die Schleppleine steiffahren. Danach weiter abfallen, um mehr Fahrt aufzunehmen. Mit einem Boot im Schlepp kann man alle Segelmanöver fahren, nur nicht sehr hoch an den Wind gehen. Die Besatzung auf dem Anhang ist jeweils über die geplanten Manöver zu verständigen. Sie hat das Schwert ungefähr dreiviertel hoch, sitzt im hinteren Drittel des Bootes und steuert im Kielwasser des Schleppers.

Es sollten stets mindestens zwei Mann an Bord des schleppenden Motorbootes sein: einer der fährt, und einer, der den Anhang nicht aus dem Auge läßt.

Segeln auf See

Wer auf Binnengewässern segeln gelernt hat, für den ist es aufregend und eine Herausforderung zugleich, auch die See zu befahren. Er muß zuvor aber lernen, die See mit Respekt zu behandeln, und wissen, daß die Gefahren viel größer sind als auf einem geschützten Binnenrevier. Man kann dort sehr schnell unbeabsichtigt außer Landsicht geraten, und wenn man Schwierigkeiten irgendwelcher Art bekommt, ist weit und breit niemand da, einem zu helfen. Man muß einiges hinzulernen für das Seesegeln, in der Theorie und auch in der Praxis. In praktischer Hinsicht hat man sich mit dem Seegang und dem Gezeitenstrom auseinanderzusetzen, in der Theorie muß man sich mit Gezeiten- und Wetterkunde befassen.

Man darf nie auf die See hinausgehen, ohne sein Boot vorher gründlich durchgecheckt zu haben, ob sich die richtige Ausrüstung an Bord befindet und in einwandfreiem Zustand ist. Man muß eine gültige (berichtigte) Seekarte des entsprechenden Gebiets an Bord haben und einen Kompaß. Wer beabsichtigt, sich weiter von der Küste zu entfernen, muß Rettungssignalmittel mitnehmen. Zur persönlichen Ausrüstung gehört: Kleidung zum Wechseln in wasserdichten Beuteln, eine Flasche mit Wasser (oder einem nichtalkoholischen Getränk) und Kraftnahrung. Jemand ist über die genaue Reiseroute und -ziel und die voraussichtliche Rückkunftszeit zu informieren, um notfalls erfolgversprechende Hilfsmaßnahmen veranlassen zu können. Natürlich muß man sich bei ihm auch zurückmelden.

Von diesen Dingen einmal abgesehen, bringt Seesegeln ungeheuren Spaß. Es eröffnet völlig neue Perspektiven und vermittelt großartige Erlebnisse. Wenn man unter Land bleibt und mit Seekarte und Tidenkalender umgehen kann, kommt man ohne große navigatorische Kenntnisse auch auf längeren Küstentörns gut zurecht.

(Der Ansicht des Autors muß entschieden widersprochen und der Standpunkt des deutschen Segelsports entgegengehalten werden, daß kenterbare Jollen nichts auf der See zu suchen haben. Siehe dazu auch die Anmerkung auf Seite 74. - Bearbeiter)

Auslaufen zu einem Tagestörn. Sorgfältige Planung ist Voraussetzung für eine problemlose und erholsame Fahrt.

Wetter

Etwas Kenntnis über Anzeichen der Wetterentwicklung ist beim Segeln auf See immens wichtig, um nicht draußen von einem Wettersturz überrascht zu werden und in eine schwierige, ja lebensbedrohliche Lage zu kommen. Bei einer Regatta auf See ist es auch ganz nützlich, vorher zu wissen, wie der Wind drehen und seine Stärke eventuell ändern wird; mit Wetterkenntnis kann man gewinnen. Man braucht nicht zu wissen, warum Wetter sich ändert oder nicht, es genügt zu wissen, nach welchen Regeln das abläuft. Die meisten Regattabahnen für Jollensegler liegen in Zonen, die von einer Folge von Tiefdruckgebieten und Zwischenhochs durchwandert werden. Erstere bringen starken, auf der Nordhälfte der Erde allmählich rechts drehenden Wind, wogegen Hochs gleichmäßiges Wetter mit meist stetigen, leichten Winden bringen. Tiefs können schon mal festliegen, meist aber wandern sie relativ schnell in östlicher Richtung. Sie kündigen sich durch anfangs hohe Schleierwolken an, denen dichtere und allmählich niedrigere Bewölkung folgt. In solchem Falle ist es ratsam, sich beim örtlichen Wetterdienst (Telefonansage) über die Stärke des heranziehenden Tiefs zu erkundigen. Die allgemeine Windvorhersage des Rundfunks für Nord- und Ostsee kann durch augenblickliche Entwicklungen überholt sein. Mit einem Tief kommt gewöhnlich Regen, der manchen vom Segeln abhält, aber im tropischen bis gemäßigten Klima seglerisch problemlos ist.
An einer offenen Küste und auch an den Ufern großer Seen entsteht an sonnigen Tagen, etwa zwei Stunden vor Sonnenmittag, die Seebrise, ein auflandiger Wind, der beträchtliche Stärke erreichen kann. Er entsteht durch schnellere Erwärmung des Landes unter der Sonne, was die Luft überm Land schneller erwärmt und aufsteigen läßt. In den dadurch entstandenen Unterdruck über Land strömt kühlere Luft vom Meer ein. Die Seebrise weht senkrecht zur Küstenlinie, wenn ihr nicht ein anderes Windsystem mit einer schrägeren Anströmung überlagert ist. Auf großen Seen, wie dem Bodensee, kann es bei Badewetter sein, daß rings um die Ufer der Wind auf Land weht und in der Seemitte totale Flaute herrscht. Nachts ist es dann umgekehrt, weil Land schneller abkühlt als Wasser, und Luft erwärmt sich praktisch nur an Oberflächen, nicht an Sonnen- und anderen Wärmestrahlen.
Beim Segeln in Küsten- oder Ufernähe muß man daran denken, daß jedes hohe Objekt, Felswand oder Hochhaus, bei ablandigem Wind einen Windschatten über das küstennahe Wasser legt. Das kann bei leichtem Wind eine Flautenzone sein, bei starkem Wind aber ist es immer ein turbulentes Gebiet mit bockigen Böen aus schnell wechselnden Richtungen, die oft auch die erfahrensten Jollenchampions reihenweise umschmeißen. Ähnlich muß man sich vor Landengen und Tälern in hohen Küsten hüten, denn aus denen pfeift ein Wind wie aus einem Jet.
Wenn Hochdruck das Wetter beherrscht, kommen rasche Drehungen des Windes und Änderungen seiner Stärke nicht vor, dafür aber kann es recht beständig einige Tage lang hart aus Nordost über Ost-, Nordsee und Ärmelkanal und die küstennahen Binnenmeere wehen. Am frühen Vormittag ist es entweder wolkenlos, oder Hochnebel läßt die Sonne nur milchig durchscheinen. Doch bald klart es auf, die milde Landbrise hört auf, ein bis zwei Stunden später setzt die Seebrise ein, und am späten Nachmittag kann es Haufenwolken mit Blitz und Donner und starken Böen geben. Der nächste Morgen ist wieder friedlich, außer es zögen hohe Brautschleier am Himmel auf, die ein herankommendes Tief anmelden.

Wellen

Wellen entstehen dadurch, daß der Wind auf eine Wasserfläche einwirkt. Wellenlänge und Wellenhöhe hängen davon ab, wie lange der Wind weht und wie lang seine Anlaufstrecke ist, ob er über einen längeren Zeitraum aus derselben Richtung kommt oder aus wechselnden Richtungen weht. Insofern unterscheiden sich die Wellen auf See beträchtlich von denen auf Binnengewässern, die schnell entstehen, aber fast ebenso schnell auch wieder verschwinden, wenn der Wind nachläßt. Auf See hingegen dauert ihre Ausprägung länger, sie stehen aber auch länger durch. Haben Wind und Strom die gleiche Richtung, bleiben die Wellen relativ flach. Steht der Wind gegen Strom, können sie sich - bei gleicher Windstärke - zu üblen Brechern aufbauen. In tiefem Wasser hat man meistens eine längere Welle, mit der man recht gut zurecht kommen kann. Kritisch wird es im flacheren Küstenbereich, wo die Wellen kürzer werden und brechen. Die Brandung kann das Boot überrollen oder kentern.

Gezeiten

Die Höhe des Meeresspiegels ändert sich durch die Massenanziehungskräfte (Gravitation) von Sonne und Mond auf das Wasser in Verbindung mit der Erddrehung. Dieser Rhythmus heißt Gezeit oder plattdeutsch Tide. An einigen Stellen der Erde gibt es täglich nur eine Tide, bestehend aus einem Hochwasser und einem Niedrigwasser, doch häufiger sind zwei Tiden je Tag mit je etwa sechs Stunden zwischen Hoch- und Niedrigwasser. Die Höhendifferenz kann zwischen einigen Dezimetern und zwölf Metern liegen, bedingt durch Topographie von Meeresboden und Küsten. Die Gravitation, die das in Bewegung setzt, ist berechenbar und damit auch das Tidenmuster, und somit kann man für sein Segelrevier Gezeitentabellen kaufen, in denen für jeden Tag steht, um welche Zeit Hochwasser und Niedrigwasser ist. In Revieren mit großem Tidenhub muß man schon die Zeit des Ablegens und der Wiederkehr nach der Gezeit richten, um sein Boot nicht über weite Strecken Strand oder Schlick schleppen zu müssen.
Da sich die Erde unter dem von Sonne und Mond geschaffenen Wasserberg hinweg dreht, kommt er an den Kontinentalküsten als scheinbare Welle an, die nicht sehr hoch ist, sich aber in tiefen Buchten und engen Durchfahrten, wie dem Englischen Kanal, und in Flußmündungen zu großer Höhe aufstaut. Dadurch entstehen Strömungen, Flut- und Ebbstrom, die ihre Richtung und Stärke beträchtlich ändern: Sie sind in Strömungsatlanten für jede Stunde mit kleinen Richtungspfeilen und zwei Geschwindigkeiten für Spring- und Nipptide in Knoten aufgezeichnet.
Bei Springtide ist die Höhendifferenz am größten, denn dann ziehen Sonne und Mond in derselben Richtung – um die Vollmond- und die Neumondzeit. Während „Halbmond” (eigentlich 1. und 3. Viertel) ist Nipptide. Im englisch-französischen Revier setzen zur Springzeit Ströme bis zu 4 Knoten, gegen die anzusegeln ein hoffnungsloses Unterfangen ist. Besser wartet man an Land oder vor Anker ab, bis der Strom in die gewünschte Richtung setzt.
Eine Tide gibt es auch in den als tidenfrei geltenden Randmeeren wie Ostsee und Mittelmeer, aber ihre Höhe ist so gering, daß ihr praktisch keine Bedeutung zukommt.
Es muß hier gesagt werden, daß die übliche Erklärung mit dem Wasserberg unter dem Zenit zwar anschaulich, aber zu einfach ist. In Wahrheit geht es um eine recht komplizierte Mathematik, und sie ist für Ozeanküsten anders als für Schelfmeere wie die Nordsee.

Hochwasser

Niedrigwasser

Segeln im Tidengewässer

Es ist beim Segeln in einem Tidenrevier ohne Frage wichtig zu wissen, wohin und mit welcher Geschwindigkeit die Strömung setzt. Aber es gibt da eine Lehre, man müsse, um an sein Ziel auf der anderen Seite der Strömung zu kommen, schräg gegen den Strom segeln, sonst mache man einen Umweg, weil der Strom einen seitlich mit sich forttrage, und man diese Versetzung auf der anderen Seite wieder gegen den Strom hinaufsegeln müsse. Der Denkfehler darin: Ob über die ganze Strombreite mit Vorhalt geradlinig über den Strom oder erst am Ende der Versetzung den Strom hinauf, das ist theoretisch derselbe Weg gegen den Strom; aber der Strom ist in der Mitte stärker als an den Rändern. Also segelt man in Strommitte langsamer, denn der Widerstand wächst mit dem Quadrat der am Boot vorbeirauschenden Wassergeschwindigkeit. Stromvorhalt sollte man auf kleiner Fahrt nur segeln, wenn dies wegen enger Durchfahrten oder einer Hafeneinfahrt nötig ist, wenn es also um Gefahrvermeidung geht, sonst ist es Unsinn.
In Tidengewässern kommt es aber auch darauf an, seinen Segelausflug so zu planen, daß man nicht zur Abendstunde, wenn man heim möchte, den Tidenstrom gegen sich hat. Darum segelt man am Morgen dorthin, wo man am Abend stromauf von seinem Heimathafen liegt.

Deckpeilungen

Bei einer Deckpeilung hält man ein näherliegendes und ein fernerliegendes festes Objekt in Deckung oder Linie, wie die Zeichnung unten rechts zeigt. Solche Richtlinien sind, wenn vorhanden, ein vorzügliches Mittel, um bei Strömung oder stark versetzendem Wind heil durch gefährliche Passagen zu kommen, indem man so steuert, daß man die Objekte immer in Linie sieht. Die Zeichnung zeigt links zwei weitere Felsen, deren Kanten man als Deckpeilung für den Kurswechsel nach Steuerbord zur Hafeneinfahrt hin verwenden kann, wobei „in Linie" nun für den Blick achteraus gilt. Freilich läßt sich nur aus der Seekarte erkennen, ob sich eine sichere Deckpeilung anbietet, oder eine erkannte durch sicheres Wasser führt. Am Auswandern einer Vordermarke gegen eine Hintermarke (Zeichnungen unten links) ist immer sicher zu erkennen, daß man von einer Strömung quer versetzt wird.

Der Felsen ist zu weit nach rechts ausgewandert. Um ihn in Deckung zu bringen, muß Steuerbord gehalten werden.

Felsen und Klippe sind genau in Linie (Deckung).

Der Felsen ist zu weit nach links ausgewandert. Um ihn wieder in Deckung mit der Klippe zu bringen, muß Backbord gehalten werden.

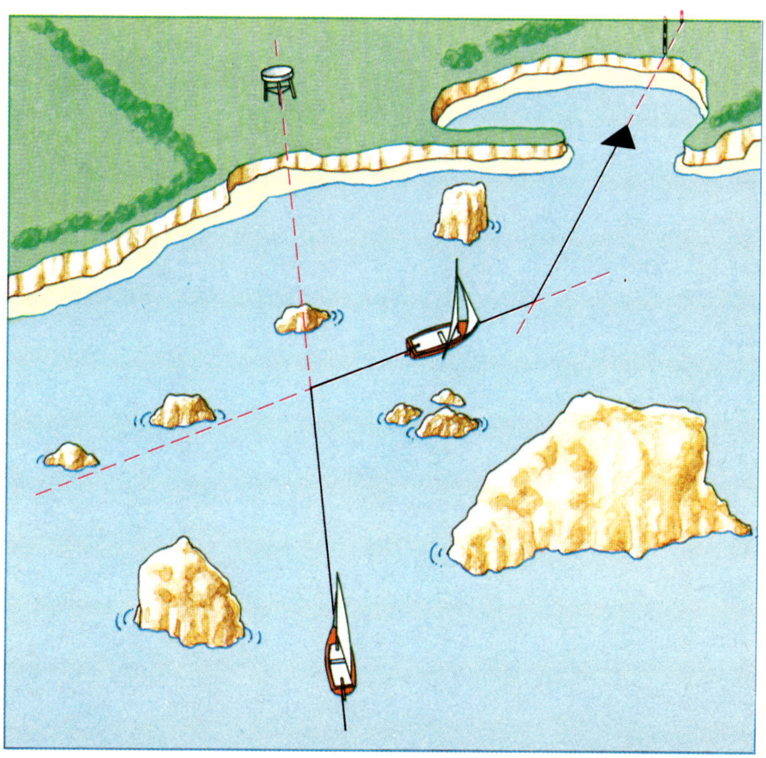

Die Wahl der Route

Wer seinen ersten Seetörn unternimmt, sollte keinen falschen Ehrgeiz an den Tag legen und sich seine Etappenziele zu weit stecken. Schon einige Stunden bei Windstärke 3 (7 - 10 Knoten Windgeschwindigkeit) zu segeln, schlaucht im Anfang ganz schön. Deshalb sollte man sicher gehen, an seinem ersten Ziel vernünftig essen und trinken zu können. Und – man muß dort auch in schäbiger oder nasser Segelkleidung als Gast willkommen sein. Stets sollte man ein näher gelegenes Etappenziel in der Hinterhand haben, falls man im nachlassenden Wind versauert. Auf einer Übersichtskarte studiert man zunächst, ob der geplante Kurs problematische Gebiete berührt. Etwa eine stark befahrene Schiffahrtsroute oder vielleicht ein Sperrgebiet, das weiträumig umfahren werden muß. Dann arbeitet man sich besser eine neue Route aus, die diese Gebiete meidet und behält bei alledem im Auge, möglichst unter Landschutz zu bleiben. Segelt man in Tidengewässern sind die Gezeitentafeln sorgfältig zu Rate zu ziehen. Man notiert sich die Zeiten für Hoch- und Niedrigwasser des betreffenden Tages und die erwartete Höhe der Flut. Dann schlägt man im Gezeitenatlas nach, um die Richtung des Stromes für das fragliche Gebiet festzustellen. Möglichst sollte man seine Fahrt so einrichten, daß der Strom die gleiche Richtung hat wie der Kurs oder ihn wenigstens nur kreuzt. Wenn die Stromgeschwindigkeit mehr als 1 Knoten beträgt, sollte man Fahrten gegenan besser vergessen. Dann ist es vernünftiger, sich eine andere Route zurechtzulegen oder Abfahrts- und Ankunftszeiten zu ändern.

Vorbereitung des Bootes

Selbst wenn man überzeugt ist, daß sich sein Boot in einwandfreiem Zustand befindet, ist ein allerletzter gründlicher Check vor einem Seetörn unerläßlich. Dabei gilt das Augenmerk vor allem dem laufenden und stehenden Gut, den Segeln, den Beschlägen und dem Ruder. Man muß sich stets vor Augen halten, daß man völlig auf sich allein angewiesen ist, wenn irgend etwas zu Bruch geht. Ein Erste-Hilfe-Kasten gehört an Bord, wie es sie speziell für Yachten zusammengestellt gibt. Wichtig ist auch ein gutes Sonnenschutzmittel, denn die Gefahr eines Sonnenbrandes ist auf dem Wasser besonders groß. Ein Satz Seenotsignale gehört zur Ausrüstung, ein Bordmesser, ein Schraubenzieher und eine Zange. Außerdem Ersatzteile für alles, was eventuell kaputtgehen könnte, Ersatztauwerk und Ersatzpaddel, falls eines zerbrechen oder verlorengehen sollte. Das hört sich ziemlich gewaltig an, läßt sich aber alles ohne Schwierigkeiten auf einer Jolle unterbringen. Selbstverständlich wird auf See ständig eine Rettungsweste getragen, auch bei nur leichtem Wind.

Eine Jolle startet zu einem Seetörn. In Erwartung eines stärkeren Windes außerhalb der Landabdeckung, ist das Großsegel vorsorglich gerefft worden.

Wetterberichte

Um das Risiko während eines Seetörns so gering wie möglich zu halten, ist es dringend erforderlich, sich vor der Fahrt alle nur zugänglichen Wetterinformationen zu verschaffen: Die Wettervorhersagen von Rundfunk und Fernsehen, die telefonischen Wetterinformationen, die Wetterkarten und Wetternachrichten bei den Hafenmeistern von Marinas und Yachtclubs. Wetterinformationen erhält man auch von der Wasserschutzpolizei, von Hafenämtern und über Sprechfunk von den Küstenfunkstellen.

Verspricht die Wetterprognose nichts Gutes, bleibt man lieber an Land und wartet ab, was kommt. Auch auf die Gefahr hin, daß der angekündigte Sturm ausbleibt und es ein verlorenes Wochenende war. Am meisten wird Nebel in der Schiffahrt gefürchtet. Deshalb niemals bei Nebel auslaufen im Vertrauen darauf, daß er sich bald auflösen wird. Wird man unterwegs von Nebel überrascht, auf dem kürzesten Weg das nächste Ufer anlaufen oder zumindest in Ufernähe ankern.

Alle Wettervorhersagen haben einen nicht unwesentlichen Nachteil: Sie umfassen nämlich verhältnismäßig große Räume. Deshalb kommt man, gerade in der nahen Küstenfahrt, kaum umhin, eigene Wetterbeobachtungen anzustellen und daraus seine Schlüsse zu ziehen. Das erfordert zugegebenermaßen neben gewissen meteorologischen Grundkenntnissen, eine scharfe Beobachtungsgabe und viel Erfahrung.

Stärke nach Beaufort	*Bezeichnung und Windgeschwindigkeit (Knoten)*	*Beschreibung der Vorgänge an Land*	*Segelbedingungen für Jollen*
0	*Windstille unter 1*	*Rauch steigt senkrecht auf. Blätter bewegen sich nicht.*	*Durch Krängung die benetzte Oberfläche reduzieren und den Segeln ein strömungsgünstigeres Profil geben. Keine plötzlichen Bewegungen.*
1	*Leiser Zug 1 – 3*	*Windrichtung nur an ziehendem Rauch erkennbar. Windfahnen reagieren nicht.*	*Das Boot macht leichte Fahrt voraus. Das Boot ist so auszubalancieren, daß der Bug etwas tiefer eintaucht und Leekrängung erreicht wird.*
2	*Leichte Brise 4 – 6*	*Wind im Gesicht fühlbar. Blätter bewegen sich. Leichte Wimpel strecken sich nicht. Windfahnen reagieren.*	*Wind reicht aus, um mit aufrecht gesegeltem Boot eine gleichmäßige Fahrt voraus zu machen. Die Segel stehen voll, müssen jedoch wechselnden Windrichtungen und Windgeschwindigkeiten angepaßt werden.*
3	*Schwache Brise 7 – 10*	*Leichte Wimpel strecken sich. Blätter in ständiger Bewegung.*	*Die meisten Jollen segeln mit Rumpfgeschwindigkeit. Leichte Jollen kommen ins Gleiten. Ideale Bedingungen für Anfänger.*
4	*Mäßige Brise 11 – 16*	*Schwere Wimpel strecken sich. Staub und Papier können hochgeweht werden.*	*Die Mannschaft reitet voll aus. Auf den meisten Kursen kommt das Boot ins Gleiten. Für Anfänger zu hart. Sie sollten ihr Boot an Land bringen.*
5	*Frische Brise 17 – 21*	*Kleine Bäume biegen sich. Baumwipfel in erheblicher Bewegung.*	*Ideale Segelbedingungen für erfahrene Segler. Boote mit weniger erfahrenen Besatzungen kentern vielfach.*
6	*Starker Wind 22 – 27*	*Große Zweige werden bewegt. Wind singt in den Drähten.*	*Sturmbedingungen für Jollensegler. Ohne Reffen ist oft kaum Fahrt voraus möglich. Nur für erfahrene Crews, die an Regatten teilnehmen.*
7	*Steifer Wind 28 – 33*	*Bäume werden bewegt. Fühlbare Hemmungen beim Gehen gegen den Wind.*	*Kein Wetter mehr für Jollen.*
8	*Stürmischer Wind 34 – 40*	*Zweige brechen ab. Beim Gehen erhebliche Behinderung.*	*Jollen müssen an Land festgezurrt werden, damit der Wind sie nicht wegbläst.*

Zurück an Land

Will man sich Boot und Ausrüstung lange erhalten, muß man pfleglich damit umgehen. Sobald man wieder an Land zurück ist, sollten sie mit klarem Wasser abgespritzt werden. Vor allem dann, wenn man in Salzwasser war, aber auch in verunreinigten Binnengewässern. Segel und Schoten müssen ebenfalls abgespült und getrocknet werden, bevor man sie verstaut. Ruder und Ausrüstung nur dann im Boot lassen, wenn man einen diebstahlsicheren Stellplatz hat. Die Segel sollte man in jedem Fall mit nach Hause nehmen. Die Fallen werden mit Stropps vom Mast zurückgebunden, damit sie nicht im Wind dagegen schlagen können. Inspektionsluken der Lufttanks zur Belüftung öffnen und ebenfalls die Lenzer. Das Boot sollte stets mit einer Plane abgedeckt und am Boden verankert werden, damit es der Wind nicht umwerfen kann.

Abgedeckte Jollen auf ihren Landstellplätzen.

Zusammenlegen des Großsegels

Dazu breitet man das Segel glatt auf dem Boden aus. Wenn man es zu zweit macht, geht es schneller und besser. Vor dem Zusammenlegen müssen die Segellatten entfernt werden.

1 *Ausgegangen wird vom Unterliek. Das Segel wird in einem Abstand von etwa 1 m zum Unterliek hin eingeschlagen.*

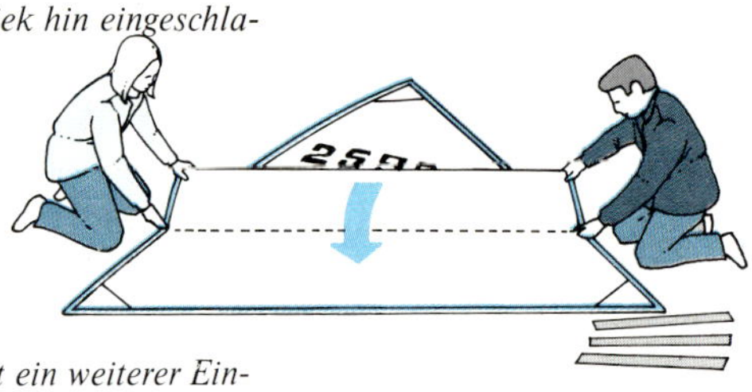

2 *Es folgt ein weiterer Einschlag.*

3 *Und so weiter schichtet man Bahn für Bahn fächerartig übereinander…*

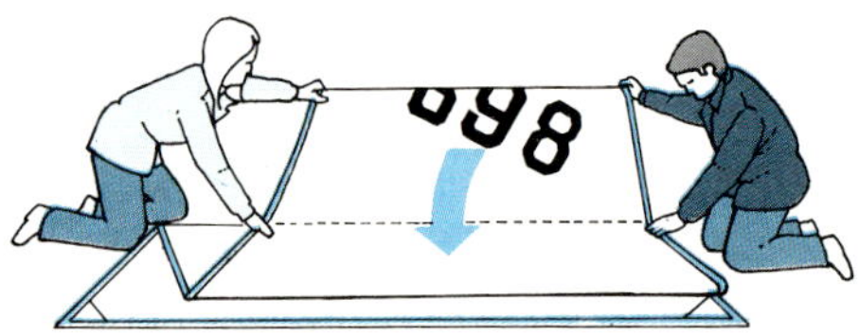

4 *…bis schließlich der Segelkopf obenauf liegt.*

5 *Nun wird das Segel von der Seite her zu einem handlichen Paket zusammengefaltet und dann im Segelsack verstaut.*

Aufrollen der Fock

Die meisten Vorsegel haben ein Drahtvorliek, deshalb sollten sie nicht eingeknickt, sondern so zusammengerollt werden, wie es hier gezeigt wird. Die Schot sollte besser abgenommen werden.

1 *Das Segel wird am Vorliek angefaßt …*

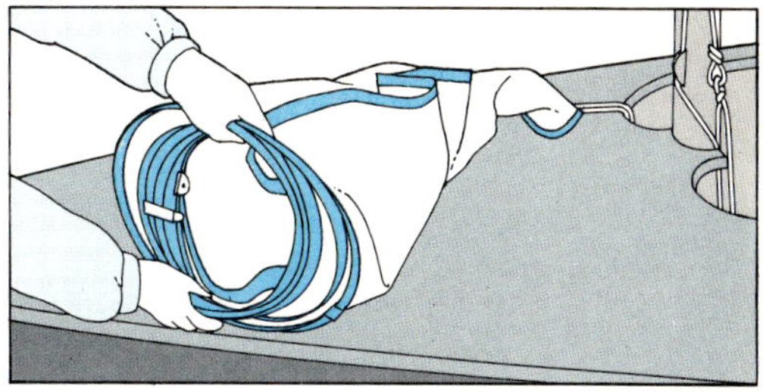

2 *… und vom Kopf zum Hals hin eingerollt.*

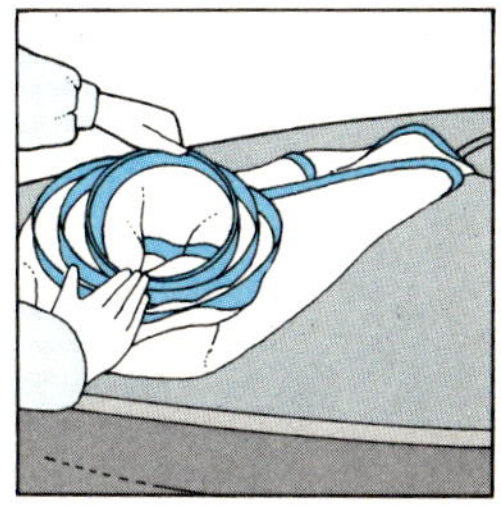

3 *Der so entstandene Schlauch wird vom Vorliek her locker zusammengelegt und im Segelsack verstaut.*

Lagern des Bootes

Nur die wenigsten Jollen haben einen Liegeplatz im Wasser, die überwiegende Mehrheit wird an Land gelagert. Wie man sein Boot lagert, hängt von der Größe und der zur Verfügung stehenden Lagermöglichkeit ab. Wo vorhanden, können kleine leichte Boote in entsprechenden Stellagen gestapelt werden. Größere Jollen lagern am besten auf ihrem Slipwagen, den Bug angehoben. So kann eingedrungenes oder Kondenzwasser zu den Lenzern im Spiegel auslaufen. Das Boot wird mit einer Plane - einer Persennig - abgedeckt.

Eine spezielle Trolley- und Trailerkombination für ein Kiel-Rennboot.

Abdecken des Bootes
Diese Jolle ist mustergültig abgedeckt und aufgebockt. Die Persennig ist mit Stropps unter dem Bootsboden gesichert, der Rumpf mit Steinen am Boden verankert. Durch die Schrägstellung kann mögliches Kondenswasser aus den Lenzöffnungen im Spiegel abfließen.

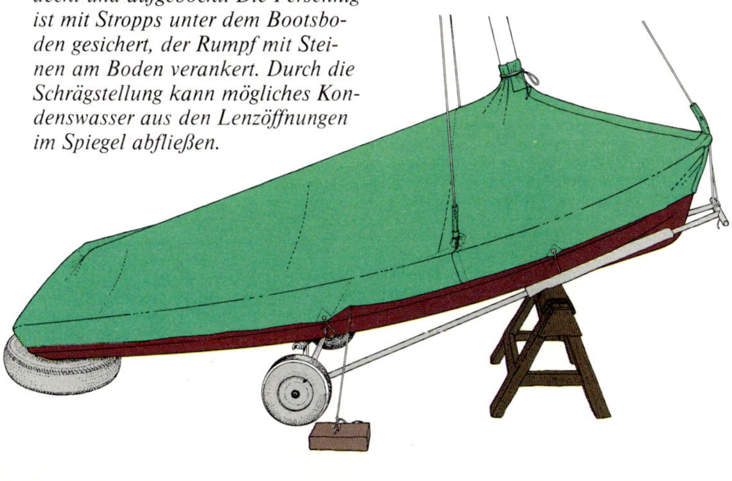

Eine unters Boot gezogene Persennig als Rumpfschutz.

Dach- und Trailertransport

Nur wenige Segler sind in der glücklichen Lage, daß sie ihr Boot nahe am Wasser abstellen können und es bei Bedarf einfach nur abzuslippen brauchen. Die Mehrzahl von ihnen muß ihr Boot weit vom Wasser entfernt abstellen. Wer sein Boot mit nach Hause nehmen muß oder Regattasegler, die ihr Boot über größere Distanzen befördern müssen, stehen vor dem Problem des Bootstransports. Am einfachsten ist es, das Boot auf dem Wagendach zu befördern, sofern es hinsichtlich Größe und Gewicht den Bestimmungen der Straßenverkehrsordnung entspricht. Zur Halterung des Bootes werden zwei gepolsterte Einzelträger auf das Wagendach montiert. Boot, Mast und Baum werden sorgfältig auf diesen Trägern gelascht. Die Segel und andere Ausrüstungsgegenstände kommen ins Auto. Ist das Boot für den Dachtransport zu groß oder zu schwer, wird es auf einem Spezialtrailer hinter dem Auto gezogen. Abhängig vom Typ des Trailers wird das Boot entweder auf dem Trailer direkt verladen, oder gleich auf seinem Slipwagen montiert auf dem Trailer befördert. Für den Dachtransport gibt es keine Geschwindigkeitsbegrenzung. Beim Trailertransport beträgt die Höchstgeschwindigkeit in der Bundesrepublik 80 km/h. Im Ausland gelten zum Teil andere Geschwindigkeitsbeschränkungen.

Verladen des Bootes

Gewöhnlich transportiert man das Boot kieloben auf dem Wagendach, so daß es mit seinem flachen Deck sicher auf den Dachträgern liegt. Muß es aus besonderen Gründen andersherum befördert werden, ist auf besonders sorgfältige Verzurrung zu achten. Außerdem sollte es gegen Regenwasser abgedeckt werden. Das Boot wird mit dem Bug voran transportiert und mit Gummistropps oder Tauwerk seitlich überkreuz mit dem Dachträger verschnürt. Bug und Heck werden mit den Stoßstangen verlascht, damit sich das Boot bei schneller Fahrt nicht abhebt. Um Schäden an Rumpf und Farbe zu vermeiden, sollten Dachträger und Haltetauwerk mit Schaumstoff oder ähnlichem unterlegt werden.

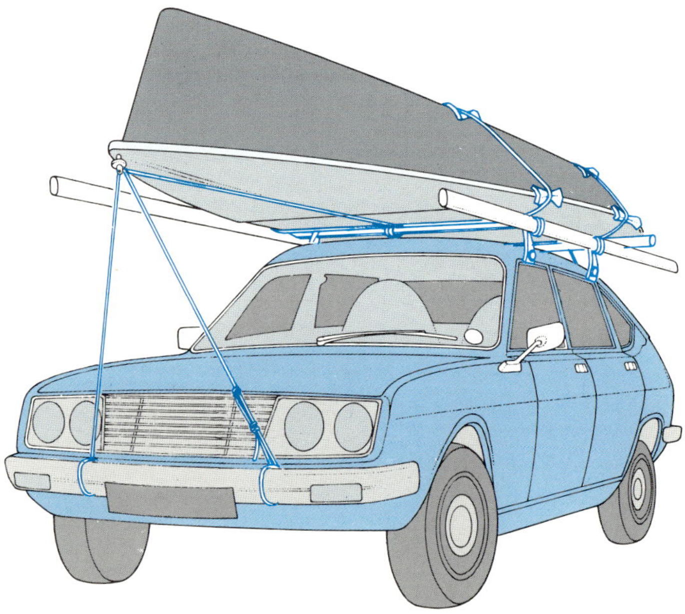

Aufladen allein

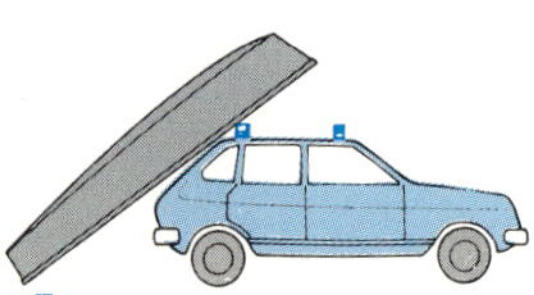

1 *Das Boot mit dem Heck so hinter dem Wagen aufstellen, daß das Vordeck auf dem hinteren Dachträger ruht.*

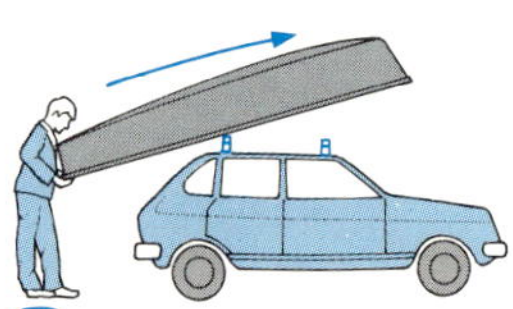

2 *Dann das Heck anheben und das Boot nach vorne schieben, bis es sicher mit seiner ganzen Länge aufliegt.*

Aufladen zu zweit

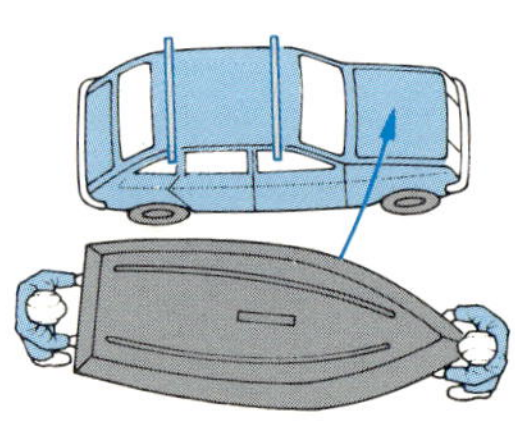

Das Boot an Bug und Heck anheben und von der Seite – das Heck zuerst – auf den Dachträger schieben.

Trailer

Man kann zwischen zwei Konstruktionsarten von Trailern wählen, denen mit einem T-Rahmen und denen mit einem A-Rahmen. In beiden Fällen lagert das Boot auf verstellbaren Auflagen oder Gummirollen. Mast und Baum liegen in einer besonderen Halterung. Der Trailer mit dem T-Rahmen hat einen starken Zentralrohrrahmen. Seine Bootshalterungen sind verstellbar. Der Trailer mit dem A-Rahmen hat den Vorteil, daß man darauf das Boot auf seinem Slipwagen huckepack befördern kann.
In jedem Fall muß der Trailer Brems-, Schluß- und Blinkleuchten, Rückstrahler und Nummernschildbeleuchtung haben und ein Typenschild der Herstellers. Er ist zulassungs- und steuerfrei, bedarf aber einer „Allgemeinen Betriebserlaubnis" vom TÜV. Bei einer Anhängelast ab 750 kg muß der Trailer eine eigene Bremsvorrichtung haben.

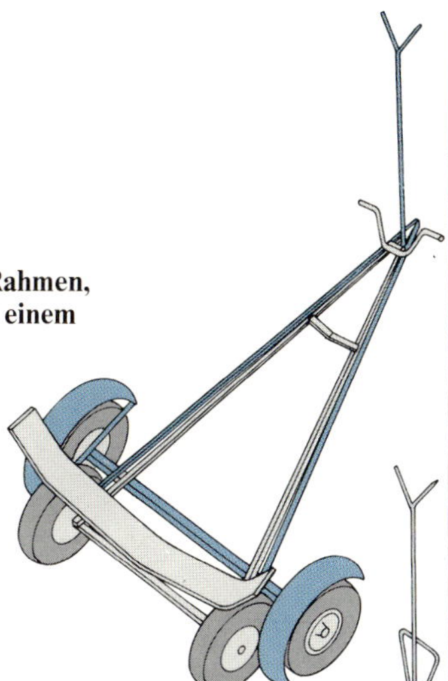

Trailer mit A-Rahmen, kombiniert mit einem Trolley

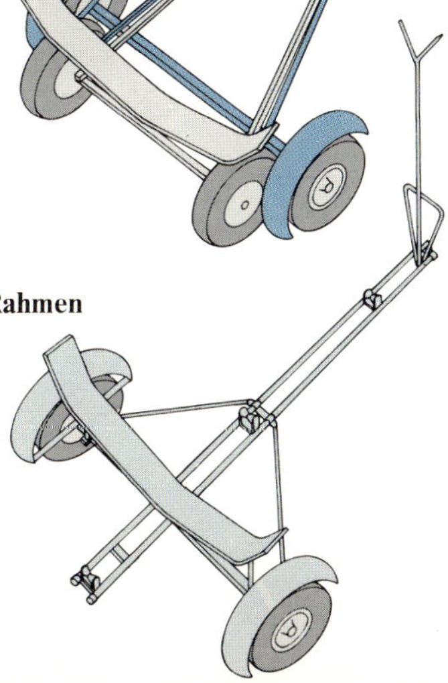

Trailer mit T-Rahmen

Beladen des Trailers

Es ist leichter, den Trailer zu beladen, wenn er bereits am Zugwagen angekoppelt ist. Wird das Boot direkt auf dem Trailer befördert, benötigt man mehrere Helfer, um es sauber auf die Auflagen zu heben. Auch ist es sorgfältig mit dem Anhänger zu verzurren, damit es nicht verrutscht. Will man das Boot auf dem Slipwagen verladen, bringt man es hinter den Trailer und zieht es so weit über den Anhänger, bis der Slipwagen auf den Rollen des Trailers aufliegt. Dann wird er so weit nach vorn gezogen, daß seine Radachsen in ihre Halterungen einrasten.

Aufladen auf einen kombinierten Trailer

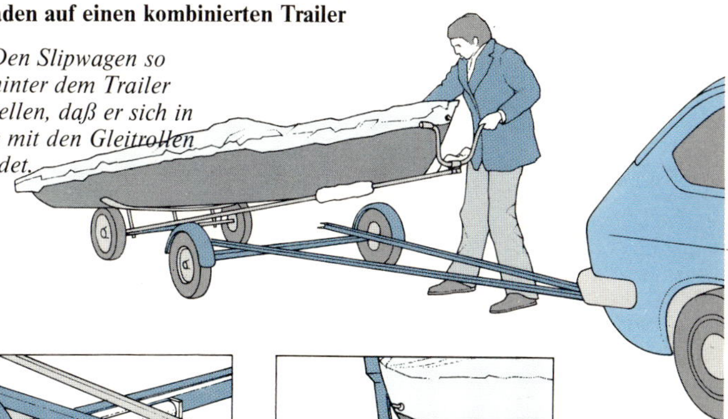

1 *Den Slipwagen so hinter dem Trailer aufstellen, daß er sich in Linie mit den Gleitrollen befindet.*

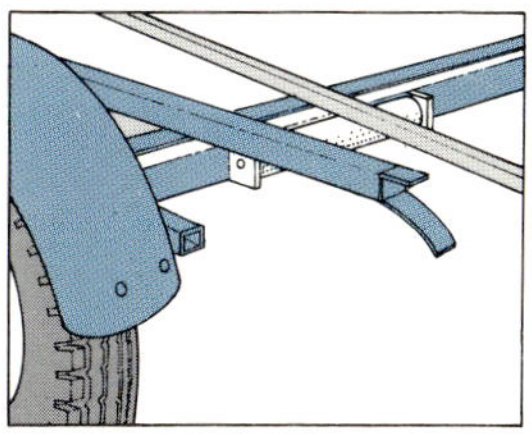

2 *Den Trolley nach vorne ziehen, bis seine Radachsen in die Halterungen einrasten.*

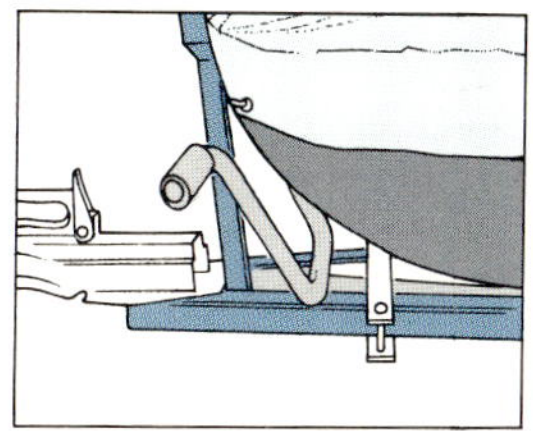

3 *Trolley und Trailer werden mit einer Falle fest verbunden und gesichert.*

Vorbereitung für den Straßentransport

Der Mast wird in seine Halterung gelegt, Wanten, Stage und Fallen werden beigebändselt oder mit Tape am Mast fixiert. Alle lose Ausrüstung wird aus dem Boot entfernt oder sicher gestaut. Boot oder Ausrüstung dürfen nicht mehr als 1,50 m nach hinten hinausragen. Beim Transport innerhalb von 100 km bis zu 3 m. Sie müssen bei Tag und Nacht markiert sein, durch ein rotes Schild beziehungsweise rotes Licht und roten Rückstrahler.

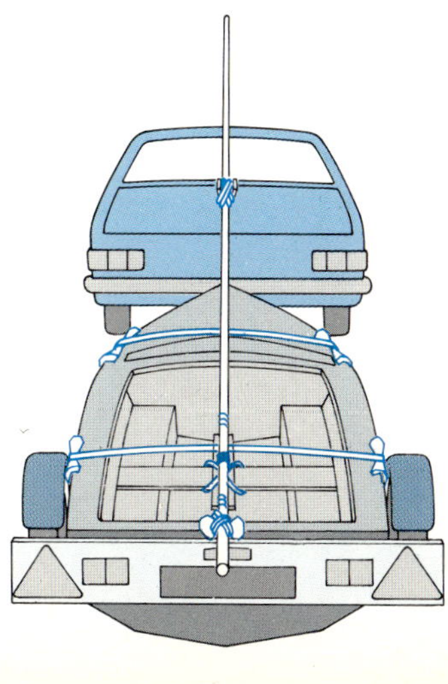

Ausweichregeln

Auch auf dem Wasser gibt es Vorfahrts- beziehungsweise Ausweichregeln. Sie weichen auf Binnen- und Küstengewässern etwas voneinander ab, doch als Grundregel gilt: Motorboote haben Segelbooten auszuweichen. Die Berufsschiffahrt hat in jedem Fall Vorrang. Auf Binnengewässern besitzt sie das uneingeschränkte Vorfahrtsrecht. Aber auch wenn der Segler Vorfahrt hat, sollte er nicht unbedingt darauf beharren, zumal Motorbootfahrer manchmal Kurs und Fahrt eines Seglers nicht richtig einschätzen können.
Fahrwasser und Schiffahrtswege sind möglichst rechtwinklig zu kreuzen. Durchgehender Verkehr hat Vorfahrt. Im übrigen hat man sich an der rechten Seite eines Fahrwassers zu halten und links zu überholen. Im freien Seeraum kann auf jeder Seite überholt werden. Für Segler untereinander gelten besondere Regeln, die hier erläutert sind. Sie gelten prinzipiell auch als Ausweichregeln bei Segelregatten (s. Seite 139).

Rechts: Ein Steuerbord-Bug-Boot (Nr. 14) kreuzt den Bug eines Backbord-Bug-Bootes in der Hoffnung, noch genug Raum zu haben. Würde es zu einer Kollision kommen, wäre die Nr. 14 schuldig.

Wegerecht

Um sicher zu sein, wer Wegerecht hat, muß man wissen, was Steuerbord- und Backbord-Bug ist. Bläst der Wind von Backbord, segelt das Boot auf Steuerbord-Bug. Kommt er von Steuerbord, segelt es auf Backbord-Bug. Es ist also jeweils die Seite, auf der der Baum gefahren wird. Zum besseren Merken kann man sich entsprechende Aufkleber auf die entsprechende Innenseite des Baums machen. Bestehen irgendwelche Zweifel am eigenen Wegerecht, passiert man den anderen hinter seinem Heck. Nie vor dem Bug vorbeilaufen.

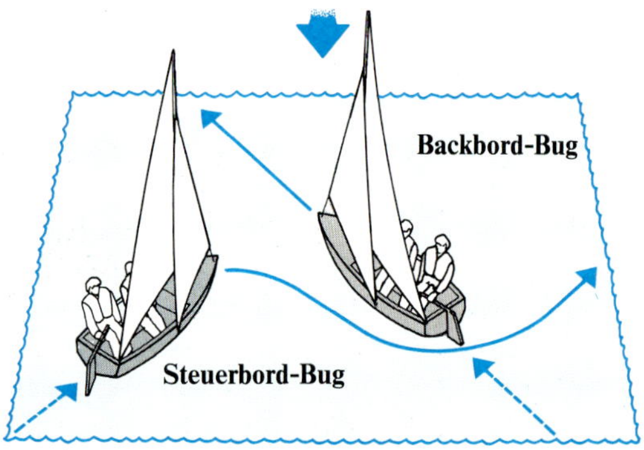

Segler auf unterschiedlichem Bug
Segeln zwei Boote auf unterschiedlichem Bug, hat Backbord-Bug Vorfahrt vor Steuerbord-Bug.

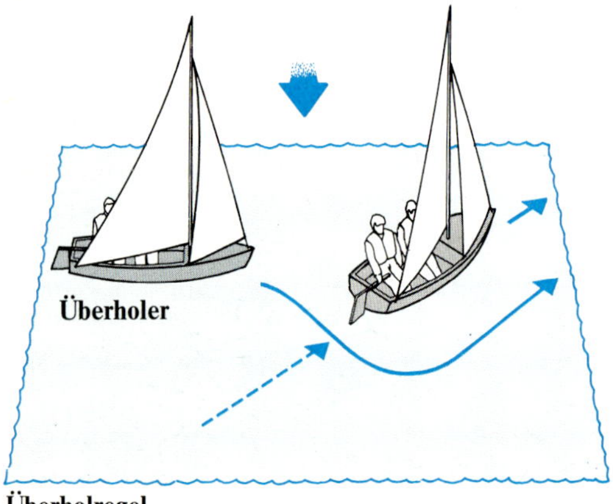

Überholregel
Der Überholer muß sich freihalten. Auf Binnenschiffahrtsstraßen darf er – abweichend von dieser Abbildung – nur in Luv überholen.

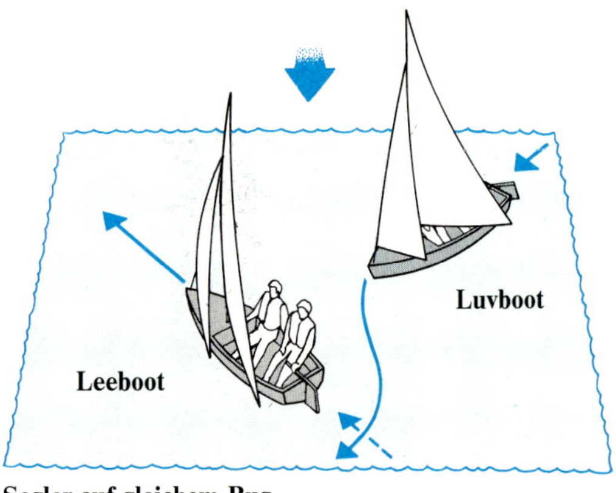

Segler auf gleichem Bug
Segeln zwei Boote auf gleichem Bug, hat das Leeboot Vorfahrt vor dem Luvboot.

16
14

Segeln für Fortgeschrittene

Beherrscht man die Grundkenntnisse des Segelns, möchte man natürlich auch schneller und sportlicher segeln können. Die Geschwindigkeit eines Bootes hängt von einer Reihe von Faktoren ab: Erfahrung und Können der Crew, Konstruktionsmerkmale des Bootes, Schnitt und Stand der Segel und optimales Rigg für die unterschiedlichen Segelbedingungen. Der erste und wichtigste Schritt zum Erfolg ist ständige Praxis, durch die man das Gefühl dafür bekommt, wie die einzelnen Trimmeinrichtungen das Verhalten des Bootes auf den verschiedenen Kursen zum Wind beeinflussen. Beherrscht man den Boots- und Segeltrimm, kann man auf ein schnelleres Boot umsteigen.

Rennjollen sind feinnervige, leichtgewichtige Segelmaschinen mit großer Segelfläche. Sie verlangen eine behutsame und erfahrene Hand. Außerdem besitzen sie eine Vielzahl sinnvoller Trimmeinrichtungen, die großen Einfluß auf ihre optimale Entfaltung haben. Fast alle Rennjollen haben ein Trapez, das der Besatzung erlaubt, noch weiter auszureiten und zusätzliches Trimmgewicht einzusetzen. Außerdem haben sie Spinnakergeschirr. Der Umgang mit dem Trapez und dem Spinnaker wird auf den Seiten 122 bis 125 und 110 bis 120 erläutert. Was man allein durch einen optimalen Trimm des Riggs unter verschiedenen Windverhältnissen erreichen kann, lesen Sie auf den Seiten 142 bis 145.

Gleiten

Alle Boote werden erheblich schneller, bringt man sie zum Gleiten. Dabei reiten sie auf ihrer eigenen Bugwelle. Die meisten Jollen kommen erst bei Windstärken um 10 kn ins Gleiten, leichtere Boote neigen schneller dazu. Im allgemeinen kommen Boote mit halbem Wind am leichtesten ins Gleiten, manche können es auch auf Am-Wind-Kurs, ja, sogar vor dem Wind, wenn es stark genug weht. Das Geheimnis, ein Boot ins Gleiten zu bringen, liegt in dem Vermögen, rechtzeitig eine einfallende Bö zu erkennen. Bevor sie da ist, fällt der Rudergänger etwas ab und fiert die Schoten leicht auf, damit das Boot nicht so stark krängt und möglichst aufrecht segelt. Hebt sich der Bug aus dem Wasser, verlagert die Besatzung ihr Gewicht weiter nach achtern. Nimmt die Geschwindigkeit zu, werden die Schoten wieder etwas angeholt, weil ja auch der scheinbare Wind vorlicher kommt. Ist die Bö vorüber, kann man das Boot im Gleiten halten, indem man etwas weiter anluvt und die Großschot etwas dichterholt. Dadurch bleibt der scheinbare Wind konstant und das Boot weiter im Gleiten.

Eine Jolle in einer Bö, auf einem Kurs voll und bei in rasanter Gleitfahrt. Die Mannschaft sitzt weit hinten und reitet aus.

Der 470er

Eine moderne Rennjolle hat gewöhnlich eine Menge von Einrichtungen, die sie von einer normalen Rolle unterscheidet. Bootsrumpf und Beschläge sind aus leichterem Material hergestellt. Die Großschot hat gewöhnlich mehr mehrscheibige Blöcke, die die höheren Zugkräfte auf die Schot durch das größere Großsegel reduzieren. Rennjollen haben gewöhnlich eine Trapezeinrichtung und können mit Spinnaker gesegelt werden. Feintrimmeinrichtungen am Baumniederholer, am Schwert oder an der Fockschotführung bieten der Besatzung eine Vielzahl von Trimmöglichkeiten für Boot und Segel.

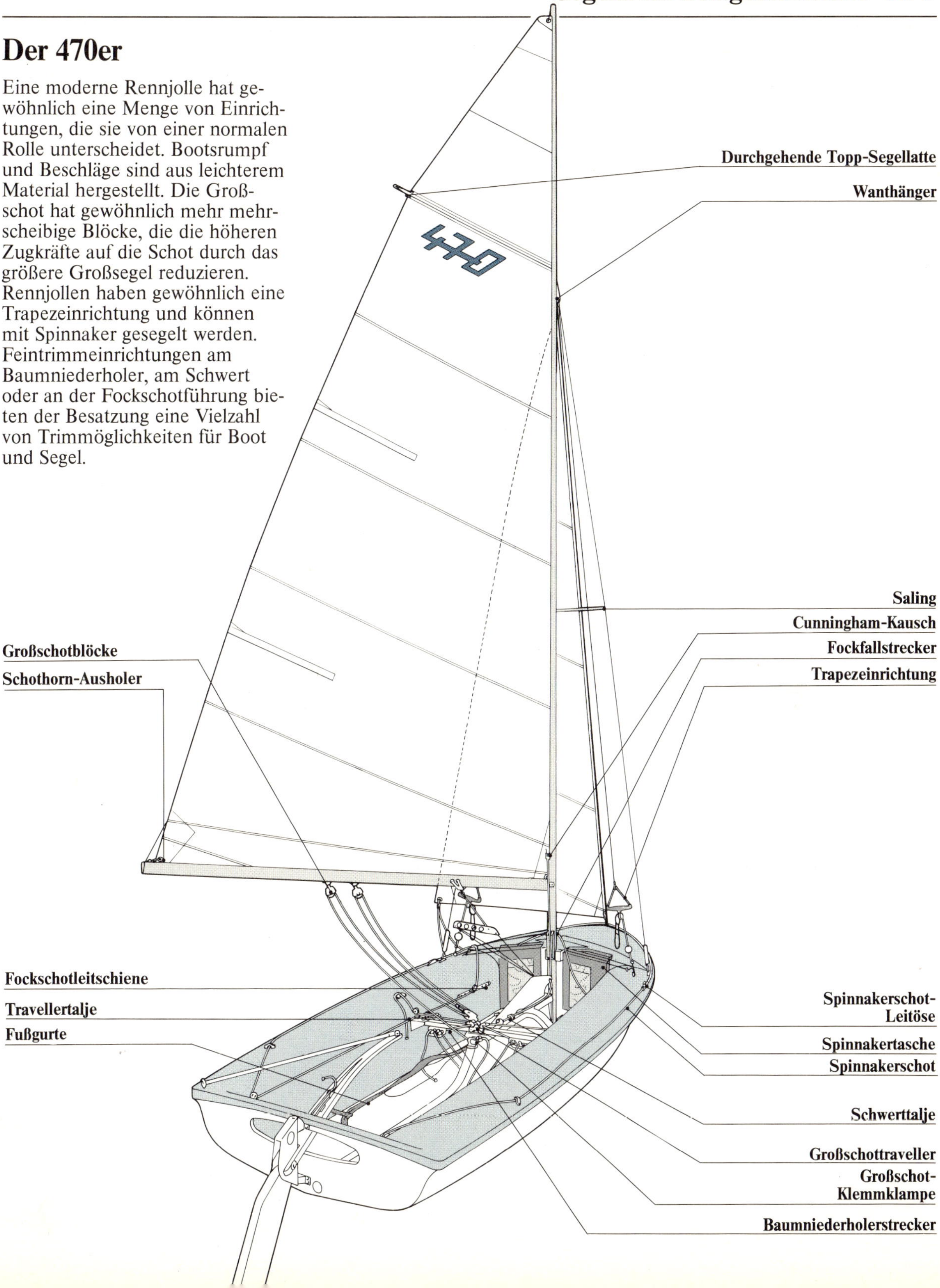

Spinnaker

Der Spinnaker – auch kurz Spi oder von den Seglern Blase genannt – ist ein dreieckiges bauchig geschnittenes Vorsegel aus leichtem Tuch. Er wird auf Raumschots- und Vorm-Wind-Kursen bei leichtem und mittlerem Wind gesetzt. Seine Fläche ist manchmal größer als die von Groß- und Vorsegel zusammen. Der Spinnakerschnitt hat sich mittlerweile zu einer speziellen Wissenschaft der Segelmacher entwickelt. Der Spinnaker wird – im Gegensatz zu anderen Segeln – nicht mit einem Liek fest angeschlagen, sondern „fliegend" gefahren. Nur der jeweilige Segelhals wird am Spinnakerbaum eingepickt.

Es gibt eine Vielzahl von Spinnakerschnitten für die verschiedenen Kurse, zwischen denen man wählen kann. Ebenso unterschiedlich und abhängig vom Bootstyp sind die Arten der Aufbewahrung und des Setzens und Bergens. Alle diese verschiedenen Systeme dienen dazu, den Spinnaker schnell zu setzen und zu bergen, ohne daß er vertörnt oder sonst unklar kommt. Die meisten Jollen bewahren ihren Spinnaker in einem Behälter im Mastbereich auf oder haben eine trompetenähnliche Öffnung am Bug, aus der heraus der Spinnaker gesetzt und in die er wieder hineingezogen wird.

Der Umgang mit dem Spinnaker erfordert sehr viel Erfahrung und gutes Zusammenspiel zwischen Vorschoter und Steuermann. Abhängig vom System besteht eine Arbeitsteilung insofern, als der Steuermann alles bedient, was achtern in seinem Bereich ist. Der Vorschoter versorgt alle Spinnakereinrichtungen im Vorschiffsbereich. Da der Spinnaker ein sehr lebendiges Segel ist und leicht außer Kontrolle geraten kann, ist es ratsam, die ersten Versuche damit bei schwachem Wind und unter Anleitung eines Spinnakerexperten zu machen.

Spinnakerschnitte

Die ersten Spinnaker waren asymmetrisch, mehr wie eine bauchige Genua geschnitten und wurden mit einer langen Spiere ausgebaumt. Um 1930 tauchten bei der 6-m-Klasse symmetrische Spinnaker auf, die mehr unseren heutigen glichen. Die ersten Spinnaker waren aus Baumwolle, ein schweres und entsprechend auch schwer zu handhabendes Tuch. Um 1950 kam Nylon als Spinnakertuch auf, ein leichtes und widerstandsfähigeres Kunstfasergewebe. In den letzten Jahren wurde eine Vielzahl unterschiedlicher Spinnakertypen entwickelt. Auf Jollen sind die üblichen Schnitte: der Horizontalschnitt, der Radial-Kopf- und der Triradialschnitt. Welchen Spinnaker man wählt, hängt von dem Jollentyp ab, den man segelt und den Wetterbedingungen, unter denen man überwiegend segelt. Der Horizontalschnitt wird für leichteres Wetter und kleinere Segel verwendet, die beiden anderen wählt man hauptsächlich für größere Segel.

Horizontalschnitt
Er dehnt sich hauptsächlich im Oberteil und eignet sich besonders für Vorm-Wind-Kurse.

Radial-Kopf
Ein Allround-Spinnaker für leichte Winde, kombiniert die Eigenschaften des Radial und Horizontal.

Triradial
Eine Kombination dreier Schnitte, universell auf allen raumen Kursen einzusetzen.

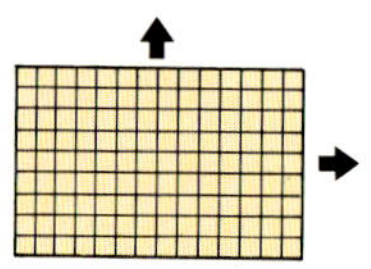

Geringe Dehnung

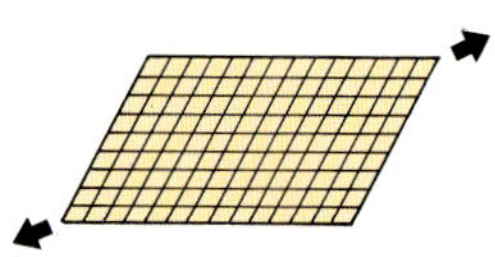

Größere Dehnbarkeit

Spinnakertuch
Spinnakertuch muß leicht und reißfest sein und darf sich wenig dehnen. Das hauptsächlich verwendete Nylon ist kaum dehnbar in Richtung von Kette und Schuß, sondern nur in der Diagonalen.

Die Spinnakerausrüstung

Außer dem Spinnaker braucht man noch einiges an zusätzlicher Ausrüstung: den Spinnakerbaum, das Spinnakerfall, eine Spinnakertasche oder Trompete aus der heraus der Spinnaker gesetzt wird, die außerhalb der Wanten laufenden Spinnakerschoten, zusätzliche Leitösen und Schotklemmen. Die Schot auf der jeweiligen Luvseite wird Achterholer genannt. Damit der Spinnaker optimal steht, sollten die Leitösen auf dem Seitendeck so angebracht sein, daß Schot und Achterholer einen Winkel von etwa 25° mit dem Seitendeck bilden.

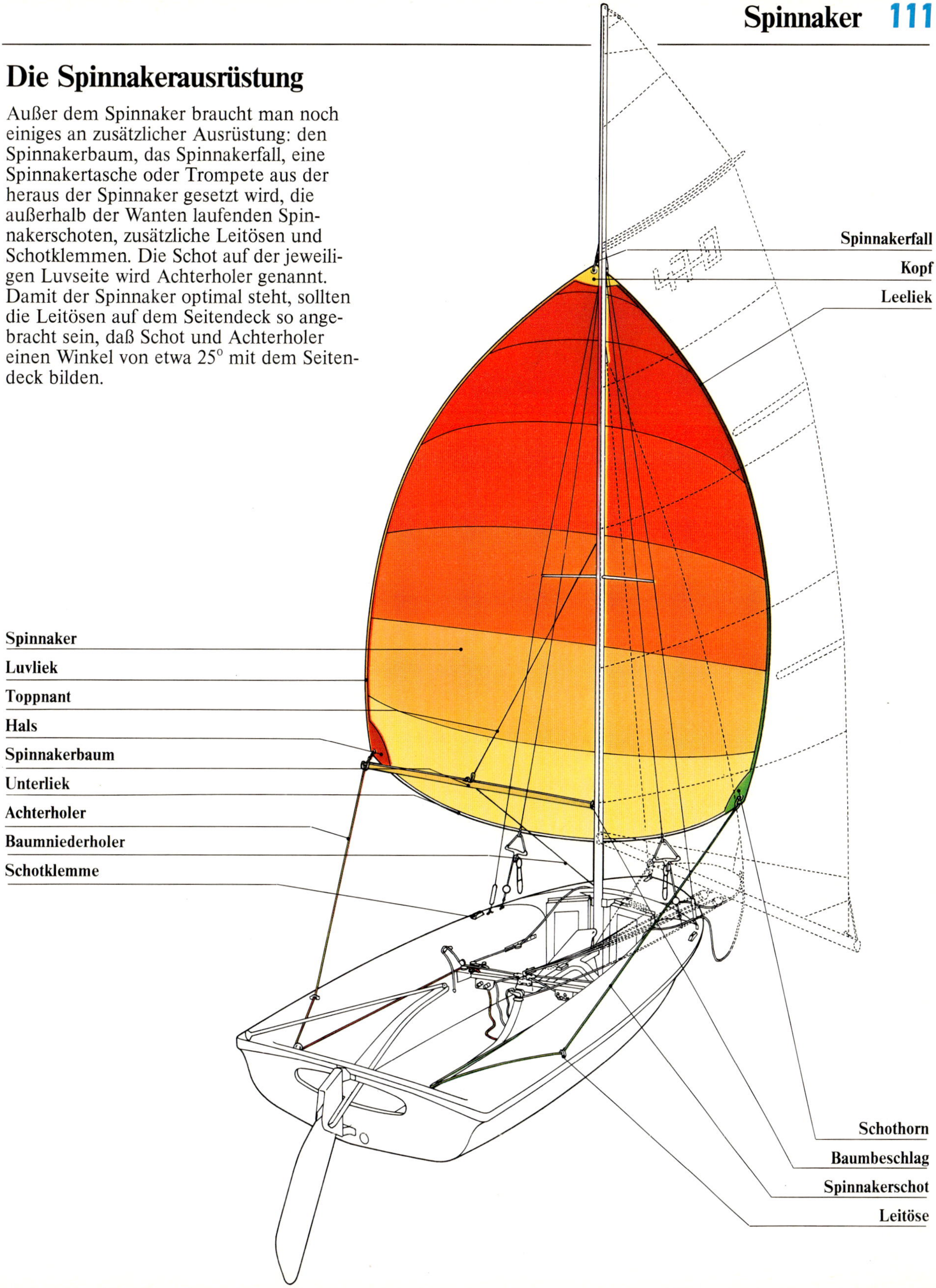

Der Spinnakerbaum

Gehalten wird der Spinnaker vom Spinnakerbaum, der mit einem seiner Enden am Hals des Segels, mit seinem anderen Ende auf der Luvseite des Bootes in den Baumbeschlag am Mast eingepickt wird. Dabei ist darauf zu achten, daß die Schnapphaken am jeweiligen Baumende mit der Öffnung nach oben eingepickt werden. Von oben wird der Spinnakerbaum durch den Toppnant gehalten, während der Niederholer ihn am Steigen nach oben hindert.

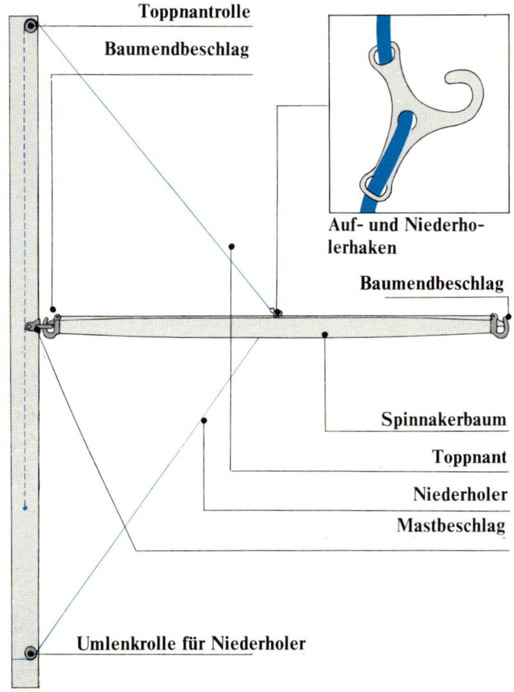

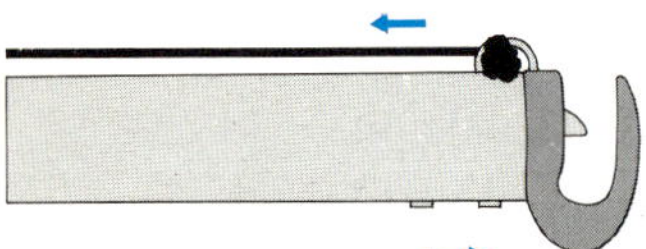
Endbeschlag offen

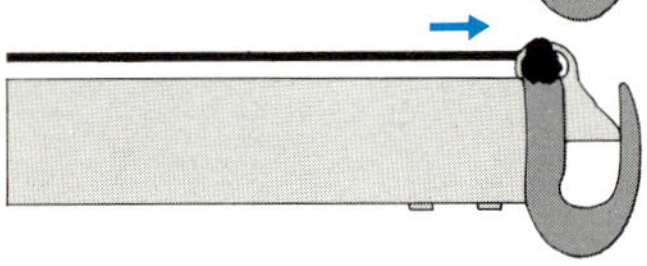
Endbeschlag geschlossen

Spinnakerbaumstellung

Der Winkel des Spinnakerbaumes zum Mast muß so eingestellt werden, daß Hals und Schothorn des Segels in einer Ebene liegen. In der Regel beträgt dieser Winkel 90°.

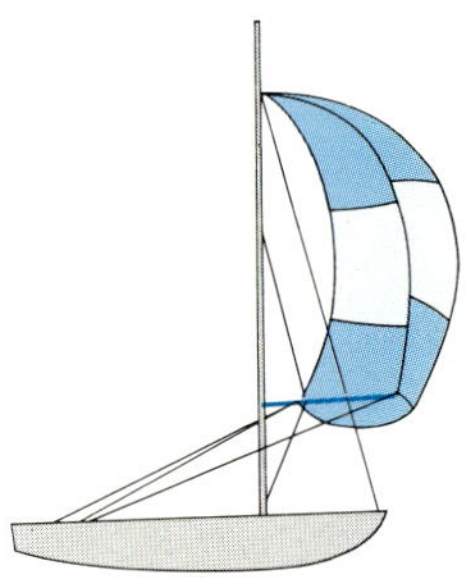
Baum korrekt gesetzt

Baum zu hoch

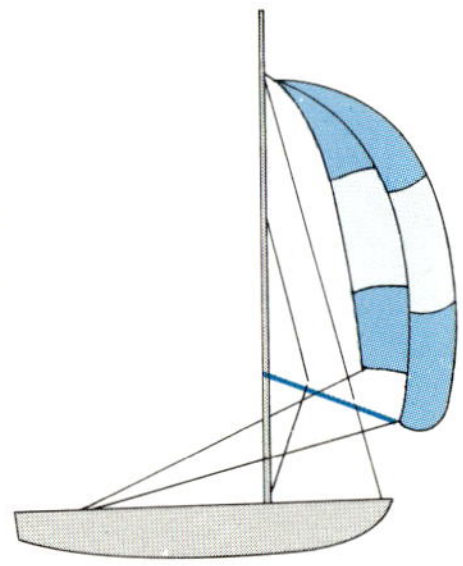
Baum zu niedrig

Oben: Auf einem Am-Wind-Kurs kann der Spinnakerbaum höher getrimmt werden, um den Spinnaker weiter und höher von Groß und Fock wegzubekommen.
Rechts: Ein perfekt gesetzter Spinnaker auf einem 505er auf Halb-Wind-Kurs.

K 5060

Spinnakertaschen

Manche Jollen haben zum Stauen des Spinnakers mit Klappen versehene Taschen an der Achterkante des Vordecks. Gesetzt wird der Spinnaker direkt aus der Tasche. Daher ist es wichtig, daß er sorgfältig klariert so verstaut wird, daß Kopf, Hals und Schothorn obenaufliegen, damit sie sofort angeschlagen werden können.

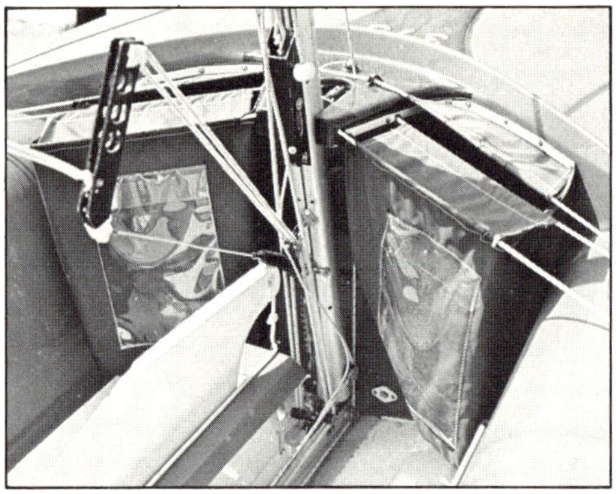

Dieser 470er hat je eine Spinnakertasche auf jeder Seite vom Mast. Jede hat eine durch Gummistropps unter Spannung gehaltene Verschlußklappe. Auf den Taschen durchsichtige Plastiktaschen.

Spinnaker stauen

Außerordentlich wichtig ist, daß der Spinnaker in der Packtasche richtig gestaut worden ist. Sonst gibt es beim Setzen bestimmt Schwierigkeiten. Wahrscheinlich wird er eine sogenannte Eieruhr bilden. Das Stauen muß zur reinen Routine werden und sollte zunächst an Land geübt werden. Am besten, man packt das Boot auf den Trolley und sezt nur den Spinnaker allein, den ein erfahrener „Packer" zuvor korrekt in der Tasche verstaut hat. Man macht das zu zweit. Einer fiert das Spinnakerfall, der andere zieht sich am Hals das Luvliek heran und stopft es in die Tasche, aber so, daß der Hals draußen bleibt. So arbeitet er sich bis zum Segelkopf vor, der ebenfalls draußen bleibt. Dann wird der verbliebene Rest des Spinnakers in die Tasche gestopft, bis das Schothorn übrigbleibt. Die drei Ecken des Spinnakers bleiben also außerhalb der Tasche, beziehungsweise obenauf liegen. Fall und Schoten bleiben angeschlagen, der Spinnaker ist – so gepackt – sofort klar zum Setzen.

1 *Der Spinnaker ist korrekt gesetzt worden. Dann fiert einer das Spinnakerfall,*

2 *während der andere Spinnakerhals und Luvliek packt und das Segel in die Tasche stopft, Hals, Kopf und Schothorn obenauf.*

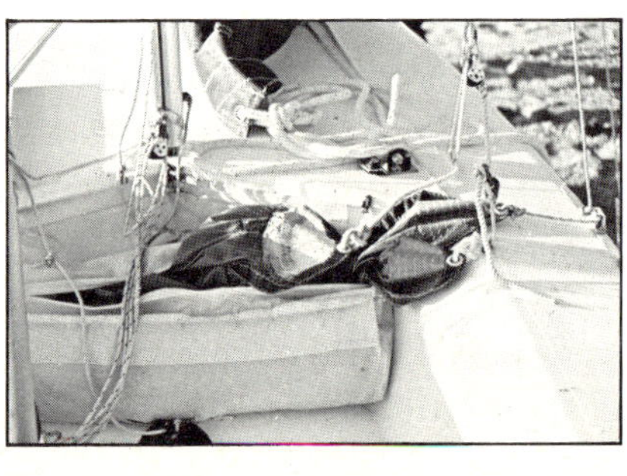

3 *So sehen Hals, Kopf und Schothorn aus der Tasche hervor. Das Fall bleibt angeschlagen, festgesetzt in der Schotklemme, damit es nicht ausweht – so ist der Spinnaker augenblicklich klar zum Setzen.*

Die Spinnakertrompete

Viele Rennjollen haben eine sogenannte Spinnakertrompete. Das ist eine trichterförmige Öffnung im Vordeck mit einem Führungsrohr, in das der Spinnaker vom Cockpit aus mit einem Niederholer hineingezogen wird. Dieses System hat den Vorteil, daß der Spinnaker nicht vertörnt und man ihn genauso wieder setzen kann, wie man ihn beim Bergen hineingezogen hat. Der Nachteil dieser Trompete ist, daß vorne überkommendes Wasser durch die Öffnung ins Boot läuft. Der Spinnaker wird an einem „endlosen" Fall gesetzt, das mit einem Ende am Kopf angeschlagen ist und mit dem anderen Ende an der Niederholerbefestigung auf der Vorderseite des Spinnakers. Dieses Ende läuft durch die Trompete nach hinten zu einer Umlenkrolle, so daß der Spinnaker beim Fieren des Falls einfällt und automatisch in die Trompete hineingezogen wird.

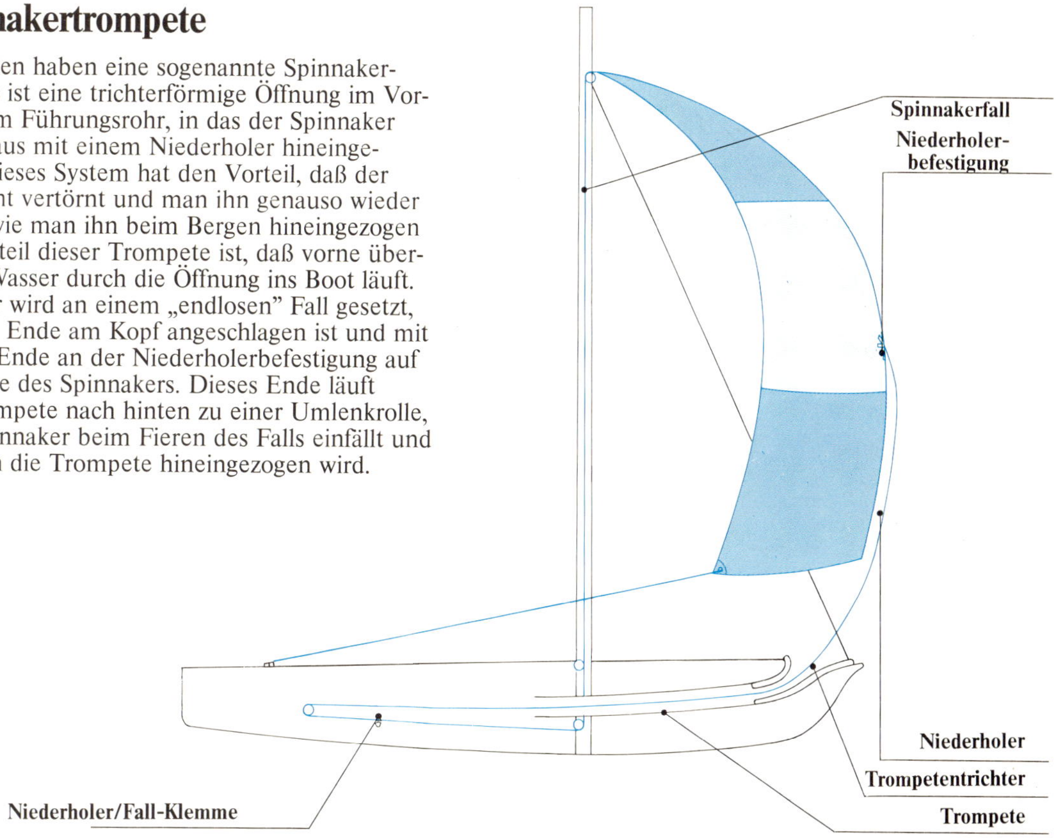

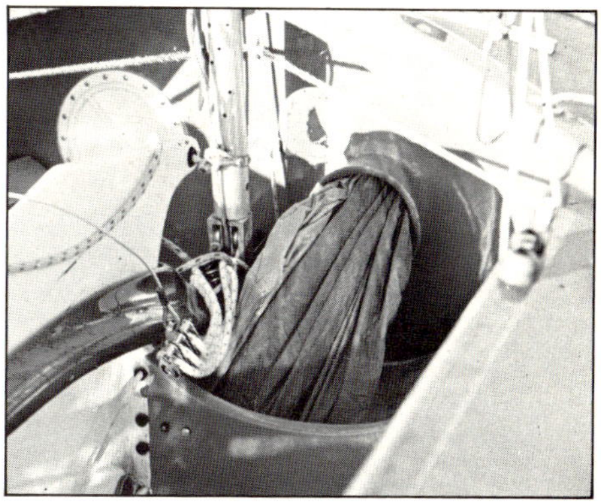

Oben und links: Die Spinnakertrompete auf einem Fireball. Man findet dieses System hauptsächlich auf Rennjollen, auf denen es bei Spinnakermanövern um Sekunden geht.

Setzen und Bergen des Spinnakers

Auch beim Setzen und Bergen des Spinnakers darf die Besatzung ihre sonstigen Aufgaben an Bord nicht vernachlässigen. Der Steuermann muß lernen, breitbeinig im Boot stehend, mit der Pinne zwischen den Beinen zu steuern, damit er die Hände frei hat, um die Spinnakerschoten zu bedienen. Die Art und Weise wie der Spinnaker gesetzt und geborgen wird, hängt vom Stausystem ab. Grundsätzlich geschieht es auf einem Vorm-Wind-Kurs. Großschot und Fockschot werden so lange belegt.

Flying Dutchmen unter Spinnaker auf einem Raumschots-Kurs während einer Regatta.

Setzen aus dem Leebehälter

Das Spinnakersetzen aus dem Leebehälter ist wesentlich einfacher, als ihn aus dem Luvbehälter zu holen. Es ist daher wichtig, vor dem Bergen zu überlegen, welcher der beiden Behälter auf dem nächsten Spinnakerkurs in Lee sein wird. Zum Spinnakersetzen geht der Steuermann auf Vorm-Wind-Kurs, während der Vorschoter noch einmal die Spinnakereinrichtung überprüft.

1 *Der Vorschoter pickt den Baum in den Hals ein, schlägt Toppnant und Niederholer am Baum an…*

2 *…und hakt den Baum in seinen Mastbeschlag ein. Währenddem setzt der Steuermann mit dem Fall den Spinnaker und bedient die Schoten. Sowie der Vorschoter vorne klar ist, kümmert er sich um die richtige Schotführung des Spinnakers.*

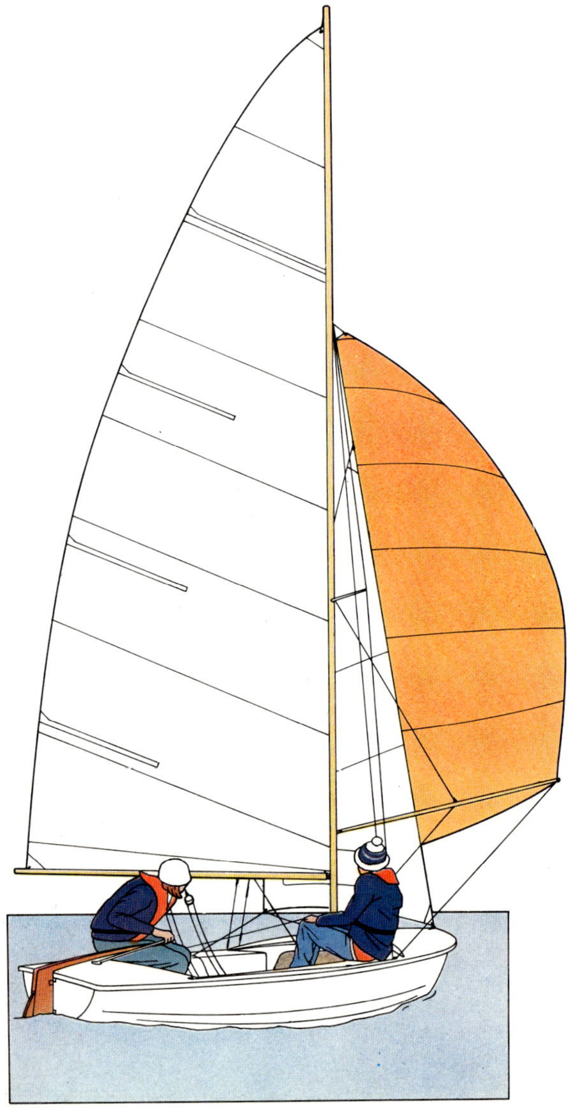

3 *Der Steuermann konzentriert sich wieder auf den Kurs, während der Vorschoter die Schoten trimmt (s. Seite 120).*

Setzen aus dem Luvbehälter

Den Spinnaker aus dem Luvbehälter heraus zu setzen, erfordert viel Geschick und etwas Glück. Deshalb ist es wichtig, den Spinnaker beim Bergen immer so zu stauen, daß er aus einem Leebehälter heraus gesetzt werden kann.

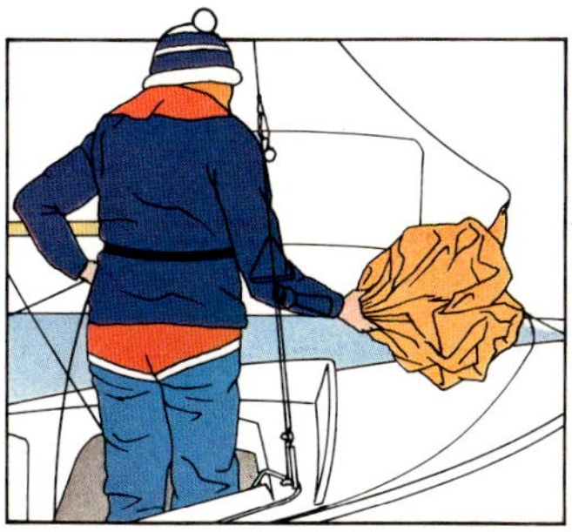

1 *Der Vorschoter holt den Spinnaker aus dem Luvbehälter und hält ihn fest gebündelt, innerhalb vom Want, in einer Hand, während die andere Hand die Leeschot klar hält. Der Steuermann übernimmt das Fall, während er mit den Knien steuert.*

2 *Der Vorschoter ruft: „Hoch!" und wirft den Spinnaker hoch und um das Vorstag herum. Der Steuermann holt blitzschnell das Fall, und durch Zug an der Leeschot bringt der Vorschoter den Spinnaker nach Lee.*

Der Steuermann übernimmt die Spinnakerschoten, und erst jetzt pickt der Vorschoter den Baum an Hals und Mastbeschlag ein und fixiert Toppnant und Baumniederholer. Dann übernimmt er die Schoten.

Mit Spinnakertrompete

Mit Spinnakertrompete ist alles einfacher. Zuerst setzt der Vorschoter die Schoten an den markierten Stellen (s. Seite 120) in den Klemmen fest. Und während der Steuermann den Spinnaker mit dem Fall setzt und dabei darauf achtet, daß er gut voll steht, pickt der Vorschoter den Baum am Mastbeschlag und am Segelhals ein und fixiert Toppnant und Niederholer am Baum. – Zum Bergen übernimmt der Steuermann den mit dem Fall verbundenen Spinnakerniederholer und zieht das Segel in die Trompete. Der Vorschoter hakt den Hals vom Baum ab, pickt Baumniederholer und Toppnant aus und den Baum vom Mast ab.

Spinnakerbergen in den Behälter

Beim Behältersystem kann der Spinnaker entweder in den Luv- oder Leebehälter niedergeholt werden. Je schneller und je zügiger das Bergen vor sich geht, desto weniger besteht die Gefahr, daß der Spinnaker sich am Rigg vertörnt. Einen Spinnaker zu bergen ist so lange kaum möglich, wie er noch voll steht. Deshalb muß zunächst der Wind aus dem Tuch gebracht werden. Man fiert Achterholer und Schot so lange, bis der Spinnaker einfällt.

Bergen in Lee
Der Steuermann geht vor den Wind und macht das Fall klar. Der Vorschoter pickt den Hals vom Baum los und zieht den Spinnaker ins Cockpit, während der Steuermann gleichmäßig das Fall fiert. Dann verstaut der Vorschoter den Spinnaker in seinem Behälter und nimmt den Baum vom Mast.

Bergen in Luv
Der Steuermann geht auf einen Halbwind-Kurs und übernimmt das Fall. Der Vorschoter pickt den Baum vom Mast, löst Toppnant und Baumniederholer und pickt den Hals ab. Dann stopft er den Spinnaker in den Luvbehälter, während der Steuermann das Fall fiert. (Eine unübliche Methode.)

Schiften des Spinnakers

Schiften bedeutet, den Baum von einer Seite auf die andere zu nehmen. Das Manöver erfordert eine gut eingespielte Crew. Auf Jollen wird meistens eine andere als die hier dargestellte Methode praktiziert: Der Vorschoter pickt den Baum am Mast aus und am bisherigen Schothorn ein. Vorübergehend, während der Steuermann den Großbaum schiftet, wird der Spinnaker mit beiden Schotecken am Baum gefahren. Jetzt den bisherigen Hals am Spinnaker auspicken und das freigewordene Ende des Baumes wieder am Mast einhaken.

Rechts: Während des Schiftens darf der Spinnaker nicht einfallen oder außer Kontrolle geraten, will man nicht eine empfindliche Geschwindigkeitseinbuße in Kauf nehmen.

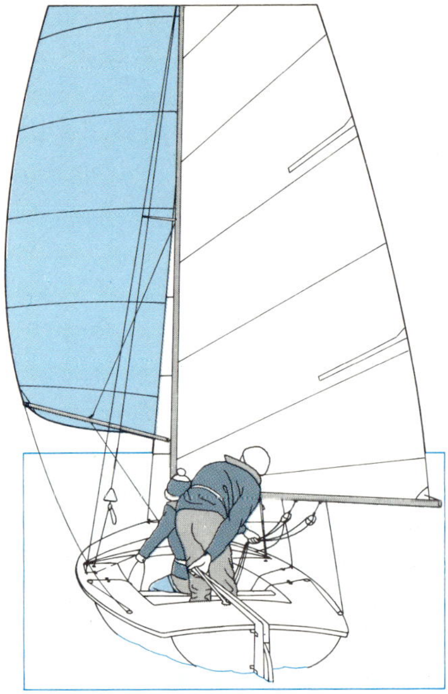

1 *Großsegel und Fock werden auf die neue Leeseite übergenommen.*

2 *Während der Steuermann mit der Pinne zwischen den Beinen Achterholer und Schot bedient, pickt der Vorschoter den Baum am Hals und Mast aus und …*

3 *… pickt ihn auf der neuen Luvseite in Schothorn und Mastbeschlag wieder ein. Die bisherige Schot ist jetzt Achterholer geworden, der bisherige Achterholer Schot.*

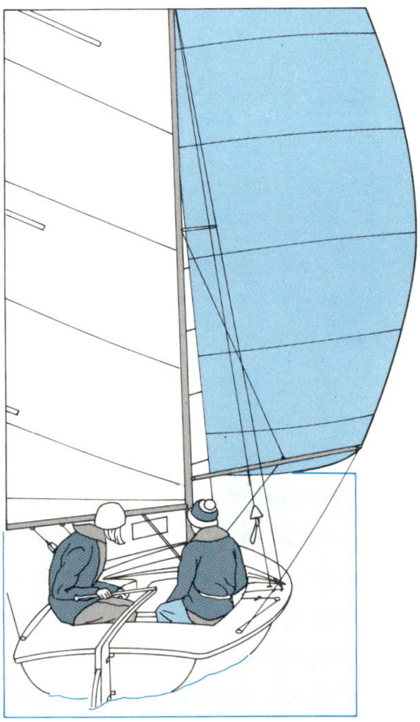

4 *Der Vorschoter übernimmt die Schoten vom Steuermann, trimmt den Spinnaker mit der Schot und belegt den Achterholer.*

693
74

Spinnakertrimm

Der richtige Stand des Spinnakers erfordert ständige Aufmerksamkeit und Korrekturen. Der Baum wird soweit es geht zur Seite ausgebracht und die Schot so weit gefiert, daß das Segel gerade noch nicht killt. Während man den Spinnaker mit der Schot trimmt, wird der Achterholer belegt, damit er nicht ausrauscht. Je höher am Wind mit dem Spinnaker gesegelt wird, desto schwieriger ist die Schotführung. Die Schot soll möglichst weit achtern und außen gefahren werden, damit sich das Leeliek öffnet. Fällt der Spinnaker ein, muß der Steuermann schnell abfallen und die Schot dichter geholt werden.

Der Spinnaker steht gut, wenn sich der Kopf im rechten Winkel zum Mast befindet. Bei starkem Wind, vor allem auf Vorm-Wind-Kurs, neigt er zum Steigen. In diesem Fall ist es besser, Schot und Achterholer weiter vorn zu fahren. Dadurch wird das Segel niedergehalten und flacher gezogen. Es pendelt nicht mehr so stark hin und her und ist so leichter zu kontrollieren. Bei mittleren Winden wird das Fall etwa 20 bis 30 cm aus dem Mast gefiert. So kommt der Spinnaker etwas mehr nach vorne und gibt dem Boot mehr Fahrt. Bei schwachen Winden, wenn das Segel nicht mehr richtig voll steht, kann man den Baum etwas tiefer fahren. In jedem Fall müssen die Unterliekecken in einer Ebene liegen.
Um den richtigen Anstellwinkel für den Baum zu finden, holt man ihn so weit nach achtern, daß der Spinnaker gerade noch nicht einfällt. Im allgemeinen heißt dies, daß der Spinnakerbaum in einem rechten Winkel zum scheinbaren Wind steht. Will der Spinnaker aber nicht voll stehen, muß der Baum vorlicher getrimmt werden. Auf keinen Fall darf er jedoch am Vorstag anliegen, er könnte dort verbiegen oder brechen.

Bei starkem und besonders böigem Wind kann der Spinnaker durchaus zu einem Kreuz werden. Als hier die Bö einfiel, war keins der beiden Boote in der Lage, daraus Nutzen zu ziehen. Eins der Boote kenterte (rechts), während das andere, um zu überleben, seinen Spinnaker fliegen lassen mußte.

Markierung der Schoten

Man kann sich die Bedienung des Spinnakers etwa erleichtern, wenn man sich für die verschiedenen Kurse die Schoten markiert. Dies geschieht mit Farbe oder verschiedenfarbigem Klebeband an den Stellen, wo, bei richtigem Trimm, die Klemmen sitzen müssen. So kann beispielsweise der Achterholer bereits vor dem Spinnakersetzen belegt werden. Hat man mehrere solcher Fixpunkte herausgefunden und markiert, braucht man nicht jedesmal wieder groß mit den Schoten zu spielen, sondern es bedarf nur noch kleinerer Korrekturen. Beim Segeln unter Spinnaker soll der Vorschoter in Luv sitzen, damit er das Vorliek des Segels ständig beobachten kann. Das bedeutet, daß der Steuermann auf Vorm-Wind- und Raumschots-Kurs in Lee sitzt, damit das Boot möglichst auf ebenem Kiel segelt. Auch auf Halbwind-Kursen sollte der Steuermann so lange es geht in Lee bleiben. Nur bei frischem Wind und beginnender Krängung wechselt er nach Luv und balanciert das Boot mit aus.

Rechte Seite: Eine Jollencrew beim Trimmen ihres Spinnakers. Geblendet vom Gegenlicht, ist es gar nicht so leicht, das Beste aus seinem Spinnaker herauszuholen.

K-7182

Das Trapez

Die übliche Trapezeinrichtung besteht aus je einem Stahldraht auf jeder Seite, der oben am Wanthänger des Mastes angeschäkelt ist. Ein am Pütting, über oder unter Deck befestigter Gummistropp hält das andere Ende der Drähte unter Spannung, so daß sie nicht frei ausschwingen können. Unten am Draht befindet sich ein Handgriff und ein Ring, in den der Trapezgurt eingehakt wird. Ein geübter Vorschoter bewegt sich blitzschnell vom Boot aus ins Trapez und wieder zurück, um so auf Böen oder Kursänderungen zu reagieren. Zu den Feinheiten der Trapezarbeit gehört es, sein Gewicht aus Trimmgründen auf der Scheuerleiste weiter nach vorn oder achtern zu verlagern oder auch mal in die tiefe Hocke zu gehen.
Tatsache ist, das Trapez verlangt schon etwas Können und viel Übung. Wer aber die Technik erst einmal richtig beherrscht, wird sich Segeln ohne Trapez kaum noch vorstellen können.

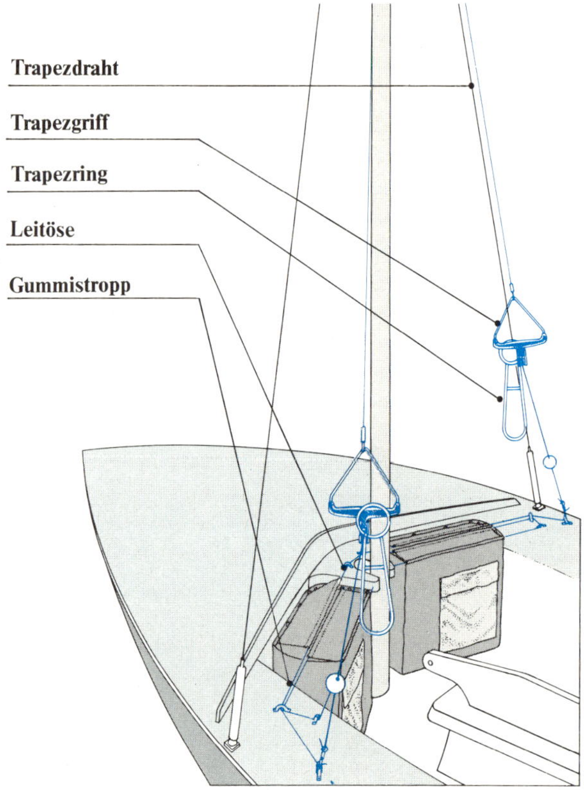

Rechts: Das Standard-Trapezsystem, wie es auf den meisten Rennjollen üblich ist. Unten: Das verfeinerte Endlos-System. Es ermöglicht dem Vorschoter, von einer Seite auf die andere zu wechseln, ohne sich ab- und wieder einhaken zu müssen.

Segeln im Trapez

Am besten beginnt man Trapezsegeln bei mittleren Windstärken mit einem trapez-erfahrenen Rudergänger, der in der Lage ist, Fehler auszugleichen. Der Vorschoter soll sich ständig bereithalten, rasch und kontrolliert ins Trapez zu gehen, wenn das Boot krängt. Der Anfänger muß zunächst das Aus- und Einsteigen und den Seitenwechsel gründlich üben. Wichtig vor allem ist die gute Verständigung zwischen Rudergänger und Vorschoter. Er muß über alle geplanten Kursänderungen verständigt werden.

So sieht ein korrekt sitzendes Trapezgeschirr aus. Das breite Rückenteil stützt den Körper und verteilt die Zugkräfte des Drahtes. Vorne, etwa in Nabelhöhe, sitzt eine Metallplatte mit dem Trapezhaken. Die Gurte sind verstellbar. (Es gibt die verschiedensten Ausführungen von Trapezgeschirren.)

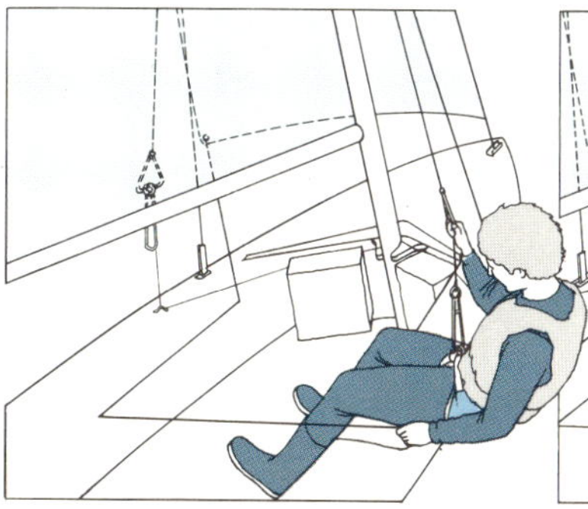

1 *Die Fock ist dichtgeholt. Der Vorschoter faßt mit seiner vorderen Hand den Trapezring und hakt ihn ein. Dann greift er mit derselben Hand den Trapezhandgriff und zieht sich hoch.*

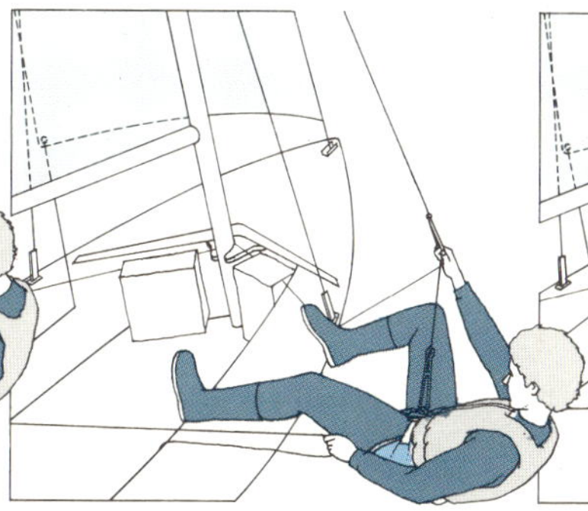

2 *Das Körpergewicht wird so weit nach hinten verlagert, bis man voll im Gurt hängt. Gleichzeitig wird das vordere Bein angewinkelt, auf den Bootsrand gesetzt und am Pütting abgestützt.*

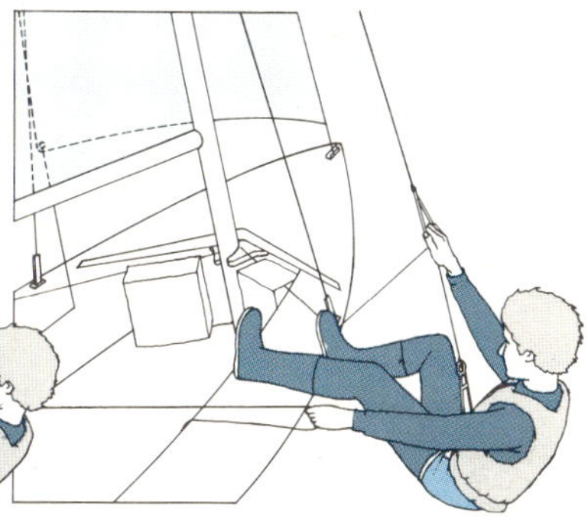

3 *Das vordere Bein wird gestreckt und dabei gleichzeitig dem seitlichen Zug des Trapezdrahtes entgegengewirkt. Dann wird das hintere Bein nachgezogen und ebenfalls auf den Bootsrand gesetzt.*

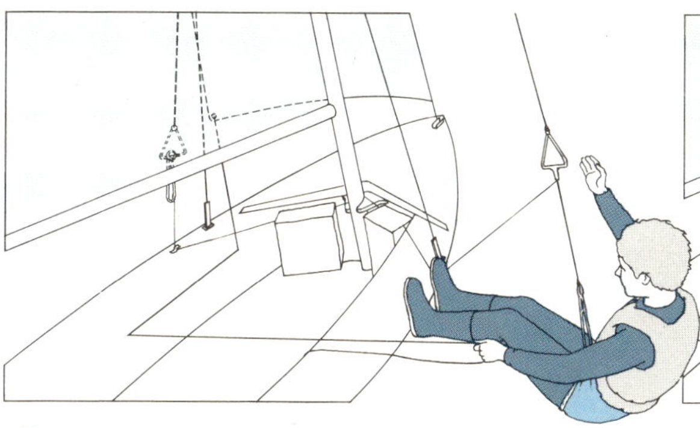

4 *Jetzt wird der Trapezgriff losgelassen, und die frei werdende Hand kann gegebenenfalls die Fockschot übernehmen.*

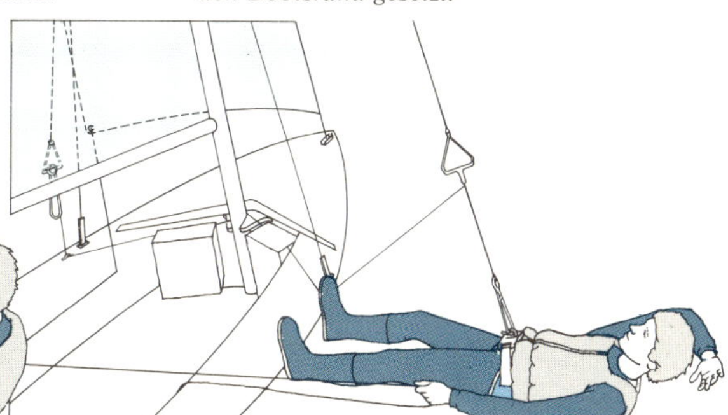

5 *Der Körper wird waagerecht gestreckt. Ideal ist die Trapezhaltung, wenn er einen Winkel von etwa 85° mit dem Mast bildet.*

Zurück ins Boot

Man wird schnell feststellen, daß es viel leichter ist, aus dem Trapez auszusteigen als einzusteigen. Ohne zu üben geht es aber auch nicht, denn man muß jederzeit schnell ins Boot zurückkommen können, wenn der Wind nachläßt oder sich der Kurs ändert. Hat der Trapezmann sich zunächst einmal mit der hier gezeigten Technik hinlänglich vertraut gemacht, kann er mit einer anderen Methode noch schneller ins Boot zurückkommen: Aus der gestreckten Trapezhaltung geht er in die tiefe Hocke, winkelt also die Beine stark an und hockt nun mit strammen Trapezdraht auf der Scheuerleiste. Dann zieht er die Füße hoch, wobei er sich gleichzeitig mit einer oder beiden Händen an der Scheuerleiste abstützen muß, und schwingt am Draht ins Boots zurück. – Hat das Trapez kein Endlossystem, muß der Gurt vorm Wechsel auf die andere Seite jeweils ausgehakt werden.

1 *Mit der Hand den Trapezgriff fassen, das hintere Bein vom Bootsrand lösen und den Körper in einer Art Kreisbogen nach hinten schwingen lassen.*

2 *Das vordere Bein wird so stark angewinkelt, daß man sich aufs Seitendeck setzen kann. Nun auch das vordere Bein ins Cockpit ziehen und gegebenenfalls den Trapezgurt aushaken.*

Um den Trapezring auszuhaken, faßt man ihn mit der Hand und drückt ihn kräftig nach unten.

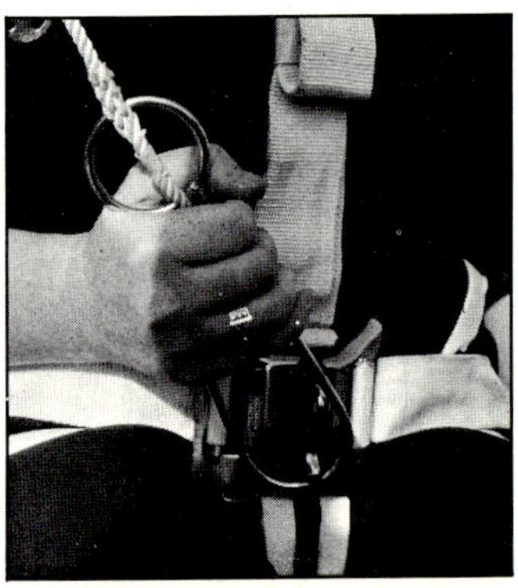

Trapeztechniken

Gewöhnlich neigt man dazu, sich im Trapez nach hinten zu lehnen, jedoch muß man immer bereit sein, sich mit dem vorderen Bein abzustützen, wenn das Boot plötzlich Fahrt verliert. Außerdem muß man seine Position ständig der Krängung anpassen, damit das Boot möglichst aufrecht segelt. Läßt der Wind nach oder fällt das Boot ab, kann man weiter ins Boot kommen, indem man die Knie beugt. Hakt man sich in das obere Auge des Trapezgurtes, hängt man etwas steiler im Gurt. Um das Boot vor- oder achterlicher zu trimmen, muß der im Trapez hängende Vorschoter seine Position auf dem Bootsrand nach vorn oder achtern verändern. Wenn das Boot gleitet, ist es wichtig, daß er ziemlich weit achtern steht (Bild unten). Bei alledem darf der Vorsegeltrimm nicht vernachlässigt werden.

Der Trapezmann steht verhältnismäßig aufrecht und weit hinten, während das Boot gleitet. So wird er nicht ständig durch die Wellen geschleift.

Das Geschick des Trapezmannes ist es, als menschlicher Hebelarm, die größte aufrichtende Kraft zu erzeugen. Gleichzeitig soll er so selten wie möglich auf die Wellen klatschen, denn das bremst jedesmal. Außerdem ist es günstig, wenn Trapez- und Steuermann sich „in Deckung" befinden (unten), um so wenig Luftwiderstand wie möglich zu verursachen. Auch sollten sie möglichst eng zusammenrücken, damit zwischen ihren Körpern keine großen Turbulenzen entstehen. Ein kleiner Nebeneffekt: Der Trapezmann hält auf diese Weise dem Steuermann das Spritzwasser ab.

Schwerwettersegeln

Es gibt keine allgemein gültigen Richtlinien, wann eine Wetterlage als Schwerwetter zu bezeichnen ist. Denn was für den einen Typ von Boot oder eine gut trainierte Besatzung noch als annehmbare Segelbedingung gilt, mag für andere Boote oder deren Besatzung schon eine Grenzsituation sein. Allgemein kann man Wind über 16 Knoten (Windstärke 5) als rauhes Wetter bezeichnen. Viel hängt dabei von dem Revier und den Stromverhältnissen ab. Steht beispielsweise Wind gegen Strom, kann die Segelei in den sehr steilen Wellen äußerst unangenehm werden. Wind von 15 Knoten und starke, steile See erschweren das Segeln erheblich mehr als Wind von 20 Knoten und eine lange See. Regatten werden häufig bei Starkwind aus Sicherheitsgründen abgesagt, und einzelne Segler werden vor dem Auslaufen gewarnt. Trotzdem ist es wichtig, daß man Erfahrung im Segeln bei Schwerwetter sammelt, denn es kann einen genausogut draußen erwischen. Um Schlechtwetterpraxis zu bekommen, sollte man sich einen erfahrenen Segler an Bord nehmen.
Je schwerer das Wetter ist, um so schwerer wird das Boot, aber auch seine Besatzung zu arbeiten haben. Wichtig ist, daß man Rigg, laufendes und stehendes Gut ständig kontrolliert und darauf achtet, daß alles in Ordnung ist. Bestehen irgendwelche Zweifel, bleibt man im Hafen. Überhaupt soll man, bevor man nach draußen geht, das Boot gründlich durchchecken. Sofern möglich, sollten die Segel gerefft sein oder zumindest so flach wie möglich getrimmt werden. Diese Maßnahme gilt für Am-Wind-Kurse. Ist man bei schwerem Wetter unterwegs, wird man feststellen, daß sich das Boot völlig anders als bei wenig Wind verhält. Die einzelnen Manöver erfolgen viel heftiger und laufen schneller ab, das Boot wird viel stärker krängen, und das Segeln mit raumem Wind ist nicht mehr erholsam, denn das Boot wird ins Gleiten kommen, und die Gefahr, daß es dabei aus dem Ruder läuft und querschlägt, ist nicht auszuschließen.

Segeln am Wind

Das Segeln hart oder hoch am Wind ist bei schlechtem Wetter der sicherste Kurs. Denn man ist in der Lage, bei Einfall einer zu starken Bö die Schoten aufzufieren oder anzuluven. Die Art, wie man am Wind bei viel Wind und starkem Seegang segelt, hängt zum Teil vom Bootstyp ab, ob es sich um eine behäbigere Familienjolle oder ein hochgezüchtetes Rennboot handelt. In jedem Fall wird die Besatzung ihr Körpergewicht zum Ausreiten voll einsetzen müssen.
Da Rennboote auch auf Am-Wind-Kursen ins Gleiten kommen, sollte man sich das zunutze machen. Dazu fällt man etwas ab, bis das Boot ins Gleiten kommt, und luvt dann wieder so hoch wie möglich an, ohne daß das Boot in Verdrängungsfahrt zurückfällt. Die Fock kann dabei etwas geschrickt werden, während der Steuermann durch Spielen mit der Großschot das Boot auf ebenem Kiel hält. Auch durch leichtes Aufholen des Schwertes kann man die Krängung reduzieren. Die ganze Aufmerksamkeit des Steuermanns gilt der Pinnenführung und muß sich darauf konzentrieren, die Wellen richtig anzuschneiden. Wird das Boot langsamer, verringert sich die Vortriebskraft des Windes, und die krängende Querkraft nimmt zu. Um wieder in Fahrt zu kommen, muß die Besatzung ihr Gewicht weiter nach vorne verlagern. Sobald eine Welle den Bug erreicht, luvt man etwas an, bis man auf dem Wellenkamm sitzt, und fällt dann auf der Rückseite der Welle wieder leicht ab. Bei großen Wellen ist die Windkraft auf dem Wellenkamm am stärksten, und die Besatzung muß daher dort besonders gut und aufmerksam ausreiten. Diese Art, durch den Seegang zu segeln, wird auch mit den schweren Familienjollen angewendet.
Eine stabile Jolle, die auch bei stärkerem Wind auf Am-Wind-Kurs nicht ins Gleiten kommt, muß etwas anders als eine Rennjolle gesegelt werden. Denn sie reagiert schwerfälliger, läuft nicht so schnell und krängt auch nicht so leicht. Man kann sie sehr gut hoch am Wind segeln, wenn man folgendes beachtet: Fällt eine Bö ein, luvt der Steuermann etwas an und fiert die Großschot so weit auf, daß sich das Boot aufrichtet. Ist die Bö vorbei, fällt er wieder auf den bisherigen Kurs ab und nimmt auch die Schot wieder dichter. Das Boot darf dabei nicht die Fahrt verlieren, weil es sonst auch seine Stabilität verlieren würde. Die Fock bleibt dichtgeholt, es sei denn, die Bö ist sehr stark.

Segeln mit halbem Wind

Das Segeln auf Halbwind-Kurs, das bei leichtem Wind am unproblematischsten ist, wird bei stürmischem Wetter zu harter Arbeit, weil ein leichtes Boot auf diesem Kurs fast ständig gleiten wird und schwierig zu steuern ist. Genau wie am Wind muß man fortgesetzt auf einfallende Böen achten, um entsprechend drauf zu reagieren und eine Kenterung zu vermeiden. Mit den Schoten muß ständig gespielt werden, auf keinen Fall dürfen sie belegt sein. Fällt eine Bö ein, fällt der Steuermann leicht ab und fiert die Schot etwas auf. Beschleunigt das Boot in der Bö, müssen die Schoten wieder etwas dichter genommen werden, da ja der scheinbare Wind durch die erhöhte Fahrt vorlicher einfällt. Auf keinen Fall darf in einer Bö angeluvt werden. Steuermann und Vorschoter sitzen eng zusammen weit achtern, damit der Bug sich hebt und entlastet ist. Je härter die Bö ist, desto weiter muß der Steuermann abfallen und die Besatzung achterlicher sitzen. Das Schwert sollte nicht mehr als zur Hälfte gefiert sein, damit das Boot bei einer langen Welle nach Lee wegrutschen kann. Ist die Bö vorbei, muß der Steuermann wieder etwas anluven, um wieder mehr Fahrt zu machen.

Segelt man parallel zur Wellenrichtung, gibt es wenig Probleme. Auf keinen Fall sollte man rechtwinklig ins Wellental hinunterfahren, da dann der Bug nur allzu leicht unterschneidet. Bei der Talfahrt wird etwas abgefallen, die Besatzung verlagert das Gewicht etwas nach vorn, und sobald das Boot beschleunigt, wird angeluvt und das Gewicht wieder achterlich verlagert, damit das Boot möglichst lange auf der Welle reitet. Nur muß man darauf achten, daß das Boot sich dabei nicht zu weit von seinem Ziel entfernt.

Unten: Segeln bei steifem Wind kann eine aufregende Sache sein, man muß nur genau wissen, wie ein Boot in einer hohen Welle mit hoher Geschwindigkeit zu handhaben ist. Gleitet es, muß es aufrecht gehalten werden und die Besatzung ihr Gewicht nach hinten verlagern, damit der Bug nicht unterschneidet.

Eine hochgezüchtete Rennjolle, wie der 470er, gleitet bereits auf einem Kurs voll und bei.

470
K 332
470
K 342
K312

Vor dem Wind

Der Vorm-Wind-Kurs ist der schwierigste. Böen können nur mit Lee-Ruder pariert werden. Platt vor dem Wind verwindet das Großsegel stark. Das führt zu heftigen Rollbewegungen des Bootes. Um dagegen anzugehen, muß der Baumniederholer so dicht wie möglich durchgesetzt und die Großschot etwas angeholt und das Schwert etwa halb gefiert werden. (Vorsicht beim Halsen.) Die Besatzung sitzt auf beiden Seiten. Ferner kann man die Fock auf die andere Seite nehmen (Schmetterling), was auch die Bewegungen des Bootes etwas stabilisiert. Beim Einmannboot hilft man sich, indem man die Großschot so weit anholt, bis die Windfäden entgegengesetzt stehen, was anzeigt, daß sich die Luftströmung am Segel umgekehrt hat. Dadurch krängt das Boot nach Lee und ist besser zu beherrschen. Bei achterlichem Wind kommen die Wellen von achtern und schieben das Boot vor sich her, das dann ins Gleiten kommt. Dabei kann geschehen, daß das Boot schneller als die Welle wird und sich mit dem Bug in die davor laufende See bohrt. Die Folge ist ein abruptes Abstoppen, während gleichzeitig der Druck aufs Rigg schlagartig zunimmt. Dadurch verliert das Boot seine Stabilität. Es kann querschlagen oder kentern. Dem kann man vorbeugen, indem man einen Raumschots-Kurs segelt, dabei die Wellen schräg abläuft und auch noch mehr Fahrt macht, da der scheinbare Wind vorlicher einfällt.
Wem ein Vorm-Wind-Kurs zu riskant erscheint, weil immer die Gefahr einer Patenthalse – eines unbeabsichtigten Übergehens des Baums – und des Querschlagens besteht, der sollte besser einen Raumschots-Kurs segeln und vor dem Wind kreuzen, um sein Ziel in Lee zu erreichen. Die längere Wegstrecke wird meistens durch die höhere Geschwindigkeit wieder wettgemacht.

Wenden und Halsen

Wenden bei starkem Wind erfordert wesentlich mehr Konzentration als unter normalen Bedingungen, denn die Manöver laufen viel schneller und „temperamentvoller" ab. Man sollte Krängungen beim Wenden oder auch das „Geigen" beim Halsen vermeiden, da sonst Gefahr besteht zu kentern.
Wichtig beim Wenden ist, daß das Boot gute Fahrt macht, bevor man durch den Wind geht, denn nur allzuleicht kann es sonst passieren, daß es im Wind stehen bleibt oder auf den alten Bug zurückfällt. Außerdem sollte möglichst auf einem Wellenberg gewendet werden. Der Vorschoter wirft die Fockschot los, sobald das Boot anfängt zu drehen, und nimmt die Fock so schnell wie möglich wieder dicht, wenn sie auf die neue Seite übergeht. Auch der Platzwechsel von der alten auf die neue Luvseite muß bei Steuermann und Vorschoter schnell und entschlossen erfolgen, damit das Boot erst gar nicht unnötig krängt. Außerdem sollten die Schoten beider Segel erst ganz dicht genommen werden, wenn das Boot wieder Fahrt aufgenommen hat.
Das Halsen bei starkem Wind und bei grober See ist kein einfaches Manöver. Es muß sehr präzise und konzentriert gefahren werden. Der günstigste Augenblick ist der Zeitpunkt, wenn das Boot Höchstfahrt läuft. Entweder auf dem Hang einer Welle oder nachdem eine Bö durchgezogen ist. Denn dann ist der scheinbare Wind schwächer und der Druck auf die Segel am geringsten. Somit geht auch der Baum leichter auf die neue Seite über. Wichtig bei diesem Manöver ist, daß der Baum nicht unkontrolliert übergeht, sondern daß man vorm Schiften die Großschot dicht nimmt und sie dann zügig auffiert, sobald der Wind das Segel auf die neue Seite drückt.

Links: Schwerwettersegeln erfordert viel seglerisches Geschick und Erfahrung. Besonders auf einem Raumschots-Kurs, wie hier, wenn das Boot in der Welle zu geigen beginnt.

Rechts: In rauher See ist es besonders wichtig, vorm Wenden keine Fahrt zu verlieren, sonst stampft sich das Boot fest und geht nicht durch [illegible]

Regattasegeln

Beherrscht man die Grundregeln des Segelns einwandfrei und beherrscht man das schnelle Segeln mit allen seinen Schikanen, kann man den Versuch machen, zu regattieren. Wettsegeln auf gut organisierten Regatten ist nicht nur ein aufregendes Erlebnis, es kann auch schnell zum Lebensinhalt werden. Vor allem ist es die beste Gelegenheit, sein seglerisches Können ständig zu verbessern.

Um in der Bundesrepublik Regatten segeln zu können, muß man den Segelschein A oder – auf Küstenrevieren – A1 des Deutschen Segler-Verbandes (DSV) besitzen. Die Regatten werden normalerweise von Clubs ausgerichtet, auf lokaler Basis, als Klassenmeisterschaften, im nationalen und internationalen Rahmen. Daran teilnehmen kann nur, wer Mitglied eines vom DSV anerkannten Club ist. Manche Clubs forcieren bestimmte Bootsklassen, so daß man nur dann eine Chance hat, aufgenommen zu werden, wenn man mit einem entsprechenden Boot kommt. Eventuell kann das bei der Anschaffung eines neuen Bootes zu einem entscheidenden Kriterium werden.

Regatten auf Club- oder nationaler Basis werden gewöhnlich als Klassenregatten, seltener als freie Regatten nach dem sogenannten Yardstick-Wertungssystem ausgeschrieben. Die Regattabahn wird von der Wettfahrtleitung festgelegt. Information darüber und auch über alle anderen wesentlichen Bestimmungen und Regeln sind in den Wettsegelbestimmungen und den ergänzenden Segelanweisungen niedergelegt. Die verschiedenen Regattakurse sind auf Seite 132/133 dargestellt.

Wichtig für jeden Regattasegler ist, daß er sich und sein Boot sorgfältig vorbereitet. Das ist eine unerläßliche Voraussetzung für den Sieg. Konditionstraining, Ausgleichssport, unermüdliches Segeltraining bei jeder Gelegenheit, bei jedem Wind und Wetter, tragen zum Erfolg bei. Auch die Kenntnis der Regattaregeln, die den Anfänger manchmal in ihrer verwirrenden Vielzahl zum Verzweifeln bringen, ist eine wichtige Voraussetzung. Sie alle wirklich zu beherrschen und alle Tricks zu kennen, setzt ein gründliches Studium und lange Praxis voraus. Doch die wichtigsten Grundregeln muß jeder kennen (s. Seite 139 bis 140), der sich mit dem Gedanken trägt, an Regatten teilnehmen zu wollen.

Es ist entschieden falscher Ehrgeiz, gleich als Steuermann segeln zu wollen. Glücklich kann sich schätzen, wer zunächst von einem erfahrenen Steuermann als Vorschoter mitgenommen wird. Und wenn man dann selbst als verantwortlicher Steuermann seine erste Regatta segelt, immer und überall die Augen offen halten. Was machen die anderen anders? Weshalb segeln sie schneller? Was habe ich falsch gemacht? Eine Regatta ist die beste Gelegenheit, von Spitzenseglern zu lernen. Als seine vornehmlichen Gegner aber sollte man sich auf diejenigen Segler konzentrieren, die in etwa das gleiche Leistungsniveau haben wie man selbst.

Ein Pulk von Optimisten rundet gekonnt eine Leemarke.

Rechts: 505er, die Probleme beim Schiften ihrer Spinnaker an der Raumschots-Marke haben.

Regattabahnen

Es gibt sehr unterschiedliche Regatten, angefangen von der kleinen Clubregatta, an der vielleicht zehn Boote beteiligt sind, bis zur internationalen Großveranstaltung, zu der Hunderte von Teilnehmern gemeldet sind. Auch die Regattakurse und Distanzen weichen voneinander ab. Sie werden von der Regattaleitung festgelegt und nach Zeit abgesegelt. Manche Regatten bestehen aus mehreren Wettfahrten, deren Gesamtergebnis den Sieger bestimmt. Die übliche Form des Kurses ist ein Dreieckskurs, bei der rechts oder links herum drei Markierunsbojen gerundet werden müssen. Es ist aber auch möglich, daß Clubs, deren Gewässer einen solchen Kurs nicht zulassen, andere Strecken festlegen. In der Regel soll der erste Kurs von der Startlinie zu einer genau in Luv liegenden Tonne führen, was für die Regattaleitung bedeutet, die Startboje bei wechselnden Winden bis zum Start laufend zu versetzen. Das Starten selber wird auf Seite 136/137 behandelt.

Lark-Jollen beim Runden einer Luvmarke in einer Meisterschaftsregatta bei schwachem Wind.

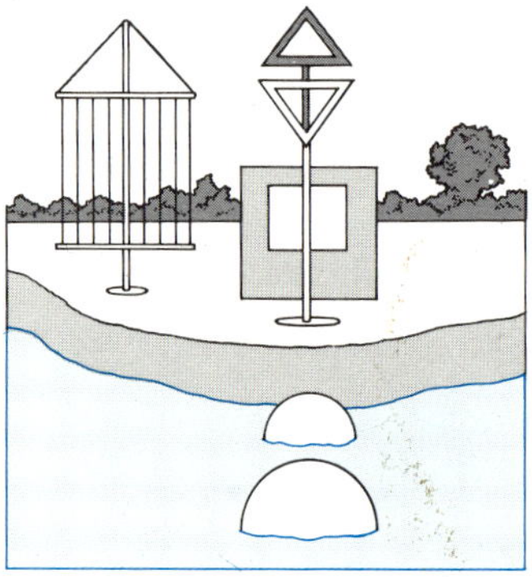

Startlinie mit Deckpeilung
Wenn sich die Dreiecke an Land in Deckung (Linie) befinden, liegt das Boot auf der Startlinie zwischen den beiden Bojen.

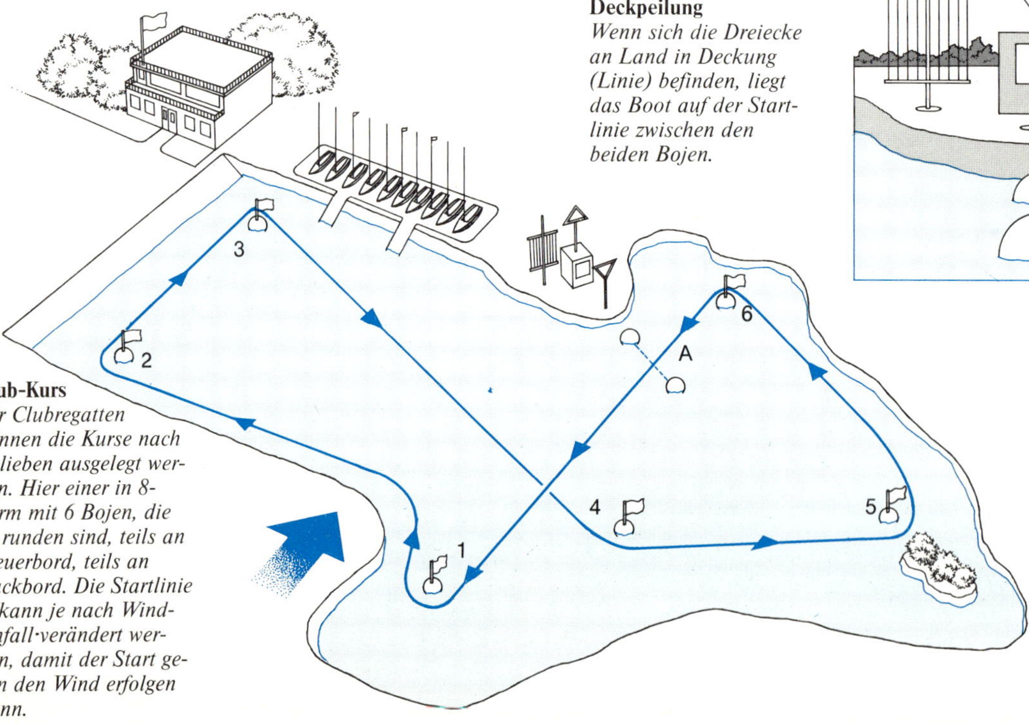

Club-Kurs
Für Clubregatten können die Kurse nach Belieben ausgelegt werden. Hier einer in 8-Form mit 6 Bojen, die zu runden sind, teils an Steuerbord, teils an Backbord. Die Startlinie A kann je nach Windeinfall verändert werden, damit der Start gegen den Wind erfolgen kann.

Der einfache Dreieckskurs

Meistens wird in Clubregatten ein einfacher Dreieckskurs gesegelt, ein olympischer Kurs (wie unten), aber ohne die dritte Runde. Die Bahn besteht aus einem gleichschenkligen Dreieck, markiert durch drei Tonnen. Die Startlinie ist so ausgelegt, daß sich die erste Tonne genau in Luv befindet. Üblicherweise besteht die erste Runde aus einem Kreuz- und zwei Raumschots-Kursen. Die zweite Runde hat einen Kreuz- und einen Vorm-Wind-Kurs und der letzte Schlag ist ein Kreuzkurs ins Ziel. Dabei werden die Tonnen jeweils an Backbord gelassen. Start ist an der Leetonne, Ziel die Luvtonne.

Der olympische Kurs

Bei nationalen oder internationalen Regatten segelt man den sogenannten olympischen Kurs. Bei ihm geht es nach der dritten Runde noch nicht ins Ziel, sondern es ist noch einmal das Dreieck abzusegeln, um sicherzustellen, daß fast die Hälfte der Regattastrecke kreuzend zurückgelegt werden muß. Internationale Regatten werden in der Regel auf offener See ausgetragen, um gleichmäßigere Windverhältnisse anzutreffen.

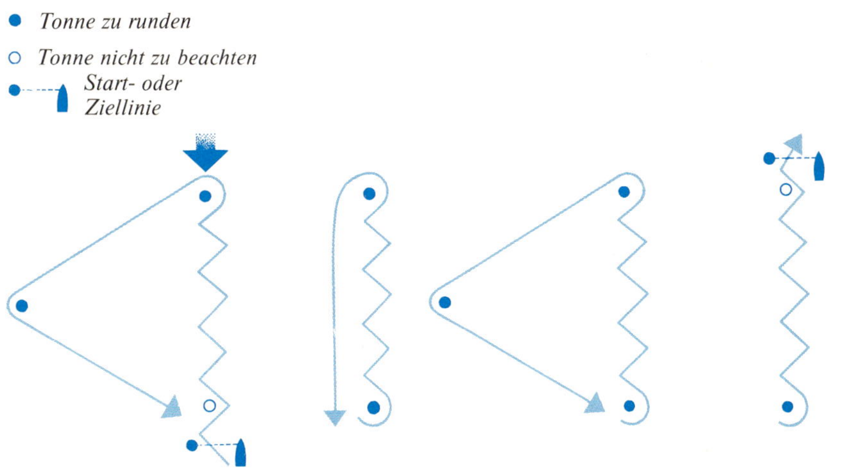

Die erste Runde hat einen Kreuz- und zwei Raumschots-Kurse.

Die zweite Runde hat einen Kreuz- und einen Vorm-Wind-Kurs.

Die dritte Runde hat einen Kreuz- und zwei Raumschots-Kurse.

Der letzte Schlag ist ein Kreuzkurs ins Ziel.

Alternativ-Kurs

Der olympische Dreieckskurs hat den Nachteil, daß auf ihm kein Halbwind-Kurs gesegelt wird. Der Alternativkurs, wie er hier dargestellt ist, gibt dem Segler Gelegenheit, sein Können auf mehr Kursen zum Wind unter Beweis zu stellen. (Zur Zeit in England in der Diskussion.)

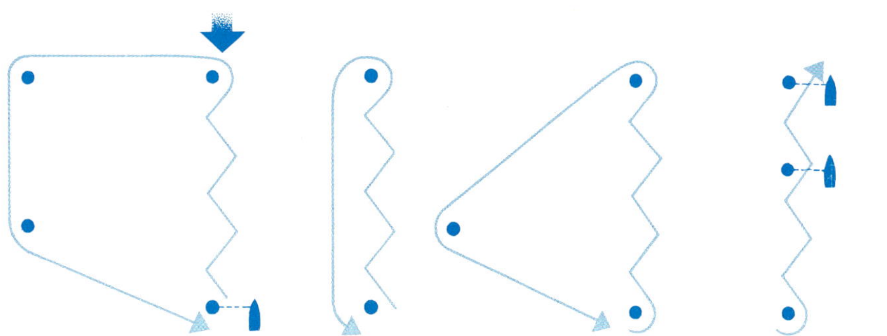

Die erste Runde hat einen Kreuz-, einen Halb-Wind-, einen Vorm-Wind- und einen Raumschots-Kurs.

Die zweite Runde hat einen Kreuz- und einen Vorm-Wind-Kurs.

Die dritte Runde hat einen Kreuz- und zwei Raumschots-Kurse.

Die Zielkreuz schließlich kann bei Bedarf verkürzt werden.

Verschiedene Arten des Wettsegelns

Das Segeln Boot gegen Boot innerhalb einer Klasse ist aufregend, aber es gibt auch Regatten anderer Art, die nicht weniger faszinierend sind. Beispielsweise Regatten, bei denen es nicht um den Einzelsieg geht, sondern um das Gewinnen im Team. Das setzt andere Regeln, andere Formen der Taktik voraus, wobei es dann auch weniger um die Schnelligkeit, sondern um die Taktik geht. Viele Clubs starten ihre Regatten auch nach dem Handikap-System, bei dem Boote unterschiedlicher Klassen gegeneinander segeln. Eine sehr seltene Art des Regattierens ist das Segeln Boot gegen Boot wie beim America's Cup.
Das Teamsegeln wird zwischen zwei Teams von drei bis vier Booten derselben Klasse gesegelt. Diese Regatta besteht gewöhnlich aus zwei Wettfahrten, zwischen denen die Boote getauscht werden. Ziel der Wettfahrt ist es, als Gruppe zu siegen. Demzufolge entscheidet weniger die Schnelligkeit des einzelnen Bootes, sondern die Taktik und das Zusammenspiel des Teams. Genaue Kenntnis der Regattaregeln ist genauso wichtig, wie das Vermögen, Kurse und Positionen des Teams zueinander und in Bezug auf den Gegner zu erkennen und entsprechend zu agieren.
Liegt man beispielsweise auf dem zweiten Platz und die Teamboote auf Platz 4 und 5, muß man versuchen, die Fahrt des Bootes auf Platz 3 soweit zu verlangsamen, daß die eigenen Boote an ihm vorbeikommen. Damit liegt jetzt das Team auf Platz 2, 3, 4 und hat eine gute Chance, das Rennen zu gewinnen. Teamsegeln vertieft nicht nur die Kenntnis der Wettsegelbestimmungen, sondern trainiert auch den praktischen Umgang mit dem Boot. (Bei uns kaum praktiziert.)
Handikap- oder Yardstick-Regatten werden häufig von Clubs veranstaltet, die viele unterschiedliche Boote haben, die zu internen Regatten zusammenkommen. Der Ausgleich der verschieden schnellen und großen Boote untereinander erfolgt durch eine Zeitvergütung, die sogenannte Yardstickzahl. Sie beruht auf den Durchschnittswerten vieler Regatta-Ergebnisse des betreffenden Bootstyps. Eine absolute Chancengleichheit gibt es dabei nicht. Zu viele veränderliche Größen, wie beispielsweise unterschiedliche Segeleigenschaften des einzelnen Bootstyps bei ungleichen Windverhältnissen, können nicht berücksichtigt werden.
Matchracing, das Wettsegeln zwischen zwei Booten gleicher Klasse, ist eigentlich die klassische Form des Rennens. In der Regel müssen dabei immer zwei Boote gegeneinander segeln. Dann segeln die jeweiligen Gewinner gegeneinander und so weiter, bis nur noch zwei Boote übrig bleiben, die um den endgültigen Sieg kämpfen müssen. Diese Match-Rennen beginnen genaugenommen bereits 5 bis 10 Minuten vor dem wirklichen Start, da während dieser Zeit die Boote bereits um die beste Startposition rangeln. Das Boot, das als erstes über die Startlinie geht, hat damit die beste Chance, das Rennen zu gewinnen, da es aus seiner Position heraus das andere Boot kontrollieren kann. Allerdings ist der Vorsprung nur so gering, daß der gerinste Fehler den Sieg kosten kann.

Einheitsklassen sind ein guter Test für die Fähigkeiten des Steuermanns, denn die Boote sind nahezu oder völlig gleichwertig.

In Regatten nach dem Yardstick-System sollte man möglichst vermeiden, sich in Kämpfe mit anderen Booten einzulassen, denn man segelt mehr gegen die Zeit als gegen Konkurrenten.

Regattavorbereitungen

Bevor man sein Boot vor einer Regatta zu Wasser bringt, ist zu checken, ob man alles Erforderliche an Bord hat, denn es ist ausgesprochen ärgerlich, wenn man auf dem Weg zum Start plötzlich feststellt, daß man irgend etwas Wichtiges vergessen hat und es nicht mehr holen kann.

Die Zeit, die man für die Vorbereitungen benötigt, hängt vom Bootstyp ab. Ein Flying Dutchman beispielsweise ist umständlicher aufzuriggen und zu trimmen, als ein Laser, der nur wenige Minuten beansprucht, um segelklar zu sein. Wichtig ist, daß der Rumpf sauber und glatt ist. Man überprüft das laufende und stehende Gut und tauscht beschädigtes Material aus. Dabei sollte man nicht knausern. Beim Riggen und Trimmen sollte man die Wind- und Wetterbedingungen der Wettfahrt berücksichtigen. Ausrüstung, die nicht den Klassen- oder Wettfahrtsbestimmungen entspricht, muß von Bord genommen werden. Andererseits muß alle vorgeschriebene Ausrüstung an Bord sein. Auch die Bekleidung sollte dem Wetter entsprechen, damit die Besatzung keine Konditionseinbußen erleidet. Sie darf weder die Bewegungsfreiheit einschränken, noch übermäßig Windwiderstand bieten. Geht man in ein längeres Rennen, sollte man an Essen und Trinken denken oder seinen Bedarf durch eine ausreichende Mahlzeit vorher gedeckt haben. Ein rechtzeitiger Gang zur Toilette erspart einem eventuelle Probleme und Nöte. Wichtig ist auch, daß man die Segelanweisungen und den Regattakurs vorher sorgfältig studiert und sich einprägt, so daß man Unklarheiten vor dem Start ausräumen kann. Die Segelanweisungen sollten an Bord mitgeführt werden. Viele Seglerkombinationen haben dafür Klarsichttaschen, die sie trocken und lesbar halten. Manchmal geben die Veranstalter Kontrollnummern an jeden Teilnehmer aus, die nach dem Rennen zurückgegeben werden müssen, damit die Regattaleitung weiß, daß alle Boote wieder zurückgekommen sind. Boote können disqualifiziert werden, die diese Anweisung nicht befolgen.

Das Punktsystem

Gewertet werden Regatten nach einem Punktsystem. Bei uns meistens nach dem des Deutschen Segler-Verbandes (DSV) oder sonst nach dem olympischen. Nach beiden Systemen gibt es für den ersten Platz in einer Wettfahrt 0 Punkte. Vom 2. Platz an differieren die Bewertungen. DSV-System: 1,6; 2,9; 4; 5; 6; 7; 8; usw. Olympisches System: 3; 5,7; 8; 10; 11,7; (7+6) 13; (8+6) 14 usw. Die schlechteste Wettfahrt kann meistens gestrichen werden. Für Aufgabe und Disqualifikation wegen eines Regelverstoßes gibt es ebenfalls Punkte. Auch bei diesen „Strafpunkten" weichen beide Systeme voneinander ab. Doch nach jedem System ist Gesamtsieger, wer am Schluß die niedrigste Punktzahl hat.

Startlinien

Die einfachste Startlinie bildet eine Deckpeilung zum Ufer. Denn wenn man die Wettfahrt auf dem freien Wasser starten will, braucht man ein Startboot. Bei fast allen Startmethoden geht man von einer festgelegten Startlinie aus, abgesehen vom sogenannten Torstart, der bei großen Jollenfeldern angewandt werden kann. Die Länge der Startlinie, sollte mindestens das $1^1/4$fache der Gesamtlänge aller am Rennen beteiligten Boote betragen.

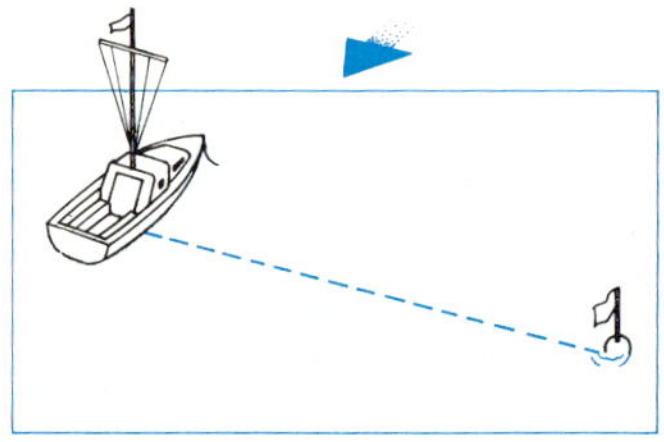

Einfache Startlinie mit Startboot
Beim Start im freien Wasser ist es mit Hilfe des Startbootes einfacher, die Startlinie genau rechtwinklig zum Wind zu legen. Die Startlinie wird gewöhnlich durch den Mast des Startbootes und eine Begrenzungsboje gebildet.

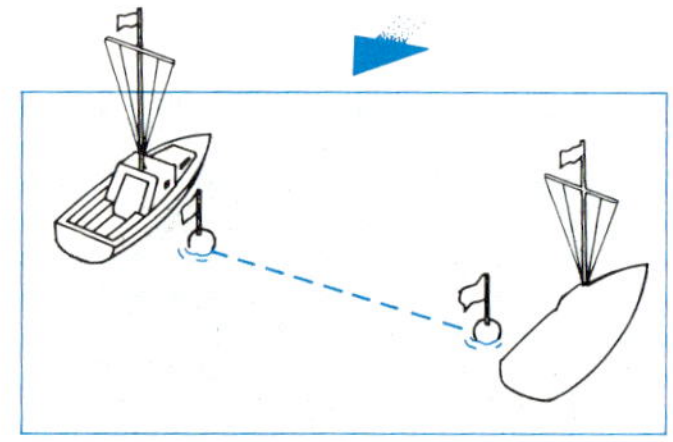

Startlinie zwischen zwei Bojen
Der Vorteil bei dieser Anordnung ist, daß das Startschiff nicht fest verankert zu sein braucht – zweckmäßig bei rauhem Wetter – und bei Winddrehungen die Bojen schnell verlegen kann. Das Startschiff kann sich rechts oders links neben den Begrenzungsbojen aufhalten.

Start eines Feldes von Fireball-Jollen mit Startboot und Backbord-Begrenzungstonne.

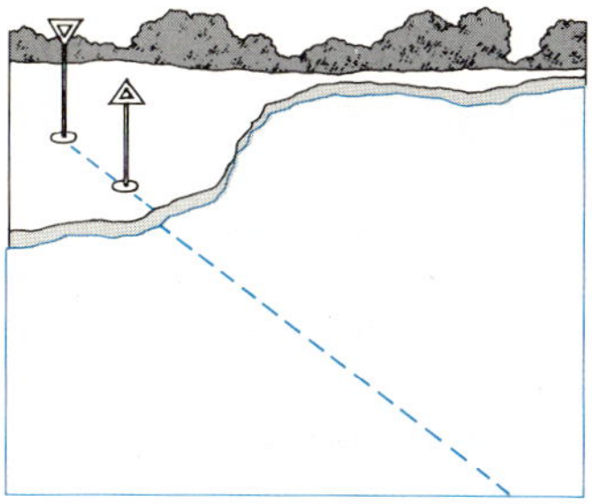

Startlinie mit Deckpeilung ohne Begrenzungsboje
Die einfachste Form einer Startlinie ist die mit einer festen Peilung an Land ohne Begrenzungsboje. Auch wenn man die Deckpeilung bei wechselnder Windrichtung verändern kann, sind die Korrekturmöglichkeiten sehr beschränkt.

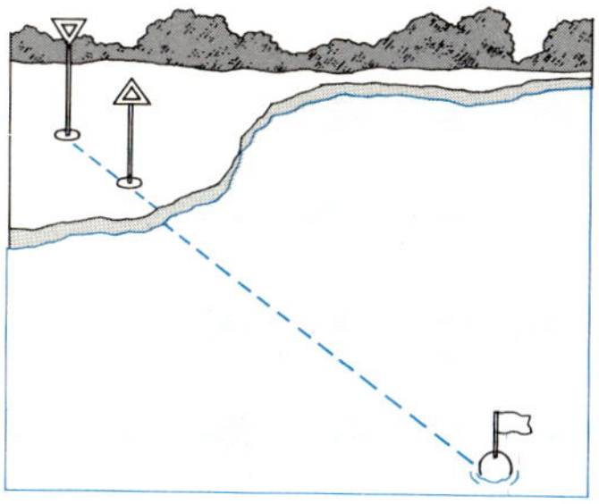

Deckpeilung mit Begrenzungsboje
Bei dieser Startlinie, gebildet durch Deckpeilung und Begrenzungsboje, sind die Segler gezwungen, innerhalb der Markierung zu starten. Die Boje braucht nicht in Verlängerung der Deckpeilung zu liegen, doch sollte sie es möglichst.

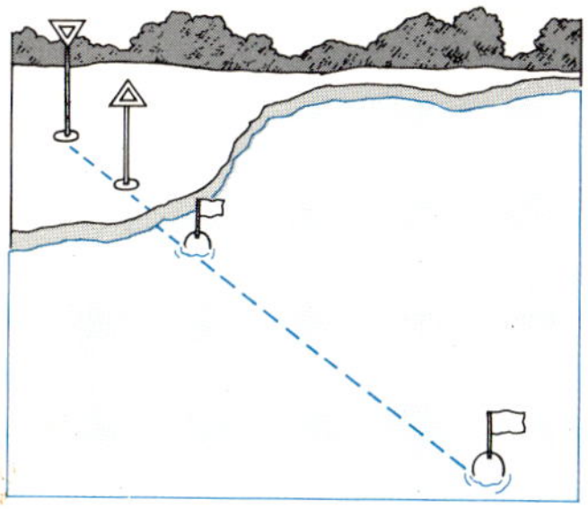

Deckpeilung mit innerer und äußerer Begrenzungsboje
Bei dieser Art der Startlinie müssen die Boote zwischen den Bojen starten. In der Regel liegen die beiden Begrenzungsbojen in Linie der Deckpeilung.

Der Torstart

Dieses Verfahren wird häufig bei großen Regattafeldern und Meisterschaften benutzt, um allen Teilnehmern ungefähr eine gleiche Startchance zu geben. Die Startlinie wird gebildet durch ein Pfadfinderboot, gewöhnlich ein Teilnehmer am Rennen, das, gefolgt von einem Torboot, am Wind vom Startschiff wegsegelt und so allmählich das Starttor öffnet. Zunächst wird die innere Boje in einem bestimmten Abstand vom Startschiff geworfen. Das Pfadfinderboot wird, um Behinderungen zu verhindern, auf seiner Leeseite von einem Wächterboot begleitet. Der zeitliche Ablauf stellt sich wie folgt dar: Ungefähr 10 Sekunden vor dem Startschuß wirft das Torboot die innere Boje, und sobald der Startschuß fällt, können die Teilnehmer durch dieses sich stetig vergrößernde Tor starten. Das Pfadfinderboot hat seinen Kurs so lange zu segeln, bis es entlassen wird und ins Rennen gehen kann. Gleichzeitig stoppt das Torboot oder wirft eine Boje, um die äußere Begrenzung der Startlinie zu markieren. Diese Art des Starts hat bei mäßigem und stetigem Wind manche Vorteile. Bei schwachen, umlaufenden Winden ist sie nachteilig.
Beim Torstart muß man darauf achten, daß man klar in Lee des Pfadfinders bleibt, damit man sich nicht plötzlich vor der Startlinie befindet und der Pfadfinder in Lee durchgeht. Eine Rückkehr aus dieser Position gibt es nicht mehr.
Beim Start ist das Heck des Torbootes hoch am Wind auf Backbord-Bug anzulaufen. Nicht raumschots, weil dann die Gefahr besteht, zwischen einem am Wind segelnden Boot und dem Torbootsheck eingekeilt zu werden.

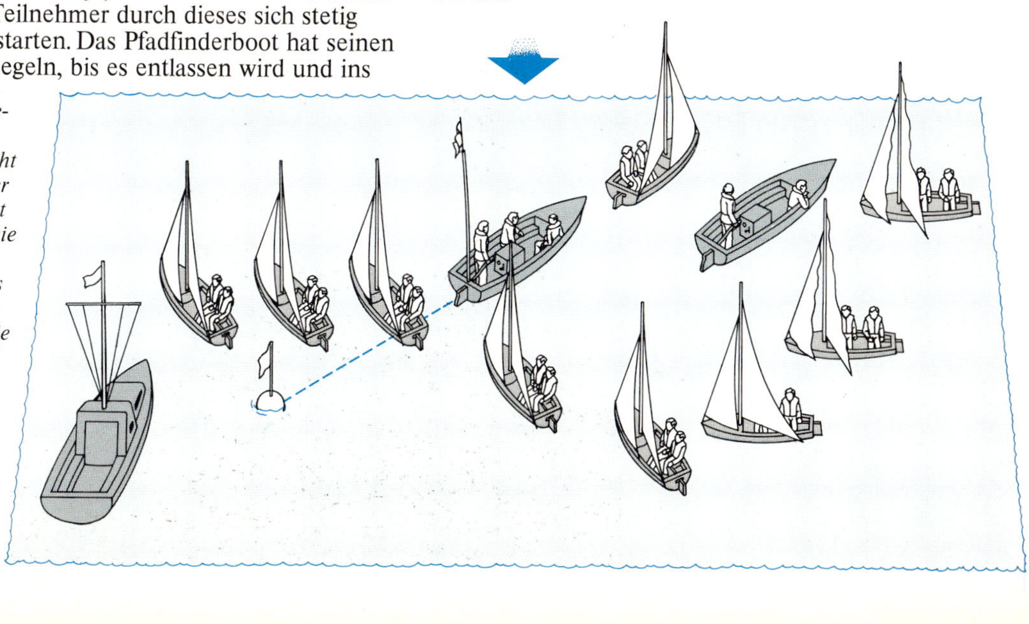

Nach Setzen der inneren Begrenzungsboje folgt das Torboot dicht hinter dem Pfadfinder mit dem Wächterboot an seiner Leeseite. Die Boote, die das Kielwasser des Torbootes gekreuzt haben, sind gestartet, während die anderen Boote noch darauf warten.

Flaggen und Signale

Vor Beginn von Regatten oder Wettfahrten gibt es Steuermannsbesprechungen, auf denen die Segelanweisungen, die während der Wettfahrt geltenden Regeln, Flaggen und Signale erklärt und alle sonstigen Informationen gegeben werden. In den internationalen Wettsegelbestimmungen gibt es auch Richtlinien für den Gebrauch von Signalflaggen und Standern des Internationalen Signalbuchs, mit denen man sich vertraut machen muß. Die Aufstellung rechts zeigt die gebräuchlichsten Flaggen und Stander, die entweder auf dem Startschiff oder dem Startmast an Land gesetzt werden. Neben diesen optischen Signalen werden auch akustische Signale (Böller u. ä.) abgegeben. Im Zweifelsfall gilt immer das optische Signal. Sinnvoll ist es, als Folie oder in einer wasserfesten Klarsichthülle ein Verzeichnis der Flaggensignale mitzuführen, ebenso eine Bahnkarte, um im Zweifelsfall schnell mal nachsehen zu können.

Golf: Torstart

Yankee: Schwimmwesten anlegen

Lima: In Rufnähe kommen

India: Ein-Minuten-Regel

Papa: Vorbereitungssignal

Hilfsstander 1: Allgemeines Rückrufsignal

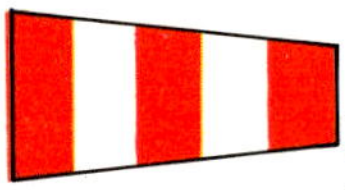
Antwortwimpel: Startverschiebung

Mit schwarzem Ball: Startverschiebung um 15 Minuten

Mit Zahlenwimpel 1: Verschiebung um 1 Stunde

Mit Zahlenwimpel 2: Verschiebung um 2 Stunden

Mit Flagge Alpha: Alle Wettfahrten sind auf ein späteres Datum verschoben

Nordpol: Abbruch der Wettfahrt

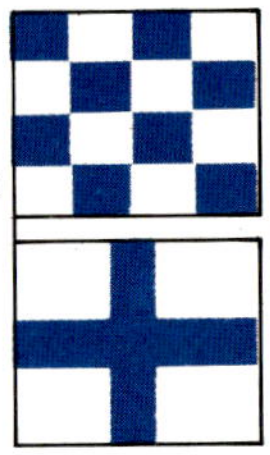
Nordpol über X-Ray: Abgebrochene Wettfahrt wird in Kürze wiederholt

Nordpol über Hilfsstander 1: Wettfahrt wird aufgehoben

Mike: Bahnmarke fehlt und wird durch den Träger dieser Flagge ersetzt

Sierra: Bahnverkürzungssignal

Ein Startschiff an der Startlinie: Das Vorbereitungssignal P zeigt an, daß es weniger als 5 Minuten bis zum Start sind.

Regattasegeln

Ein Anfänger muß die Wettsegelbestimmungen wenigstens so weit beherrschen, daß er weder Mitsegler behindert, noch sich einer Disqualifikation aussetzt. Wer hingegen häufiger regattiert, muß sich eingehend mit den Einzelheiten der Regeln beschäftigen. Sie sind international und werden von der International Yacht Racing Union (IYRU) herausgegeben und in Deutschland durch die Zusatzbestimmungen des Deutschen Segler-Verbandes ergänzt. Eine goldene Regel für den Anfänger: Im Zweifelsfall lieber Raum geben, anstatt in blindem Vertrauen auf sein vermeintliches Wegerecht drauflos zu segeln.

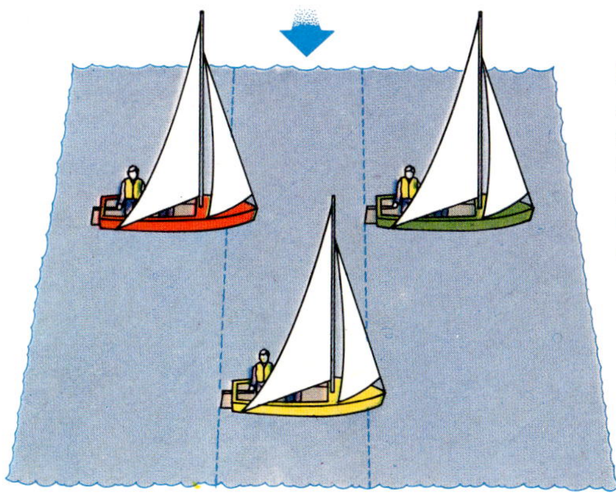

Klar achteraus
Ein Boot ist klar achteraus, wenn es mit keinem anderen Boot überlappt. (Gelb überlappt Grün, Rot überlappt Gelb.)

Auf unterschiedlichem Bug
Das Boot auf Steuerbord-Bug muß dem Boot auf Backbord-Bug ausweichen (Regel 36).

Auf dem gleichen Bug
Segeln zwei Boote auf dem gleichen Bug, muß das luvwärtige dem leewärtigen Raum geben (Regel 37).

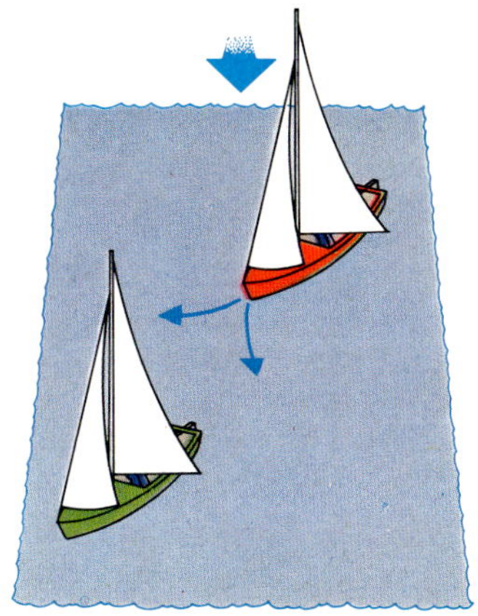

Klar achteraus
Ein Boot, das klar achteraus liegt, muß sich von dem klar vorausliegenden Boot freihalten (Regel 37).

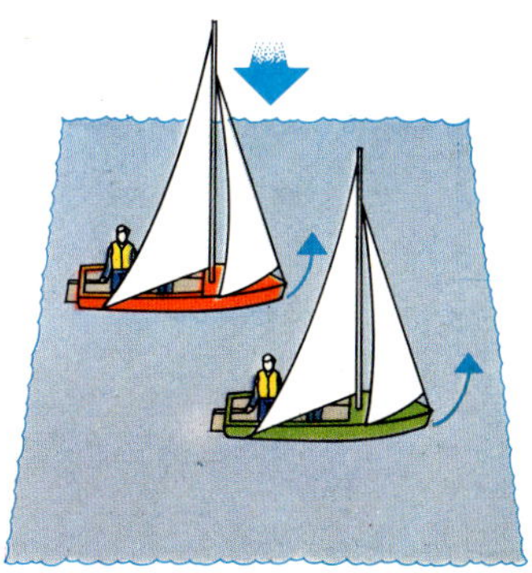

Luvkampf
Ein Boot klar voraus oder in Lee kann den Gegner ausluven, ausgenommen Regel 38 (rechts). (Grün kann anluven, Rot muß sich freihalten.)

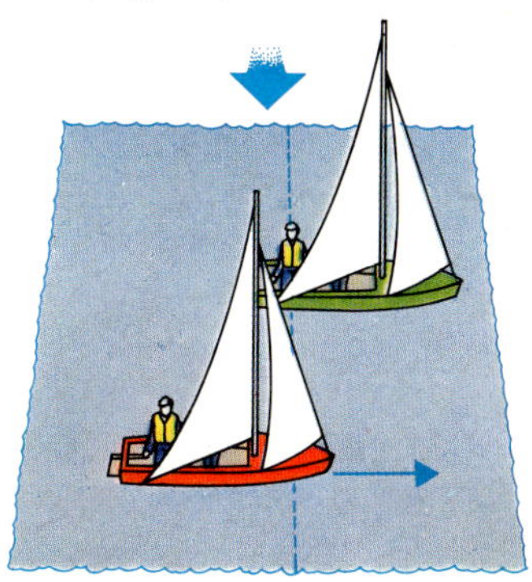

„Mast querab"
Ein Leeboot (Rot) darf nur so lange anluven, bis sein Mast querab vom Steuermann des Luvbootes (Grün) ist (Regel 38).

Protest

Wer schuldhaft gegen eine Regel verstoßen hat, nimmt die in den Segelanweisungen dafür vorgesehene Buße auf sich. Ist man aber von der Schuld eines anderen überzeugt, muß die Flagge Bravo des Internationalen Signalbuchs als Protestflagge im Want gezeigt werden. Protestieren darf auch, wer einen Regelverstoß als Zeuge beobachtet hat.

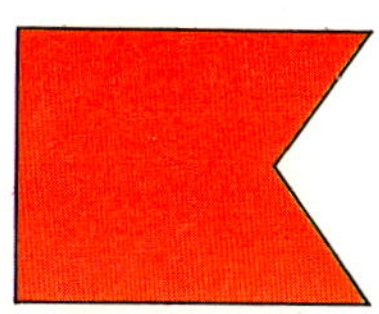

Hindernisse und Bahnmarken

Die kritischen Stationen bei einer Wettfahrt sind die Bahnmarken. Das sind die Punkte, an denen sich die Boote ballen und um ihre Vorteile ringen. Hier gilt es besonders, seine Rechte zu kennen, denn abgesehen davon, daß auch geblufft wird, geht es ja darum, sich in die bessere Position zu manövrieren oder sie zu halten, aber auch um Kollisionen zu vermeiden. Es gibt eine Reihe von Regeln für das Runden von Bahnmarken, aber auch um Zusammenstöße zu vermeiden. Schon bevor man an die Boje herankommt, sollte man die anderen Boote aufmerksam beobachten und bereit sein, schnell zu reagieren, wenn ein Gegner Raum verlangt.

Starboote an der Wendemarke. Das Boot im Vordergrund ist in der Klemme, und blockiert die von hinten aufkommenden Boote. Einige Boote segeln auf Steuerbord-Bug und haben kein Wegerecht gegenüber denen auf Backbord-Bug.

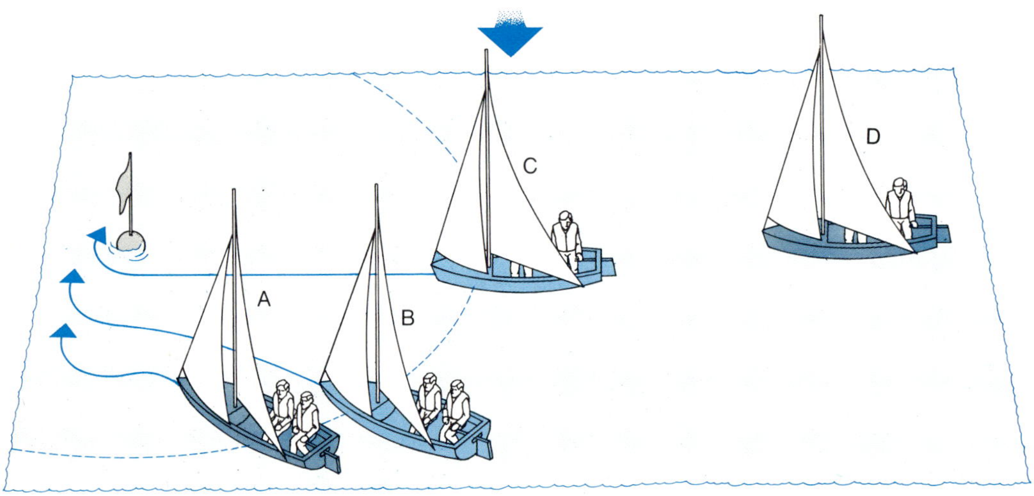

Runden der Bahnmarken
Nähern sich mehrere Boote einer Bahnmarke, so müssen die jeweils außenliegenden Boote dem innenliegenden Boot Raum geben, sofern mindestens zwei Bootslängen vor Erreichen der Bahnmarke eine Überlappung hergestellt wurde. A muß B und C Raum geben, B nur C. D kann keinen Raum verlangen, denn es liegt noch klar achteraus von allen anderen Booten (Regel 42).

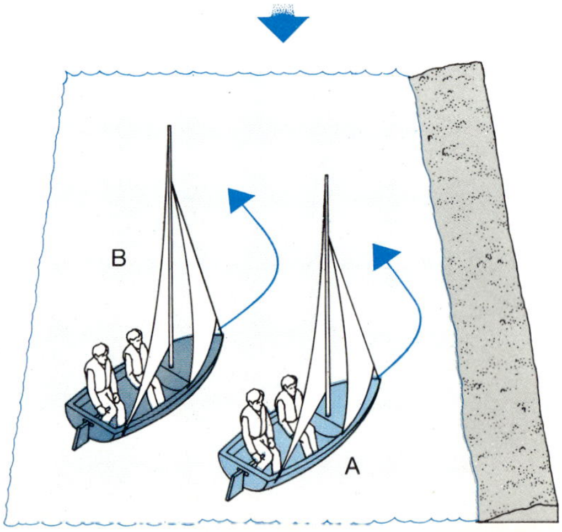

Raum bei Hindernissen
Segeln zwei Boote auf dem gleichen Bug, kann das Leeboot (A) Raum verlangen, wenn die sichere Schiffsführung ein Ausweichen vor dem Hindernis verlangt (Regel 43).

Rechte Seite: Drei Gull-Jollen nähern sich einer Wendemarke. 1863 liegt klar voraus, aber 1939 muß 2202 Raum geben, weil eine Überlappung besteht.

1863
1939

Wie man ein Boot schneller macht

Wer das Beste aus seinem Boot herausholen will, muß Mittel und Wege finden, die Antriebskräfte optimal zu nutzen und zugleich den durch Rigg und Rumpf verursachten Wind- und Reibungswiderstand so weit wie möglich zu reduzieren. Der Stärke der Antriebskraft ist eine Grenze gesetzt. Sie liegt dort, wo die Mannschaft nicht mehr in der Lage ist, ein Boot auf einem Am-Wind-Kurs auszureiten. Weil man auf einem Am-Wind-Kurs am besten die Wirksamkeit des Riggs feststellen kann, sollte man mit dem Bootstrimm auf diesem Kurs beginnen. Bauchiger getrimmte Segel bringen mehr Vortrieb als flachgeschnittene Segel, verursachen jedoch mehr Krängung. Früher hatte man eine Vielzahl von Segeln für die verschiedenen Bedingungen. Heute kann man den Segelbestand durch die verschiedenen Trimmöglichkeiten von Rigg und Segeln kleiner halten. Nicht alle Boote werden vom Hersteller mit sämtlichen Trimmeinrichtungen geliefert, und man muß sich eine Reihe von zusätzlicher Ausrüstung hinzukaufen oder einbauen. Bei manchen Klassen sind Trimmeinrichtungen sogar bewußt eingeschränkt.

Ist ein Boot neu oder hat man es noch nie gesegelt, ist es gut, wenn man ein schnelles Boot vom gleichen Typ mitsegeln lassen kann und seins dann genauso trimmt.

Ein Teil der notwendigen Korrekturen kann auf dem Trockenen vorgenommen werden, der überwiegende Teil des Trimms aber muß auf dem Wasser erfolgen. Für den Trimm auf dem Trockenen legt man das Boot am besten auf den Bootswagen, setzt die Segel und dreht es, bis es in einer Am-Wind-Position steht. Dann setzt man den Schothornstecker so weit durch, daß möglicherweise vorhandene vertikale Falten entlang des Baumes verschwinden. Die Cunningham-Kausch wird nur dichtergenommen, wenn sich Falten entlang des Mastes am Vorliek zeigen. Dann wird die Großschot so weit angeholt, bis die obere Segellatte etwa parallel zur Bootslängsachse steht. Nun holt man die Fockschot so weit dicht, bis ihr Achterliek in seiner Gesamtlänge parallel zum Großsegel steht. Die Form dieser Düse, die hier zwischen Fock und Großsegel entsteht, und die Spannung in der Achterlieken der beiden Segel sind wichtige Kriterien für einen optimalen Segeltrimm. Die Fock muß so eingestellt sein, daß die Windfäden alle gleichmäßig in derselben Richtung und waagerecht stehen. Die entsprechenden Fixpunkte werden markiert.

Die verbleibende Feineinstellung muß beim Segeln auf dem Wasser vorgenommen werden. Bei leichtem Wind und Seegang ist ein etwas bauchiger getrimmtes Segel vorteilhafter. Es gibt mehr Vortrieb. Dazu fährt man den Mast so gerade wie möglich und den Schothornstrecker etwas loser. Nimmt der Wind zu, muß das Großsegel flacher gefahren werden. Das erreicht man, indem man den Schothornstrecker steif durchsetzt und durch Biegung des Mastes. Zum Teil ergibt sie sich von allein bei stärkerem Wind. Sie kann aber auch durch mehr Spannung auf den Want- und Stagspannern erreicht werden. Bringt man den Traveller der Großschot außerdem weiter nach Lee und verändert die Fockschot-Holepunkte, so bewirkt das eine Verwindung in den oberen Teilen des Segels. Dadurch reduziert sich der Winddruck aufs Segel und damit auch die Krängung des Bootes. Die zunehmende Mastbiegung bei starkem Wind macht nicht nur die Segel flacher, sondern sie erweitert auch die Düse zwischen Großsegel und Fock und verringert die Spannung in den Achterlieken beider Segel. Dadurch verringern sich die Kräfte aufs Rigg ebenfalls.

Die Düse zwischen Groß- und Vorsegel muß stets offengehalten werden.

Der Mast

Der Mast ist eine wichtige Trimmeinrichtung für den Stand der Segel und auch für die Kursstabilität eines Bootes. Einrichtungen am Mast, wie die Salinge oder der verstellbare Mastfuß, verändern den Stand und die Krümmung des Mastes und damit natürlich auch die Wölbung im Segel. Bei normalen Segelbedingungen, wenn das Segel bauchig gefahren wird, soll der Mast möglichst gerade stehen. Wünscht man das Segel flacher, trimmt man den Mast im oberen Bereich nach hinten und im mittleren Bereich nach vorn. Man kann aber auch den Mast seitwärts biegen und damit auch die Segelform verändern. Holt man den Masttopp nach Lee, öffnet sich das Segel durch stärkere Verwindung im oberen Bereich, damit läßt der Druck im Segel nach und die Krängung verringert sich.

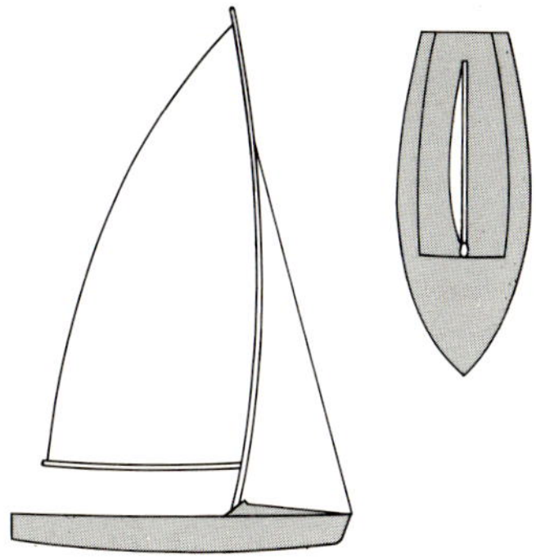

Mast im mittleren Bereich nach vorn und im oberen Bereich nach achtern getrimmt: flacheres Segel.

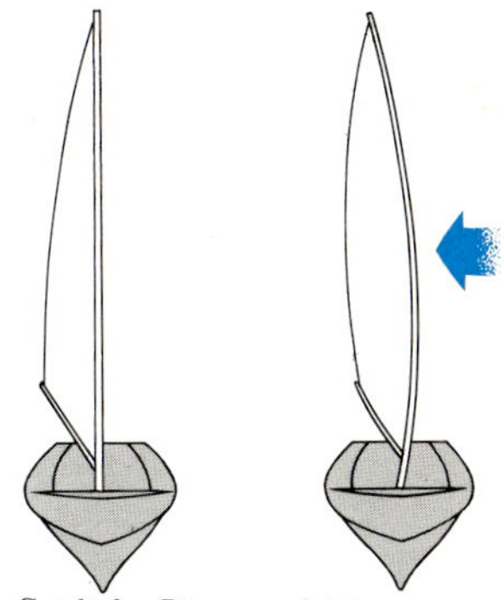

Seitliche Biegung: Links gerader Mast, rechts Mastbiegung nach Lee.

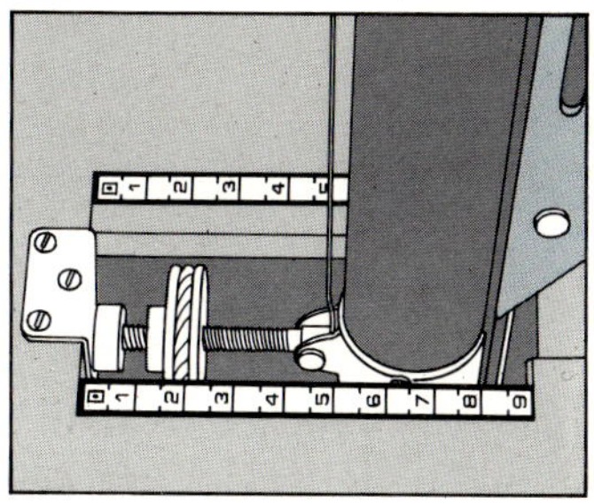

Mastkontroller
Er dient zur Kontrolle der Mastbiegung in Deckshöhe. Bei leichtem Wind wird der Mast im Deck zurückgehalten. Bei zunehmendem Wind läßt man ihn langsam nach vorne kommen. Dadurch erhält er mehr Biegung. Der Beschlag besteht aus einem Nylonrad auf einem Gewindebolzen.

Die Saling

Die Saling ist eine der wichtigsten Trimmeinrichtungen des Mastes, mit der man seine Biegung verstärken oder verhindern kann. Der Winkel, um den sie die Wanten aus ihrer Geraden wegspreizt, beeinflußt das Verhalten des Mastes unter Segeln. Dabei darf nicht vergessen werden, daß beim Segeln nur Luvwant und -saling unter Beanspruchung stehen und eine Biegung des Mastes verursachen. Salinge können während des Segelns nicht verändert werden. Sie müssen vor dem Mastsetzen eingestellt werden.

Der Winkel der Salinge zur Längsachse des Mastes beeinflußt seine Biegung nach vorn und achtern. Werden sie so eingestellt, daß die Wanten ungespreizt zum Topp laufen, haben sie keinen Einfluß auf die Biegung des Mastes. Da sich der Mast normalerweise im Mittelbereich biegt, nimmt er auch die Saling mit, soweit es die Wanten erlauben. Verläuft der Spreizwinkel der Saling nach achtern, werden die Wanten aus ihrer geraden Zuglinie gedrückt. Kommen die Wanten dann unter Spannung, versuchen sie, die Saling und den mittleren Bereich des Mastes nach vorn durchzudrücken. Steht die Saling nach vorn, werden die Wanten aus ihrer normalen Zugrichtung nach vorn gespreizt. Sie drücken dadurch Saling und Mast im mittleren Bereich nach achtern und wirken auf diese Weise der natürlichen Mastbiegung entgegen.

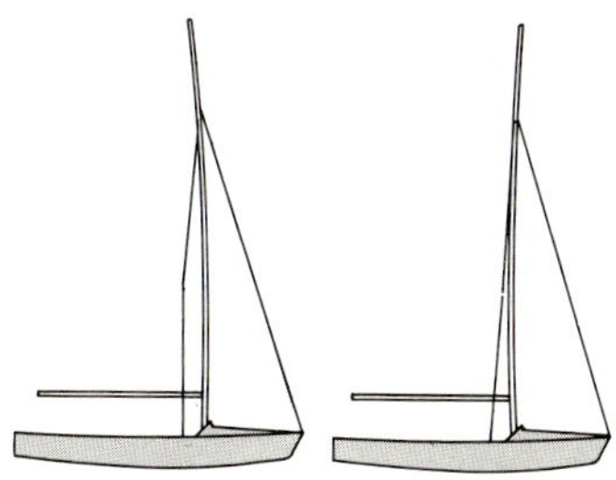

Salingswinkel
Die Saling links ist nach achtern abgewinkelt und drückt den Mast im Mittelbereich nach vorn. Die Saling nach vorn gewinkelt (rechts) drückt den Mast im mittleren Bereich nach achtern durch.

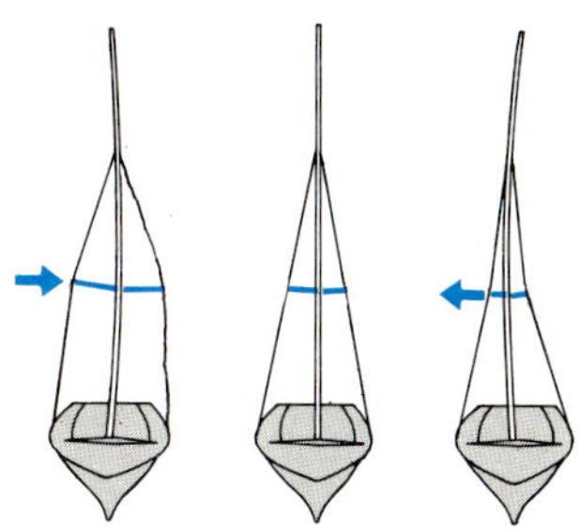

Salingslänge
Saling unter Druck (links), neutral (Mitte) und unter Zug (rechts).

So wie der Winkel der Saling zum Mast seine Biegung bestimmt, kann auch die Länge der Saling den Masttrimm beeinflussen. Je länger die Saling ist, desto steifer macht sie den Mast gegen eine seitliche Biegung. Die kurze Saling hingegen gibt dem Mast genügend Flexibilität zur Seite, die mit Hilfe der Wanten kontrolliert werden kann.

Großschotführung

Die Großschot kann einen fest auf dem Cockpitboden oder Schwertkasten sitzenden Fußblock haben oder einen verstellbaren, der mit einem Schlitten auf einer Travellerschiene gleitet. Der Traveller erlaubt zahlreiche Trimmöglichkeiten des Großsegels. Wird der Traveller nach Lee gebracht, wirkt der Schotzug senkrechter, das Segel wird flacher, der Mast biegt mehr durch. Traveller mittschiffs bewirkt ein etwas bauchigeres Segel. Man kann mit dem Traveller das Achterliek mehr öffnen und schließen und – in gewissen Grenzen – auch das Steigen des Baumes verhindern. Um dem Mast eine stärkere Biegung geben zu können, kann man die Großschotblöcke am Baum weiter nach hinten versetzen. Ein senkrechter Schotzug holt den Masttopp nur geringfügig nach achtern. Eine schräg in Richtung Mastfuß wirkende Zugkraft der Schot übt gleichzeitig einen gewissen Biegedruck auf den mittleren Bereich des Mastes aus.

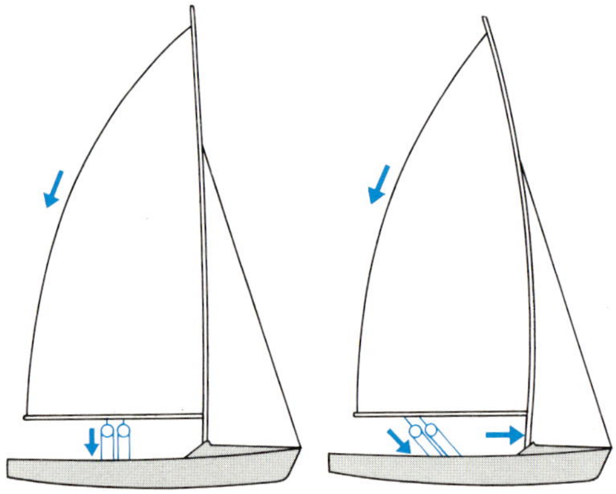

Senkrechter Zug der Großschot nach unten ermöglicht nur den Masttopp leicht nach hinten zu holen. Schräger Zug der Großschot, durch Versetzen der Blöcke nach hinten, ergibt eine stärkere Biegung des Mastes.

Großschotführung mit Traveller, der einen senkrechten Zug ausübt.

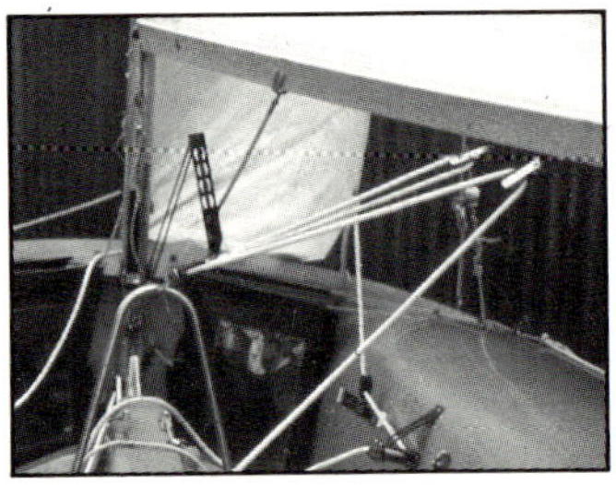

Großschotführung mit schrägem Zug. Sie wirkt auch weitgehend als Baumniederholer.

Segellatten

Es wird häufig übersehen, daß auch Segellatten den Segeltrimm beeinflussen, denn sie sorgen für einen guten Stand des Achterlieks. Sie werden, je nach Bedarf, aus unterschiedlichem Material mit unterschiedlicher Biegsamkeit, dem Segel entsprechend gefertigt. Ein bauchiger geschnittenes Leichtwettersegel beispielsweise benötigt weichere Latten als ein flaches Schwerwettersegel. Nicht durchgehende Latten sollen am inneren Ende dünner werden, damit sie im Segel keinen Wulst bilden. Durchgehende Latten sollen über ihre ganze Länge gleichmäßig elastisch sein. Sie können auch durch loseres oder festeres Einbinden in die Tasche den Bauch des Segels verändern. Jede Segellatte sollte in der Reihenfolge ihrer Verwendung numeriert und am vorderen oder hinteren Ende markiert sein.

Schothornstrecker (-ausholer)

Mit dieser Einrichtung kontrolliert man die Spannung des Großsegelunterlieks. Auf vielen Jollen besteht diese Streckvorrichtung nur aus einem Bändsel am Schothorn, das man durch das Auge an der Baumnock zieht und festmacht. Auf Rennjollen oder größeren Booten besteht die Streckeinrichtung aus einer kleinen Talje, die, je nach Bedarf, durchgesetzt oder gefiert werden kann. Ein gestrecktes Unterliek macht das Segel im unteren Bereich flacher, so daß der Segelschwerpunkt nach achtern rutscht. Bei der Grundeinstellung sollte das Unterliek so weit gestreckt werden, daß es keine vertikalen Falten mehr zieht, aber noch keine horizontalen.

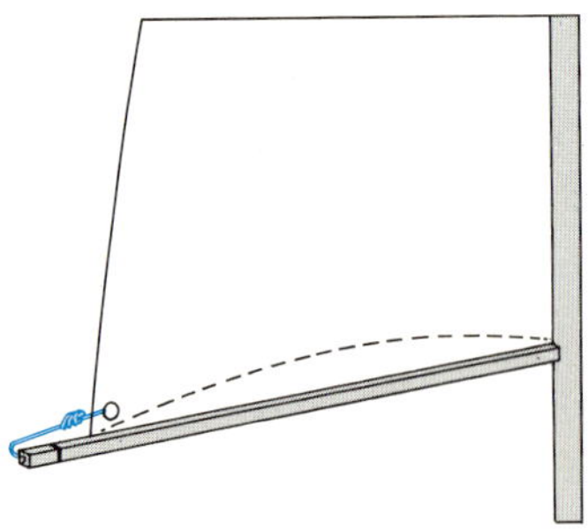

Ist das Schothorn nur leicht durchgesetzt, bleibt das Segel bauchig.

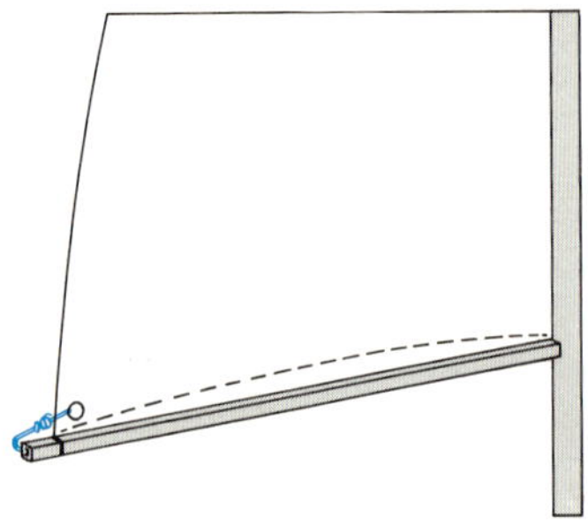

Bei stramm durchgesetztem Schothornstrecker wird das Segel flach.

Cunningham-Kausch (-Hole)

Diese Einrichtung besteht aus einer kräftigen Kausch ein bis zwei Handbreit über der Halskausch, durch die ein Stropp als holende Part einer kleinen Talje mit Zug nach unten geschoren ist. Das feste Ende ist am Lümmelbeschlag belegt. Mit dieser Einrichtung kann man den Segelschwerpunkt verändern. Nimmt der Wind zu, wandert der Schwerpunkt im Segel, weiter nach achtern, holt man die Cunningham-Kausch dicht, kommt der Schwerpunkt wieder nach vorn zurück. Als Faustregel gilt, daß man sie anholt, bis alle Falten am Vorliek des Segels verschwunden sind.

Baumniederholer

Der Baumniederholer verhindert das Steigen des Baumes auf Kursen mit raumen Winden und das Verwinden des Großsegels im oberen Bereich.
Er muß jederzeit leicht regulierbar sein. Bereits kleine Veränderungen in der Einstellung des Niederholers können große Wirkungen haben. Fiert man ihn beispielsweise auf einem Am-Wind-Kurs etwas, verwindet sich der obere Teile des Großsegels – das Boot segelt sofort aufrechter.

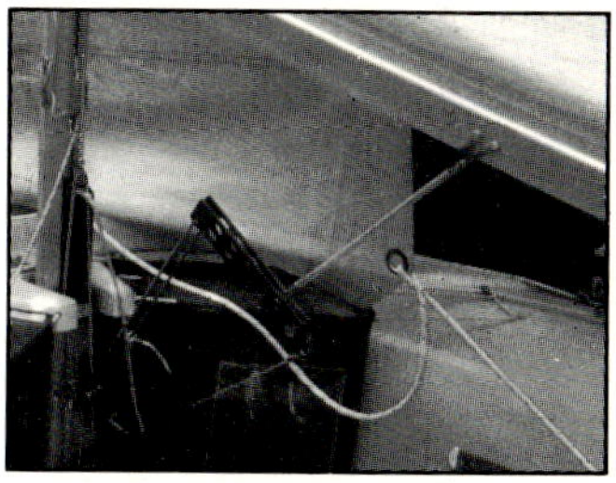

Ein wirkungsvoller Baumniederholer mit einer Hebelwaage, wie man ihn auf Rennjollen findet. Über ein doppeltes Streckerfall kann er von jeder Seite des Bootes aus bedient werden.

Das Fockfall

Besonders wichtig ist, daß der Zug des Mastes nicht vom Vorstag, sondern vom Vorliek der Fock aufgenommen wird. Fallen sollten daher aus Stahldraht sein, damit man sie genügend durchsetzen kann und das Vorliek nicht nach Lee durchhängt. Denn dadurch wird das Segel zu bauchig. Bei Booten, die keine verstellbaren Wanten haben, ist das Fockfall die einzige Möglichkeit, um die Wantenspannung zu variieren. Daher sollte es einen Strecker haben, der vom Steuermann bedient werden kann.

Fockschotführung

Die Einstellung der Fockholepunkte für die richtige Schotführung ist abhängig von Kurs und Windstärke. Sie sollen daher nach vorn, achtern, aber auch seitlich verstellbar sein. So kann man Achter- und Unterliek der Fock trimmen und die Düse zwischen Groß- und Vorsegel dem Wind entsprechend verändern und verhindern, daß sich das Segel stark verwindet. Bei starkem Wind wird der Holepunkt mehr auswärts gefahren, bei leichtem Wind weiter einwärts.

Zusammenwirken der Trimmeinrichtung

Nur beim richtigen Einsatz all dieser Einrichtungen ist es möglich, die Segel optimal und effektiv zu trimmen. Die nebenstehenden Zeichnungen demonstrieren die beiden Extreme des möglichen Segeltrimms. Das linke Bild zeigt ein Boot mit gerade getrimmtem Mast. Baumniederholer lose, Schot dicht, Schothornstrecker nur leicht angeholt und die Cunningham-Kausch lose, die oberste Segellatte stramm eingebunden. Das Resultat ist ein sehr bauchig stehendes Segel. Auf der rechten Zeichnung ein Boot, bei dem der Mast bis zum möglichen Maximum des Segelschnitts gebogen ist. Dafür müssen Schot, Schothornstrecker und Baumniederholer ganz steif durchgesetzt sein, ebenfalls die Cunningham-Kausch. Das Resultat ist ein extrem flaches Segel.

Links: Sind alle Trimmtaljen nur leicht durchgesetzt, bleibt der Mast gerade und das Segel bauchig.

Oben rechts: Setzt man alle Trimmtaljen stramm durch, peitscht der Mast nach hinten und das Segel wird flach.

Tauwerk und seemännische Knoten

Tauwerk ist ein lebenswichtiger Teil der Ausrüstung eines Bootes, und Ersatz geht ziemlich ins Geld. Der Umgang mit Tauwerk und die Pflege von Tauwerk zählen zum täglichen seemännischen Handwerk. Man kann die Lebensdauer seines Tauwerks erheblich verlängern, wenn man stets darauf achtet, daß es nirgends scheuert. Gibt es Scheuerstellen, sollten sie sofort herausgeschnitten und die Enden zusammengespleißt werden. (Weit besser ist es, beschädigtes Tauwerk durch neues zu ersetzen.) Auf das Ende einer Leine kommt ein sogenannter Takling, der sie vor dem Aufdrüseln bewahrt.
Im Laufe der Zeit haben die Seeleute eine Vielzahl von Knoten entwickelt. Die Auswahl auf diesen Seiten zeigt die hauptsächlich gebrauchten. Einige sind universell zu verwenden, andere mehr für spezielle Zwecke. Wie beispielsweise der Stopperstek, der nur in einer Zugrichtung funktioniert. Seemännische Knoten müssen unbedingt halten, sich zugleich aber leicht wieder lösen lassen. Auch in nassem Tauwerk.

Teile des Knotens

Wenn man sich mit seemännischen Knoten befaßt, muß man die entsprechenden Fachausdrücke kennen. Ein Ende in Haarnadelform heißt Bucht. Der Teil, über dem die Bucht geformt wird, heißt feste Part, und das Ende der Leine wird Tampen genannt.

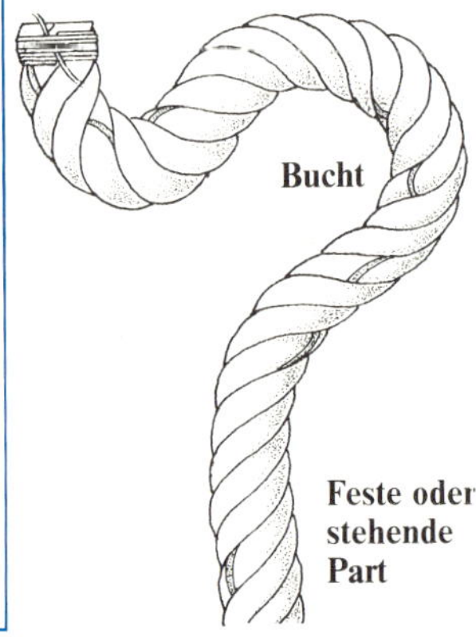

Achtknoten

Der Achtknoten ist schnell und leicht herzustellen. Er wird in den Tampen eines Endes gemacht, um unbeabsichtigtes Ausrauschen zu verhindern. Mit ihm werden Schoten gesichert.

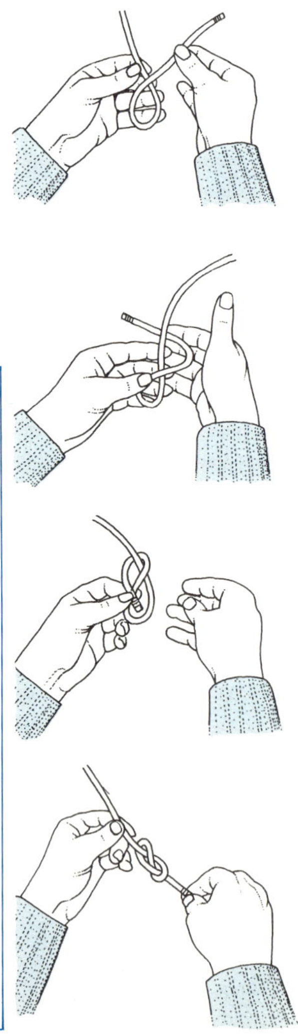

Tauwerksarten

Früher wurde Tauwerk ausschließlich aus Naturfasern hergestellt. Heute wird praktisch nur noch synthetisches Tauwerk verwendet. Es ist weitaus strapazierfähiger, doch lösen sich herkömmliche Knoten auch leichter, weil die Kunstfasern eine glatte Oberfläche haben. Das einzelne Tau besteht aus Kardeelen. Die Kardeele werden zu Enden geschlagen – das heißt, verdrillt – oder geflochten. Für Festmacheleinen und Fallen wird meist dreikardeeliges geschlagenes Tauwerk genommen, für Schoten geflochtenes. Es ist lehniger und griffiger, hat aber auch mehr Reck als geschlagenes Tauwerk. Material und Stärke hängen vom Verwendungszweck an Bord und von der Bootsgröße ab.

Polypropylen 3-kardeelig

Nylon 8-geflochten

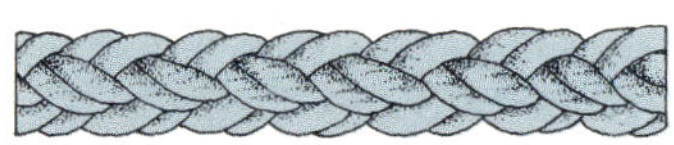

Nylon doppel-4-geflochten

Polyester 3-kardeelig

Nylon Mantelgeflecht

Kreuzknoten

Dieser Knoten besteht aus zwei Überhandknoten, die so gegeneinanderlaufen, daß die Parten jedes Tampen nebeneinander und auf derselben Seite aus der Bucht des anderen Tampen kommen. Verlaufen die beiden Überhandknoten in derselben Richtung, entsteht ein sogenannter Altweiberknoten, der nicht hält.

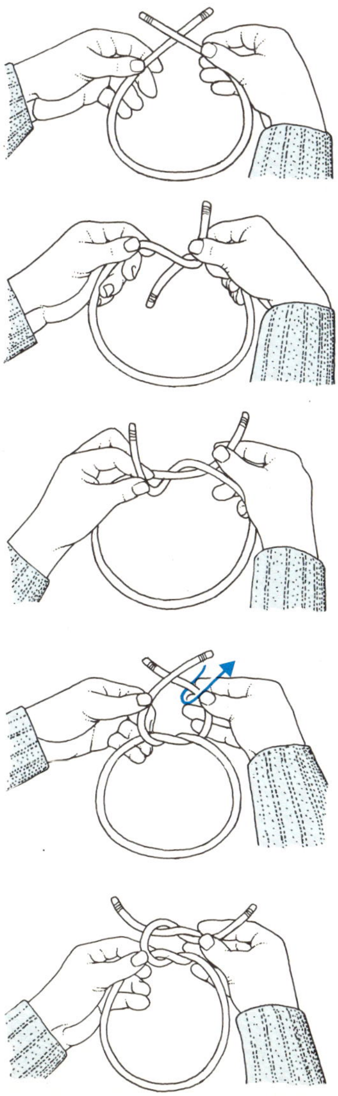

Lösen eines Kreuzknotens

Der Kreuzknoten wird auf folgende Weise schnell und leicht gelöst: Fassen Sie einen Tampen des Knotens mit einer Hand und die feste Part mit der anderen Hand und ziehen Sie den Knoten auseinander. Schieben Sie nun den Knoten von der festen Part her über den Tampen.

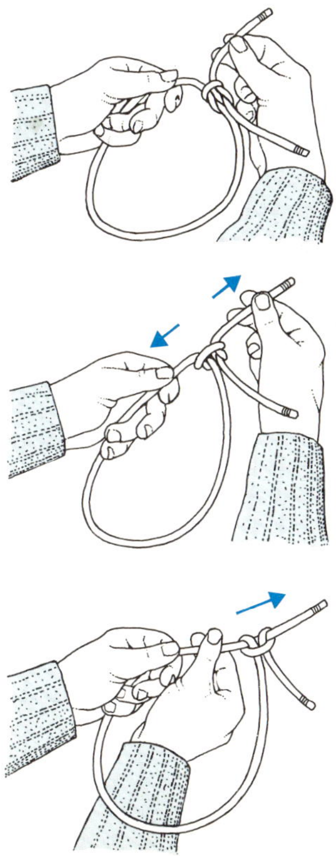

Einfacher Schotstek

Den Schotstek verwendet man in der Regel zum Zusammenstecken zweier ungleich starker Enden (hält nicht in glattem Kunstfaser-Tauwerk). Zum Lösen wird der Knoten umgebogen und die Bucht auseinandergezogen.

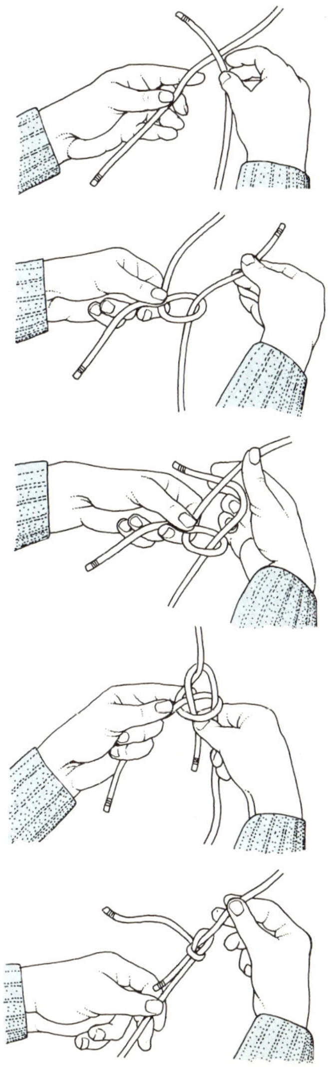

Eineinhalb Rundtörn und zwei halbe Schläge

Dies ist der gebräuchlichste Knoten, um ein Ende, auf dem nicht viel Kraft steht, an Spieren, Handläufen und Wanten festzumachen. Der Knoten ist schnell und leicht angefertigt und läßt sich genauso schnell wieder lösen.

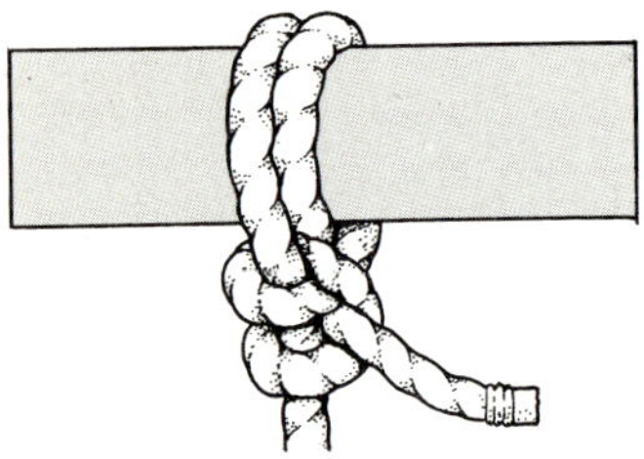

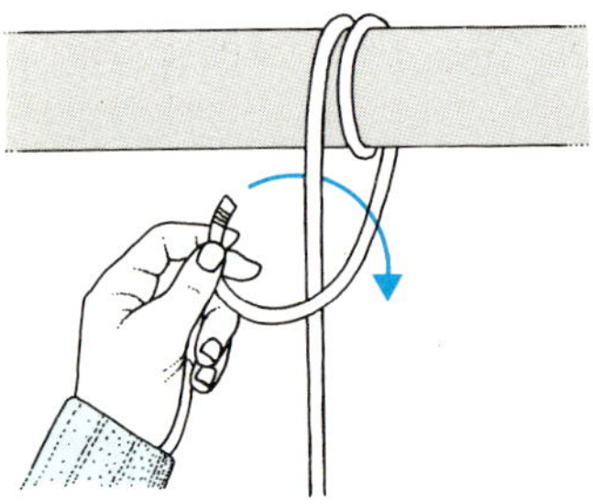

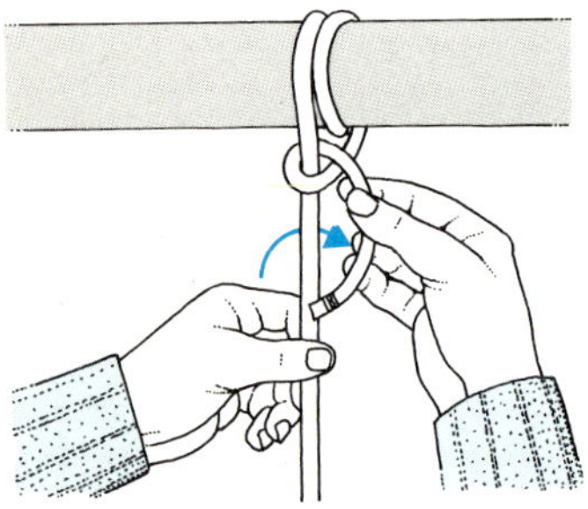

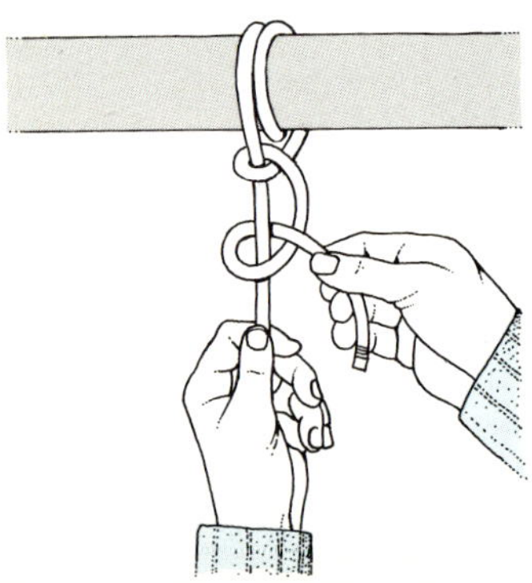

Webeleinstek

Der Webeleinstek dient zum vorübergehenden Belegen an einem Rundholz. Er läßt sich schnell und leicht anfertigen, hält jedoch nur dann dauerhaft, wenn der Zug im rechten Winkel erfolgt.

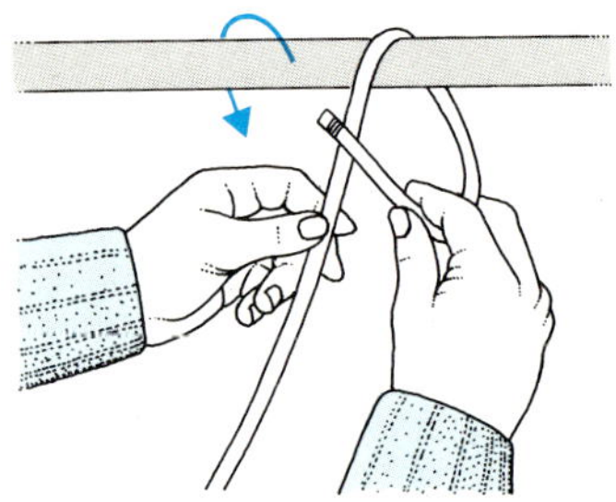

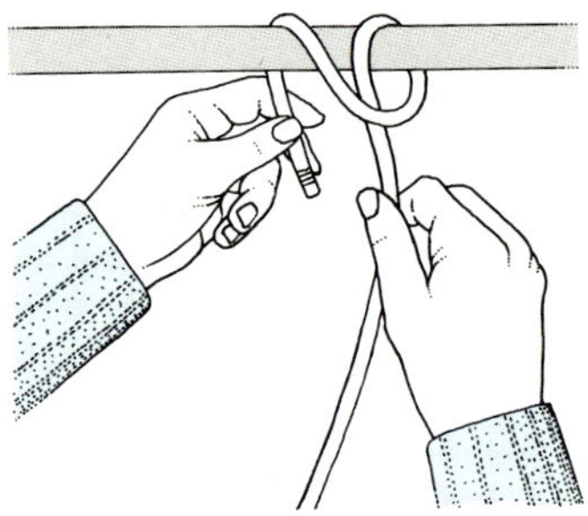

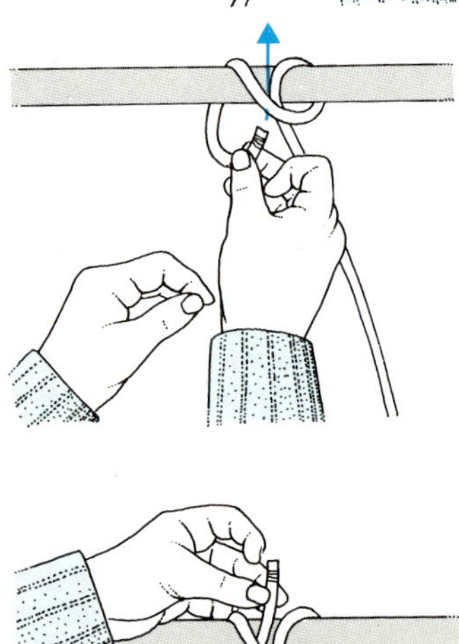

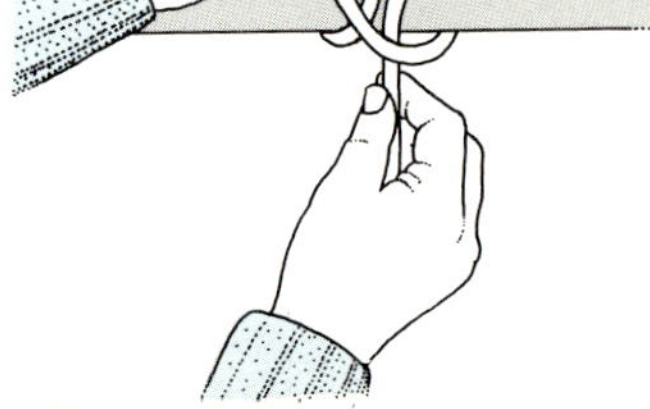

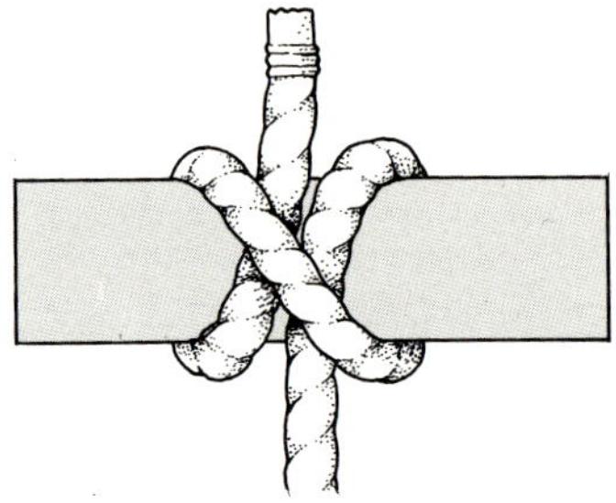

Webeleinstek um einen Poller

Auf die folgende Weise kann mit dem Webeleinstek schnell an einem Poller festgemacht werden. Das Ende wird wie hier gezeigt in zwei Buchten gelegt und dann über den Poller geworfen. Zusätzlich unbedingt durch zwei halbe Schläge sichern.

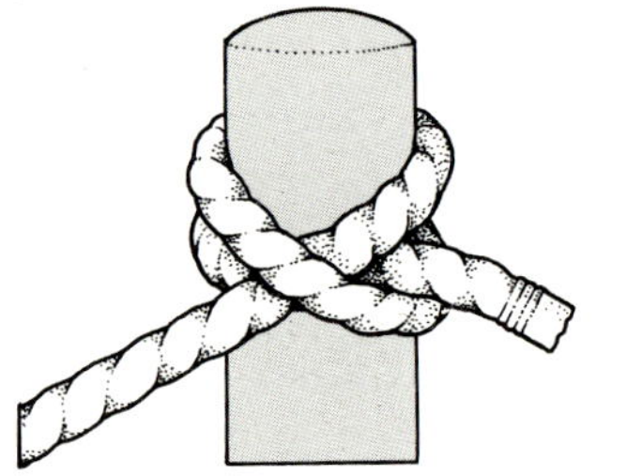

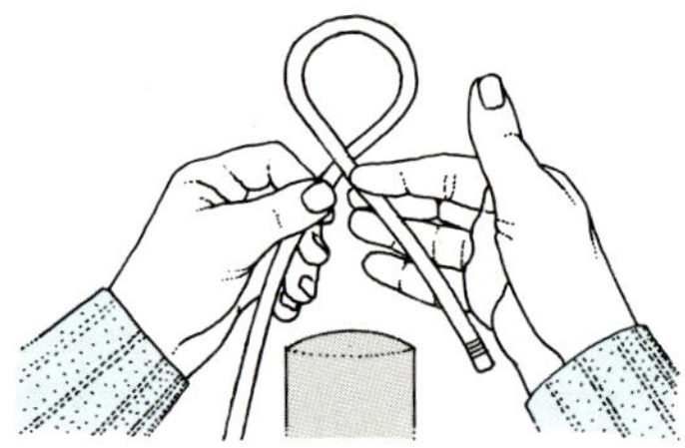

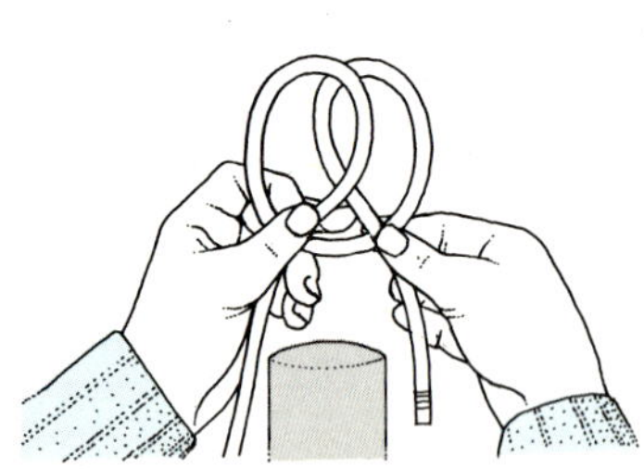

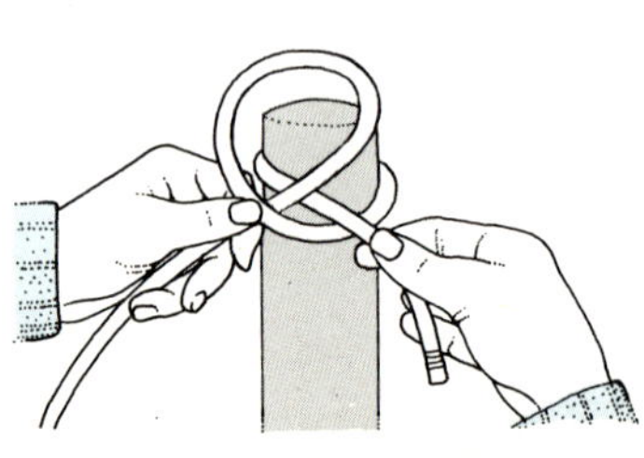

Einfacher Palstek

Man erhält ein Auge im Tampen, das sich nicht zusammenzieht. Hat man durch Drehen der rechten Hand in der festen Part ein Auge gebildet sind die folgenden Vorgänge einfach zu bewerkstelligen. (Bei uns wird er anders herumgemacht, den Tampen außerhalb des Auges.)

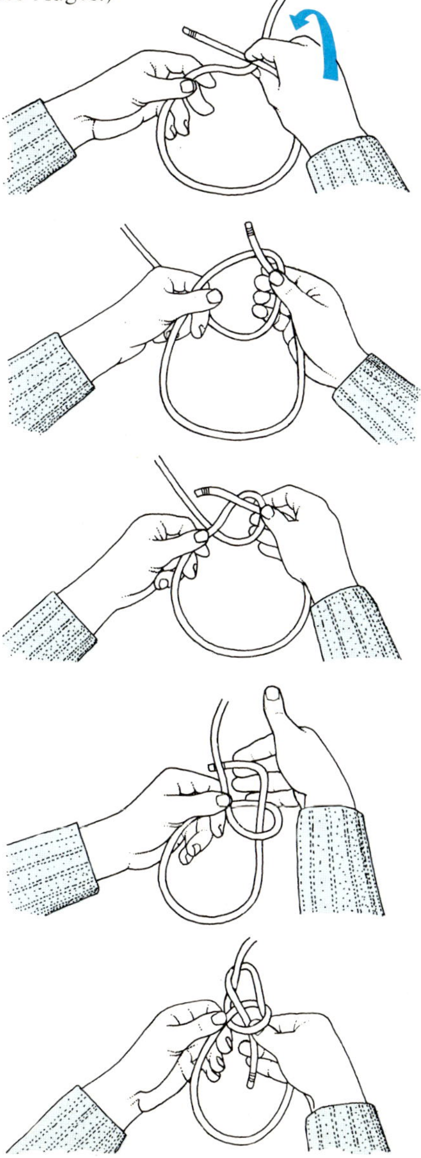

Stopperstek

Der Stopperstek dient zum Anstecken eines Tampens an einer vertikalen Spiere, wie z.B. dem Mast, da der Knoten nicht nach unten rutscht, solange Kraft auf der holenden Part steht.

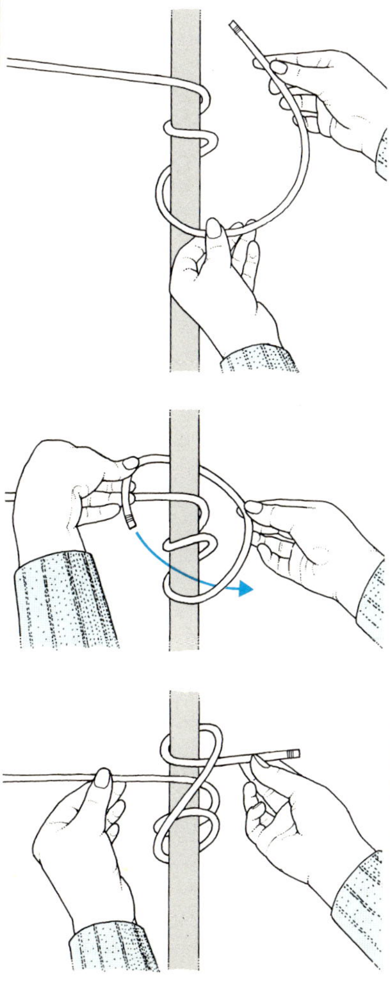

Doppelter Schotstek über festem Auge

Er dient zum Festmachen eines Endes an einem festen Auge oder einem Haken. Bis Phase drei gilt er als einfacher Schotstek, der aber nicht sicher hält.

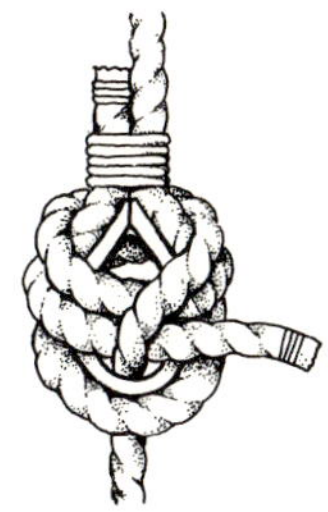

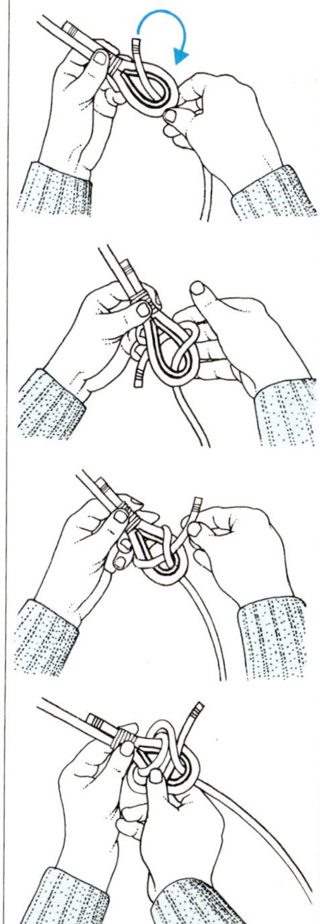

Eineinhalb Rundtörn mit Slipstek

Es gibt verschiedene Knoten, die sich so bekneifen, daß sie durch einfachen Zug schnell gelöst werden können. Meist wird eine durchgesteckte Bucht der laufenden Part bekniffen. So auch bei diesem Knoten. Zu größeren Sicherheit kann man mit der Bucht noch einen halben Schlag draufsetzen. Er löst sich dann aber nicht mehr auf Zug.

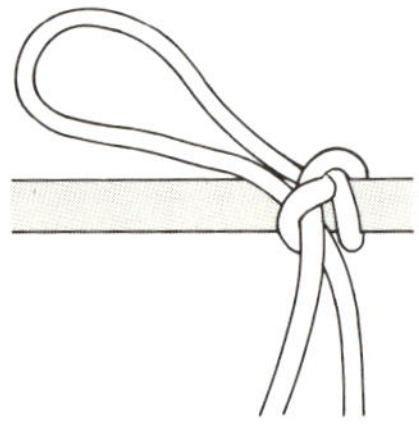

1 Man macht eineinhalb Rundtörn,

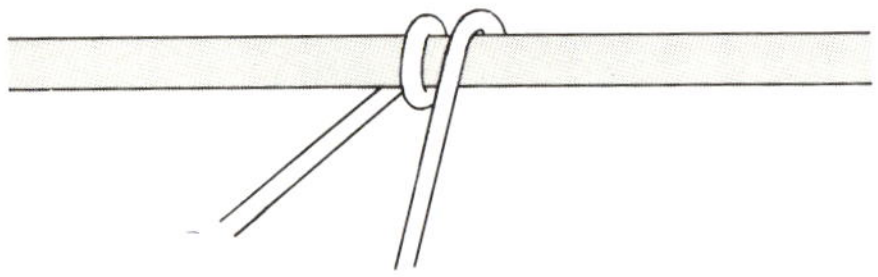

2 verdoppelt das Ende zu einer Bucht und legt sie über die feste Part,

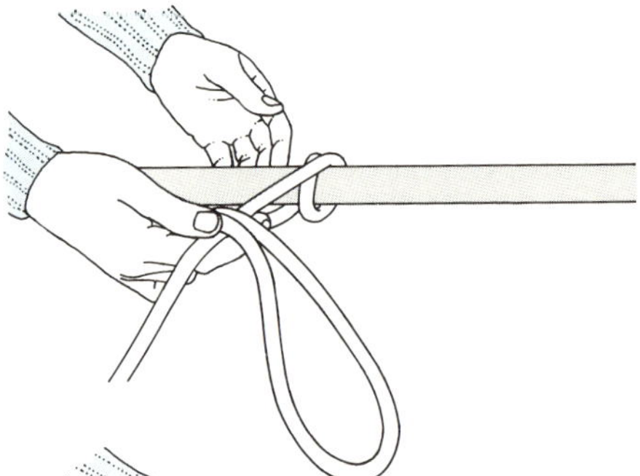

3 macht dann einen halben Schlag mit der Bucht um die feste Part und zieht ihn zusammen.

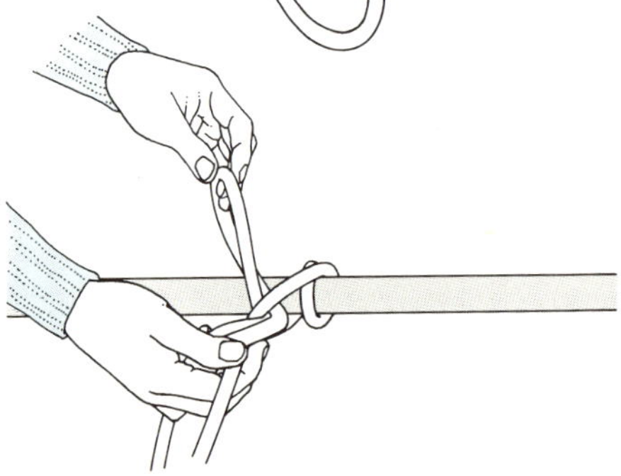

4 In diesem Stadium kann der Knoten schnell gelöst werden, indem man einfach am Ende zieht.

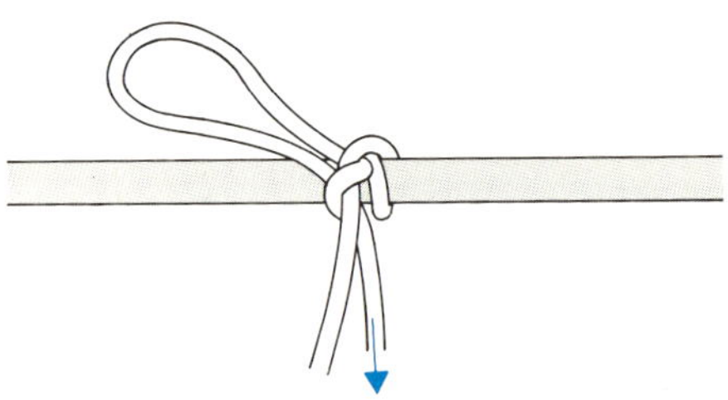

Zur größeren Sicherheit kann noch einmal ein halber Schlag draufgesetzt werden. Der Knoten läßt sich dann aber nicht mehr auf Zug lösen.

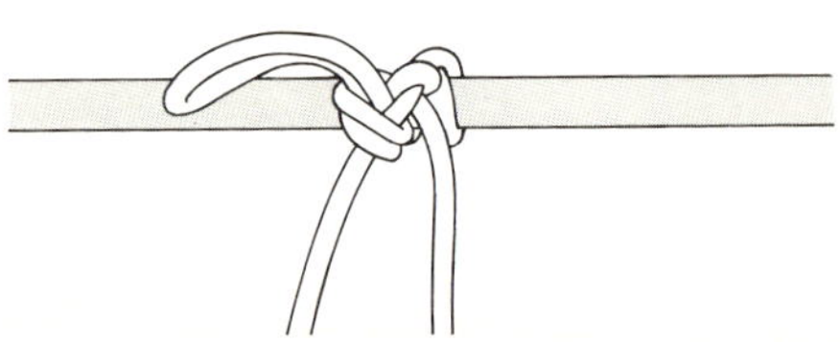

Roringstek mit halbem Schlag

Er dient zum Festmachen einer Leine an einem Ring oder einer Stange.

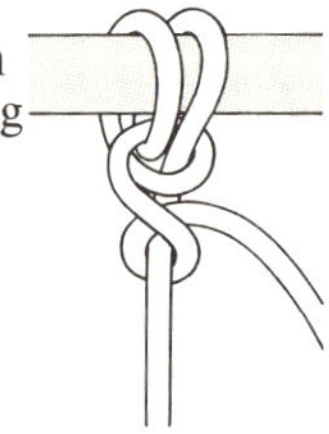

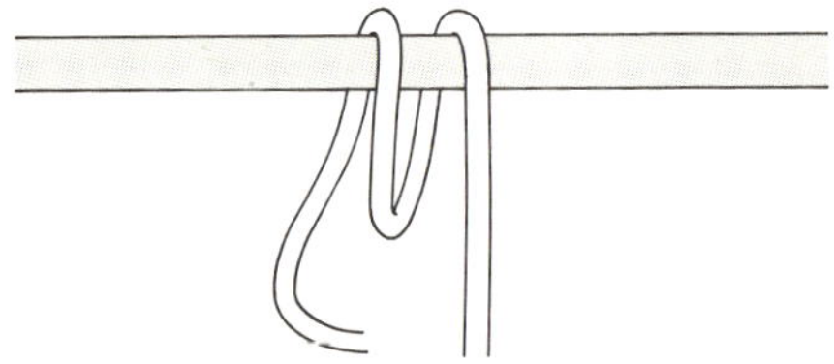

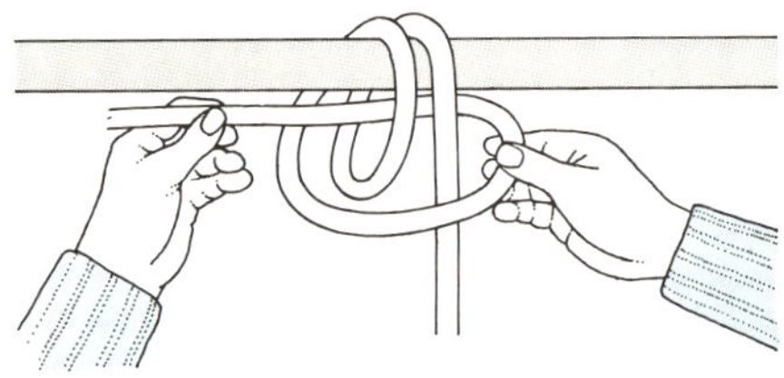

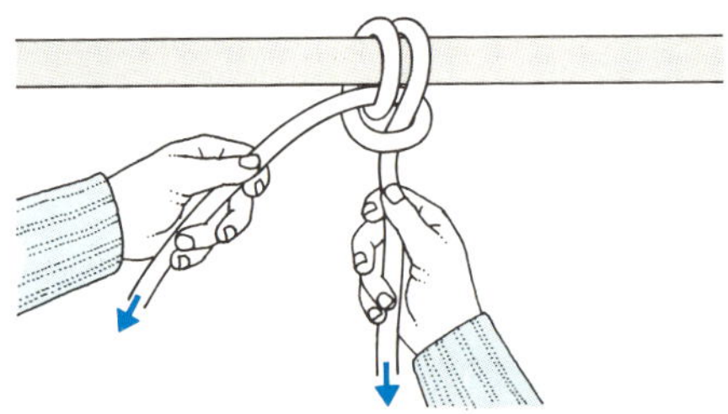

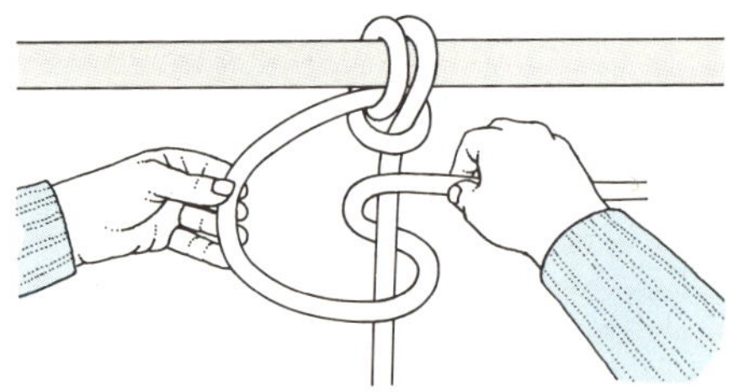

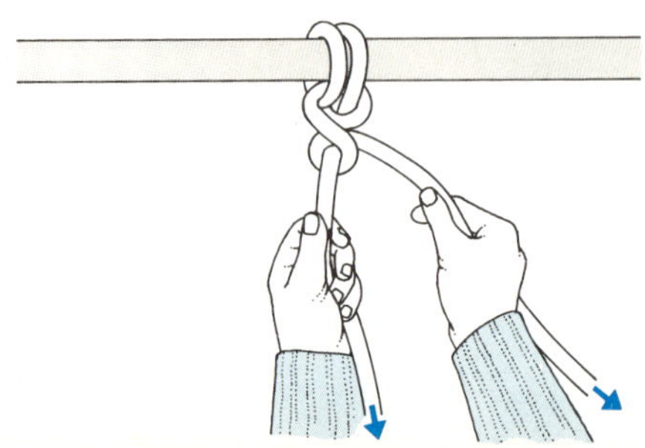

Der Takling

Um Tampen vor dem Aufdrüseln zu sichern, muß mit Takelgarn ein Takling, entgegen der Drehrichtung des Tauwerks, aufgesetzt werden. Hier der Behelfstakling.

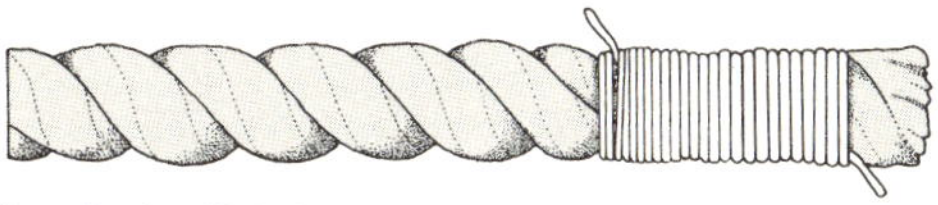

Der fertige Behelfstakling

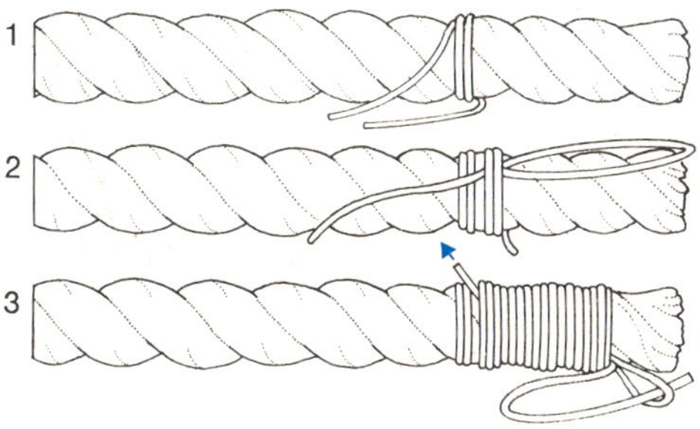

Spleißen

Als Spleißen bezeichnet man das Verflechten zweier Enden. Man braucht dazu einen Marlspieker, um die Kardeele auszudrehen. Erlernen läßt sich spleißen nur in der praktischen Anschauung.

Der fertige Kurzspleiß

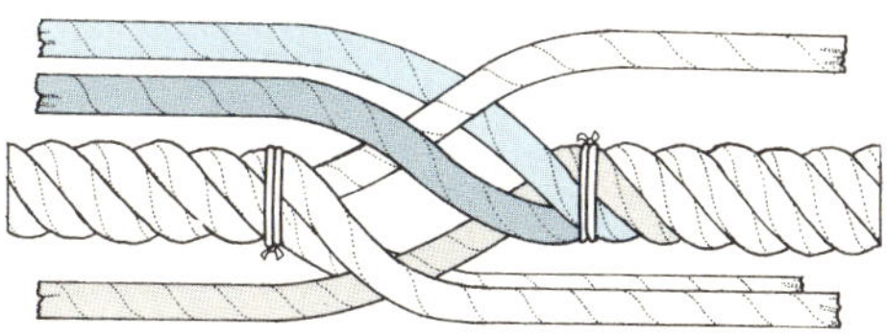

1 *Beide Tampen werden etwa 6 Törns aufgedreht. Um ein weiteres Aufdrüseln zu verhindern, kommt ein Bändsel rum.*

2 *Nun eins der Kardeele des linken Tampens nach rechts spleißen – über und unter ein Kardeel – gegen den Schlag, in dem die Kardeele zusammengedreht sind. Dann die beiden übrigen Kardeele auf die gleiche Weise nach rechts einspleißen. So werden mit allen Kardeelen jeder Seite 6 Runden gespleißt. Die herausragenden Kardeelspitzen sauber abschneiden.*

Augspleiß

Da ein Spleiß besser hält als jeder Knoten, sollten die Festmacher an einem Ende einen Augspleiß erhalten. Dazu müssen die Kardeele lang genug aufgedreht werden, um jedes fünfmal durchstecken zu können. Der Spleißanfang wird durch einen Takling gesichert, damit die Leine nicht weiter aufdreht.

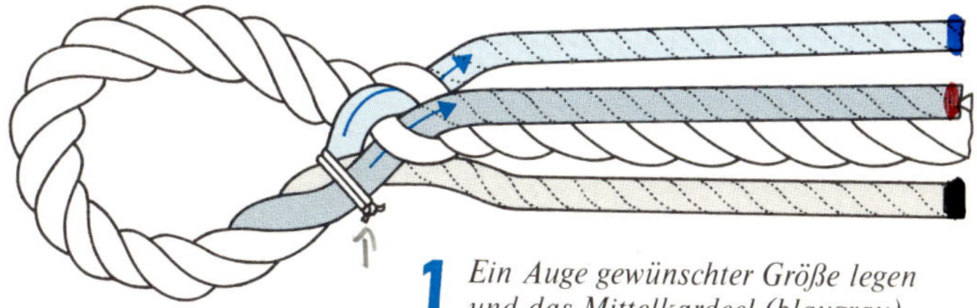

1 *Ein Auge gewünschter Größe legen und das Mittelkardeel (blaugrau) unter das oberste Kardeel der stehenden Part am Kreuzungspunkt stecken. Nun das linke Kardeel (blau) links unter das nächst weitere Kardeel stecken. Beide Steks nicht zu fest dichtziehen.*

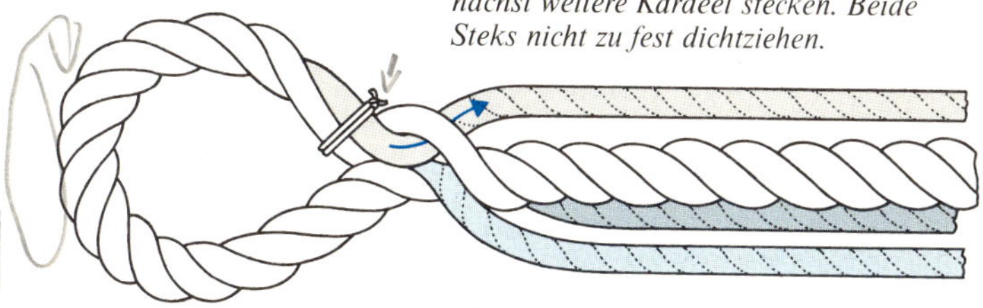

2 *Nun das rechte Kardeel unter das stehende Kardeel rechts vom stehenden Kardeel stecken, unter dem das mittlere Augkardeel steckt.*

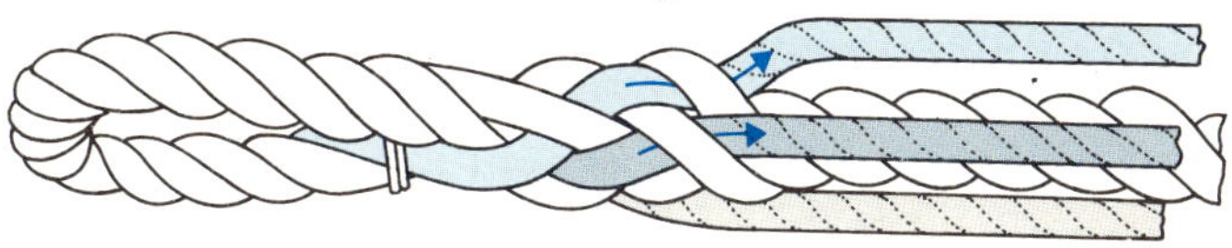

3 *Nun werden die Kardeele der Reihe nach immer von rechts nach links gegen den Schlag durchgesteckt, je fünfmal, und jede Stekrunde wird dichtgezogen.*

4 *Der Anfängerfehler wird immer beim ersten Stecken des rechten Kardeels gemacht. Merke: Rechts und rückwärts vom ersten Stek. Zum fünften Stek kann man die Kardeele etwas verjüngen. Überstehendes wird abgeschnitten.*

Der Umgang mit Tauwerk

Damit das Tauwerk keine Kinken wirft und klar läuft, muß man wissen, wie es richtig aufgeschossen wird. Nicht gebrauchtes Tauwerk wird sofort aufgeschossen. Nichts lose als Knäuel irgendwo herumliegen lassen. Leicht kann jemand darauf ausrutschen, und außerdem vertörnt es sehr schnell und unentwirrbar. Kunstfasertauwerk ist zudem empfindlich gegen UV-Strahlung. Ist es mit Chemikalien – Lösungsmittel, stark verschmutzte Binnengewässer – in Berührung gekommen, sollte es so bald wie möglich mit Süßwasser abgespült werden. Gelegentlich wird man eine Leine an Land oder zu einem anderen Boot hinüber werfen müssen. Das klappt niemals, wenn sie nicht vorher richtig zum Werfen aufgeschossen worden ist.

Eine bunte Auswahl der verschiedensten Tauwerksarten aus Kunstfasern.

Belegen auf einer Klampe

Auf einer Klampe muß so belegt werden, daß sich das Tauwerk unter Zug nicht bekneift. Zunächst legt man einen vollen Rundtörn um den Steg der Klampe, dann zwei weitere Törns in Achtform um die Klampe. Zuletzt sichert man den Tampen von Festmachern mit einem Kopfschlag, nicht jedoch die Tampen von Fallen und Schoten.

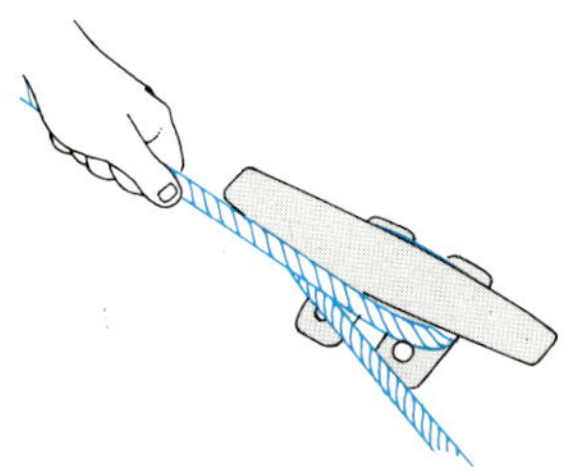

1 *Zuerst wird ein Rundtörn um den Klampensteg genommen.*

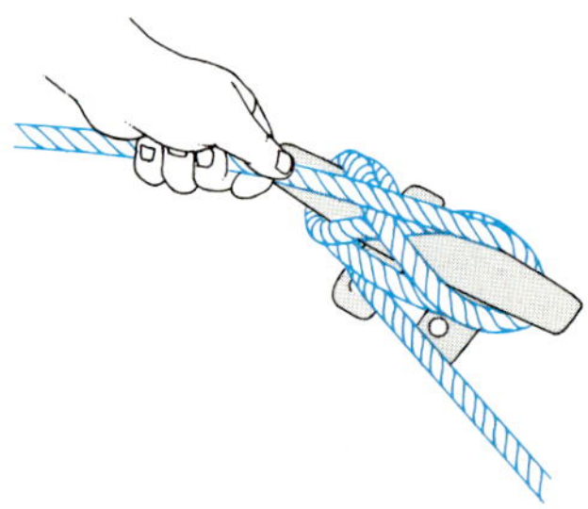

2 *Dann werden zwei Achttörns um die Klampe gelegt.*

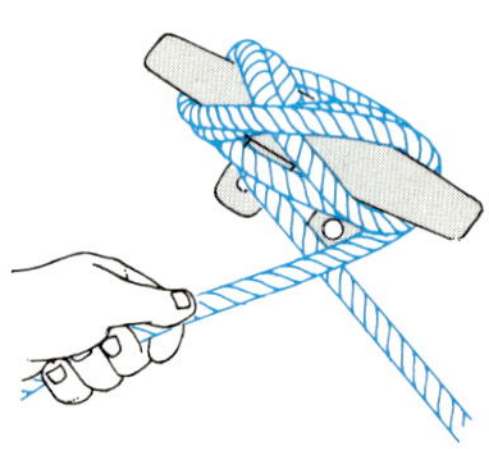

3 *Zuletzt wird mit einem Kopfschlag (bei Festmacheleinen und mit einem Rundtörn bei Fallen) belegt.*

Beim Belegen auf einer Festmacheklampe ist es notwendig, den Tampen mit einem Kopfschlag zu sichern. Anstelle des Kopfschlages kann man auch einen Slipstek setzen, der sich durch Reißen am Ende blitzschnell lösen läßt.

Aufschießen einer Leine

Aufgeschossen wird eine Leine in ungefähr armlangen Buchten und in Laufrichtung der Kardeele. Schießt man entgegengesetzt auf, gibt es ärgerliche Kinken – die Leine verwindet sich in sich. Eine stehende Leine wird stets in Richtung zum losen Ende aufgeschossen. Die Bildfolge zeigt, wie man ein Fall am Mast aufschießt.

1 *Die feste Part, dicht hinter der Klampe, über die Handfläche legen und die Leine in Buchten in der Handfläche im Uhrzeigersinn (bei rechtsgeschlagenem Tauwerk) aufschießen...*

2 *...bis die Leine zu Ende ist.*

3 *Mit der anderen Hand durch die Buchten hindurchfassen und den Anfang des Bunsches nach vorne holen.*

4 *über Kreuz „verdrillen"...*

5 *...und das so gewonnene Auge über das obere Horn der Klampe hängen.*

Werfen einer Leine

Gelegentlich ist es notwendig, eine Leine an Land oder an ein anderes Boot zu übergeben. Dabei läßt sich nicht vermeiden, daß man sie werfen muß. Am besten ist es, die Leine für den Wurf neu aufzuschießen, damit man sicher ist, daß sie klar ausläuft. Wie die Abbildung zeigt, nimmt man in jede Hand ungefähr die Hälfte der Buchten und wirft nur einen Teil mit der Wurfhand hinüber. Den anderen Teil gibt die zweite Hand im Flug hinterher.

1 *Die aufgeschossene Leine wird geteilt, bei längeren Leinen der kleinere Teil in die Wurfhand genommen.*

2 *Geworfen wird mit weitausholendem Arm über das Ziel hinweg.*

3 *Dabei müssen die Buchten aus der anderen Hand glatt und ungehindert auslaufen.*

Kleines Segellexikon

A

Abdrift (auch Abtrift) Seitliches Versetzen eines Bootes durch Wind oder Strom.

abfallen Eine Kursänderung vom Wind weg. (Gegenteil: anluven.)

ablandig Wenn der Wind vom Land in Richtung See weht. (Gegenteil: auflandig.)

abschlagen Das Abnehmen der Segel. (Gegenteil: anschlagen.)

abtakeln Die gesamte Takelage vollständig abnehmen, also stehendes und laufendes Gut mit dem Mast, etwa um das Boot einzuwintern. (Gegenteil: auftakeln.) Oft fälschlich verwandt für Segel abschlagen.

achteraus Alles, was hinter einem Boot liegt. (Gegensatz: voraus.)

Achterholer Jeweils die Spinnakerschot, die sich in Luv befindet, also am Spinnakerbaum.

Achterleine Festmacherleine, die vom Heck eines Bootes schräg nach achtern an Land oder zu einem Pfahl führt. Bisweilen auch als Heckleine bezeichnet. (Gegenteil: Vorleine.)

Achterliek (das) Die hintere Kante eines Segels.

Achterstag (das) Vom Masttopp zum Heck verlaufendes Stag, das die nach vorne gerichteten Kräfte des Mastes aufnimmt. (Gegensatz: Vorstag.)

anluven Eine Kursänderung höher an den Wind heran. (Gegenteil: abschlagen.)

anstecken Einen Gegenstand mit einem Ende oder zwei Enden miteinander verbinden.

aufbrisen Der Wind nimmt an Stärke zu.

auffieren Dem Zug auf einer Leine nachgeben, ohne sie ausrauschen zu lassen. Häufiger auch nur: fieren.

aufklaren Das Wetter „klart auf", es wird besser. – 2. An und unter Deck, im Spind Ordnung schaffen.

aufkommen 1. Mit Ruderlage mittschiffs die Drehbewegung des Schiffs allmählich verringern. –
2. Ein voraus laufendes Schiff einholen. –
3. Schlechtes Wetter, Gewitter, Sturm oder dergleichen kommt auf.

auflandig Wenn der Wind von See in Richtung Land weht. (Gegenteil: ablandig.)

aufschießen 1. Mit dem Boot in den Wind drehen, um es zum Stehen zu bringen. –
2. Eine Leine in regelmäßigen Buchten zusammenlegen.

auftakeln (auch aufriggen) Die gesamte Takelage (Rigg) an Bord bringen und aufrichten. (Gegenteil: abtakeln.) Oft fälschlich verwandt für Segel setzen.

auftuchen Ein Segel oder auch eine Abdeckplane ordentlich zusammenlegen.

Auge Seemännische Bezeichnung für verschiedene Arten von Ringen, Ösen, Löchern oder Schlingen. In Wortverbindungen entfällt das „e" (Augspleiß, Augbolzen).

B

back (engl.) Zurück, Rückwärts. Wird ein Segel back geholt, fällt der Wind von der „Rückseite" ein. Entweder segelt das Boot dann rückwärts oder man erhöht dadurch das Drehmoment beim Wenden.

Backbord (Bb) in Fahrtrichtung gesehen die linke Seite eines Bootes. Links.

Baum Eine Stange aus Holz, Kunststoff oder – heute meistens – Aluminium, an der die untere Kante eines Segels angeschlagen (Großbaum) oder auch „fliegend" gefahren wird (Spinnakerbaum).

Baumniederholer Unten am Mast angreifende Talje, die ein Steigen des Baums auf Vorm-Wind-Kursen verhindert.

beidrehen Eine Yacht hoch am Wind, durch entsprechende Segelstellung, etwa das Backholen der Fock, nahezu zum Stehen bringen.

beiliegen Beigedreht einen Sturm abwettern, aber auch längere Zeit annähernd an einer Stelle liegen bleiben, um etwas zu bergen oder eine Reparatur auszuführen.

bekneifen Festklemmen (von Leinen).

belegen Eine Leine festmachen.

Beplankung (die) Außenhaut eines hölzernen Schiffes.

bergen 1. Die Segel herunternehmen. –
2. Einen Gegenstand in Sicherheit bringen. – 3. Ein in Seenot geratenes Schiff einbringen. Die Besatzung oder Ladung von einem gestrandeten Schiff herunterholen (abbergen).

Bermuda-Rigg Bezeichnung für die Hochtakelung, die von Fischerbooten der Bermuda-Inseln stammt. Das dreieckige Hochsegel löste in den 30er Jahren das viereckige Gaffelsegel als Yachttakelage ab.

Bindereff (auch Bändselreff) Die Segelfläche wird bei starkem Wind verkleinert, indem man das Tuch auf den Baum herunterholt und dort festbindet.

Block Gehäuse aus Holz, Metall oder Kunststoff mit einer oder mehreren Rollen über die Leinen laufen.

Boje 1. Im Grund verankerter Schwimmkörper zum Festmachen von Booten. –
2. Nicht ganz korrekte Bezeichnung für Tonnen, die als Seezeichen oder Wendemarken bei Regatten dienen.

Bord (der) Eigentlich die Schiffsseite (Backbord, Steuerbord), besonders deren Oberkante, daher „über Bord" fallen. „An Bord" heißt allgemein sich auf einem Schiff befinden.

brechen 1. Seemännischer Ausdruck für das Reißen von Leinen und Ketten (nicht jedoch für Segel). –
2. Das „Überkämmen" der Wellen, wenn sich auf einer Welle eine Schaumkrone bildet.

Bucht 1. Zurückspringendes Küstenstück. –
2. Schleife in einer Leine. Sie wird „in Buchten" aufgeschossen.

Bug (der) Das vordere Ende eines Schiffes. Steuerbord-, bzw. Backbordbug bezeichnet jedoch jeweils die Seite einer Yacht, auf der der Großbaum geführt wird.

C

Cockpit (das) Vertiefung im Deck, in der sich während des Segelns die Besatzung aufhält. Auf Jollen der gesamte nicht eingedeckte Raum.

Cunningham-Hole (auch C.-Kausch) Nach seinem Erfinder, dem Amerikaner Briggs Cunningham, benannter Vorliekstrecker am Großsegel. Eine zweite Kausch, etwa 15 cm über dem Segelhals, durch die ein Niederholer führt, mit dem das C-Hole auf den Baum heruntergeholt werden kann. So läßt sich die Großsegel-Wölbung unterschiedlichen Windverhältnissen anpassen.

Curryklemme Nach ihrem Erfinder, Dr. Manfred Curry, benannte gezahnte Federklemme, die sich unter Zug bekneift. Vorwiegend zum Festsetzen von Schoten und Streckern verwendet.

D

Deckpeilung (die) Zwei Objekte (Landmarken) werden in Deckung gebracht. Die Deckpeilung zweier bekannter Objekte ergibt eine terrestrische Standlinie.

Deutscher Segler-Verband (DSV) 1888 gegründeter Dachverband der deutschen Segelclubs und oberste Segelsportautorität der Bundesrepublik.

Dolle (die) Gabelförmiges Auflager aus Metall oder Kunststoff für den Riemen (von Landratten fälschlich als Ruder bezeichnet) beim Pullen (Rudern).

Draggen (der) Kleiner vierarmiger Anker, auch als Suchdraggen zum Auffischen über Bord gefallener Gegenstände verwendet.

Ducht (die) Quer oder längs liegendes Sitzbrett in einem offenen Boot.

dwars Querab, rechtwinklig zur Fahrtrichtung.

E

Ende Leine, Tau; ausgenommen sehr dicke Taue. Sie heißen Trossen. Die Enden eines „Endes" bezeichnet man als Tampen oder auch Tamp.

F

Fahrwasser An engen Stellen oder zwischen Untiefen, Sandbänken usw. die durch Seezeichen markierte Fahrrinne mit tiefem Wasser.

Fall (das, Mehrz.: Fallen)
1. Leinen oder Drähte zum Setzen der Segel. Entsprechend Großfall, Fockfall oder Spinnakerfall. –
2. Der Fall = Neigung eines Mastes nach vorne oder achtern.

Fender (der) Polster aus unterschiedlichen Materialien, um die Bordwand vor Beschädigungen an Stegen, Nachbarschiffen oder ähnlichem zu schützen.

fieren Dem Zug auf einer Leine nachgeben, ohne sie ausrauschen zu lassen. Häufig auch: auffieren.

Fock (die) Dreieckiges Vorsegel. Es gehört zu den Haupt- oder Arbeitssegeln.

Fockroller Mechanische Vorrichtung, um die Fock, vom Cockpit aus, auf das Vorstag aufzurollen.

Freibord (der) Höhe der Bordwand über der Wasserlinie.

G

Gaffel (die) Rundholz an dem das viereckige Gaffelsegel mit seinem Oberliek angeschlagen wird.

Gatchen (auch Gattchen) Kleines, meist mit einer Metallkausch eingefaßtes Loch in Segeln oder Planen, durch das Bändsel, Strecker oder ähnliches gezogen werden können.

geigen Schaukeln des Bootes um die Längsachse, besonders vor achterlichem Wind.

Genua (die) Eine große Fock für leichtere Winde. Sie zählt zu den Beisegeln. Regatta-Yachten haben bis zu vier Genuas unterschiedlicher Größen und Tuchstärken, die meist römisch beziffert werden. Also Genua I, II usw.

GFK Abkürzung für glasfaserverstärkter Kunststoff, das Baumaterial, aus dem heute die meisten Jollen hergestellt werden. Andere gebräuchliche Bezeichnungen: Fiberglas- oder Polyesterharz-Boote.

Gezeitenstrom-Atlas Vom Deutschen Hydrographischen Institut herausgegebene Sammlung von Gezeitenstrom-Karten, die Richtung und Stärke des Tidenstromes an bestimmten Bezugsorten enthalten.

Gezeitentafel Vom Deutschen Hydrographischen Institut herausgegebene Tabellen, die für verschiedene Bezugsorte die Zeiten für Hoch- und Niedrigwasser und die Tidenkurven angeben.

gieren Seitliches Ausscheren eines Bootes aus seinem Kurs, besonders vor achterlichen Seen.

gleiten Ein Zustand, der von leichten Booten (Jollen) durch einen teilweisen dynamischen Auftrieb erreicht wird. Dabei reiten sie auf ihrer Bugwelle und können ein Mehrfaches ihrer Rumpfgeschwindigkeit erreichen.

Gut (das) Das gesamte Faser- und Drahttauwerk der Takelage eines Segelbootes, unterteilt in „stehendes Gut" – dazu zählt die feste Verstagung des Mastes mit Vorstag, Wanten und Achterstag – und „laufendes Gut". Dazu gehören die Fallen zum Setzen der Segel und die Schoten zur Segelführung.

H

Hahnepot (die) Ein gespreiztes Ende, das die in seinem Scheitel angreifende Kraft auf zwei Punkte verteilt.

Hals Die vordere untere Ecke eines Segels.

halsen Mit dem Heck durch den Wind gehen.

Havarie Beschädigung einer Yacht durch Grundberührung, Kollision oder Sturm.

Heck (das) Das hintere Ende eines Schiffes.

heißen/hissen Das Hochziehen eines Segels oder einer Flagge.

holen Das Ziehen an einem Ende (anholen, durchholen, einholen, ausholen, aufholen). (Gegensatz: fieren.)

I

International Yacht Racing Union (IYRU) 1907 in London gegründeter Welt-Segler-Verband, dem heute die nationalen Segelsportverbände aus rund 70 Ländern angehören.

J

Jolle 1. Allgemein ein kleines offenes Boot. –
2. Ein offenes Segelboot mit Schwert im Gegensatz zum Kielboot.

K

Kat 1. Eine Takelung mit einem Mast und nur einem Großsegel, also ohne Vorsegel. – 2. Gebräuchliche Abkürzung für Katamaran.

Kausch (die) Eine ring- oder auch herzförmige Metall-oder Kunststoff-Verstärkung für ein Auge.

kentern Umkippen eines Bootes, nachdem es den Kenterpunkt überschritten hat. Alle Schwerboote können kentern.

killen Flattern der Segel.

Kinken (die) Eine in sich verdrehte Leine hat Kinken. Aus den Kinken treten = jemand aus dem Wege gehen.

Klampe (die) Eine doppelarmige Knagge aus Holz, Metall oder Kunststoff zum Belegen von Leinen.

Knickspanter Boote, deren Rümpfe einen eckigen Querschnitt haben. Es kann ein einfacher oder ein doppelter Knickspant sein. (Gegensatz: Rundspanter.)

Knoten (kn) Nautische Geschwindigkeitsbezeichnung für Seemeilen pro Stunde. Der Ausdruck stammt von der Markierung der Logleine des alten Handlogs mit Knoten.

Kopf Die obere Ecke eines Segels, an der man das Fall anschäkelt.

Kopfschlag Beim Belegen auf einer Klampe wird das letzte Ende so über Kreuz gelegt, daß es sich bekneift.

Krängung Schräglage (eines Bootes).

Kreuzen Mit Zickzack-Kurs auf ein Ziel in Windrichtung zusegeln.

L

Lateralplan Die Silhouette des Unterwasserschiffs von der Seite gesehen. Je nachdem ob der Kiel lang, kurz oder tief ist, spricht man von einem langen, kurzen, tiefen oder auch flachen Lateralplan.

laufendes Gut Alles Tauwerk, das beweglich ist und über Blöcke, Scheiben und dergleichen läuft (Fallen, Schoten, Dirken, Flaggleinen usw., aber nicht Backstagen).

Lee Die dem Wind abgekehrte Seite.

leegierig Ein Boot, das die Eigenschaft hat, ständig abzufallen.

lenzen 1. Ein Boot leerpumpen oder ausschöpfen. –
2. Mit einem Schiff vor einem Sturm herlaufen.

Liek (das, Mehrz.: Lieken) Die verstärkten Kanten eines Segels (Vor-, Achter-, Ober-, Unterliek).

Lippe (Lippklampe) Klauenartige Durchführung für einen Leinen im Schanzkleid oder auf Deck.

Lose Wenn ein Ende nicht dichtgesetzt ist, hat es Lose. Lose geben heißt, mit einem dichtgesetzten Ende nachgeben.

Lümmel Die Verbindung zwischen Baum und Mast, bestehend aus dem Lümmelbeschlag am Baum und dem Lümmellager am Mast. Das kann ein einfacher Haken sein, ein rundum schwenkbarer Zapfen, eine Steckbolzen-Verbindung, ein Schlitten mit Manschette und ist – sofern vorhanden – mit dem Patentreff kombiniert.

Luv Die dem Wind zugekehrte Seite.

luvgierig Ein Boot, das die Eigenschaft hat, ständig in den Wind zu drehen.

M

Marlspieker Ein starker Stahldorn, zum Arbeiten mit Drahttauwerk, hauptsächlich jedoch zum Öffnen festgefressener Schäkelbolzen verwendet.

Mastspur Eine Ausnehmung im Kielschwein oder ein Beschlag, der den Mastfuß hält und mitunter in der Längsschiffsrichtung verstellt werden kann, um den Mast weiter nach vorne oder achtern zu trimmen.

N

Nock (die) Das Ende des Baumes, nicht aber des Mastes. Das heißt Topp. Auch die Enden der Kommandobrücke auf Großschiffen werden als Brückennock bezeichnet.

O

Ösfaß Gefäß zum Wasserschöpfen (ösen), meist aus Kunststoff.

P

Patenthalse Unfreiwilliges Halsen, verursacht durch Unaufmerksamkeit des Rudergängers oder starkes Gieren oder Rollen des Bootes. Auf Jollen kann sie leicht zum Kentern führen, auf schweren Kielyachten zu Bruch in der Tagelage.

Patentreff (auch Rollreff) Die Segelfläche wird verkleinert, indem man das Tuch auf den Baum wickelt.

Persenni(n)g (die) Eine wasserdichte Abdeckplana für die Segel, das Cockpit oder das ganze Boot.

Pinne (auch Ruderpinne) Waagerechter Hebelarm am Kopf des Ruderschaftes, oft klappbar. Gelegentlich wird das Steuern auch als Pinnieren bezeichnet.

Plicht (die) Seltenere Bezeichnung für das Cockpit, der Vertiefung im Deck, in der die Crew, die Besatzung, sitzt.

Poller (der) Starker, kurzer Pfahl aus Holz, Metall oder auch Stein zum Festmachen von Leinen an Land. Auch die kleineren Versionen an Deck heißen Poller. Man unterscheidet, je nach Form, einfache, Doppel-, Kreuz- und Doppelkreuzpoller.

Protest Einspruch einer Yacht gegen eine andere, die in einer Regatta gegen die Wettsegelbestimmungen verstoßen hat. Er wird durch eine Protestflagge angezeigt.

pullen Seemännische Bezeichnung für rudern.

Pütting (das; auch Rüsteisen) Beschlag, mit dem die Wanten am Bootsrumpf befestigt sind.

R

raumen Eine günstige Winddrehung mehr nach achtern. (Gegensatz: schralen.)

reffen Ein Segel verkleinern.

Regatta Ursprünglich die venezianische Bezeichnung für das Wettrudern der Gondolieri, heute zum Begriff für segelsportliche Wettkämpfe geworden. Eine Regatta umfaßt im allgemeinen mehrere Wettfahrten, die an einem Tag hintereinander oder auf mehrere Tage verteilt ausgetragen werden.

Reitbalken Eine quer übers Cockpit laufende Strebe, unter die man beim Ausreiten des Bootes die Füße haken kann.

Riemen Seemännischer Ausdruck für „Ruder" mit denen nicht gerudert, sondern gepullt wird.

Rigg (das) Moderne Bezeichnung für Takelage. Sammelbegriff für Masten, Bäume, stehendes und laufendes Gut. Entsprechend wird eine Yacht „geriggt" oder „aufgeriggt".

rollen Die Bewegung einer Yacht im Seegang um ihre Längsachse.

Ruder Seemännischer Ausdruck für „Steuer", auch „Rohr" genannt. Verballhornung des flämischen Roer. Man steuert mit dem Ruder. Jollen haben meist einen Steuermann, Yachten dagegen einen Rudergänger.

Ruderblatt Der unter Wasser befindliche Teil des Ruders.

Rumpfgeschwindigkeit Jedes Schiff hat eine konstruktiv bedingte Rumpfgeschwindigkeit, die es nicht überschreiten kann. Sie ist leicht zu errechnen: Wurzel aus der Wasserlinienlänge in Metern x Faktor 2,43 = Geschwindigkeit in Knoten. Nur bei Gleitfahrt wird die Rumpfgeschwindigkeit überschritten.

Rundspanter Boote, deren Rümpfe einen runden Querschnitt haben. Er kann sehr schmal oder auch extrem breit sein. (Gegensatz: Knickspanter.)

Rüsteisen Pütting (s. dort)

Rutscher (auch Schlitten) Gleitschuh am Vorliek eines Segels, der in der Gleitschiene an der Rückseite des Mastes läuft.

S

Saling (die) Waagerechte Streben am Mast, die im oberen Bereich die Wanten abspreizt, um eine bessere Mastverspannung zu erzielen.

Schäkel (der) Durch Schraub- oder Steckbolzen verschließbare Metallbügel unterschiedlicher Größen und Stärken, um stark beanspruchte Teile an Bord miteinander zu verbinden. Beispielsweise den Anker mit der Kette oder das Fall mit dem Segel.

schamfilen Scheuern, reiben.

scheren 1. Ein Ende durch einen Block, ein Auge oder eine Leitöse führen. – 2. Im Sinne von „laufen". Ein Schiff schert aus dem Kurs.

schiften Den Baum von einer Seite auf die andere nehmen.

Schlag Die zwischen zwei Wendemanövern beim Kreuzen zurückgelegte Strecke.

schlingern Eine periodische Bewegung um die Längsachse.

Schot (die) Leine zum Regulieren der Segelstellung. Entsprechend Fockschot, Großschot oder Spinnakerschot.

Schothorn Die hintere untere Ecke eines Segels.

Schotring Ein runder Bügel am Großbaum, an dem die Schot angreift.

schralen Eine ungünstige Winddrehung mehr nach vorne. (Gegensatz: raumen.)

schricken Etwas fieren. „Einen Schrick in die Schot geben".

Schwell (der) In Häfen hineinstehende schwache Dünung. Von vorbeifahrenden Schiffen verursachter Wellenschlag.

Schwert Senkrecht in einem Schwertkasten steckende Platte auf Jollen, die beim Segeln der seitlichen Abdrift entgegenwirkt. Es gibt Steckschwerter und drehbar gelagerte Senkschwerter.

schwojen Das Pendeln eines Bootes um seinen Anker oder seine Muring, hervorgerufen durch Wind oder Strom.

Seemeile (sm) Sie ist 1852 m lang. Das entspricht der Länge des 60. Teiles eines Längengrades, also einer Längen- oder Meridianminute. In der Seefahrt werden alle Entfernungen in sm angegeben.

slippen 1. Das Zuwasserbringen eines Bootes auf einem Slip, einer Bootsrampe. – 2.Schnelles Loswerfen einer Leine. „Auf Slip belegen."

Spant (das; Mehrz.: Spanten) Die Quer- und Längsrippen eines Schiffes. Der Kunststoff-Bootsbau kommt weitgehend ohne sie aus. Längsspanten werden auch Stringer genannt.

Spiegel Der Abschluß des Hecks. Ist er einwärts geneigt, spricht man von einem einfallenden Spiegel, bei Neigung nach auswärts entsprechend von einem ausfallenden.

spleißen Das dauerhafte Verflechten von Tauwerk. Entweder um zwei Enden miteinander zu verbinden oder um ein Auge zu bilden.

Spring Zusätzliche Festmacheleinen zu der Vor-und Achterleine, die eine Bewegung des Bootes in der Langsrichtung verhindern. Die Vorspring verläuft vom Vorschiff schräg nach hinten, die Achterspring vom Achterschiff nach vorne.

Stag (das) Drahttauwerk zum Abstützen und Versteifen der Masten nach vorne und achtern. – Über Stag gehen, dasselbe wie wenden.

Stander 1. Für bestimmte Zwecke fertig gespleißtes Drahtende, z.B. der Bojenstander. – 2. Kurze dreieckige Flagge (Vereinsstander), im Gegensatz zum Wimpel, der auch dreieckig, aber lang und schmal ist.

Steuerbord (Stb) In Fahrtrichtung gesehen die rechte Seite eines Bootes. Rechts.

Steven Vorderer und hinterer Abschluß des Bootsrumpfes, entsprechend Vor- und Achtersteven.

Stringer Versteifung des Bootsrumpfes in Längsrichtung (s. Spanten)

T

Takelage Sammelbegriff für Masten und Bäume, stehendes und laufendes Gut. Moderne Bezeichnung: Rigg

Takelung Die Art und Weise, wie ein Boot getakelt oder geriggt ist: Slup, Kutter, Ketsch usw.

Tamp(en) Die beiden Enden einer Leine (seemännisch: eines Endes).

Tide (die) Eine Tide oder auch Gezeit umfaßt Flut und Ebbe. Sie reicht von einem Niedrigwasser über das Hochwasser zum darauffolgenden Niedrigwasser.

Tonne Bezeichnung von „schwimmenden Seezeichen". Je nach ihrer Form bezeichnet man sie als Baken-, Spieren-, Spitz-, Stumpf-, Kugel oder Faßtonnen. Unter den Bakentonnen gibt es wiederum Heul-, Leucht- und Glockentonnen.

Topp Spitze des Mastes

Toppnant Aufholer für den Spinnakerbaum.

Törn 1. Eine Segelfahrt. – 2. Ein ungewollt in eine Leine eingedrehtes Auge. Eine vertörnte Leine = unklare Leine.

Trailer Ein- oder doppelachsiger Bootsanhänger. Bis zu einer Achsbelastung von 375 kg kann er ungebremst sein, darüber hinaus muß er eigene Bremsen haben.

Trapez Ein auf Rennjollen oben im Mast befestigter Draht mit einem Gurt, in dem sich der Vorschotmann weit nach Luv aus dem Boot hängt, um als „lebender Ballast" die Stabilität zu erhöhen.

Traveller (engl. Laufkatze) Genaugenommen der Schlitten, an dem der Großschot-Fußblock auf einer Schiene oder einem Rohr gleitet. Inzwischen aber hat sich die Bezeichnung für die gesamte Einrichtung eingebürgert, die dem besseren Trimm des Großsegels dient.

trimmen (der Trimm) Alle Maßnahmen, die ein Boot schneller machen und sein Seeverhalten verbessern.

U

über Stag gehen Eine andere Bezeichnung für „wenden".

V

verholen Ein Schiff mit Leinen von einem Platz zu einem anderen bringen.

Verklicker Drehvorrichtung für einen Stander am Masttopp zur Windrichtungsanzeige.

Verstagung Dasselbe wie „stehendes Gut". Sammelbegriff für die Masthalterungen: Vor- und Achterstag und Wanten.

Vorschiff Der vor dem Mast liegende Teil eines Bootes. Entsprechend das Vordeck.

Vorschoter Derjenige, der nicht steuert, sondern die Vorschot bedient.

Vorsegel Alle Segel vor dem Mast, also Fock, Genua, Klüver, Spinnaker.

W

Want (das; Mehrz.: Wanten) Das stehende Gut rechts und links vom Mast. Kleine Boote haben nur ein Wantenpaar, größere Yachten mehrere (Topp-, Ober-und Unterwanten).

wenden Mit dem Bug durch den Wind gehen.

Wirbelschäkel Schäkel mit einem drehbaren Auge oder drehbar verbundene Doppelschäkel.

wriggen (auch wricken) Ein Ruderboot mit einem Riemen am Spiegel durch schraubenartige Bewegung vorwärtsbewegen.

Y

Yardstick Von dem Engländer Zillwood Milledge 1951 ausgeknobelte Handikap-Methode, nach der Jollen und Yachten, Einrumpf- und Mehrrumpfboote gegeneinander segeln können. Jedes Boot erhält eine empirisch ermittelte Yardstick-Zahl, durch die die gesegelte Zeit geteilt wird.

Z

zeisen Zusammen- oder anbinden, etwa aufgetuchte Segel. - Beschlag-Zeiser = Bänder zum Zeisen der Segel.

zurren Zusammenschnüren, festbinden. Etwas seefest zurren.

Stichwortverzeichnis

Quellenhinweise

Fotos
(O = oben, M = Mitte, U = unten, L = links, R = rechts)

Avon Inflatables Ltd: 149
R. R. Baxter: 120
Beken: Titel 13, 14R, 15
Alastair Black: 3, 10, 11, 14L, 27, 46, 47, 49, 71R, 108UR, 109, 111, 113, 117, 119, 121O, 129
Bob Bond: 41U
Jack Coote: 19L
Dick Everitt: 18OR
Bob Gordon: 53
Ambrose Greenway: 146
Colin Jarman: 18BR, 19BR, 75, 114, 115U, 121U, 135
National Maritime Museum: 12
Mike Payton: 140
Sue Rawkins: 143O
RNLI: 147
Stephen Sleight: 37, 99, 128
M. A. Stock: 18L
John Watney: 17, 19OR, 20, 21, 29, 71L, 100, 103, 104, 125, 127, 143U, 148
Rodger Witt: 141
Steven Wooster: 7, 23, 25, 33, 35, 36, 39, 40OL, 40OR, 41, 42, 43, 44, 45, 50, 51, 52, 54, 56, 57, 58, 59, 60, 61, 63, 64, 65, 66, 67, 68, 72, 73, 74, 76, 77, 79, 80, 81, 83, 84, 86, 87, 88, 92, 93, 96, 98, 101, 107, 108UL, 108M, 110, 112, 115OL, 115OR, 115ML, 115MR, 118, 124

Illustrationen
David Ashby
David Etchell
Andrew Farmer
John Ridyard
Les Smith
Venner Artists